Being Interior

New Cultural Studies

Series Editors

Joan DeJean
Carroll Smith-Rosenberg
Peter Stallybrass
Gary A. Tomlinson

A complete list of books in the series
is available from the publisher.

Being Interior

Autobiography and the Contradictions of Modernity in Seventeenth-Century France

Nicholas D. Paige

PENN

UNIVERSITY OF PENNSYLVANIA PRESS

Philadelphia

10 9 8 7 6 5 4 3 2 1

Published by
University of Pennsylvania Press
Philadelphia, Pennsylvania 19104-4011

Library of Congress Cataloging-in-Publication Data

Paige, Nicholas D.
   Being interior : autobiography and the contradictions of modernity in
seventeenth-century France / Nicholas D. Paige.
      p.   cm. — (New cultural studies)
   Includes bibliographical references and index.
   ISBN 0-8122-3577-0 (cloth : alk. paper)
   1. Autobiography.   2. Authors, French—Biography—History and criticism.
3. France—Biography—History and criticism.   I. Title.   II. Series.
CT25 .P35   2001
840.9′492—dc21   00-041802

The inner world is somehow more my own than the outside world. It is so *warm*, so *familiar*, so *intimate*. What a pity it is so vague and dreamlike. Does what is truest and best have to seem so unreal?

—NOVALIS

Contents

A Note on Sources

In my transcriptions of early modern sources, with the exception of Montaigne, I have modernized spelling (while preserving capitalization). I have occasionally modified punctuation for clarity. Translations, which unless otherwise indicated are my own, subordinate fluidity to exactitude, in an attempt to maintain the specificity of the early modern lexicon of subjective states. Furthermore, the English-speaking reader should keep in mind that the original French in many of these passages is more than convoluted: the average seventeenth-century writer could not compete with the lapidary precision of a Pascal or a La Rochefoucauld, but showed, rather, a fondness for the run-on sentence that it is impossible to rein in entirely. All quotations from the Bible refer to the Revised Standard Version.

Introduction: *Inside the* Grand Siècle

Amid accounts of military exploits and affairs of state, Louis XIV pauses for a moment in his memoirs to give his son some advice on religious matters: "[L]'extérieur sans l'intérieur," he writes, "n'est rien du tout" (The exterior without the interior is nothing).[1] The immediate context of the passage makes the king's meaning clear enough: Louis exhorts the Dauphin not to pay mere lip service to religious duties, for religion, at bottom, sanctions the power of the monarch. But with his usual *l'état c'est moi* knack for putting his finger on the transformations of his age, the Sun King—that very emblem of gilt and lace, pageantry and parade, light and visibility—reminds us here that the spectacle of royal power had its underside, or rather, its inside, and that this inside was religious. And indeed, just as the French state expanded outward into new colonies and conquests, many individuals set out for what they thought of as uncharted spiritual terrain, a land that lay inside them and which was formed as if by opposition to a devalued exterior. This is a book about the development, in the course of the seventeenth century, of a cultural imperative to "be interior," and specifically the alternately self-evident and intractably problematic connection between this new human interiority and the rise of autobiographical writing.

A particularly rich account of one of the many inner voyages undertaken in these years can be found in a long letter written in 1632 by the Jesuit exorcist and mystic Jean-Joseph Surin. Describing to a colleague the experiences of a laywoman, Marie Baron, to whom he was giving spiritual guidance, Surin writes:

[Baron] disait que le matin, à son réveil, elle se trouvait comme dans un pays étranger. Il lui semblait qu'elle n'était plus de ce monde, et elle s'en sentait comme bannie et confinée dans son intérieur, comme dans une profonde solitude qui lui présentait de vastes espaces pour se cacher aux yeux des hommes. Ce seul mot d'«intérieur» la ravissait hors d'elle-même. Elle conseillait aux personnes spirituelles d'agrandir et de dilater incessamment leur intérieur et de n'y rien souffrir qui pût le rétrécir et le borner. C'était là où elle habitait et où l'amour la tenait occupée, hors des atteintes de toutes les choses extérieures.
([Baron] said that in the morning, upon waking, she found herself as if in a foreign

country. It seemed to her that she was no longer of this world, and she felt as if banished and confined in her interior, as if in a deep solitude that offered her vast spaces to hide herself from the eyes of man. The mere word "interior" was enough to ravish her out of her senses. She advised spiritual people to enlarge and dilate their interior incessantly, and not to allow anything to shrink or limit it. It was there that she lived and that love kept her busy, safe from all exterior things.) [2]

The swoons of Marie Baron mentioned here stand in for those of countless readers of the time: the word "interior," lending a talismanic presence to title after title, littered the pages of the century's immense output of devotional literature. In itself, it seemed to guarantee success, from a text contemporary with Surin's letter, Jean-Pierre Camus's 1631 *Traité de la réformation intérieure*, to Jean de Bernières's *Chrétien intérieur* (1661), which went through some fourteen editions in as many years and spawned a cohort of imitators. And if Baron's enthusiasm for interiority was widespread, so was Surin's enthusiasm for her enthusiasm: he was far from the only male ecclesiastic of the period who willingly reported on a woman's inner travels. On the contrary. As much as women reigned over the novelistic geography of Madeleine de Scudéry's subjective land of "Tendre," they symbolized religious interiority as well, at least to men like Surin.[3] Surin's eager dissemination of Baron's call to subjective "dilation" was repeated over and over again in the following decades, as the mystic graces of nuns and laywomen like Baron fueled the burgeoning genre of religious biography.

This book is about the inner refuge that fascinated Surin, but it is also about what Surin did not yet, in 1632, think to make an issue in his letter on Marie Baron—namely, the association of the subjective depths of human beings with first-person writing. We are told, in Surin's words, only of what Baron "would say" (the imperfect "disait" giving the nuance of repeated action); we are told of what she "would advise" fellow seekers, and of what "it seemed to her" when she set off for her inner *terra incognita*. Yet Surin gives us no excerpts of her own letters, no written exchanges with her spiritual director, no transcriptions from her journals. Curiously, these documents existed, for he refers to them from time to time elsewhere in the letter. Yet Surin never takes the step of associating interiority with the *writing* subject; Baron simply speaks with the authority of an oracle dispensing counsel. As the century wore on, no self-respecting biographer would be able to refrain from giving verbatim transcription of first-person writing if it existed; and it did often exist, precisely because directors like Surin took ever more care to assure that their most talented aspirants leave written records of what were touted as their "interior and secret dispositions." In a few decades, this association would start

to harden, and Surin, in step with the spirit of the changing times, would en-
vision the publication of his biographical letter on Baron along with a partial
but lengthy transcription of her journal, which he had preserved.[4]

Between 1632, when Surin wrote this letter, and 1660, when he envisioned publishing Baron's journal, something had changed, something that
in this case concerned not so much autobiographical practice (the journal,
after all, had existed all along) but the place of that practice in the culture of
modernity: it was in these years that autobiography became truly *readable*, in
the sense that it was constructed as the locus of an experience-based identity.
My subject here is in part the history of this readability, of a dawning recognition that writing like Baron's might have interest — and might indeed be more
interesting than the words of any mere biographer. *Being Interior* has, however, a second movement which accompanies this historical argument, and
that leads us back once more to a last look at the letter on Marie Baron: interiorized subjectivity, and the autobiographical writing that was increasingly
inseparable from it, arose out of and embodied a tension peculiar to, and, I
will argue, even constitutive of modern subjectivity. The inner space Surin
lauds is, after all, foundationally paradoxical. Paradoxical, first, because, as
one commentator has pointed out, human insides acquire here characteristics
more commonly associated with the outside — vastness, openness, infinite expansion — as if characteristics of the divinity had been transferred onto and
introjected into the subject.[5] As we shall see, the rhetoric of human depth in
these formative years was in large part appropriated from the unknowability
of a God who was, with the advent of modernity, to be found deep in the heart
rather than in the manifest world.[6] More significant is a second paradox: when
the inner landscape that Baron calls a "foreign country" opens up, this "vast
space" is both a haven of love ("where love kept her occupied"), safe from
the reach of the "external" world, as well as an exile to which the subject is
"banished and confined." Interior space, then, is a Janus in that it is both desired and imposed: the individual *wants* to withdraw, to cultivate interiority
through a process of "dilation," while at the same time she is *forced* to hide
herself, far from the prying "eyes of men." This ambiguity, so characteristic
of spiritual writings in these years, would not fade in the following centuries.
As interiority gained wider, secular resonance, new subjective tropes such as
the prison cell or the island would be marked by the same inextricable mixture of deprivation and plenitude, confinement and self-presence, hostility
and happiness.[7] In this respect, Surin's paradox illustrates the modern process of "subjection" itself: "[T]aken to be the condition for and instrument
of agency," Judith Butler has recently argued, "[the subject] is at the same

time the effect of subordination, understood as the deprivation of agency."[8] Hence being interior, both in the seventeenth century and in ours, will so often feel good and bad at the same time: the space of our authenticity is also the evidence of our alienation.

Being Interior consists, then, of two interlocking arguments, made, as Surin's example suggests, through reference less to the familiar canonical figures of Montaigne or Descartes than to the religious literature where concern for autobiographical interiority flourished best and earliest. First, retracing the dawning interest in autobiography, this book aims to account for how a type of writing came to imply a mode of being and, conversely, how something people were learning to call "inner experience" seemed to produce, as if naturally, authoritative books. Then, I try to show how what might appear from our point of view a naïve confidence in the readability of the human interior only obscures a contradiction of which writers of the period were acutely conscious: in drawing the line between interior and exterior, autobiography became the signature text of an always embattled subjectivity. *Being Interior* tells the story of how a world turning its back on institutional authority and scholastic tradition, invented the voice of experience and learned to read interiority, but it also anatomizes a culture in which autobiography would always be suspected of not keeping its many promises.

Thinking Through Autobiography: On the Tracks of a Literary Mentality

Not long ago, any inquiry into interiority and the writing and reading practices it stimulated might have automatically partaken of a familiar "unmasking of constructs." For a while at least, during the 1970s and 1980s, autobiography seemed one of poststructuralism's many victims.[9] If the author were really dead and the referentiality of language but a mirage, if the text had in fact no "outside," what terrain could be left for autobiography to occupy? If the cult of the interior so fervently practiced by phenomenological critics such as Gaston Bachelard, Jean Rousset, and Jean Starobinski were indeed, as Michel Foucault seemed to suggest, part and parcel of disciplinary institutional practices, who would want to make space for it anyway?[10] Moreover, as Katherine Eisaman Maus has noted, New Historicists too have been reluctant to accord importance to early modern tropes of inwardness, in part out of a desire to preserve the supposed otherness of a period not yet tainted by the many evils of Cartesian subjectivity.[11] All these factors would seem to limit approaches to the development of both interiority and autobiography to those of a few scholars who persist in their nostalgic belief in the "self," or, on the contrary, to poststructualists documenting the flimsiness of its modern tyranny.

In part, *Being Interior* is intended to suggest that these two mutually exclusive positions are more symbiotic than they first appear, for the "self" shimmers so attractively because it is labile, protean. But autobiographical interiority also deserves more than mere defense or critique because of its omnipresence and sheer heuristic value. To this day, what I will call the "autobiographical mentality" — an odd hybrid which stubbornly blends concrete cultural practices and states of mind — continues to underwrite everything from psychoanalysis to the tell-all TV talk show, and to unite bookstore shelves as seemingly unrelated as business and New Age. What accounts for this extraordinary persistence, this diversity of uses? How has autobiography become not only, in the words of one of its best historians and theorists, an unspoken human right, but a tool for demanding rights that have been denied?[12] That the right to the autobiographical "I" might deserve exercise, notably on account of its political expediency, is abundantly evident inside academe, where Foucault's famous and utopian appropriation of Samuel Beckett's rhetorical query "What does it matter who is speaking?" has been countered again and again by those who maintain that it is very important indeed.[13] And thus autobiography is much more than a dead object of study whose incoherence critics are wont to rehearse. When scholars exhume forgotten autobiographies and promote them as voices from the past or from the margins, they posit once again the link between identity and autobiography, the seductive aura of authenticity that has, for hundreds of years, emanated from this type of text.[14] Still more noteworthy (and oft-noted) is that autobiography has become a mode of scholarship in itself, a way of proceeding at a time in which critical interest in identity has made it vital to know who is speaking, from what position, and based on what personal experience; especially in matters of race, class, and gender, the autobiographical voice speaks today with unrivaled authority.[15] One of my main concerns here is to understand the history of the contestatory gesture that autobiography continues to embody: if the first person preserves its critical function vis-à-vis the juggernaut of tradition, it is in part because, as I will suggest, the "I," at least in its modern guise, was from its very inception inseparable from that critical function.

The autobiographical "I" seems to seize on each attack on its authority to better infiltrate our mental and literary landscape; indeed, it can scarcely do much good, I argue, to declare the dramatic "end" of a subjectivity whose foundation is crisis itself. Yet strangely, we know relatively little about how this perplexing state of affairs has arisen. Among the myriad studies of individual works, there have been, of course, attempts at grappling with the question of how we have come to think autobiographically and to predicate authority on the first-person discourse of experience. Two approaches here have long dominated investigations into the genre's historicity. On the one hand, a select few have aimed at the exhaustive and encyclopedic goal of gathering evidence of autobiography since classical times; the general thrust of these neo-Hegelian arguments is to portray the practice as being in germ always and everywhere, waiting patiently to be "discovered" with the advent of modern consciousness.[16] On the other—and these attempts comprise a much larger subset—lie chronological interrogations of a few familiar "great precursors"—Augustine, Montaigne, Teresa of Avila, and John Bunyan put in frequent appearances—who are shown to lead up to someone like Rousseau, who in his turn is superseded by a pivotal twentieth-century anti-autobiographer, such as Malraux.[17]

The works of Rousseau's predecessors do enable us to take some measure of the changes in subjectivity that made Rousseau's work possible. Given the persistent resonance of autobiographical thought, however, given its diffuseness, the variety of its forms, and its effect on high and low culture alike, the limitations involved in analyzing only a few convenient ur-texts are evident. Such efforts leave us far from an account of how autobiography came to transform, massively, the way members of a culture of literacy, great thinkers or not, thought about themselves, their experiences, and the relation of these selves and experiences to the printed word. The widespread nature of this transformation is precisely what suggests that the history of autobiography might be better understood less as a genre but as psycho-textual hybrid—a way of thinking and a range of material practices that mutually constitute one another. This is what I refer to as the autobiographical mentality, a term that deliberately echoes the familiar *histoire des mentalités* used by the Annales school, a group of historians and sociologists who trace their lineage back to Lucien Febvre, Marc Bloch, Lucien Lévy-Bruhl, and the journal *Annales d'histoire économique et sociale*, founded in 1929.

Although the influential *histoire des mentalités* has over the years come under attack—notably for a naïve belief in the transparency of documentation pertaining to "average people," and for privileging quantitative methods in a way that evacuated the question of the subject which had been so important for founders like Febvre and Georges Duby—the term "mentality" seems to me particularly appropriate for a study of autobiographical interiority. The historians of mentalities were mistrustful of historiography based on "great events" and the men whose individual will was supposedly responsible for bringing them into being, and equally critical of a history of ideas in which the theories of disparate "great thinkers" were seen as part of an ongoing dialogue. Emphasizing discontinuous ruptures over evolutionary continuity, and the collective over the individual, the *mentalités* school sought to scrutinize the different types of "mental hardwiring" (to update Febvre's suggestive term *outillage mental*) that separated epochs. These historians would go beyond events and get down to what we now think of as the problem of subjectivity. As Duby put it, "feelings, emotions, moral values, and even the workings of thought also have their own history."[18] All of these characteristic elements of Annales-based history are particularly relevant to a phenomenon as nebulous and persistent as autobiography. Invocations of an enduring pantheon of key texts that seem to furnish evidence of generic evolution — for example, Montaigne's *Essais*, Descartes's *Discours de la méthode*, the *Confessions* of Rousseau — bear responsibility for an understanding of autobiography as the innovation of a few great minds, toiling away in their libraries, in close, heated rooms or in sylvan isolation. Yet such autobiographical autonomy emerges as purely illusory after a more thorough examination: a subject that thinks itself through autobiography does so in large part in response to large-scale transformations of material life — transformations in law, government, and print culture, to name but a few. More generally, can an understanding of modernity, conceived of as a set of materially rooted *practices*, really be delivered by a history of ideas in which a few philosophers appear to establish the ground of all that would come? After all, the "Cartesian subject" may well be representative of modernity, but it was but one particle of a much larger and diverse nebula, one containing not only other conflicting ideas but other types of thinking and acting altogether.[19] Close attention to seventeenth-century reading and writing habits reveals that the subjective trends described philosophically by a Descartes or a Hobbes — say, the effort to overthrow the authority of books or to circumscribe God's "sphere of influence" — were appearing simultaneously in complementary guises elsewhere on the cultural map of the early modern period, and to different effect.

Second, a literary mentality, while certainly governing the way writers, great or pedestrian, invest themselves in certain texts, also involves *readers* in this process of investment. Autobiography in a generic sense could exist only once a culture knew how to recognize it, how to control its production, diffusion, and consumption. The study that follows, heeding Roger Chartier's call for a history of reading practices, is in part an archaeology of the material recognition given to autobiography as it started to force its way into print.[20] If, as Philippe Lejeune has argued, autobiography's defining principle is less its (often dubious) referentiality than a "pact" formed between the author and the reader, then a history of the construction of the autobiographical pact remains to be written.[21] How is a reading public groomed for a new mode of relating to texts? How do authors, editors, and even typesetters modify their practices to conform to—and change—a given audience's horizon of expectations? Questions such as these can help us to appreciate the fact that seismic upheavals on the order of Rousseau's *Confessions* are often preceded by years and years of cultural continental drift. The literary event can take place only in the context of slowly changing material practices.[22]

Widespread interest over the last two decades in the topic of subjective modernity and its relation to reading practices has opened up considerably the possibility of thinking about autobiography as something other than a literary genre whose practitioners echo or subvert the body of work bequeathed by predecessors. Productive use of a wide variety of material—from women's conduct books to literary anthologies—has demonstrated how subjectivity is produced through certain reading practices and vice-versa.[23] Concern with how autobiography fits into this picture, however, has been partial in both senses of the word. Following the models of Ian Watt and Jürgen Habermas, scholars have almost inevitably regarded the Enlightenment, and more specifically the English Enlightenment, as providing the two conditions necessary for the development of autobiographical thinking—Protestantism and a rising bourgeoisie; hence eighteenth-century London has emerged relatively unchallenged as the birthplace of autobiography, indeed as the literary and subjective epicenter of the modern world.[24] Drawn this way, however, this portrait of modernity, and of autobiography's place within it, loses in interest what it gains in sharpness. If the modern—that shorthand for a cluster of phenomena to which autobiography and interiority belong—is the bourgeois, is the Protestant, is the Enlightenment, then by the same token it must also be, implicitly, a phenomenon open to easy causal explanations and a phenomenon just as easily left behind once "exposed." Subjective interiority was too implicated in the new and ubiquitous technology of print, too bound up with the vicissitudes of a vocabulary evolving over many centuries, and too able to infiltrate the most seemingly incompatible positions—mysticism and skepticism, Protestantism and Catholicism, and others—to owe its existence solely to the activities of a specific national culture, class, or creed.

Autobiography and interiority were part of an evolution in subjectivity whose long-sought "origins" seem quite a bit more foggy—and intriguing—

once one looks a bit further afield than do the customary studies of "great books," once we adventure beyond hypotheses that predicate modernity on isolated ideas. It is in this sense that the *mentalités* approach to the problem of autobiographical subjectivity can be of help, for it implies the analysis of many texts, and ones from domains usually overlooked in traditional literary history—more "popular" social strata, and notably, religious communities. It also entails revising or nuancing the old typologies used to separate off into distinct categories so-called genres such as the memoir, the journal, and auto-biography "proper."[25] A model of this type of approach is James Amelang's thorough study of early modern artisan autobiography. While providing a broad typology of different types of "life writing," Amelang is nonetheless at-tentive to the blending that is not simply symptomatic of the inevitable break-down of all generic categories under close scrutiny, but, more specifically, characterizes a time when "[personal] writing was not a 'normal' cultural practice or expectation."[26] His work, along with that of Jonathan Dewald on aristocratic memoirs, goes some way toward dispelling tempting conclusions regarding the link between creed or class and autobiographical practice, and toward giving us a picture of how the work of someone like Rousseau might be considered a product, not cause, of popular autobiographical writing.[27]

At the very least, then, *Being Interior* builds on the research of historians like Amelang and Dewald, and expands work on the history of autobiogra-phy to a habitually neglected corpus, that of French religious writing.[28] Filling gaps, however, is not my principal aim. By arguing for revised spatial and temporal limits for the phenomena that make up modernity, I do not merely seek to assert that France, too, knew the changes that did England, or knew them first, or knew them even in a different socio-economic context. The most useful effect of such a displacement is, rather, to nuance our concep-tion of just what an autobiographical, interiorized subject might have been, to go beyond the weary caricatures of the "modern subject" too prevalent in contemporary academia—that autonomous master of the objective world, a being secure within the new genre of autobiography that reifies his unique-ness. This is the autobiographer as straw man—a being so improbably naïve and quaint that it is little wonder that poststructuralists spent a gleeful decade exposing his foundations as illusory, and that many think it will be so easy to move beyond him.[29] Perhaps—and this is a point to which I will return—we might do well to speak of modern subjectivity, indeed modernity more gen-erally, much in the way Gilles Deleuze has accustomed us to speaking of capi-talism: as a cultural formation capable of endlessly reinventing itself *because* it is unstable, and which persists not in spite of its contradictions and weaknesses, but as a result. Autobiography, in its manifestly problematic promise to make identity readable, is part of the contradictions of modernity.

Religious Topography: In, Out, and In-Between

Autobiography thrives not because of a naïve belief in the subject's autonomous development or in the compatibility of an "authentic" self and language, but because it was founded on a division that has been a potent organizing principle of reality for the last five or so centuries—the division between interior truth and exterior appearance. Especially since Foucault, in *Les Mots et les choses*, argued that the idea of depth—of nature, of the subject—characterized the modern *episteme*, scholars have shown human interiority to be one of the most pervasive metaphors uniting all sorts of cultural products, from the metaphysical to the architectural.[30] *Being Interior*, which fits into this constellation of work, asks how the autobiographical text was instrumental in effecting this new sense of the interior, and does this by reversing the marginalization of the religious in traditional literary history. If political memoirs of the seventeenth century, for instance, do not figure in the following study, this is not because I assume that they are not part of the autobiographical nebula, but simply because *Being Interior* insists on the importance of the inner-outer divide to autobiographical culture. And, though one could no doubt search with some success secular memoirs of the time for signs of the trope, it was principally among the French adepts of religious interiority that, over the course of the seventeenth century, autobiographical writing came to constitute the privileged mediation between the interiorized subject and the exterior world.

Given that scant serious consideration has been given to the mine of cultural data that is to be had in the religious domain, it is little wonder scholars have overlooked this key intersection of a discursive practice and a psychological metaphor. In the case of France, the separation between religious literature and its secular counterpart has been especially acute—a separation that holds less in Spain and England, where religious autobiographies such as Teresa's *Life by Herself* (pub. 1588) and Bunyan's *Grace Abounding to the Chief of Sinners* (1666) have achieved canonical status. Witness, for instance, Philippe Lejeune's justification for excluding what he calls spiritual autobiography from his first study of the genre's development in France: "Regarding the history of autobiography, it must be emphasized that [spiritual autobiography] is an autonomous corpus: it had no influence on the birth of modern autobiography; moreover, after the end of the eighteenth century, this tradition has continued without modern autobiography having had much influence on it."[31] And yet, aside from the rather obvious objection regarding the position of Augustine's *Confessions* in the Western literary tradition,[32] one might well note the importance of the religious domain in general for any history of the book. Representing a significant proportion of the books printed in the seventeenth century, religious writing is perhaps the ideal terrain for an investigation into early modern reading and writing habits.[33]

As the rapturous testimony of Surin I evoked at the outset demonstrates, in the devotional vocabulary of the period, the very term "interior" knew remarkable success, used everywhere as an attribute, imprecise but definitely laudatory. The multiple valences of the term will become clear in the course of this study, so I will not lay them all out here. For the moment, a typical use will suffice. In her *Life* (published 1720), Jeanne Guyon writes of an inspirational meeting with "un homme fort intérieur": for many like Guyon, the highest religious aspiration was not to be saintly, nor virtuous, but to be, like this man, "very interior."[34] This qualification had little or nothing to do with patristic theories of what, in the Pauline Epistles, was called the "inner man." If, following Paul, Augustine had indeed spoken of a *homo exterior* and a *homo interior*, these categories of his theological system were attributes of every person, and designated certain universal faculties. The "interior man" referred to the faculty of reason, whereas the "exterior man" encompassed those faculties, such as the senses, that man shared with animals.[35] Guyon's use of "interior" is quite different; the term is opposed not to the animal or the licentious side of man, nor even, as one might expect, to the libertine or the hypocritical *faux-dévot*; her "very interior man" was viewed instead as the contrary of the erudite theologian, who might be well versed in the study of sacred texts and commentary, and yet lack the direct *experience* of God. Hence, Guyon was setting up a split between elements of the same religious community—between a lettered elite and spiritual cognoscenti—whose ways of knowing she supposed to be essentially different.

"Interior" could as well connote a metaphorical space inside the subject, hidden from view by duplicitous appearances. The seventeenth century has often been characterized as a time of particular semiotic malaise, in which the social order increasingly seemed a system of signs anchored in no absolute.[36] Social signifiers such as dress could be modified; one still needed a sword to enter Versailles, but swords, after all, could be rented outside the palace gates. Even power, Louis XIV intuited, was not a thing in itself, a function of military strength, but an effect that could be produced through judicious use of spectacle and mise-en-scène.[37] This malaise extended into the religious domain as well, for the Church, too, was perceived as an institution that produced signs that might well be empty—signs such as the Eucharist, which served as a point of convergence for contemporary semiotic anxieties.[38] In the same way, a place in that institution's hierarchy might not guarantee spiritual worthiness nor even efficacy: being a member of the caste implied only claims on a purely "exterior" domain and had nothing to do with interior piety.[39] In a word, virtue itself was not readily readable in outward acts: just as a novel such as *Don Quixote* (1605–15) encouraged readers to mock a hero lost in an epic past where "doing" (acts) still implied "being" (virtue), many readers of the religious press were loath to confuse acts of piety and spiritual merit. The aspiring early modern saint was acutely aware that charity and self-mortification belonged to the now devalued domain of the spectacle, of representation.

These convictions opened up quite different possibilities for what was now a "subject"—a being who no longer took its legitimacy from its place in the cosmic (or social) order, but who depended on self-legitimation. On the one hand there developed what Daniel Roche has memorably called a "culture of appearances," a culture in which selves could be "fashioned" (to use Stephen Greenblatt's influential notion).[40] Early modern characters and types such as Iago, Don Juan, the picaro, and even Puss 'n Boots all sought to profit from social and semiotic malaise by turning the slippage of signs to their advantage and fashioning their own identity. Conversely, others reacted in a quite different way to semiotic disorder. Some Church reactionaries would steadfastly assert the stability of signs—the correspondence between institutionalized signifiers and the truth they represented—but the autobiographers discussed here took a different tack: they constructed the interior as mystical in the sense of "hidden from view," in other words, as a truth without signposts. The authentic subjective space of interiority could be deepened through the efforts of dilation evoked by Marie Baron—adepts were frequently invited to "work on their hearts," as one translator of Augustine put it[41]—but the deeper it became, the more invisible it was, and the more immune to contamination by the world outside. Yet there had to be a "way in," and this was autobiographical writing, which continuously and emphatically gestured to the hidden interior. The existence of this space could only be detected by a Happy Few who were privy to autobiographical writing; the identity of the individual, esoteric and not exoteric, acquired thereby a semblance of stability—but, as we shall see, just a semblance.

This was what "being interior" meant, then—cultivating a relationship with God that was thought to be experiential rather than bookishly scholastic, lived rather than learned; it was to mistrust the institutional and the hierarchical, and to shy away from the duplicity of a virtue gauged by outward acts or miracles. But most significantly—and this aspect of modernity remains hidden if the latter is always construed as fundamentally skeptical or secular—being interior entailed transferring ideas of the unsoundable depth of God to the human subject, and then taking this interior domain of "experience" as the object of autobiographical writing. Those who were interior proclaimed the merits of first-person testimony, and theorized a relationship between the depths of subjective authenticity and a form of writing that would allow the reader to peer into this abyss.

Being Interior is divided into two parts, the first of which traces how and why this autobiographical dream was fabricated in seventeenth century France. I say "dream," for many of the works discussed here do indeed hold forth the utopian promise of transparency between interior and exterior via the autobiographical text. At the same time, however, autobiographical and interior utopias were—"always already"—unstable, defensive; they held down one side of a dialectic in which every assertion of autobiographical transparency ran headlong into anxiety over the proliferation of opportunities for incomprehension, and this is the subject of this book's second part. If autobiography reified self, it also put that self into circulation among readers who might or might not know how to interpret the subject's newfound uniqueness: to the inherent inadequacy of language was added the potential alienation of print—the very condition of modern autobiographical practice. Indeed, although virtually none of the autobiographers discussed in these pages wrote explicitly for print—many pointedly refused it, and restrained their readership as much as possible—print was nevertheless the horizon against which the autobiographical project was defined. It made autobiography thinkable, but at the same time it also made it problematic. Alternately transparency and obstacle (to use Jean Starobinski's concise characterization of Rousseauian subjectivity), it is little wonder, then, that autobiography came to be figured as the martyrdom, as much as the medium, of the modern subject.[42] Hence my sense of the lessons to be drawn from the works of writers for whom autobiography, not yet institutionalized and still without even a name, was never a given: each autobiographical act demanded to be interrogated, and these interrogations survive, traces of a constitutive tension between readers, writers, and the society that joined them only at the perverse price of an uneasy separation.

Autobiography and interiority were, and are, utopias, but they had, then, their infernal dimensions as well. If at times—for reasons that range from the personal to the political—one might like to solidify one's identity, at other times equating oneself with a thing (a book, a narrative) opens up dystopias of alienation, slander and judicial pursuit. For this reason, my study tends to thread between a somewhat Foucauldian picture of how the autobiographical mentality fit in with modern practices of "governmentality" (the techniques, from confession to poll-taking, by which subjects are governed but more important learn to govern themselves), and a less dismissive position that seeks to understand the psychological and social heuristics of the practice: in other words, what interests me in autobiography is its undecidable relation to institutional power.[43] In a sense, I wish to temper the historical assessment of autobiographical interiority as inherently complicitous with the modern "production" of subjects of power—such was the argument to be found in some of the most powerful pages of *The History of Sexuality*, volume one—with a sense of the myriad ways in which discipline trips up in its own instruments.[44] If the practice of autobiography might well be envisioned as a sort of literary panopticon—that "architectural figure"[45] of the process of internalization wrought by exposure to the disembodied gaze of power—it deserves to be understood in addition as something other than a monolith: as much rubble, in a sense, as edifice. Like the mis-named "individual" it appears to solidify, autobiography is in fact the sign of a fracture. By this I mean not only that the genre, read with close attention to the deconstructive meanders of textuality, can be said (in Paul De Man's formulation) to "de-face" the subject.[46] More important, an autobiography is also a book that serves, socially, as a site of contention; it establishes itself at the modern fault line separating private from public, female from male, individual from society, manuscript from print, accused from accuser. It is resistance and repression, agency and subjection, all rolled into one, and there is no reason to regard either of these poles as the hidden truth of the other.

What follows, then, is a history of the many roles played by the autobiographical mentality in early modern culture—the conflicts it both echoed and engendered, the asylums it proposed and deferred, the powers it simultaneously perturbed, reversed, and reinscribed. Hence *Being Interior* is not conceived of as a celebration of personal spaces, but argues, rather, that those spaces could only enclose paradox and conflict. Sometimes naïve, sometimes deeply mistrustful, flowing through but also against institutions like the Church and the judiciary, this emerging practice was effectuated both via the very material medium of print, as well as in the putatively autonomous space of scriptural self-presence. Because autobiography sat astride—uncomfortably—a reality cloven into interior and exterior halves, it would alternately figure plenitude and dispersal, transparency and opacity, centrality and marginality, authority and vulnerability, order and contestation; such contradictions were its constitutive condition.

The four chapters that comprise the present study are an attempt to provide a fuller picture than we currently possess of how and why autobiography took hold of our collective imagination, and they advance by lending an ear to the many moments in the seventeenth century when autobiographical writing did not "go without saying." For before it became routine to think in terms of human interiority, before autobiography was a recognized genre, writers and readers could only but leave traces of their grapplings with these new metaphors and practices. In other words, rather than paying attention to the life-story we are told, I have adopted the tactic of attending to the gaps in the narrative—to the moments writers pause to redefine or justify their work, and to the manifest efforts of editors to fit these new practices into existing conceptual categories.

No one methodology is entirely sufficient to the task, but as I have hinted, perhaps the most useful tool for heightening our sensitivity to these gaps is to be had by paying attention to the material forms early autobiography assumed on its journey from writer to reader—briefly, the way it was "packaged," even "sold." Chapter 1 does just this, by looking at the seventeenth-century French transmission of two books that modern readers have come to recognize (or perhaps misrecognize) as autobiographical and interior landmarks—Augustine's *Confessions* and Montaigne's *Essais*. Understanding the early modern history of autobiography entails knowing more than that Montaigne and Augustine were popular reading in the seventeenth century, and thus might have "influenced" the development of the genre. It is essential, I maintain, that we excavate *how* these works were being read: Who was reading them? What did this precise reading public like best about them? What did they contain that was ignored or unreadable? What values did they come to represent? These questions have answers, and they suggest that if the modern propensity to read Montaigne and Augustine as if they were autobiography is anachronistic with respect to the texts themselves, it is an anachronism whose origins reach back to the seventeenth century. By way of a demonstration that wends its way among other points of interest as well—we will see, for instance, how the *Essais* themselves seem divided on the relations they posit between writing and self, and how already in the fourth century Augustine was rewriting Pauline conceptions of what the "inner man" might be—I mostly want to show how editors and translators increasingly held these two works of Augustine and Montaigne up to readers as texts emanating from the depths of subjective experience, as instruments of what Foucault has termed a "hermeneutics of self."

Chapter 2 approaches the problem of autobiography's arrival not through considering the seventeenth century's repositioning of texts of the past, but rather by looking at how contemporaries were taught and brought to write autobiography themselves, and how this writing seeped little by little into print. Within convent walls, much autobiographical writing was produced, predominantly as private exchanges between a nun and her spiritual director. Yet from approximately 1650 on, this writing started to acquire visibility as such exchanges gained the status of publishable documents. The growing thirst for autobiographical texts is evident in religious biographies, which — expanding on Surin's work on Marie Baron — became vehicles for the transmission of a type of text that had heretofore commanded no editorial attention. As they transposed autobiographical texts verbatim into their works, biographers invented a fascinating typographical array of ways to call attention to the now sensational fact that their subjects were speaking of their own accord. In the short space of a few decades, the presence of quoted passages became so intrusive as to reduce biographers to mere cutters and pasters of autobiographical fragments. Here too, other stories are inseparable from this main narrative, above all the story of the gendering of autobiographical interiority: the culture of autobiography was set up by men as well as women as feminine, and the transfer of authority from the biographer to the autobiographer represented at the same time a transfer from men such as Surin to women like Baron. It is no wonder, I maintain, that our culture remains fascinated with autobiography as "a voice from the margins," for it was invented as such.

Thus Part I of this study, "Reading In," charts the Western investment in a mode of thinking that associates the first-person discourse of experience with authority, authenticity, and self-presence. Part II, "Frictions," is concerned with the more somber underside of modern subjectivity — difference, madness, marginality, and all manners of persecution. For if some envisioned a world in which the inviolate space of quotation marks might guarantee soul-to-soul communication, others recognized that texts were distressingly mobile, subject to misappropriation and misinterpretation. The works of three important mystics situated on the embattled fringes of the Catholic Church — Jean de Labadie (1610–1674), Antoinette Bourignon (1610–1680), and Jeanne Guyon (1648–1717) — demonstrate how the insistent wish for transparency was inevitably overtaken by a recognition that a book, even an autobiographical one, was fatally exterior. Their mistrust sprang from autobiography's emerging status as an instrument of judicial attack and defense: it was the willingness of the courts to look to a defendant's biography for proof of heterodoxy that led writers to the formulation of autobiographical ripostes. Whence the sense, in the work of these writers, of the Faustian bargain of autobiography, which emerges as the symptom, perhaps even the agent of a friction, the trace of subjects forever driven to justify themselves before society, and yet forever misread even in their attempts to be transparent. Early examples of autobiography, I argue, are irreplaceable because they read as particularly lucid chronicles of the very forces that contributed to and defined their production.

The final chapter is an attempt to historicize a category of knowledge we usually take for granted — "experience," an unavoidable concept that rushes in to fill the void left by a modern propensity to view institutions, historical models and exemplars, and "book-knowledge" itself as bankrupt, inapplicable to the individuals we feel ourselves to be. Here I examine a single text, the strange autobiography of Jean-Joseph Surin, who was not only Marie Baron's spiritual director but also the star exorcist in the most notorious case of possession in seventeenth-century France. In the wake of the Loudun possession of the 1630s, Surin experienced acute physiological and psychological disturbances; his *Science expérimentale des choses de l'autre vie* (1663) tells the story of his twenty-year battle with aphasia, delirium, and most of all a haunting and painful sense of his own personal difference. Yet Surin's difficulties were anything but infirm relics of a more superstitious age. On the contrary, Surin's breakdown occurred precisely at the moment the authority of the Church and its entire interpretive tradition was wavering, unable to make sense of the "individual"; his difficult task was to theorize autobiography as the book one clings to when all other books fail, a self-authorizing space where one undertakes the analysis of the ineffable quality of "experience."

It remains to point out what should be obvious from my title: that this is a study of in fact two phenomena — autobiography and interiority — that do not precisely coincide. An inclusive work on the metaphor of interiority in early modern France would need to take into account interests as far removed from religious self-exploration as mining treatises, which also helped spread belief in a "deep," subterranean world.[47] Likewise, a complete study of autobiography would need to take account of the aforementioned domains of aristocratic and artisan memoirs, as well as judicial confessions and even possession narratives. *Being Interior* aims at neither of these goals. I have striven, rather, to isolate a particularly potent combination of concepts and practices—interiority, autobiography, experience—that can and do appear in other contexts, independently of one another. But because my subject is confluence, isolation can never be total, and it is inevitable that issues that come up with much force in some chapters—the gendering of autobiography, the wavering of doctrinal authority, and so on—overflow into or serve as background for others. As such, although the chapters can be read separately, each one is designed to develop subjects only anticipated in earlier chapters, and to echo themes already set forth.

A final word on what some readers may view as an overly proleptic or teleological cast to my arguments. Leaving aside the more theoretical problem of whether or not it is even possible to think historical change without the proleptic unconscious hidden in every use of the terms "still" or "not yet," "then" and "now," I can say that this book persistently argues against viewing the "modern" as a stable, self-contained epoch that resulted from an absolute rupture (situate it where one may) with a premodern past. At the same time, and in complementary fashion, I insist that those who would maintain the absolute otherness of the premodern past are mostly engaging in the utopian exercise of erecting a world magnificently untainted by our own (supposedly) unhealthy conceptual categories. Once this is stated, the problem then becomes: to what extent is it legitimate to sift through the past in search of relics that resemble what we now recognize as a (more or less) stable practice? My first answer, rather abstract, is that the legitimacy of such methods is directly proportional to the attentiveness with which we sift and classify, and to the amount of nuance we can bring to our characterizations of both past and present. A more concrete response, however, can be found in the material I am proposing to explicate: the more one listens with care to the hemming and hawing that is literature—discourses traversed, like a city, with old passageways and bright boulevards, an accretion of dead metaphors, new figures of speech, obsolete and innovative book-making procedures, and so on—the more evident it becomes that looking to the seventeenth century for the beginnings (or at least some of the beginnings) of autobiography and the culture of interiority is anything but anachronistic. On the contrary, and rather uncannily, what these texts have to explain to us is no less than our own desire to excavate them, and our pressing need to understand the vexed but always promising history of autobiography.

Part I
Reading In

Chapter One
The History of an Anachronism
Montaigne, Augustine, and the Becoming of Autobiography

Historians do not care much for anachronisms, and for good reason: on the one hand, anachronism strikes at what they hold dearest, namely, rigorous attention to historical specificity; on the other hand, it serves as a disquieting reminder that interpretations of the past can be articulated only from the perspective of an inescapable present. Notwithstanding this cause for anathema—anachronism as that which must but cannot be eliminated if the historian is to exist—we should keep in mind that anachronisms, being as much the products of temporality as any other cultural formation, are open to historical inquiry. No doubt they have their stories to tell.

Take the example of a book that most Montaigne scholars would regard as a particularly egregious anachronism—a volume published in 1935 by Marvin Lowenthal under the title of *The Autobiography of Michel de Montaigne*. Lowenthal's project was as touchingly naïve as it was critically hopeless: he aimed to assemble a "continuous narrative" of Montaigne's life by extracting those sections of the *Essais* where the author spoke of himself, banishing thereby the digressions and "rank confusion" that for a modern public mar the reading experience: "Aided by scissors, paste, and patience, I have let [Montaigne] retell his life-story."[1] But would Montaigne really have understood what it might mean to tell his "life-story" in the form of a "continuous narrative"? As many recent commentators have hastened to point out, Montaigne's text betrays little sympathy for this steadfastly modern belief in the importance of personal chronology.[2] Armed with famous snippets from the *Essais* ("C'est un sujet merveilleusement vain, divers et ondoyant, que l'homme" [Truly man is a marvelously vain, diverse, and undulating object (I, 1: 9; 5)], "Si je parle diversement de moi, c'est que je me regarde diversement" [If I speak of myself in different ways, that is because I look at myself in different ways (II, 1: 335; 242)], and so on),[3] scholars of late have tried, in the face of readings such as Lowenthal's, to assert the otherness of Montaigne's view of self, a self rooted not in an organically unified life history but in contingency, exemplarity, and palimpsestic infinitude.[4] These corrections, numerous and persuasive, do make the autobiographical anachronism seem a pitfall that threatens a proper understanding of Montaigne and, more generally, of a time in which people did not yet function as self-realizing, coherent subjects.[5] And yet it would be a shame to dispatch too rapidly, as many have, the whole question of Montaigne's "autobiography." For it remains to wonder how that other time gave way to our own: what were the historical antecedents for Lowenthal's disrespect for Montaigne's text? Since when have readers wished he had written his own *Life*?

Lowenthal, it turns out, had a number of cutting and pasting predecessors in the seventeenth and eighteenth centuries. Starting with Pierre Charron, who pillaged the *Essais* to compose his enormously successful *De la sagesse* (1601), there followed at least three attempts to make Montaigne palatable for a contemporary readership.[6] Yet there was a great difference, for these compilers invariably *cut out* precisely those portions that Lowenthal wanted to highlight, producing not an autobiography but collections of thoughts — like the popular *ana* of the time, collections of witticisms organized into topics.[7] One might be prompted to conclude from this that an autobiographical reading of Montaigne has only become possible in the last century or so, but there is more. Lowenthal's enterprise was in fact uncannily congruent with a reading practice that dates to within a mere sixteen years of Montaigne's death, for it was in 1608 that appeared for the first time, appended to the *Essais*, a short (some 175 lines) text entitled *Sommaire discours sur la vie de Michel seigneur de Montaigne*. The *Sommaire discours*, reproduced in many editions of the *Essais* over the next two centuries, was a virtual template for Lowenthal's edition: it pieced together a biography of the author simply by quoting from the *Essais*. Catherine Magnien-Simonin has pointed out this text's innovation: the *Sommaire discours* was a purely chronological exposition of Montaigne's life, lifted from his own writings, whereas the biographical blurbs common at the time normally followed the rules of the *enkomion*, divided as they were into the tripartite "biens extérieurs, biens du corps, biens de l'âme." According to Magnien-Simonin, it was the *Sommaire discours* that more or less put into circulation the legend of Montaigne wanting to depict himself "tout entier, et tout nud," as he put it in his "Au lecteur."[8] More precisely, we might say that the *Sommaire discours* indicates that a moment had come in which the self-portraiture that Montaigne himself evokes in his "Au lecteur" was expected to be chronological — a notion quite foreign to Montaigne's own text.

The *Sommaire discours* does not, of course, "prove" that Montaigne wrote his autobiography after all, nor that his contemporaries wished that he had. But its existence is troubling because it complicates greatly the traces of reception furnished by the seventeenth-century compilers who ignored the biographical elements in Montaigne's work (say, his fall from his horse in "De l'exercitation" [II, 6]) in favor of his philosophizing. As a document, the *Sommaire discours* betrays the ambiguity of a moment in which biography and autobiography blended strangely: like Lowenthal, it let Montaigne tell his own life story, but only while simultaneously substituting the third person for the first in its transpositions—"Mon livre est toujours un" (My book is always one) becomes "Son livre a toujours été un" (His book was always one). It reminds us, then, that just as the *Essais* themselves were a deformation of the Renaissance practice of the commonplace book,[9] the reading of the *Essais* was also deformed over time, and these deformations hold clues as to the evolution of modern reading practices.

The question of chronologically understood identity is, however, but one component, vital as it may be, of reading autobiographically. Another component, and the one that will govern the following reading of Montaigne's and to a lesser degree Augustine's seventeenth-century reception, is interiority and its relation to writing. I mean interiority here in a rather specific sense, not simply as a vague term of approbation applied by modern scholars in an attempt to make early texts seem "relevant" to twentieth-century readers, even—and perhaps especially—when the metaphor is entirely absent from the works in question.[10] Interiority is a metaphor, and the question of autobiographical anachronism is linked to the metaphor's use: since when have Montaigne and Augustine seemed to readers to express their inner selves on the printed page?

Reading Montaigne with Rousseau's Eyes

In 1774, or, by the literary calendar, roughly halfway between Rousseau's undertaking of his *Confessions* (1764) and their initial publication (1782), Montaigne's *Journal de voyage* appeared in print for the first time.[11] This record of Montaigne's travels in Europe had lain forgotten in a trunk until a historian of the Perigord region named Joseph Prunis happened upon it while searching the château of the author of the *Essais*. The then-owner of the château, Charles-Joseph Ségur, entrusted the *Journal*'s publication to Prunis, who commenced by drawing up a preface for the projected edition. The reader of Prunis's preface is taken on a tour of Montaigne's fabled library; the editor points out the inscriptions painted on the walls, and laments the disappearance of the library's books — precious relics of the great man. By Prunis's day, Montaigne's pronouncement that he had, with the *Essais*, produced a "livre consubstantiel à son auteur" (a book consubstantial with its author [II, 18: 665; 504]) had become decidedly modest. For Prunis, all of the library was a sanctum; all of these books were somehow one with their owner. Even the inscriptions Montaigne had copied onto his walls were of interest, and Prunis saw to their publication, announcing: "Tout ce qui a trait à Montaigne est précieux" (Everything that has to do with Montaigne is precious).[12]

Anticipating the activities of the modern institution of the literary fan club, Prunis scoured the home of the great author, uncovering all the textual relics he could find. This obscure eighteenth-century historian's enthusiasm for Montaigne's work — any and all of it — brings to mind changes in what Michel Foucault has called the author-function. For Foucault, this term designates an ensemble of discursive practices — "the way we handle texts, the comparisons we make, the traits we extract as pertinent, the continuities we assign, or the exclusions we practice."[13] In publishing Montaigne's inscriptions, for example, Prunis was claiming for the corpus of the author's official "work" material that had previously been outside it. Montaigne was no longer simply a man who wrote a book called the *Essais*; he was the Author of a network of textual traces that needed to be piously conserved. But the story of the *Journal de voyage* continues, and it is this continuation that is of special importance for autobiography's history.

If, as Foucault maintains, our ideas of what an author is always involve an ideologically motivated selection, it follows that not all members of a reading community share precisely the same conception of authorship. And indeed, Prunis's selection, though clearly made with a mind to the concept of the author, was more limited than some at the time would have liked. Claiming that the *Journal*'s countless descriptions of "la moindre humeur vitieuse" (the slightest ill humor)[14] might bore (or embarrass) readers less enthusiastic than himself, he made plans to publish only selections from the *Journal*. Ségur, the official owner of the manuscript, was less than pleased by Prunis's editorial choice, and turned to Anne-Gabriel Meunier de Querlon, in charge of manuscripts at the Bibliothèque Royale in Paris. To Querlon, then, Ségur gave orders to proceed with complete publication, a task realized by the edition of 1774. Despite Prunis's recognition of the author's importance, his editorial restraint would no longer do: everything about Montaigne had to come out in the open.

Like Prunis, Querlon added a preface, but rather than provide a few anecdotal details and descriptions, he availed himself of these pages to set up a way of reading the *Journal*. Querlon argues that, in contrast to the *Essais*, which were intended for publication, the *Journal* was private writing. "Ce journal (il faut bien le répéter) n'avait été fait que pour lui, pour son usage particulier" (He wrote this journal [I must repeat] only for himself, for his private use). And repeat it he does: Querlon reiterates several times that it is here, in this long-lost text, not in the *Essais*, that the reader is to find the most potent example of Montaigne's stylistic *négligence*. Given their public nature, the *Essais* are "un peu plus soigné[s]" (a little more polished) than the *Journal*, which is compared to a "[t]ableau croqué sans le moindre soin" (a picture sketched without the least care) by an artist "[qui] ne crayonne que pour lui seul" ([who] is only scribbling for himself).[15] Querlon warns adepts of the travel journal genre not to expect the usual long descriptions of artworks and edifices, nor digressions on local politics and manners: the *Journal* contains none of that. And so, faced with the necessity of justifying the relevance of this text to the interest of his readers, Querlon comes up with the following argument:

[C]e qui rendra ce Journal intéressant pour les Lecteurs qui cherchent l'homme dans ses écrits, c'est qu'il leur fera beaucoup mieux connaître l'Auteur des *Essais* que les *Essais* même. . . . Ici [in the *Journal*] l'on ne voit plus l'Ecrivain, non pas même dans le moment le plus froid de la composition la moins méditée: c'est Montaigne lui-même. On le voit mieux que dans ses *Essais*, parce que c'est bien moins lui qui parle, qui rend témoignage de lui-même, que les faits écrits de sa main pour la décharge de sa mémoire, sans autre vue, sans la moindre idée d'ostentation prochaine, éloignée, présente, ou future.[16]

(This Journal will be of interest to Readers who seek the man in his writings, because it will allow them to know the Author of the Essays better than the Essays themselves do. . . . Here [in the *Journal*] one no longer sees the Writer, not even in the coldest moment of the least concerted composition: it is Montaigne himself. One sees him more clearly than in his Essays because it is less he who is speaking and giving testimony, than facts written in his hand in order to discharge his memory, without any other purpose, without the least idea of ostentation, whether immediate or far away, present or future.)

This argument is the extension of Querlon's previous distinctions between private and public writings, between carefree and careful styles. Whereas the author of the *Essais* speaks incessantly of himself, he does so knowingly; his book is thus a construction, the work of a professional writer ("l'Ecrivain"). The *Journal*, on the other hand, is spontaneous discourse, on the surface less concerned with Montaigne himself, but in reality contiguous with him in a way that "concerted" ("méditée," i.e., self-reflexive) writing could never be: "C'est Montaigne lui-même."

In these prefaces—prescriptions for tackling works whose readability was clearly in question—both Prunis and Querlon give clear illustrations of the application of the author-function to a text created in an authorial environment quite different from that of the 1770s. But Querlon's reading is particularly intriguing, for it demonstrates the extent to which autobiographical thinking was bound up with the institution of authorship: in that web of works spun out by the creature we know as the author there is one sensitive autobiographical spot where the author can be seen, naked and spontaneous, free even of the weight, the immense professional responsibility, of authorship itself. Querlon is much more specific than Prunis, who associates Montaigne with *all* of the texts he might have come in contact with—books owned, authors cited, and so on. Querlon argues that the author is not, in fact, reflected in all texts equally, for there are public texts and private texts, each having its own relation to the individual who produced them. Querlon reads the *Essais*, first, as a public discourse; and second, as so obsessively self-reflective that no clear portrait of Montaigne emerges from the jumble of brush strokes. Conversely, upon the *Journal de voyage*, Querlon projects his desire for a private text, linked intimately to an author who was writing for himself alone; this private writing is seen to be a spontaneous "discharge of memory" revealing the true Montaigne. The format of the *Essais* scatters the subject, while the private *Journal* restores his wholeness. The latter provides the raw center around which the rest of Montaigne's work gravitates.

Any reader of the *Journal* would probably find Querlon's reading aberrant—it is after all a dryly impersonal text, the first third of which appears to have been written not by Montaigne at all, but rather by an anonymous "secretary" who refers to his employer in the third person. But it is the very outrageousness of Querlon's judgment, its strained quality, that alerts us to the urgency transfiguring reading practices in the same years that Rousseau, following the prohibition of his public reading of the *Confessions* in May 1771, was hard at work on *Rousseau juge de Jean-Jacques*. The example of Querlon's preface to the *Journal* hints at the existence of a reading public training itself to project values—authenticity, privacy, and transparency, for instance—upon certain texts held to be experiential, and to accord those texts pride of place in the network of an author's production.

If by appealing to the autobiographical urge Querlon hoped to sell books, he must have been disappointed. In a review article in the *Correspondance littéraire* on the occasion of the *Journal*'s publication, Querlon's potential readers could read: "Il n'est pas étonnant que les *Voyages* de Montaigne aient été attendus avec tant d'empressement; il l'est moins encore qu'ils aient fait si peu de sensation depuis qu'ils ont paru" (It is not surprising that the *Voyages* of Montaigne were so eagerly awaited; but it is even less surprising that they have caused so little sensation since they appeared).[17] The expectation explains the burst of five editions (in different formats) in 1774 and 1775; the lack of subsequent interest explains why no others were forthcoming. But this failure must not be interpreted as a rejection of Querlon's values, for the reviewer for the *Correspondance littéraire* — probably Grimm — thirsts as much as Montaigne's editor for an intimate, autobiographical rapport with the author; it is just that for him that rapport comes from the *Essais* and not the *Journal*. Echoing ideas that had become commonplace by the eighteenth century, the reviewer writes:

On aime à suivre Montaigne dans l'intérieur de sa maison, à s'enfermer avec lui dans sa chambre, à s'asseoir à ses côtés au coin de son feu, et à écouter ainsi toutes les confidences qu'il se plaît à nous faire de ses opinions, de ses idées, de ses sentiments, de ses goûts particuliers, de ses affections et de ses pensées les plus secrètes.[18]
(We enjoy following Montaigne into the interior of his house, being closed up with him in his room, sitting down next to him by the fire, and listening to all the confidences he wishes to accord us concerning his opinions, his ideas, his feelings, his private tastes, his affections and his most secret thoughts.)

What this sentence proposes is nothing less than a topography of the autobiographical subject: taking us from the outside to the inside, to the bourgeois space of subjectivity as it was developing in the 1700s (house, fireside), we as readers of the *Essais* are also brought through a clear progression from the implied exteriority of the cerebral to the emotional/experiential, passing from opinions and ideas to feelings, taste, and secret thoughts. These last are, more precisely, Montaigne's "*most* secret thoughts": reading autobiographically implies navigating this graduated topography, plumbing the depths of a subject who is not simply constructed of appearance and underlying reality, but who is layered, a human onion.

Is Montaigne Shallow or Deep?

Bringing up the issue of Montaigne's interiority may well seem pointless to Montaigne scholars of whatever persuasion — both to the group of critics who find his interiority self-evident, and to those who find it hopelessly anachronistic. For the former group, concerned with the problem of the self in the

Essais, Montaigne's frequent use of a term such as "dedans" cannot but imply the existence of subjective space, and open up to us thereby a phenomenological understanding of the Montaignian relation between self, world and text. These observations rapidly lead to a kind of received wisdom in Montaigne studies—namely, that the *Essais* are, in the words of Richard Regosin, "interiority externalized, . . . the invisible made visible." [19] This insistence on Montaigne's modernity, his ability to speak directly to us after some four hundred years, is a point of irritation for those who prefer to emphasize the historical particularity of Montaigne's *moi*, and to applaud Montaigne's quite un-modern, indeed sometimes postmodern, insight into the self's inherent performativity: the author, the *Essais* seem to prove, is not "expressed" in a text of which he is the referent, but constituted in the very act of writing. How else can one interpret the utter circularity of the famous "Je n'ai pas plus fait mon livre que mon livre m'a fait, livre consubstantiel à son auteur" (I have no more made my book than my book has made me—a book consubstantial with its author [II, 18: 665; 504])? [20]

An enormous gulf separates these two readings of Montaigne's ubiquitous *moi*—the gulf, I would argue, of depth itself. As Foucault has shown in his later work on sexuality, all reflexive first-person discourse does not necessarily take its place in the same continuous and ever-increasing concern with "individuality." On the contrary, he argues: the West has known two radically different "technologies" of the self. One, which dominates particularly the modern world, and defines the type of autobiographical reading of Montaigne I have been exploring, Foucault calls a "hermeneutics of self." For the West, the self is conceived of as something pre-existing that people (notably the subject him or herself, but also someone like a psychoanalyst) strive to interpret; it is the locus of a hermeneutic act undertaken in the conviction "that there is something hidden in ourselves and that we are always in a self-illusion which hides the secret." Confession, autobiography, psychoanalysis, the TV talk show—all would be unthinkable without the hermeneutic lure of discovering, Foucault writes, "the truth that inhabits the individual." [21] All form the library of our culture of avowal, "a literature ordered according to the infinite task of extracting from the depths of oneself, in between the words, a truth which the very form of the confession holds out like a shimmering mirage." [22] To this hermeneutics, which turns the self into the subject of the discourse of truth, Foucault opposes a concept that characterized most of the ancient world and only slowly mutated into the hermeneutic imperative— care of the self. To take care of the self (the Greek precept *epimeleisthai sautou*) is not to discover a buried truth, but to engage in a daily ascetic regimen.

Rather than revealing the extradiscursive truth of the subject, caring for the self involves an *assimilation* of truth — for instance, a memorization of laws of conduct so complete that desired actions (fearlessness in the face of death, indifference to pain or pleasure, and so on) become automatic. Last, according to this Stoic view there is no essential division between what I am and what I appear to be; I can become what I want, for "I" is nothing else but a blank slate ready for inscription. Care of the self, therefore, has as little use for the metaphor of depth as a hermeneutics of self depends on it.

If I mention Stoicism here, it is certainly not by way of resurrecting Pierre Villey's now unfashionable theory of the "evolution" (from Stoic to Skeptic to Epicurean) in Montaigne's thought.[23] No doubt there is in the *Essais* a certain tension between competing Classical "ideas" from which Montaigne produces an uneasy (or happy) synthesis, but this philosophical tension appears as somewhat of an epiphenomenon next to the discordant technologies of the self that govern each appearance of the Montaignian *moi*. It is this opposition — between self as a practice and self as the locus of a pre-existent truth (i.e., an interiorized subject) — that accounts for the deceptiveness of Montaigne's interiority. Because the *Essais* mark the intersection or overlapping of two different models of identity, even Montaigne's most inward turns are doggedly shadowed by the ethic of the malleable self. Moreover, the coexistence of these competing models for an "I"-centered world has made inevitable the split in critical writings concerning the subject of Montaigne's "self" — between partisans of a modern, autobiographical Montaigne, and supporters of a flat pre- or postmodern nonsubject.

Admittedly, distinguishing the self-as-practice from the hermeneutic subject is not always a simple matter, especially given the insistence with which modern readers view any mention of reflexivity as a primitive form of an evolving concern with individuality. That is, given the subsequent subjective developments of which we ourselves are a product, we tend to read all Montaigne's pronouncements on himself as if they involved a hermeneutics, a discovery of something deep and hidden. A perfect example is "De la solitude" (I, 39), which begins with the common Montaignian opposition between *particulier* and *publicq*, which translates, here and elsewhere in the *Essais*, the problematic possibility of what Timothy Hampton has described as "productive social action." Because of this opposition, Hampton writes, Montaigne becomes two — "the solitary Montaigne, who is able to create and recreate himself through the process of writing in the protected space of his study, and Montaigne the actor, who finds himself misunderstood and misinterpreted by those around him."[24] This disjunction leads Montaigne to a

series of proclamations that one is tempted to read as interiorizing: "[I]l faut
ramener [l'âme] et [la] retirer en soy" ([W]e must bring [the soul] back and
withdraw it into itself [I, 39: 240; 176]); "Il se faut reserver une arriere boutique toute nostre" (We must reserve a back shop all our own [241; 177]); "La
plus grande chose du monde, c'est de sçavoir estre à soy" (The greatest thing
in the world is to know how to belong to oneself [242; 178]); "Nos forces nous
faillent; retirons les et resserrons en nous" (Our powers are failing us; let us
withdraw them and concentrate them on ourselves [242; 178]); "Retirez vous
en vous" (Retire into yourself [247; 182]). Indeed, the repetition of the pronoun "en" with personal pronouns, coupled with the architectural metaphor
of the "arriere boutique," do seem to suggest a turn inward: Montaigne, here,
might be read as prefiguring those moments of inner monologue when the
Princesse de Clèves withdraws to her *cabinet* in order to sort out her feelings
for the Duc de Nemours. What could be more modern than this retreat into
a private space?

And yet the whole enterprise of retreat for Montaigne has little to do
with introspection as such, if one understands that term, as I believe we must,
as literally as possible — as the search for a truth located metaphorically inside
each one of us.[25] Instead, retreat here is a matter of engaging in a practice of
self-government ("[se] gouverner" [247]) by which one prepares oneself for
misfortune through the contemplation of hypothetical events or exemplary
figures: "presentez vous tousjours en l'imagination Caton, Phocion et Aristides" (keep ever in your mind Cato, Phocion, and Aristides [247; 183]) he ad-
vises the reader of "De la Solitude." Withdrawing into his "arriere boutique"
is thus flight from public action, and, furthermore, a means of "bridl[ing]"
("bride[r]" [I, 8: 21; 32]) the disorderly flux of the mind, of establishing "a
definite organization in [one's] head" ("certaine police en sa teste" [II, 1: 333;
240]), of "train[ing] [one's] life . . . toward a definite goal" ("dress[er] . . . sa
vie à une certaine fin" [II, 1: 337; 243, translation modified]). This is undoubtedly a self-reflective turn, in that social action, action on the stage of history,
is discredited in favor of a care of the self; but no reiteration of the simple
words "en moi" would make this a hermeneutic introspection, as the briefest
comparison with Rousseau would suggest. When Rousseau writes of the plea-
sures of solitude, the act of retreat makes possible a type of self-cultivation in
which the subject, and not some exterior idealized model, is the point of origin. Hence, Rousseau writes of his idyllic stay at "Les Charmettes" as follows:

La méditation me tenait en cela lieu de connaissance, et une réflexion très naturelle
aidait à me bien guider. . . . Ne sachant à quel point le sort ou la mort pouvaient arrêter

mon zèle, je voulais à tout événement acquérir des idées de toutes choses, tant pour sonder mes dispositions naturelles que pour juger par moi-même de ce qui méritait le mieux d'être cultivé.[26]
(In that way meditation took the place of knowledge for me, and a very natural reflection contributed to my guidance . . . Not knowing at what point fate or death would put a stop to my zeal, I wanted as a measure of precaution to acquire ideas about everything, so that I could both sound my natural dispositions and judge for myself what most deserved to be cultivated.)

Solitude enables Rousseau to "sound" the depths of his "natural" reflections and dispositions, to substitute for mere book-knowledge a guidance that seems to take root in the autonomy of the subject. Similarly, he leaves the throngs in order to come face to face with an authentic experience of being that the agitations of social life occlude: on the island of Saint-Pierre, he experiences an enjoyment "[d]e rien d'extérieur à soi, de rien sinon de soi-même et de sa propre existence" (of nothing exterior to oneself, of nothing but oneself and one's own existence).[27] Retreat is thus a gesture that the modern subject will re-appropriate and invest with subjective qualities absent two centuries earlier, when it was still associated with scholarly study and aristocratic *otium*.[28]

Readers familiar with what Villey called Montaigne's "Epicurean phase" know that Montaigne will come to critique Stoic exercises of the type that appear in "De la solitude," founded on the idea of imitation: "Mes actions sont reglées et conformes à ce que je suis et à ma condition" (My actions are in order and conformity with what I am and with my condition) he writes in the 1588 edition, admitting that since he is "ny Ange, ny Caton" (neither an angel nor Cato [III, 2: 813; 617]), he may as well try to be neither.[29] But if the crisis of exemplarity leads Montaigne to reject imitation, does the breakdown of this identity paradigm cause him to envisage truth as lying at the bottom of individual experience? Does Montaigne replace a Stoic care of the self with a hermeneutics, thus opening up an interior space, the space of modern subjectivity? The answer is complex.

On the one hand, a number of critics, generally inspired by deconstructive critiques of reference, have argued that the breakdown in previously accepted identity paradigms — notably imitation, but also the citation of prior authorities — leads the Montaignian *moi* into something of a closed loop. In other words, Montaigne cannot predicate his identity on a correspondence between the *moi* and an ideal, because all ideals — such as honor ("De la gloire" [II, 16]) — are a type of false money or empty signifier; he therefore imagines a kind of self-presence-through-writing. This self can exist *only* in writing; there is nothing to imitate, but neither is there something "there," in the subject, before the act of writing itself. The author is not "expressed" in a text of which he is the referent; instead, Montaigne presents us with an endlessly reiterated self-reflexivity, qualitatively different from "subjectivity," which, following Descartes, would be assumed to precede language and to found the latter's referentiality.[30] The mirror relation of absolute similitude, the pure tautology that Montaigne claims to exist between his person and his book ("tout le monde me reconnoit en mon livre, et mon livre en moy" [everyone recognizes me in my book, and my book in me (III, 5: 875; 667)]) precludes the idea of hermeneutic quest.

Seen in this way, as part of a history of subjectivity, the proliferation of the *moi* in Montaigne has been portrayed not so much as the beginnings of an autobiographical consciousness, but rather as a sort of primordial soup from which such a consciousness would be able subsequently to emerge. According to Antoine Compagnon, for example, Montaigne sits astride two radically different modes of attributing authority to texts: the *Essais* represent a moment of *dérive* following the "fabulous mobilisation of the text"[31] provoked by the invention of the printing press, after which the medieval practice of copying and commenting institutionally approved authorities (such as Aristotle) could never be the same; and they precede the Cartesian *res cogitans*, which will anchor all discourse in the self-evident experience of thought. In this subjective no-man's-land, Montaigne can but oscillate between citation and assertions of originality, between the half-fetishized, half-disenchanted discourse of the Latin Other which he is driven to incorporate into his own text, and the anxious repetition of a *moi* menaced by this discourse's proliferation.[32] Compagnon concludes by comparing Montaigne's situation to that of French philosophy a century later:

> The reference, still potent at the time, which Montaigne attempted to avoid was that of the great man, the *auctoritas* who would confer on him an identity. For Malebranche this no longer exists and the reference is completely different: it is the subject itself; any subject is its own reference. . . . Montaigne refused the test and the guarantee of tradition, but he did not know of a new one. This is why he was unable to do anything other than speak, tirelessly and incessantly, of himself.[33]

This is also why, according to such arguments, Montaigne's abundant concern with himself should not necessarily be taken for a step on the road to the "discovery of the individual." All first-person pronouns are not alike, and the advent of the subject can be read in the movement from the direct object pronoun in Montaigne (by which the individual takes refuge from duplicity by closing itself within an infinitely repeating circuit) to the Cartesian "I" (which takes as its object the world itself). Since this Cartesian subject has not yet been articulated, Montaigne is led to multiply self-reflexivity in the anxious quest for a ground for the "I": "le plus seur estoit de me fier à moy-mesme de moy" (the surest thing was to entrust myself . . . to myself [III, 12: 1045; 799]).[34]

In spite of accounts such as Compagnon's, which situate Montaigne squarely beyond or before the advent of "modern subjectivity," it is difficult not to recognize another trait of the *Essais* that some might prefer to reject as anachronistic—Montaigne's repeated if inclusive gesturing towards an in-choate depth. Montaigne manages to combine both unbridled self-reflexivity —a reflexivity which admits of nothing outside of the textual practice that constitutes the "I" — *and* a persistent deployment of topographical tropes that from time to time open up an experiential subjective world of which the *Essais* are the hermeneutic tool. I have argued in the case of "De la solitude" that Montaigne, in writing of that need to "ramener [l'âme] et [la] retirer en soy" (bring [the soul] back and withdraw it into itself [I, 39: 240; 176]), often stops short of the opening of an interior space. At other moments, however, Montaigne shifts from the ethic of the care of the self to a more interiorizing vo-cabulary, as in the justly famous passage that follows:

Le monde regarde tousjours vis à vis; moy, je replie ma veue au dedans, je la plante, je l'amuse là. Chacun regarde devant soy; moy, je regarde dedans moy: je n'ay affaire qu'à moy, je me considere sans cesse, je me contrerolle, je me gouste. Les autres vont tousjours ailleurs, s'ils y pensent bien; ils vont toujours avant,
    nemo in sese tentant descendere,
moy je me roulle en moy mesme.
(The world always looks straight ahead; as for me, I turn my gaze inward, I fix it there and keep it busy. Everyone looks in front of him; as for me, I look inside of me; I have no business but with myself; I continually observe myself, I take stock of myself, I taste myself. Others always go elsewhere, if they stop to think about it; they always go forward;
    No man tries to descend into himself;
as for me, I roll about in myself.) (II, 17: 657–58; 499)

Here, a centripetal divorce between self and world is replaced by what can be described as a scopic movement ("je replie ma vue") in which a still vague in-terior ("dedans," "dedans moy") is taken as a object of interest; the metaphor of interiority is furthermore enhanced by the citation from Persius's fourth Satire, according to which "no one tries to descend into oneself." But is there truth to be discovered in these depths? At first glance, no: this object of *inter-*

est is not an object of *inquiry*, in that at the moment Montaigne lexically looks inward—literally, introspects—he can only but assert the familiar tautological self-presence resulting from a proliferation of reflexive verbs and object pronouns ("je me roulle en moy mesme"). And yet, just when the reader is about to conclude that what introspection there is here comes to naught (in that nothing is really uncovered), Montaigne continues: "Cette capacité de trier le vray, quelle qu'elle soit en moy" (this capacity for sifting truth, whatever it may amount to in me), suggesting that Montaigne may well occupy a hermeneutic stance with respect to his depths after all.

The numerous modern commentaries on this passage have done little to throw light on Montaigne's hesitation here, on the inconclusiveness of his metaphors of interiority. Jean Starobinski, in his long gloss of the passage does highlight the paradox that nothing is in fact to be discovered in the indeterminate inner space Montaigne creates. Yet for Starobinski, paradox can be ascribed only to the insight of the author. Montaigne's pronouncements on the self, in other words, should always be read with an eye to reconstructing the ultimately consistent phenomenological world view that is their origin. Hence, given the difficulties involved in reading Montaigne, here and elsewhere, as describing a self-as-hidden-truth, the critic opts for a synthesis that restores Montaigne's unique and rigorously consistent perspective on selfhood: "Our true self is not the obscure and insubstantial reality toward which the incomplete effort at knowledge tends," Starobinski writes, "it is this very tension and incompletion."[35] Starobinski's reading, in this respect, ignores the possibility that Montaigne's textual pronouncements on and descriptions of his *moi* are traversed by the contradictions of a historical moment and partially determined by metaphors that have origins and fates that lie outside of the text itself. For in this passage and others, one can witness both a subjectively "modern" Montaigne *and* his pre-modern double, the Montaigne of those who view the *Essais* both as "interiority externalized, . . . the invisible made visible,"[36] *and* as the text of a self that is not yet a subject.

My point, then, is that Starobinski's attempt to offer an alternative to each of these dominant readings of the Montaignian self succeeds no better than they do in describing a text in which many conflicting ideas of selfhood come into play, often in one and the same passage. If Montaigne's thought varies ("Si je parle diversement de moy, c'est que je me regarde diversement" [If I speak of myself in different ways, that is because I look at myself in different ways (II, 1: 335; 242)]), it is not only because, say, his ideas or perspectives change, but also because he is writing at a moment when human beings were starting to metaphorize themselves in a very specific way. To appreciate the contradictions of the text one must read it against the evolving vocabulary of inwardness that one sees, for instance, in Renaissance debates on imitation and authorship. As Terence Cave has shown in his discussion of Erasmus's and Dolet's quarrel over Ciceronianism, it is precisely to Renaissance questions on the attribution of authenticity to texts that one can trace one of the earliest occurrences of a reflexive use of the verb "to express" ("exprimere"): "If you want to express Cicero totally," Erasmus writes in his *Ciceronianus* (1528), "you cannot express yourself. If you do not express yourself, your discourse will be a lying mirror." Du Bellay in a similar context avails himself of the trope of interiority that will from time to time surface in Montaigne's *Essais*, as for instance when he maintains that the good translators must "pénétrer aux plus cachées et intérieures parties de l'auteur qu'ils se sont proposé" (penetrate into the most hidden and interior parts of the author they have taken up).[37] Metaphors such as these are inseparable from the development of the autobiographical mentality, even if they here occur in treatises with no personal content. Montaigne's originality, if he must have one, is to have begun the deployment of interiorizing tropes in a first-person text still massively dedicated to the care of the self.

Innards

The distinguishing feature of the hermeneutic self is its hiddenness, the difficulty the subject as well as the observer has in accessing secret truths. It is this difficulty in "getting it out" that guarantees the authenticity of the confession, the truth of the utterance, and the depth of the subject.[38] Certainly, Montaigne speaks often of the possibility of transparency, of the restoration of a world in which inside and outside were in fact no different — this is the promise of sincerity that will so often accompany autobiographical avowal in the modern age.[39] Hence, in his discussion of dissimulation he offers the maxim, "Un coeur genereux ne doit point desmentir ses pensées; il se veut faire voir jusques au dedans" (A generous heart should not belie its thoughts; it wants to reveal itself even to its utmost depths [II, 17: 647; 491]); and "Du repentir," obsessively centered on the "dedans" as a space of authenticity, concludes with the wish, "Je me veux presenter et faire veoir par tout uniformément" (I want to present and show myself uniformly throughout [III, 2: 816; 620]). Yet wholeness remains always tantalizingly out of reach, only to be projected nostalgically on a Classical past that in all probability never existed in the first place. The logic of interiority requires, on the contrary, a remainder of the hidden, a resistance to transparency, something that, at best, can be pointed to but not "expressed": "Or, autant que la bienseance me le permet, je faicts icy sentir mes inclinations et affections. . . . Ce que je ne puis exprimer, je le montre au doigt. . . . Je ne laisse rien à desirer et deviner de moy" (Now, as far as decency permits me, I here make known my inclinations and feelings. . . . What I cannot express I point to with my finger. . . . I leave nothing about me to be desired or guessed [III, 9: 983; 751]). It is at moments such as this last, in which Montaigne admits of something that problematizes the consubstantiality of his book, that a subjective world opens up, a world to be shown, peered into, scrutinized, in search of some secret—"jusques à noz intimes et plus secretes ordures" (even to our inmost and most secret filth [III, 5: 888; 677]), as he writes in "Sur des vers de Virgil," a chapter concerned precisely with the voicing of the hidden and censored.

One of the most significant moments in which the Montaignian text starts to take human hiddenness as its subject occurs in a passage, added to the 1595 edition, that would feel familiar to a modern reader even if it had not been so extensively cited, usually as proof of Montaigne's modernity:

C'est une espineuse entreprinse, et plus qu'il ne semble, de suyvre une alleure si vagabonde que celle de nostre esprit; de penetrer les profondeurs opaques de ses replis internes; de choisir et arrester tant de menus airs des ses agitations. Et est un amusement nouveau et extraordinaire, qui nous retire des occupations communes du monde, ouy, et des plus recommandées. Il y a plusieurs années que je n'ay que moy pour visée à mes pensées, que je ne contrerolle et estudie que moy; et, si j'estudie autre chose, c'est pour soudain le coucher sur moy, ou en moy, pour mieux dire.
(It is a thorny undertaking, and more so than it seems, to follow a movement so wandering as that of our mind, to penetrate the opaque depths of its innermost folds, to pick out and immobilize the innumerable flutterings that agitate it. And it is a new and extraordinary amusement, which withdraws us from the ordinary occupations of the world, yes, even from those most recommended. It is many years now that I have had only myself as object of my thoughts, that I have been examining and studying only myself; and if I study anything else, it is in order promptly to apply it to myself, or rather within myself.) (II, 6: 378; 273)

Like so many other parts of the *Essais*, this one deals with flux, specifically, the flux of the mind; one can easily associate it with dozens of other sections of the *Essais* in which Montaigne comments on the state of continual passage that characterizes history as much as the individual.[40] Two elements of this particular text, however, deserve closer scrutiny—those elements that impart a subjective familiarity to the passage. The first is a metaphor, the metaphor of the fold, sandwiched between two metaphors of movement: this "alleure si vagabonde" and these "agitations" the self-observer seeks in vain to "arrester" are separated by "les profondeurs opaques [des] replis internes" of the mind, a depth the observer tries to "penetrer." If movement and folds can certainly be thought of as staples of "Baroque" aesthetics—characterized by change and inconsistency—much, nevertheless, separates them. Movement *undoes* the notion of unified truth, while the fold suggests that something lurks inside: the fold at once marks a scission between exterior and interior and sets up a meandering relation between the two.[41] Montaigne's justly famous movement is a metaphor for a selfhood not yet anchored in the depths that hide truth; it is a vivid metaphor indeed, but only for someone already equipped to map experience in terms of inner and outer does it imply interiority. It is only these internal, subjective folds—which may well seem unremarkable to the reader accustomed to, say, the labyrinthine metaphors of a Racine— that present the reader with one of the *Essais*'s most explicit references to the subject's depth and its relation to writing.[42]

This deepening is something that strikes Montaigne himself as worthy of emphasis; it cannot "go without saying," as the tell-tale hesitation at the end of the citation makes clear: "c'est pour soudain le [i.e., an exterior object of study] coucher *sur* moy, ou *en* moy, pour mieux dire." Montaigne frequently uses the preposition "en" with the pronouns "moy" or "soy." Yet a false-start of this sort ("ou en moy, pour mieux dire") underlines that the preposition "en" is to take its meaning from the foil of "sur"; in other words, it alerts the reader to a moment of semantic shift in which the preposition "sur," with its connotations of superficiality, is explicitly declared inadequate. But we can go further: it also suggests that ideal conduct or belief is no longer seen as something the individual *applies to* himself as if it were a mask ("coucher sur"); rather, the individual must *incorporate* ("coucher en") this exterior ideal.[43] Hence Montaigne, in his hesitant move from the care of the self to a hermeneutics of the self, might be said to demonstrate the process by which the modern subject internalizes cultural norms and values and comes to view them as arising within him or herself. Montaigne describes an incorporation that will eventually erase its origin, leaving the individual as self-regulating subject, forgetful of the fact that this standard has come to him from outside.[44]

Replacing "sur" by "en" in a context in which we have already been invited to penetrate the opaque folds of the subject hardly appears, then, an accident; and it appears still less so when later on in the same addition of the Bordeaux copy we hear a strong echo of the metaphor of the fold. Speaking of the task of painting "[s]es cogitations, sujet informe" ([his] cogitations, a shapeless subject), Montaigne writes: "Je m'estalle entier: c'est un *skeletos* où, d'une veuë, les veines, les muscles, les tendons paraissent, chaque piece

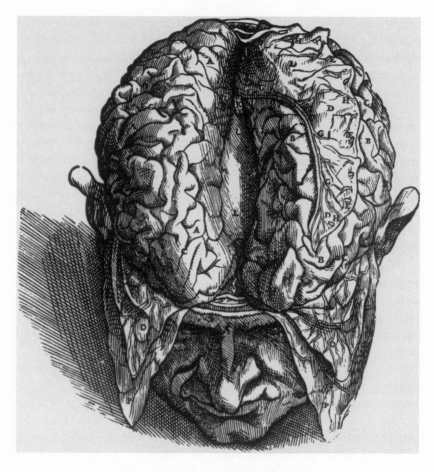

Figure 1. Vesalius's cranial folds. From *De Humani Corporis Fabrica* (1543).

en son siege" (I expose myself entire: my portrait is a cadaver on which the veins, the muscles, and the tendons appear at a glance, each part in its place [379; 274]). Not only does this passage explicitly relate writing to the anatomical uncovering of internal bodily organs,[45] but it also leads us to suspect that the previous metaphor of the mind as fold ("les profondeurs opaques de ses replis internes") might be something closer to an anatomical description of the brain than simply a variation on a Baroque topos. Vesalius's seminal *De Humani Corporis Fabrica* (1543), for example, contains a number of plates depicting the cranial folds of the brain. Montaigne's text here may well found itself on the same epistemic ground as the Renaissance science of anatomy, given to understanding what Foucault has described as "the tangible space of the body, which is at the same time that opaque mass in which secrets, invisible lesions, and the very mystery of origins lie hidden."[46]

The occasional but nonetheless insistent invitation to penetrate metaphoric opacity, the suggestion that under the fold might lie some secret truth that writing will make available, are often in Montaigne just such an anatomical affair. Unsurprisingly for someone afflicted with kidney stones, his concern with the internal (e.g., "interne vergogne" (inner shame) [II, 17: 648; 491], "constitution interne" (inner constitution) [III, 2: 810; 614], "interne santé" (inner health) [III, 13: 1079; 826]) is inseparable from the modern science of the subject that is medicine. In this, he delivers much more than he promises in his "Au lecteur," where he declares he will present himself as naked ("tout nud"), for truth, he discovers, is not skin deep. Instead, it seems to lie "au dedans et dans [l]a poictrine" (within, in his own bosom) (III, 2: 808; 613). Something inhabits the hidden world of Montaigne's "entrails" and "veins" (III, 10: 1004; 767). Thus when Montaigne writes that his heart is unknown to the world ("Les estrangers ne voyent que les evenemens et apparences externes; chacun peut faire bonne mine par le dehors, plein au dedans de fiebrve et d'effroy. Ils ne voyent pas mon coeur, ils ne voient que mes contenances" [Strangers see only the results and outward appearances. Any man can put on a good face outside, while full of fever and fright within. They do not see my heart, they see only my countenance (II, 16: 625; 474)]), the reader would do well to restore the anatomical specificity of the reference. Certainly the heart had long occupied a key symbolic place in Western culture, but what attracts Montaigne—and so many mystics of the following century, as well as the partisans of Enlightenment *sensibilité*—to the organ is its interiority.[47] The heart is true because it is physically hidden; inside, invisible, it demands unveiling. What remains to be determined is the extent to which contemporaries of Montaigne came to conceive of his writing as the instrument of subjective dissection.

From Aristocrat to Penitent

In 1669, the year before Pascal's attack on Montaigne's "sot projet . . . de se peindre" (foolish project . . . of portraying himself) appeared in his posthumous *Pensées*,[48] the last complete edition of the *Essais* for the next fifty-odd years appeared in France. While Arnauld and Nicole were, along with Pascal, chastising Montaigne for his excessive use of the first person, only "chop jobs" would appear under Montaigne's name; books like the *Esprit des Essais* (1677) and *Pensées de Montaigne* (1700), by carefully excising content deemed too personal, promised to dispense with all that was offensive to Classical sensibilities.[49] What happened, after decades and decades of frequent reprints? Was it a question of Classicism's victory over Montaigne's subversive Renaissance individualism, a containment of his Baroque ebbs and flows? Perhaps in part, but I would like to show in this section how Montaigne did not precisely go out of fashion or become unreadable in these years. Rather, his sudden exit from the seventeenth-century scene was due to the fact that little by little, the *Essais* could no longer be read as moral philosophy, but instead became a repository of inner truths that were best kept hidden.

Scholars who have traced Montaigne's reception in France—and there have been many—have not failed to point out the extent to which his contemporaries appear to have appreciated the *Essais* for reasons the average twentieth-century reader might find strange.[50] Witness La Croix du Maine (1584), who glosses Montaigne's choice of title as meaning "discours pour se façonner sur autrui" (discourses for modeling oneself after another),[51] Pasquier's statement (c. 1602) that the book is above all "un vrai séminaire de belles et notables sentences" (a veritable school of beautiful and notable sayings),[52] or the very un-modern title choice given to Florio's 1603 English translation: *The Essayes or Morall, politike and millitarie discourses of Lo[rd] Michaell de Montaigne*. These are but a few examples of a climate in which self-knowledge was equated with (aristocratic) moral philosophy, with the care or fashioning of a self not yet deep.[53]

Statements such as these, however, mingle from the very outset with a biographical consciousness that puts emphasis on the personal nature of the text: the *Essais* are also, especially in the third book, "une ample Déclaration de la vie . . . de Montaigne" (a full Declaration of Montaigne's life) (La Croix du Maine again),[54] "une histoire de ses moeurs et actions" (a history of his mores and actions) (Pasquier),[55] and, as Marie de Gournay hinted in her objection to the inclusion of the aforementioned *Sommaire discours* in the volume, a virtual biography: "Aussi suis-je contraire à cette vie de l'Auteur, qu'ils [the editors] ont logée en tête, étant complète dans le volume" (Thus I am opposed to this life of the Author which [the editors] have placed at the beginning of the work, for it is contained completely in the volume).[56] More important for the history of a hermeneutics of self, however, is the increasingly interiorizing reading that accompanied this biographical consciousness. To passing allusions to Montaigne as, for instance, "celui qui sait le plus aisément exprimer le monde intérieur" (the man who is able to express the inner

world with most ease),[57] will be added a much more precise understanding—
which was partially a misunderstanding—of the *Essais* as the expression of a
secret self.

It is in the pages of admirers such as Jean-Pierre Camus and Marie de
Gournay that Montaigne's occasional metaphors of interiority undergo an
amplification indicative of a shift in the manner in which the *Essais* were
read. Many of those who have looked into the question of Montaigne's reception have attempted to gauge contemporary reaction to and appreciation
of Montaigne's *peinture du moi*—that is, did his readers "grasp" his radically
individualist project or not? What interests me in remarks such as those of
Pasquier and La Croix du Maine is something more specific, to wit, the extent to which self-portraiture came to imply the effort to express a hidden
truth. "The private," as Habermas has noted, originally designated not the
hidden subjective richness which moderns tend to associate with the term,
but simply the life of men having no public (i.e., political or military) role.[58]
Yet "vie privée" in Guez de Balzac's judgment on Montaigne, for example,
takes on quite different shades of meaning from this traditional use:

Ce qu'il dit de ses inclinations, de tout le détail de sa Vie privée, est très agréable. Je
suis bien aise de connaître ceux que j'estime, et s'il y a moyen, de les connaître tout
entiers, et dans la pureté de leur naturel. Je veux les voir, s'il est possible, dans leurs
plus particulières et leurs plus secrètes actions. Il m'a donc fait grand plaisir de me
faire son Histoire domestique.[59]
(What he says of his inclinations, of all the details of his private Life, is quite pleasing.
I am delighted to know those whom I esteem, and, if there is a way, to know them
entirely and in the purity of their natural bearing. I want to see them, if possible, in
their most particular and most secret actions. For this reason it was a great pleasure
to have him relate to me his domestic History.)

On the one hand, private life here seems to be simply the way one is at home
("son Histoire domestique"); but on the other, it is clear that the home is now
the locus of "natural" man, a man with "particularities" and "inclinations"
which can be read if one can only peer into this "secret" sphere. "Du Repentir" contains a similar passage in which Montaigne writes of the necessity to
keep order "jusques en son privé, . . . où tout est caché, . . . en sa maison
[et] en ses actions ordinaires" (even in private, . . . where all is concealed, . . .
in our own house [and] in our ordinary actions) (III, 2: 808; 613); this is the
same passage in which, as we have seen, Montaigne makes his anatomical
gesture towards an inner space, "au dedans et en sa poictrine" (within, in his
own bosom). At moments like these, then, something like *privacy* displaces
the dominant meaning of the private; and the *Essais* emerge as the key-hole

onto the double space of a concatenated interiority, the home and the subject himself.[60]

Guez de Balzac also includes two qualifications—"s'il y a moyen" and "s'il est possible"—which are also essential elements of the developing discourse of interiority: expression of the depths must be aleatory, a promise but not a guarantee. Too great a transparency between inside and outside and the distinction itself collapses: this is the phantasmatic limit of the autobiographical mentality, the promise of restored totality and of an end to division, a limit that can never be realized precisely because of the autobiographical text itself. Balzac's qualification enables us to distinguish his reading from Pasquier's comment that proclaimed Montaigne's death to be "un beau miroir de l'intérieur de son Ame" (a beautiful mirror of the interior of his Soul).[61] Pasquier here uses the word interior, but continues to deploy it within the Medieval context of the mirror of the soul, a context in which the soul and body are exact reflections of one another. This contention Montaigne himself had taken pains, especially in "De la physionomie," to refute: mirrors, he notes in his critique of imitative exemplarity, are "vague" (hazy) (III, 13: 1088; 834). Yet for Guez de Balzac, no refutation is even in order because a new solution to the problem of misleading appearances has been developed— the truth of personality can be discovered slowly, uncovered layer by layer as more information is gathered through the observation of privacy.

If the *Essais* had any direct literary descendant, it was surely Jean-Pierre Camus's *Diversités* (1609–18). Under Montaigne's spell and wanting to emulate the *Essais*, Camus, the future proponent of "devout humanism," had conceived of the *Diversités* as the work of a lifetime. Like Montaigne, Camus shunned overarching architecture by assembling independent chapters, each devoid of fixed subjects and filled with citations from classical authors. In addition, Camus was as attuned to Montaigne the self-portraitist as to Montaigne the compiler: "Mais de se peindre soi-même, son corps, son esprit, ses humeurs, ses vices, ses vertus, ses défauts, sa valeur, cet auteur est le Phénix en cette matière" (But in portraying oneself, one's body, mind, humors, vices, virtues, faults, and worth, this author is in these matters a Phoenix). As in the case of Balzac, however, this self-portraiture is once again inflected in the direction of interiority: Montaigne's "étude de soi" (self-study) was no mere aristocratic care of the self, but promised rather to "pénétrer plus profondément dans les secrets cachots et recoins d'un esprit" (to penetrate more profoundly into the secret dungeons and recesses of a mind). The *Essais* emerge as part and parcel of a hermeneutic act that can only be undertaken by the subject himself: "Qui peut mieux parler de lui que lui? Qui l'a mieux connu qu'il s'est connu soi-même? C'est un[e] erreur populaire de croire plutôt un tiers parlant d'un autre, que celui qui parle de soi-même" (Who can speak of him better than he? Who knew him more than he knew himself? It is a popular error to believe a third party who speaks of another rather than he who speaks of himself).[62] Sentences such as these will gain increasing currency as the seventeenth century wears on and the speaking subject, displacing the "tiers parlant," will become the locus of a discursive authority inseparable from and predicated on the idea of interiority.

Balzac and Camus only provide us with passing references, indications that formulations which were vague or unusual in Montaigne's own work were being picked up, sharpened, and used to qualify the *Essais* as a whole. If these sentences were buried in much longer works, however, and can hardly be supposed to have influenced a seventeenth-century readership, the same is not true for Marie de Gournay, who in two prefaces (1595 and 1635) to the *Essais* provided a blueprint for reading that would accompany most editions until 1669. In proposing what she herself called "quelques règles pour se gouverner en cette lecture" (some rules for guiding oneself in this reading), Gournay goes the furthest toward eliminating the old aristocratic view of the *Essais* as reading for soldiers and statesmen, and substituting a new understanding of the *Essais* as the discourse of an interiorized subject.[63]

In the wake of increasing interest in Montaigne's "fille d'alliance," or (figuratively) adopted daughter, the story of Gournay's original preface to the first posthumous edition of the *Essais* in 1595 has become fairly well known. Shortly after the appearance of the 1595 edition, Gournay expressed shame at her long and sometimes shrill preface, going so far as to rip it out of copies sent to her friend Lipsius. The next edition (1598) bore only a short note retracting the previous preface, and it was this that appeared until 1617, when it was replaced in its turn by a partially reworked version of the original 1595 version.[64] Scholars have recently focused attention on how this reception, and indeed the 1595 preface itself, seem to mime what François Rigolot has called "the twists and turns . . . of marginalized feminine discourse in the seventeenth century."[65] Writing as a woman, Gournay could not limit herself to advancing the cause of Montaigne's book, but in addition had to defend the very right of a woman to speak; and once she did speak, she immediately experienced guilt over her transgression.[66]

The fate of the 1595 preface does indeed suggest such conclusions, but this text, and the almost entirely new one that replaced it in 1635, can tell us much as well about modes of reading, and specifically about the predicating of textual authority on interiority. Though the original preface contains little or nothing in the way of interior metaphors of the sort that will be used by Balzac or Camus, it does betray a particularly acute attention to the person of the author. Gournay does not so much adumbrate the usual considerations evinced by contemporaries regarding the seemliness of self-portraiture, but instead attempts to theorize the person as author; she analyzes the link that joins person and text. Hence, when Gournay discounts attacks on Montaigne's belief in God by saying, "C'est à moi d'en parler; car moi seule avais la parfaite connaissance de cette grande âme, et c'est à moi d'en être crue de bonne foi, quand ce livre ne l'éclaircirait pas" (It is for me to speak of this; for only I had a perfect knowledge of this great soul, and one must believe me in good faith in those places where the book does not adequately shed light on it),[67] this is more than hysterical presumption (as a whole misogynist tradition of Gournay's critics have claimed), and more too than a proto-feminist strategy (as modern scholars have correctly maintained). It is a gesturing toward the person of the author as unifying principle that can be known either through his text or personally—the two being situated somehow on the same plane. If the book isn't quite clear, Gournay seems to say, appeal can be made to his life so as to assemble a coherent view.

Like Querlon's reading of Montaigne's *Journal de voyage* over 150 years later, Gournay's remarks furnish a perfect illustration of Foucault's theory of the author-function, or, as he defines it, "the manner in which a text apparently points to this figure who is outside and precedes it."[68] Thus, while Balzac will merely regret that Montaigne did not include more biographical information—for instance, what kind of mayor he was—Gournay does far more than highlight the "personal" nature of the work. Instead, she proposes a mode of reading founded upon a newly reversible relationship between subject and text: the person of the author guarantees the text, and conversely, the text can and should be explained by the person of the author. But this reversibility can only imply a second, similar rapport, this time linking author and reader. Hence the following remarkable statement of Gournay's, which constitutes a veritable theory of readerly identification with the person/author Montaigne:

[J]e ne puis faire un pas, soit écrivant ou parlant, que je ne me trouve sur ses traces; et crois qu'on cuide souvent que je l'usurpe. Et le seul contentement que j'eus oncques de moi-même, c'est d'avoir rencontré plusieurs choses parmi les dernières additions [of the Bordeaux copy] que tu [the reader] verras en ce volume, lesquelles j'avais imaginées toutes pareilles, avant que les avoir vues.[69]
(I cannot take a step, whether in writing or speaking, without finding myself on his

track; and I believe it is often suspected that I am usurping him. And my only source of pride is to have found several things among the last additions [of the Bordeaux copy] which you [the reader] will see in this volume, things which I had imagined that way ever before having seen them.)

In reading, one slips into the skin of the author; one is able, somewhat in the manner of Borges's Pierre Ménard rewriting from scratch Cervantes's masterpiece, to generate the whole of the work from one of its parts. Richard Regosin, who reads Gournay's text as "both express[ing] and perform[ing] the insistent and unending desire for the other in friendship," casts this same passage as a female reappropriation of a long tradition of male friendship literature; nevertheless, its subjective specificity merits special emphasis.[70] For if it can be argued that readerly empathy lies at the root of modern novelistic reading practice (one thinks of the reception of Lafayette's *La Princesse de Clèves* and Rousseau's *Julie, ou la nouvelle Héloïse*),[71] autobiography certainly shares this foundation. Hence it comes as no surprise that the conversion experience that Gournay underwent upon reading the *Essais* for the first time necessarily leads to a two-year thirst for meeting "leur auteur même" (their very author).[72]

In a sense it is entirely logical that the 1595 preface has been so insistently read with reference to the facts surrounding the real-life relationship between Gournay and Montaigne, for the empathic theory of reading proposed is completely particularized. Gournay's 1635 preface, with many cuts to and amplifications of the original version, takes a different tack: whereas in 1595, Gournay founded the authority of the text on her own privileged relation to it, forty years later Montaigne's whole literary enterprise is offered as exemplary of a general will to interiority that each and every reader must—the imperative is Gournay's own—exercise with respect to him or herself. That Gournay's consideration of the question of self-portraiture will be treated differently the second time around is evident even in the small changes imparted to the vocabulary used in the first version. In 1595, Gournay had qualified Montaigne's action as that of "se produire nu devant le peuple" (showing himself naked before the people); the second preface, however, changes the phrase to "produire sa vie nue aux yeux du monde" (showing his naked life to the eyes of the world).[73] A small change, without a doubt, but an important one, if one pauses to reflect that the second metaphor implies writing and readership whereas the first seems modeled after monarchical representation. Montaigne no longer just stands naked, he offers up a naked life (or *Life*), and this not before the crowd, like a king, but before the eyes of the world. The evolution is slight but perceptible, in that the implied mediation of textuality in the act of "producing oneself" becomes central to Gournay's concerns.

The significance of this change would be imperceptible if it were not for a further array of additions that shift attention away from a previous defense of self-portraiture on grounds of pedagogical utility—the *Essais*, according to the 1595 preface, taught the reader to become an "honnête homme" (well-bred man), and were a necessary apprenticeship for any "grand chef d'armée et d'état" (great military or state leader).[74] This justification, which involves what I, following Foucault, have described as a care of the self, subsists in Gournay's second preface, but it is extended by a long excursus on the necessity of confession and public avowal that greatly amplifies and sharpens Montaigne's own brief allusion to confession.[75] Here, we learn that Montaigne's critics think themselves superior because "ils se gardent d'avouer leurs vérités" (they are careful not to confess their truths), and that all evils of the world come from the disguising of one's true self: "levez le masque d'entre nous," Gournay proclaims, "car les hommes seraient bons par tout, si par tout on les voyait" (lift the mask from between us, for men would be good on all sides, if one could see them from all sides). Like Montaigne, Gournay inserts the *Essais* into the Christian tradition of confession, citing the example of Augustine; but she goes further still, founding the possibility of any and all justice, secular as much as divine, on the exhumation of hidden truth. In the same astonishing breath, the Catholic Church's prescription of confession and the judicial use of torture emerge together as ancestors and analogs of Montaigne's text, now seen as the corollary of these institutional practices:

[L]a Justice ne tire son effet que de la découverte des crimes: donnant la ghéhenne aussi, pour y contraindre les hommes: et l'Eglise parfait sa confession auriculaire, par la générale et publique. Chacun au reste se doit constituer Juge sur soi-même: comme tel, mon Père [Montaigne] déclare et fouette ses vices, non en privé seulement, mais en public.[76]

(Justice derives its effect only from the discovery of crimes: it also provides for torture, so that men will be so obliged: and the Church perfects and completes its auricular confession by the general and public one. Each man must moreover make of himself a judge of himself: as such, my Father [Montaigne] declares and lashes his vices, not only in private, but also in public.)

The *Essais*, then, are no longer a tool for caring for ourselves so that we may become wise gentlemen; the reader is required, rather, to follow the hermeneutic lead of this "scrutateur universel de l'homme intérieur" (universal inspector of the inner man) who offers us a surgical guide to subjective truth, "l'Anatomie parfaite d[es] passions et mouvements intérieurs" (the perfect Anatomy of the passions and inner movements).[77] The duty is imperative: "Il faut voir son vice, et l'étudier pour le redire: ceux qui le cèlent à autrui, le cèlent ordinairement à eux-mêmes: ils ne le tiennent pas pour assez couvert, s'ils le voient" (One must see one's vice, and study it in order to repeat it in words: those who conceal it from others ordinarily conceal it from themselves: they do not think it is sufficiently covered up, if they themselves still see it).[78] Gournay's advocacy of avowal is not quite an anti-Machiavellian tirade against willful deceit, for her language here is redolent of what Charles Taylor has seen as "the assumption behind modern self-exploration"—the idea "that we don't already know who we are."[79] Here, the hidden is not hidden as if behind a curtain that one pulls strategically around one's true motives; instead, evils lurk inside, deep down, in the anatomical depths of a subject driven to come clean. "Voilà pourquoi," Gournay writes, presenting the view as Montaigne's own, "il les faut souventefois remanier au jour: les ouvrant et les éventrant du fond de nos entrailles, d'une main impitieuse" (That is why one must repeatedly bring them back into the light: opening them up and cutting them out from the depths of our entrails, with a pitiless hand).[80] By 1635, the *Essais* had metamorphosed into the exemplary tool of a hermeneutics of self.

The image of Montaigne as self-flagellating penitent glaringly contradicts what many modern commentators like to think of as the spirit of the *Essais* themselves—say, an equanimous acceptance of one's own shortcomings seen for what they are. And yet Gournay here can not be accused of total projection, in that she is simply extending a specifically anatomical metaphor already present in Montaigne's own discussion of the *Essais* as confession: "Ceux qui se mescognoissent, se peuvent paistre de fauces approbations; non pas moy, qui me voy et qui me recherche jusques aux entrailles" (Those who have a false opinion of themselves can feed on false approbations; not I, who see myself and search myself to my very entrails) (III, 5: 847; 643–44). Nor is this the only place Montaigne understands subjective flux as visceral: he refers elsewhere to "la presse domestique que j'ay dans mes entrailles et dans mes veines" (the domestic pressures that oppress my entrails and veins) (III, 10: 1004; 767). But that which is isolated or occasional in Montaigne becomes central for Gournay, the linchpin of an entire way of reading that cannot but dictate a renewed interest in textual authenticity. Once the text is considered not as a work linked to other works by the intertextual play of citation, but as a unified manifestation of a subjective truth, it becomes increasingly important to explain, as Gournay attempts to do, why Montaigne's use of Classical authorities does not "usurper la propriété de son Oeuvre" (usurp the ownership of his Work). Her response is that any reader can distinguish the *Essais* from a mere compendium such as that of the "perpétuel copiste" (inveterate copyist) Charron's *De la sagesse*, for one can "sentir au Génie d'un Livre qu'il est tout d'une main" (sense in the Genius of a Book that it is all from one hand).[81]

If the autobiographical anachronism, then, was partially present in Montaigne's very text, it was in the course of the seventeenth century that the uncovering of the hermeneutic self—the notion of identity founded on the secret depths of the subject and manifested in an authentic text—became *the* goal of reading. In order to express these depths, Gournay reached for a confessional vocabulary of sin and crime—those secrets that religious and judicial authorities, respectively, sought to uncover. No documents exist that would help us take the measure of how influential this reading was; of the ten subsequent editions of the *Essais* that would appear before 1669, her 1635 preface appears in six.[82] As I have alluded, the only subsequent editions of Montaigne, the *Esprit des Essais* of 1677 and the *Pensées de Montaigne* of 1700, would steer as far clear from the confessional as possible, selecting only "les choses historiques et divertissantes" (things historical and entertaining) that were capable of serving "l'utilité publique" (the public good).[83] But rather than view the eclipse of Montaigne's "confession" as proof of a lack of interest in the hermeneutic self, one might propose quite the contrary—that this self had become, in Pascal's famous words, "haïssable" (hateful) only because it had finally been "born." For indeed, Montaigne's concern for the interior, to the extent that it originally existed in the *Essais* and was amplified by glosses in the first half of the seventeenth century, was not forgotten, nor was it in any way "unreadable" by a public still somehow behind Montaigne's times: it was more or less *repressed* in a gesture that, rather than contradicting the developing obsession with interiority, only exacerbated it.

The *Logique, ou l'art de penser* of Antoine Arnauld and Pierre Nicole (1662) illustrates how, by the second half of the seventeenth century, even attacks on the deep self tended to be waged in interiorizing terms. For the profoundly Cartesian thinkers of Port-Royal, an interiorized self is one that solipsistically attributes truth to its own utterance alone; with this insight, and a remarkable degree of prescience, they describe the nature of the person we might call the "modern subject." Such a localization of truth, however, is "hateful" in that it can only represent a threat to God's order, not to mention the institution of the Church, and this is why, broadly speaking, the *Logique* condemns Montaigne for speaking of himself. Thus, when Arnauld and Nicole read Montaigne's proclamation that "mes actions sont reglées, et conformes à ce que je suis et à ma condition" (my actions are in order and conformity with what I am and with my condition), they must exclaim: "Paroles horribles, et qui marquent une extinction entière de tout sentiment de Religion" (What horrible words, which reflect a complete extinction of all religious sentiment). Yet the paradox of this critique is that it only contributes to the depth of the subject: an increasingly reified hermeneutic self, Arnauld and Nicole maintain, needs to be kept bottled up, as it were, lest it obscure divine truth:

[C]'est pourquoi les personnes sages évitent autant qu'ils peuvent, d'exposer aux yeux des autres, les avantages qu'ils ont; ils fuient de se présenter en face, et de se faire envisager en particulier, et ils tâchent plutôt de se cacher dans la presse, pour n'être pas remarqués, afin qu'on ne voie dans leurs discours que la vérité qu'ils proposent.[84]
(This is why the wise avoid as much as possible exposing their advantages to the eyes of others; they flee from presenting themselves directly and from being seen alone, and they try instead to hide themselves in the throng to escape notice, so that we may see in their words nothing but the truth which they put forth.)

This critique, then, manages to cause interiority to become impacted; the subject as ground of truth — a truth that, according to Arnauld and Nicole, competes with the Christian truth — is sentenced to banishment, but the subject can be so banished only if its censors first concede its existence. The gesture that consigns the self to the realm of the hidden ("se cacher . . . pour n'être pas remarqués"), at least in the *Logique*, opens the door to the self's existence.

Somewhat counterintuitively, the success of Gournay's hermeneutic reading of the *Essais*, therefore, might be said to lie in the resistance Montaigne encountered in the latter half of the seventeenth century. Montaigne had to be eliminated as soon as the implications of subjective depth became clear to the keepers of the religious flame; but the grounds proposed for his elimination ironically confirmed the victory of interiority. And as with Montaigne and Gournay, this victory can be read in the *Logique*'s metaphors. Arnauld and Nicole gesture repeatedly at the depths, more insistently than Montaigne ever did because by their time it seemed self-evident (but still novel enough to rate considerable interest) that the something was lurking "dans le fond du coeur des hommes" (in the depth of men's hearts), something secret ("une secrète complaisance, . . . une aversion secrète"), unruly ("[les] désordres"), and evil ("cette disposition maligne et envieuse") that one can either show ("découvr[ir]") or hide ("cacher," "cel[er]").[85] Although some supporters of Port-Royal, Arnauld and Nicole report, could go as far as advocating the avoidance of the first person pronoun, by dint of the Foucauldian paradox elaborated in *The History of Sexuality*, *not* talking about oneself only drives the truth deeper; one of interiority's characteristics is its production in interdiction. "Soupirs d'autant plus doux qu'il les fallait celer" (Sighs all the sweeter for having to be hidden), wrote Racine (*Bajazet* I, 1), who had been educated at Port-Royal, where the language of interiority seemed to prosper in direct proportion to hatred of the *moi*.[86]

Modernizing Augustine

The language of interiority, so prevalent among Jansenists, derived at least partially from their use of Augustine, on whom Cornelius Jansen had written the work that gave the movement its name. I would hasten to establish from the outset, however, that I do not believe that this is merely a question of "influence," and even less of "doctrine." First, the importance of interiority for modern culture and subjectivity comes out of its pervasiveness, its ability to transcend denominational, national, and gender barriers and to transform how people wrote, independent of beliefs best characterized as epiphenomenal. The case of Montaigne, who may well not even have read the *Confessions*,[87] and who nonetheless still sketches out the beginnings of metaphorical depth, speaks volumes about the limits of an exclusively intertextual understanding of subjective phenomena. Second — and this will be the thrust of the remainder of this chapter — one might say that seventeenth-century readers (some but not all of them Jansenists) influenced Augustine as much as Augustine influenced them, in that they took the *Confessions* out of the Latin culture of scholasticism and, in four separate translations, pushed his concept and language of interiority further than he ever had. The *Confessions'* popularity, I will argue, was due to a perceived degree of harmony between Augustine's concerns and those that were reconfiguring, twelve centuries later, the subjective landscape.[88]

The question of the "inner" in Augustine's works has been approached many times, especially by scholars of religion whose accounts inevitably seem to credit Augustine with the triumphant "discovery" of inner space.[89] These studies, however, like those of critics who neglect to consider the lapses and contradictions in Montaigne's equally reputed interiority, do little to probe the limits of Augustine's idea of depth, or to situate it with respect to the modern "hermeneutics of self" which was transforming the seventeenth century's understanding of the *Essais*. The following brief account of the *Confession's* Latin is meant to provide background for an inquiry similar to that brought to bear on Montaigne's reception. These two canonical examples complement each other nicely, for while Montaignian interiority was perceived, exaggerated, but ultimately occulted by a secular readership that valued pithy reflections or maxims above an interiorized relation between subject and text, Augustine's work, penetrating into a totally different milieu, found acceptance based on the very same qualities for which Montaigne was censored. For among a religious readership, the vogue for interiority turned Augustine's text into a cornerstone of a new type of mystic literature of the heart that purported to make accessible the most remote parts of subjective experience.

Augustine derived his conception of the "inner man" from Saint Paul, who employs the expression three times in his Epistles. These uses, however, are only crudely related to the modern metaphor of psychological depth, because the "inner man" for Saint Paul is an essentially allegorical expression that opposes the spirit to the sinful body: "For I delight in the law of God in my [inner man], but I see in my members another law at war with the law of my mind and making me captive to the law of sin which dwells in my members." [90] Doctrinally speaking, it is this understanding of the "inner" that Augustine elaborates on when he defines, in *De Civitate dei* (13.24.2) and *De Trinitatae* (12.1.1), *homo interior* as the soul, as that which distinguishes man from animals, and *homo exterior* as the body. It follows, therefore, that this "inner man" differs substantially from the alternately anatomical and psychological notion of the interior or inside of man, as represented by Montaigne and Gournay's "entrails." For Saint Paul, and Augustine, the soul is represented allegorically as a "little man inside," a man with metaphorical ears, eyes, and so on. [91]

The concept of inner space as it starts to develop in the early modern period finds a corollary or antecedent less in these theological distinctions than in Augustine's literary language itself, which developed around them. Metaphorical interiority of the sort I have spoken of regarding Montaigne is perhaps best visible in Augustine's discussion of memory in book X of the *Confessions*. In a famous passage, memory (which for Augustine is both a repository of personal sense impressions and a Platonic *anamnesis*, or remembrance of past existence) is compared to "vast palaces" (lata praetoria memoriae) (X, 8, 185). [92] The palace of memory possesses "profundity" (X, 8, 187), or, more literally, an inner sanctum, the Latin word for which, "penetralis," coming from the verb "to penetrate," of necessity connotes a space of depth that can be explored. [93] Memory, then can have this architectural interiority, that of a structure composed of "recondite receptacles" (de abstrusioribus quibusdam receptaculis) (X, 8, 185). [94] The spatial conception of memory actually ends up blending with the inner-outer distinction as inherited from Paul. In the following passage, the outer is still associated with the body and the senses, but the "man within" is now clearly a subjective *region* that can be entered into:

> To the best of my powers of sense-perception, I traveled through the external world. Starting from myself I gave attention to the life of my own body, and examined my own senses. From there I moved into the recesses of my memory, manifold vastnesses full of innumerable riches in wonderful ways.
> (lustravi mundum foris sensu, quo potui, et adtendi vitam corporis mei de me sensusque ipsos meos. Inde ingressus sum in recessus memoriae meae, multiplices amplitudines plenas miris modis copiarum innumerabilium.) (X, 40, 217)

Memory's recesses, for Augustine, are infinitely deep: "Who has plumbed [memory's] bottom?" (Quis ad fundum eius pervenit?) (X, 8, 187). The *Confessions* contain an array of Latin expressions centering around the heart that suggest subjective depth—"intimus cordi est" (IV, 12), "ex intimo cordis meo" (IV, 13), "a fundo cordis mei" (IX, 1)—much as in English one would speak "from the bottom of one's heart." Both the case of the deep heart and that of memory are in harmony with the idea of the inner man as that part of us that enables us to know divine truth.[95] Thus, Augustine's famous apostrophe to God as He who was "more inward than my most inward part and higher than the highest element within me" (tu autem eras interior intimo meo et superior summo meo) (III, 6, 43) makes clear that this particular interior trajectory does not, in fact, establish man as the ground of his own truth. As Etienne Gilson has put it, the Augustinian path "lead[s] from the exterior to the interior and from the interior to the superior."[96] Augustinian interiority, then, would seem to leave us somewhat short of a hermeneutics of self, in that the truth discovered in introspection is not the subject's own at all. The end-point of all language, and all subjective desire, as John Freccero insists, is God himself.[97] This point is certainly supported by the structure of the *Confessions* as a whole, for the text, in the last three books, becomes rigorously impersonal as the individuality of the autobiographical "I" whose story occupied the previous books is eliminated.[98]

At many moments, however, man's insides lack this divine clarity, and that which is deep or inner is associated with the base, with sin. These are the moments when Augustine has become a "problem" for himself (mihi quaestio factus sum) (X, 33, 208), bent on introspecting not so much to see God as to discover his own iniquities: "From a hidden depth a profound [consideration] had dredged up a heap of all my misery and set it in the sight of my heart" (Ubi vero a fundo arcano alta consideratio traxit et congessit totam miseriam meam in conspectu cordis mei) (VIII, 12, 152). Man has within a "deep darkness" (hac profunda caligine) (III, 11, 49) and the causes for his actions are an abyssal mystery: "Who can untie this extremely twisted and tangled knot?" (Qui exaperit istam tortuosissimam et inplicatissimam nodositatem?) (II, 10, 34), he asks, contemplating his motives for stealing a pear. If Paul had indeed written that "before [God] no creature is hidden, but all are laid bare to the eyes of him with whom we have to do" (Heb. 4:13), Augustine is much more specific, in that in his hands God's gaze penetrates the inner depths of every person, an idea absent from the Pauline text: "Indeed, Lord, to your eyes, the abyss of human consciousness is naked. What could be hidden within me, even if I were unwilling to confess it to you?" (Et tibi quidem, domine, cuius oculis nuda est abyssus humanae conscientiae, quid occultum esset in me, etiamsi nollem confiteri tibi?) (X, 2, 179). In other words, God's omniscience in Paul (He sees everyone) becomes, in Augustine, a penetrating gaze that sees *inside* each one of us. Augustine's proto-"hermeneutics of self" is all the more convincing because he does not simply *choose* to hide sin; rather, the opacity of the human interior is such that one can never be sure subjective truth has been discovered:

That is how I see myself, but perhaps I am deceived. For there are those deplorable blind spots where the capacity that lies in me is concealed from me. My mind on examining myself about its strengths does not regard its findings as easy to trust. What lies within is for the most part hidden unless experience reveals it.
(Ita mihi videor; forsitan fallar. Sunt enim et istae plangendae tenebrae, in quibus me latet facultas mea, quae in me est, ut animus meus de viribus suis ipse se interrogans non facile sibi credendum existimet, quia et quod inest plerumque occultum est, nisi experientia manifestetur.) (X, 32, 207)

Interiority, here, represents something more than, and even the contrary of, the doctrine of the "inner man," for it is now human sin and desire that are hidden within.[99]

Already, then, the tropes and concepts of hermeneutic selfhood are present; but the autobiographical mentality that assembled these building blocks some twelve centuries later transformed unambiguously the *Confessions* into a text of deep experience. This was accomplished in two ways: first, the translations themselves "modernized" Augustine's own language of interiority; and second, the imperative of subjective interiority was dictating changes in the way seventeenth-century translators attempted to situate the *Confessions* for a new public. For the sake of brevity, I will restrict myself to a few particularly telling examples of the vicissitudes of translations. The first comes from Arnauld d'Andilly's 1649 version, the language of which probably does the most to "deepen" Augustine's text.[100] In book X, chapter 6, Augustine inquires into what he loves in God, excluding any criteria that would have to do with the outer man—that is, the senses. He then concludes that the object of his love must be something else, something beyond though to some extent analogous to the sensory universe of light, sound, smell, taste, or touch:

[T]here is a light I love, and a food, and a kind of embrace when I love my God—a light, voice, odor, food, embrace of my inner man, where my soul is illuminated by a light which space cannot contain, where there is a sound that time cannot seize, . . . and where there is a bond of union that no satiety can part.
(et tamen amo quandam lucem et quandam vocem et quendam odorem et quendam cibum et quendam amplexum, cum amo deum meum, lucem, vocem, odorem, cibum, amplexum interioris hominis mei, ubi fulget animae meae, quod non capit locus, et ubi sonat, quod non rapit tempus, . . . et ubi haeret, quod non divellit satietas.) (X, 6, 183)

The "interiority" of this passage is limited to that of the allegorical "inner man" ("interioris hominis") who shares the senses of the outer man but transposes them to a spiritual plane. Yet in the hands of Arnauld d'Andilly, however, Augustine's inner man starts to become the interior of Augustine himself:

Mais cette lumière, cette harmonie, cette odeur, cette viande, et cette volupté ne se trouvent que dans le fond de mon coeur, dans cette partie de moi-même qui est toute intérieure et toute invisible, où mon âme voit briller au-dessus d'elle une lumière que le lieu ne renferme point.[101]
(But this light, this harmony, this smell, this food and this voluptuousness are found only at the bottom of my heart, in this part of myself that is all interior and invisible, where my soul sees shining above it a light that space cannot contain.)

The inner man has subtly but unmistakably metamorphosed into the "invisible," "interior" part of Augustine lying at the "bottom of his heart."

Indeed, "the bottom" ("le fond") and "the deep" ("le profond") surface with remarkable regularity in Arnauld d'Andilly's translation, rendering Augustine's rare "fundus" ("a fundo cordis mei" [IX, 1]) and "intimo cordis" (cf. IV, 12 and IV, 13), as well as his more common "intus" ("inside," "inwardly"). Hence a phrase such as "Inwardly I said to myself" (dicebam enim apud me intus) (VIII, 11, 150) becomes "Car je disais en moi-même du plus profond de mon âme" (for I said within myself from the deepest part of my soul).[102] Arnauld d'Andilly's predilection for "le fond," however, inevitably accentuates Augustine's metaphoric interiority: in this last example, the translator is given to adding the idea of depth of soul, even when the "je disais en moi-même" had already rendered accurately Augustine's Latin. Similarly, "le fond"is wont to appear unsummoned: hence, while Augustine asks, "What else has stirred my mind to ask and discuss and consider this question?" (quid est, quod mihi venit in mentem quaerere et discutere et considerare?) (II, 8, 33), Arnauld d'Andilly's French transforms the mind's curiosity into a sounding of the subject's depths: looking into the question, Augustine "examin[e] la disposition de [s]on esprit, et sond[e] le fond de [s]on coeur" (examine[s] the disposition of [his] mind, and sound[s] the depth of [his] heart.) [103]

This passage, in which Augustine searches for the causes that drove him in his youth to steal a pear for the sole pleasure of stealing, can be taken for representative of a general trend among the French translations, that of an increasing willingness to impose a modern vocabulary of interiority onto Augustine's language. Goibaud du Bois, for example, in his 1686 translation, follows Arnauld d'Andilly in interpreting Augustine's questioning as a hermeneutic act the subject performs upon his own interior: "Que se passa-t-il donc en moi, et par où puis-je pénétrer quel fut le vrai motif de cette méchanceté?" (So what happened in me, and how can I penetrate the true motive of this wickedness?).[104] By contrast, the two French translations that had preceded Arnauld d'Andilly's had been quite sober renditions of the original. "[D'où] me vient maintenant cet[te] humeur de vous demander cela, mon Dieu, d'en rechercher la raison, et de la considérer si avant" ([Whence] comes to me now this penchant to ask you this, my God, to search for its cause, and to pursue my speculations?), asks Aemar Hennequin's Augustine in 1582,[105] whereas in 1638, René de Cérisiers's enquires only: "[D]'où me vient ce dessein d'examiner cette matière?" (Where did I get the idea of examining this matter?).[106] Only a complete reading of Arnauld d'Andilly's or Goibaud du Bois's translations can give the reader a feel for the combined effect of these apparently minute changes, but these few examples of interiorizing exaggerations and improvisations should be sufficient to suggest the metaphorical trends at work.

More than the lexical minutiae of the translations themselves, however, it is the paratexts accompanying the French Confessions that serve as a barometer for the rapid changes the notion of human interiority underwent in the relatively short space of a century. Translation required the sensitizing of a new reading public — vernacularization demanded vulgarization — and thus translators availed themselves of prefaces and dedications in order to elaborate on what made the text so accessible to those with no theological training. If the Confessions were to become such popular reading in the seventeenth century — and the holdings of major libraries suggest printings in almost every year from 1649 on — this was only possible once the book was wrenched from its traditionally theological, elite readership, and moved into the domain of devotional literature. To achieve such a displacement, translators appealed to an incompatibility that Michel de Certeau has pointed to as a structuring feature of the seventeenth century's spiritual landscape — the irreducible opposition of the doctrinal and the experiential, the mind and the heart.[107] This perceived divorce was responsible for the *Confessions'* exceptional status as a paradigmatic text of interiority, and necessitated a double editorial isolation. For translators separated the *Confessions* from the rest of Augustine's writing, deemed cerebral, and then effected a further and internal separation between the work's first ten books — where Augustine's experiential "I" is most in evidence — and the last three, more theological in scope. In this way, just as Augustine himself had appropriated Pauline ideas in ways that Paul would have found foreign, the seventeenth century could only read, and transmit, the *Confessions* based on its own evolving understanding of the very concepts that Augustine's work had helped put in circulation.

Judging by the scarcity of the early editions of Aemar Hennequin's 1582 translation, the *Confessions* took some time to find an audience other than scholastic and Latinate.[108] Hennequin dedicates his innovative enterprise to none other than Henri III, whom he praises for his work against the heretics who, unlike the French monarchy, have rejected the sacrament of confession. Describing Augustine as "un des plus grands Evêques, plus digne[s] Confesseur[s], plus excellent[s] Docteur[s] que nous avons eu[s] dans l'Eglise" (one of the greatest Bishops, most worthy Confessor[s], [and] most excellent Doctor[s] we have had in the church), Hennequin's presentation conjoins a purely sacramental reading of the *Confessions'*s title and assertions of Augustine's double — institutional and theological — orthodoxy.[109] Augustine's first foray into the vernacular is, then, inseparable from the context of the religious wars and the nascent Catholic League; the reader is summoned to appreciate how, eleven hundred years in advance, this great confessor "a combattu, écrit, et disputé contre les Lutheriens d'Allemagne et les Calvinistes de France" (fought, wrote and argued against the Lutherans of Germany and the Calvinists of France).[110]

Hennequin's polemical preface acts as a perfect foil to those that would follow, for little in it hints at the devotional and interiorizing uses to which the *Confessions* were soon put, starting with the Jesuit René de Cérisier's translation, published for the first time anonymously in 1638 and reprinted at least a dozen times until 1709. Part of this inflection consists of reconceiving elements already present in Hennequin's version. If, as in Hennequin, the *Con-*

fessions are assimilated to the penitential act of avowal, Cérisiers goes much further than his predecessor in that confession is metaphorically described as an exteriorization, an uncovering of secrets and shadows:

Tous les courages ne sont pas assez grands pour publier des péchés qu'on n'a faits qu'en cachette: souvent on a autant de véritable peine de (*sic*) les exposer, qu'on a eu de faux plaisir à les faire. [Mes fautes] sont de cette nature, ils aiment les ténèbres, et ne peuvent souffrir la lumière.[111]
(Not everyone has enough courage to make public the sins one has committed only in secret: often exposing them causes as much real pain as committing them has given false pleasure. [My faults] are of this sort, they love the shadows and cannot tolerate the light.)

Cérisiers's insistence here on sin as the element the subject makes public even as he claims to want to keep it hidden certainly takes its place in the Foucauldian narrative of avowal (in *The History of Sexuality*) that spans the whole of the modern age, from the prescription of private confession once a year in 1215 all the way to the work of Freud. But Cérisier's preface contains much more than a mere confirmation of Foucault's thesis, for the "interior turn" that the *Confessions* take over the course of the century—indeed the entire culture of interiority that characterizes modernity—is not at all limited to an exacerbated sensitivity to concupiscence. Things other than darkness lay in the depths within.

If for the seventeenth century the *Confessions* seemed a "deep" text, it was above all because the work was increasingly assimilated to the mystical discourse of experience, a discourse that will, as will become more clear in the following chapter, relentlessly seek out autobiographical testimony to contact with the divine within. Cérisiers's preface is rife with the devotional, eroticized language of seventeenth-century mysticism ("Jouissez donc du cher objet de vos amours, goûtez à loisir la dévotion de ce Séraphin visible, consumez votre bon coeur des saintes ardeurs de ses flammes" [Take pleasure then in the dear object of your love, taste at leisure the devotion of this visible Seraph, consume your delighted heart with the holy ardor of his flames]), a language that clearly indicates that the *Confessions* were finding a new audience composed of readers searching for certain values that devotional currents will label "interior." Augustine's pages, for example, are full of "feux invisibles" (invisible flames) that are said to melt all but the hardest readers. Cérisier cautions his readers against reading the *Confessions* as a narrative exposition of sin, and casts them instead as a salutory divine fire: "Partout cette excellente Confession n'est pas tant un [lavoir] où on peut nettoyer ses taches, qu'une fournaise où l'on doit embraser ses froideurs" (This excellent Confession is throughout not so much a [wash basin] where one can cleanse one's stains, as a furnace where one must set one's chills ablaze). In this, Cérisier's preface demonstrates how ideas of hidden depth and difficult avowal contain not only the rhetoric of sin but also a more happy double, the language of affective mysticism that promised experiential plenitude with every turn inward. If the hermeneutic self is such an attractive idea to moderns, it is surely because the promised truth within is not *only* sexual sin, that "privileged theme of confession" — though it is certainly that too.[112] The object of what Foucault has characterized as a *scientia sexualis*, the human interior constitutes itself as a zone of happy authenticity only when it becomes the object of another science, what seventeenth-century mystics called "la science expérimentale," the science of experience.[113]

The *Confessions*, then, emerged as the book of two interrelated concepts of interiority — the interior as dark center of the secretive subject, but also the interior as the burning, experiential heart visited by mystical graces. This doubly interior reading persists and deepens in what was by far the most popular seventeenth-century translation of the *Confessions*, that of Robert Arnauld d'Andilly, the elder brother of the important Port-Royalist Antoine Arnauld. Once again, the reader is invited to embark on a hermeneutic approach to the hidden self, one in which Augustine's "clear" and "penetrating" gaze peers, "avec une séverité de Censeur" (with a Censor's severity), "jusques dans les replis les plus cachés de son âme pour y découvrir les moindres défauts et les moindres faiblesses" (down into most hidden folds of his soul to discover in it the most minor faults and weaknesses).[114] Once again, too, the translator moves the *Confessions* in the direction of the mystical relation of graces. From the very outset of Arnauld d'Andilly's long "Avis au lecteur," the translator argues for a break between a literature of the heart and one of the mind, a break that has situated the *Confessions* squarely among the former: "l'unique fin des livres de dévotion doit être d'élever à Dieu l'esprit et le coeur de ceux qui les lisent, et beaucoup plus encore le coeur que l'esprit" (the unique aim of devotional books must be to raise towards God the minds and hearts of their readers, and much more their hearts than their minds). Whereas in other works Augustine spoke the reasoned language of men, in the "ravissements" (ravishments) of this "ouvrage d'amour" (work of love) he forgets his self-control ("[s]a retenue") and gives in to an "effusion" of mystic proportions: "[S]i partout ailleurs [dans son oeuvre] il paraît des étincelles de ce feu céleste qui le consumait, il en paraît ici des flammes qui sont capables d'échauffer les plus froids et de fondre la glace des âmes les plus endurcies" (if everywhere else [in his work] there appear the sparks of this celestial fire that consumes him, here appear flames that are capable of warming even the coldest and of melting the ice of even the most hardened souls).[115] This devotional vocabulary is essentially that of Cérisiers, and the fact that the reading of the *Confessions* that the Jansenist Arnauld d'Andilly proposes so firmly reinforces the de-theologizing and interiorizing started by his Jesuit predecessor demonstrates how immaterial sectarian differences can be where subjective trends are concerned.

Both of the last two translations I will be discussing, that of Philippe Goibaud (or Goibaut) du Bois (1686) and Simon-Michel Treuvé (1703), participate in this same vogue for works that touch the heart; their prefaces are filled with the devotional language contained in the previous two versions of the *Confessions*.[116] Their works are particularly significant, however, on account of their amplification of an idea already present in Cérisiers's commentary—to wit, that the *Confessions* are in fact two books, one speculative and cerebral, one experiential and cordial, and that the division between the two occurs precisely where the autobiographical account of the first ten books gives way to the meditations on time and Genesis in books XI to XIII. Cérisiers had warned his reader not to put off by the "subtile recherche" (subtle inquiry) of the books that followed the "histoire de sa vie" (story of his life), and Goibaud du Bois, too, speaks to the increasing difficulty the work's hybrid composition poses to its new readership: "La plupart de ceux qui lisent les Confessions de s. Augustin en demeurent au dixième livre, et laissent les trois derniers" (Most of those who read the *Confessions* of St. Augustine stop at the tenth book and leave the last three [unread]).[117] Goibaud's goal seems to be to encourage his readers to overcome this thorny ("épineux") difficulty, which he excuses through recourse to historical explanations. If book XIII, for example, appears incongruous, this is, he argues, owing to the necessity of allegorical interpretation in Patristic times.

Treuvé, however, in an editorial decision that provides a fitting climax to the trends that had brought the *Confessions* very far indeed from where Hennequin had first positioned them over a century earlier, felt no need to reconcile his modern readership with passages that had clearly lapsed into irrelevance. Treuvé, another relation of Antoine Arnauld's, and much appreciated in Jansenist circles, had already authored two highly successful devotional works—*Instruction sur les dispositions qu'on doit apporter aux sacrements* (1676) and *Le Directeur spirituel pour ceux qui n'en ont pas* (1691). The latter especially appealed to a burgeoning market for books we might think of as "self-help," that is, inspirational books for those who profess themselves weary of or excluded by institutional mediation. Treuvé's *Confessions* were aimed at just such an audience: he proposed an abridged version in which, as his title read, "l'on n'a mis que ce qui est le plus touchant et le plus à la portée de tout le monde" (we have included only what is most touching and most accessible to everyone).[118]

What was most "touching" and "accessible" in Augustine's work? Treuvé's translation amputates the last three books entirely, and condenses what remains into five books that leave out what the translator views as extraneous historical material, such as the account of Augustine's disputes with the Manicheans or his biographical sketch of his mother in book IX. The result is a volume that guarantees that the moving and tender qualities of the work triumph over those that might dry out ("déséch[er]") the heart.[119] Treuvé's editorial project, aimed at bringing the strangeness of Augustine's work in line with the expectations of contemporary readers, bears more than a passing resemblance to Martin Lowenthal's production of Montaigne's "autobiography" that I evoked at the outset of this chapter.[120] And his early example of the autobiographical anachronism was far from a historical anomaly: it was preceded as far back as 1638 by an English translation (printed in Paris): *The Kernel or Extract of the Historical Part of S. Augustine's Confessions, Together with All the Most Affectuous Passages Thereof, Taken out of That Whole Book and Severed from Such Parts as are Obscure, Device, or Ornament*. In 1660, Abraham Woodhead even offered a *Life* of Augustine in two parts, the first volume of which was autobiographically entitled *The Life of S. Augustine. Written by Himself in the First Ten Books of His Confessions*.[121]

The appearance of Treuvé's abridged *Confessions* at the opening of what was to be the century of *sensibilité*—an age in which emotional response founded not only the standard of literary worth but the very possibility of a scientific approach to the human body—was supremely appropriate.[122] The *Confessions* had become an intimate experience, one of reader identifying with writer through the precious material mediation of the portable book. For Treuvé also vaunts his translation for its physical properties, which are something like the material complement of its touching content: "on pourra facilement le porter toujours avec soi, et avoir la commodité d'en lire quand on voudra quelque chapitre" (one may easily carry it with oneself at all times and have the convenience of reading it whenever one wishes). It goes without saying that people had carried the *Confessions* with them for private reading before this time (the case of Petrarch comes to mind).[123] But Treuvé's explicit reference to the advantage of portability marks the *Confessions'* definitive move out of the ecclesiastical domain, and their journey into the private world of "literature," where they would enjoy, until this day, their status as the West's first autobiography.

Becoming Autobiography

I have tried to suggest that Augustine's and Montaigne's use of metaphoric interiority, and the deliberate enhancement of that interiority during the seventeenth century, offer some insight into the origins of the anachronism that is autobiographical reading. Martin Lowenthal's "autobiography" of Montaigne is the result of changes that lead back to readers who enjoyed Treuvé's edition of Augustine, readers who would certainly sympathize with picking and choosing those bits of Montaigne's own work that echo their own concerns. But I have also tried to show, via my discussion of the texts of Augustine and Montaigne themselves, that if these readings were incomplete, they were also startlingly perceptive in the way they zeroed in on aspects of these authors' work that would for centuries define their popularity. Thus, the modern tendency to privilege autobiographical readings can and should be understood not as something totally foreign to the texts themselves, but rather as part of a diachronic process in which these important works have *become*, bit by bit, autobiographies. There is never any one moment in which an expressible "inside" becomes suddenly thinkable, a moment in which the hermeneutic anachronism becomes possible; rather, in a long series of re-positionings, the present takes from the past something that it recognizes as its own, and brings it into harmony with prevailing expectations. Historical difference is suppressed, and likeness enhanced, but the latter is no more a complete fabrication than the past is "in fact" totally other. Indeed, it is this eerie mixture of familiarity and difference that even Foucault, the theorist of "epistemic rupture," came to appreciate most when working with texts of Antiquity.[124]

Yet there is a paradox here, one that hints that the origins of this anachronism are more complicated, that there is more in this than a sweeping narrative of the advent—good or bad—of a hermeneutic, interiorized subject that expresses itself through writing. This paradox is that at the same time Augustine and Montaigne were subject to the same interiorizing logic, the comparative fates of the *Confessions* and the *Essais* in the seventeenth century were quite divergent. Judging by their publication history and the many texts that aimed to frame the works for their readers, one can remark an inverse relationship in the popularity of the two authors—Montaigne's fortunes turned sour just as Augustine's were hitting a high point. Here are two of the works most likely to be mentioned as ancestors of modern autobiographical practice, and yet they could not have been treated more differently even as they were read in similar ways. Why did the *Confessions* excite such enthusiasm in the second half of the century, while the *Essais* attracted only opprobrium, if they both were seen as manifestations of a deep self?

Beneath the diachronic narrative of the rise of human interiority as a paradigm for modern subjectivity lie synchronic discrepancies, tell-tale signs of the diverse and contradictory social forces in which interiority was, and remains, embedded. Although interiority is indeed part of the general fabric of early modern culture, from science to literature to religion, certain developments, such as the important link between writing and the inner world, seem to prosper in one or another specific terrain. Before the rhetoric of autobiographical interiority moved out into secular literature in the eighteenth century, that terrain was religious. Marie de Gournay's foregrounding of the penitential sincerity with which Montaigne exposed his "entrails" and made the hidden interior readable was in this light no accident. In moving to separate the *Essais* from the then-popular works on aristocratic self-fashioning with which they were often lumped (e.g., Nicolas Faret's *L'Honnête homme ou l'art de plaire à la cour* [1630], who cites Montaigne) and in trumpeting them instead as confession, Gournay showed tremendous prescience, for the subjective future belonged to interiority and interiority was, for the moment, preeminently religious.

Of course, Gournay's efforts to portray Montaigne as an exemplary penitent came to nothing, and he fell from favor: the *Essais* did not make a good devotional text. Explanations for this failure are not hard to come by—Montaigne's skepticism, his worldliness, his lack of contrition (in spite of Gournay's assertions), and, most of all, his conception of a God far removed from the goings-on of men. The devotional milieu demanded not only confessional penitence—of which the *Essais* offer little—but also first-person narratives of mystic experience. For if Augustine met with approval, it was certainly not because his text somehow implied, as one modern commentator has put it, "the destruction of the speaking subject." [125] On the contrary, I hope to have shown how that destruction, in the last four books of the *Confessions*, left his readers "cold," to use the same expression as his translators, and they disregarded it. Rather, Augustine offered a text of experience—man's experience of God as something lived and within that can be expressed through writing.

So while Montaigne may well—on occasion, at least—have looked within himself, and been appreciated for so doing, the Augustine of the seventeenth century actually found something there—something sinful, yes, but also a hidden brightness that moored his identity and demanded to be exposed.

In its thirst for inner experience, however, the devotional public did not limit itself to the reading of one exemplary man's canonical text. Unlike "heroic virtue" (one of the saintly traits necessary for canonization by Rome), and unlike theological sophistication, experience belonged to everybody. Experience's seductive charm was that it could not simply be learned, nor imitated, as one might imitate a supreme act of charity; instead, it had to be "caught," like a divine fever. "Je souhaite, mon cher Lecteur, que ce feu de l'amour divin qui a embrasé le coeur de Saint Augustin, et qui lui a fait produire un si excellent ouvrage, jette de si vives étincelles dans le vôtre" (Dear Reader, may this fire of divine love that set Saint Augustine's heart aflame, and that made him produce such an excellent work, cast such bright sparks into your own), writes Arnauld d'Andilly with a logic that can only suggest that those flames in the hearts of Augustine's readers would be, in their turn, autobiographical.[126] The inner pleasure of experience implied that contemporaries too do what Augustine did, and indeed, as I shall show in subsequent chapters, by the second half of the century, large amounts of what were repeatedly touted as autobiographical "gémissements intérieurs" (inner moanings) would for the first time find their way into print. Yet the rest of this book will also attempt to highlight a paradox that lies in wait at every turn in the investigation of our culture of interiority. The type of experiential, collective enthusiasm that Arnauld d'Andilly hoped Augustine's *Confessions* inspired was always dogged by the contrary hope *not* to be understood: my experience, after all, is only mine if it is not quite yours. As an anonymous compiler put it, with regard to Augustine's "gémissements inénarrables" (unspeakable moanings), "ces délices des âmes fidèles sont si intérieures, si secrètes, si cachées, si inconnues, qu'il n'y a que les personnes mêmes qui les éprouvent qui les puissent comprendre: et même après l'expérience que l'on en a faite, on n'est point encore capable de les expliquer" (the delights of faithful souls are so interior, so secret, hidden and unknown, that only the same persons who experience them can understand them: and even after the experience one has had of them, one is still incapable of explaining them).[127] Somewhat contradictorily, then, experience was both readable and hidden, common to all and yet specifically one's own; it couldn't be had through books and at the same time reading and writing about it were an integral part of its cultivation. Such was a logically untenable position, certainly, but it is precisely this friction—between assertions of irreducible depths and extravagant hopes for textual communities united by a commonly ineffable experience—that fired the dream of autobiography, a book that was not quite a book, an ostensibly transparent window nonetheless tantalizingly opaque.

Chapter Two
Verbatim
Print, Gender, and the Death of the Biographer

To what extent does the reception of a work tell us as much if not more about generic evolution than the characteristics of the work itself? Or, to restate the question by paraphrasing a favorite children's conundrum: if an autobiography falls in a forest and no one cares to read it, is it still an autobiography?

Consider the fate of the Capuchin Benoît de Canfeld's *Véritable et miraculeuse conversion*, a fairly short text (150 pages), written in 1596 and clearly modeled on Augustine's *Confessions*. Its first appearance, in a Latin translation under the title *Soliloquum grave*, was in a biographical compendium of the Capuchin order, the *Annales capuccinuum* (1610). Here, lost among numerous third-person biographical sketches, was an autobiographical narrative, inconspicuously filling a spot in a perfectly conventional editorial practice — the annals of a religious order. When Benoît's original French text first saw print in the 1614 Nantilly edition of his best-selling mystic treatise *Règle de perfection*, it again reoccupied a biographical space — the space of the common biographical sketch or elegy that accompanied an author's collected works. In this precise case, this sketch is one of several heterogeneous texts tacked on to the *Règle*. The complete title of the volume, which mentions these subordinate texts "coat-tailing" their way into print, reads *Règle de perfection contenant un abrégé de toute la vie spirituelle . . . , augmentée en cette septième édition de sa miraculeuse conversion, et un sommaire discours de son heureuse vie et mort; plus une sienne méthode et adresse de l'oraison, avec une lettre qu'autrefois il a écrite au P. Ange de Joyeuse.*[1] In the title, the autobiographical text (the "miraculeuse conversion") and the biographical text (the "sommaire discours") commingle, functioning analogously; nowhere on the title page is there any indication that the "miraculeuse conversion" was in fact a work of Benoît de Canfeld himself, utterly unrelated to the "sommaire discours." They complemented the volume, as did the single letter to Père Joyeuse. Not the focal point of an edition, autobiography could be considered a complementary "extra" or bonus — a bonus that differed in no way from a biographical sketch, a letter, or a fragment on prayer.

The editorial frames for Benoît's text were not yet exhausted. In 1621, Jacques Brousse published a *Life* of Benoît, which included the complete text of the 1614 edition of the *Conversion*—right down to the chapter titles. The title page here reads *La Vie et conversion miraculeuse du R. P. Benoît de Canfeld, Anglais, Predicateur Capucin.*[2] Again, the autobiographical status of the text is passed over as it is made to function silently as biography; not until the end of the first chapter does Brousse even bother to make it apparent that his *Life* includes a very large autobiographical segment. The 1666 edition of the *Règle de perfection* gave a final blow to the status of the *Conversion*. The edition reprints it in its customary place, but the title page does more than dissimulate, as before, the text's autobiographical origins—it no longer makes any mention at all of the *Conversion*. The title now reads: *Règle de perfection . . . , revue, corrigée, et augmentée en cette dernière edition de la vie de l'auteur, et d'un éclaircissement nécessaire pour bien entendre la volonté de Dieu.*[3] Typographically speaking, biography had displaced autobiography: though the text was still in print, its autobiographical nature had been completely obscured, or rather forgotten, for the first person did not seem to interest anyone enough to make the effort actually to repress or hide it, as had been done with the interiorizing content of Montaigne's *Essais*.

If one analyzes the *text* of the *Véritable et miraculeuse conversion*, one finds what is very arguably an autobiography—here, Benoît de Canfeld, though skipping his childhood, tells of his vocation, of his doubts and hesitations faced with both the attractions of the world and the Protestant heresy, and finally of his religious conversion and entry into the Capuchin order. On the whole, the text strongly recalls Augustine's—one finds the same interspersed invocations of God, the same attention to the temptation of heretical doctrine, the same conversion long postponed and finally realized, and in the company of a friend no less. The author cites Augustine, and uses expressions typical of the Augustinian *homo interior*: "vous avez entonné dans l'intérieure oreille de mon âme ces très saints et salutaires propos, *fiat lux*" (you have intoned in the inner ear of my soul these most holy and salutary words, *fiat lux*).[4] And the whole narrative is framed by considerations on the religious wars that make clear that this *Conversion* was being inserted into the very same social context as the first (1582) translation of the *Confessions*, in which Aemar Hennequin claimed that the work would, above all, combat heresy.[5] For all these textual reasons, then, one has every reason to regard Benoît de Canfeld's text as an autobiography in the line of Augustine's *Confessions*. Yet as soon as one looks at the lackluster fate of the work, questions come to mind. Here was a phenomenally successful author (the *Règle de perfection* was reprinted regularly throughout the century and translated into some five languages), one of the main players in the burgeoning mystic circles of early seventeenth-century France, and yet his autobiography fell on deaf ears. As Augustine's *Confessions* gained an ever-widening devotional audience, the *Véritable et miraculeuse conversion* went out with a whimper. Why?

Certainly, explanatory causes are to be found in the text itself, notably in the organizing principle of the Catholic-Protestant doctrinal opposition, so topical at the turn of the century, but incapable of striking the devotional chords of a mysticism increasingly given to outpourings of the heart which seemed to bypass entirely thorny theological problems. But there are other reasons as well, reasons that recall Montaigne's similar fall from favor: to a large extent, the success or failure of a text depends on the readership it is able to find, rather than on the content of the text itself. Montaigne's text was interiorizing, but not religious, and I have suggested in the previous chapter that in the seventeenth century, there was little place for an interiorized auto-biographical "I" save in the religious press. Benoît de Canfeld's text was aimed at the right readership, but the author's concern with questions of doctrine (will I stay a Catholic or give my mental ascent to the reasoning of the Protes-tants?) hurt its chances of being labeled "interior" by the devotional public. Augustine was such a canonical figure that his text was treated differently, with its doctrinal aspects either being downplayed or edited out entirely.

In addition, Benoît de Canfeld's reception is explained by one of the main arguments of this book—to wit, that there was no one moment at which autobiography suddenly became thinkable, but rather a slow process by which writers, readers and editors learned to recognize the autobiographi-cal document as a text worthy of special attention and publication. Given its effacement, Benoît de Canfeld's text can be situated on one end of the pub-lication spectrum: although it *was* indeed printed, judging from paratextual clues, it made no particular claim upon the reader's attention. It would take until the eighteenth century for the other extreme to be reached, for it was only then that independent works started to appear in France under titles that advertised their status as autobiographies.[6] Between these two extremes lies the intriguing fate of substantial amounts of autobiographical material that was the object of obvious enthusiasm even as it remained, like the *Véri-table conversion*, squarely in the shadow of biography. Even Teresa of Avila's autobiography (published 1588), virtually a publishing hapax in that it stood on its own and under its author's (as opposed to editor's) name, could not quite escape from this biographical shadow: the French translations of the Teresa's *Vie et oeuvres*, especially toward the beginning of the century, often included not the autobiography that one would expect, but a translation of a 1590 biography of the mystic—which in turn incorporated extracts from her autobiographical writing. There are two ironies here: biography and autobiography were confused to the point where religious men and women claiming to have been influenced by the *"Vie de Thérèse"* may well be referring to her *biography* rather than her autobiography; and her influence qua autobiographer owed perhaps as much to the first-person snippets furnished by her biographer than to her own autonomous autobiography.[7] Since readers of the period had only just begun to differentiate autobiography from biography, the fact that Benoît de Canfeld's text was fitted into a biographical space and then forgotten there comes as no surprise.

One last reason, however, for Benoît de Canfeld's eclipse can be stated more baldly: he was a man, at a time when "being interior" implied, among other things, being a woman. Augustine was a partial exception to this rule— "partial" because the success of his *Confessions* over the course of the seventeenth century depended on a devotional public that, as I shall show, was gendered feminine. Indeed, this is a detail I left out of my previous consideration of the *Confessions'* growing popularity, and one that, as much as the religious gulf, distinguished them from the *Essais* of Montaigne. For Marie de Gournay may have been the author of important protofeminist texts, but she destined her *Essais* for a male readership at the same time she interiorized them: "[J]e vous consigne cet orphelin qui m'était commis, afin qu'il vous plaise désormais de lui tenir lieu de Tuteur et de Protecteur" (I give over to you this orphan who was entrusted to me, so that it may please you henceforth to stand in as its Tutor and Protector), she writes, dedicating a book described as "entièrement fils de son Père" (entirely the son of its Father) to none other than the Cardinal Richelieu.[8] René de Cérisiers, by contrast, introduced his interiorized reading of the *Confessions* by dedicating them to a woman, the Duchesse de Guillon, whose "belle passion pour S. Augustin" (impressive passion for Saint Augustine) had apparently led her to suggest the translation in the first place.[9] Vernacularization of the *Confessions* took them out of the hands of the scholastic male elite and made them accessible to those in search of the tender and the touching. In his translation of the *Soliloquies*, also dedicated to a woman, Cérisiers explicitly genders this select and interior group feminine. Certain that "Saint Augustin ne parlera pas inutilement Français à ceux qui n'entendent pas le Latin" (it will not be useless for Saint Augustin to speak French to those who do not understand Latin), he is equally sure that these "ceux" will in fact be "celles," for he specifies that "les femmes . . . sont le principal sujet de cette version" (women . . . are the main motivation behind this version). Cérisiers concludes with a devotional commonplace that was frequently invoked in the latter half of the century to justify the publication of thousands of pages of women's autobiographical writings: "Si les hommes connaissent Dieu, les femmes l'aiment" (If men know God, women love Him).[10] This love came from the heart and overflowed—with the blessing and through the instigation of many a confessor such as Cérisiers—onto the printed page. Inner spaces and the writing they appeared to generate were the special province of women.

By extension of this feminization of piety, Augustine, no matter how in favor or assiduously promoted by translators, could do only so much for the evolving discourse of autobiographical interiority. "Experience" was properly a female domain, and thus it was Teresa of Avila's *Life*, rather than the *Confessions*, that formed a template for the production of autobiographical material during the following century. "Very soon after [Teresa's] death, one can observe the birth of a veritable vogue of written confession," writes one scholar of Spanish Catholic autobiography;[11] in seventeenth-century France, the phenomenon was no less impressive. Indeed, Teresa's overwhelmingly popular *Life* seems the obvious choice for an explanation of the significant numbers of mystical first-person texts in the seventeenth century. Immeasurably more than Augustine's *Confessions*, the *Life* was an obligatory reference both in autobiographical writings (where it was usually listed among favorite devotional readings) and in the various paratexts that accompanied these writings into print (where an explicit comparison was often drawn between it and the writings at hand).

Yet I would stress that the "intertextual model"—according to which one great book is immediately recognized and imitated, thus transforming the literary landscape forever—is not precisely what I think Teresa's popularity corroborates. This model seems weak in at least two respects. First, it is a classic example of question begging, for it does not explain why Teresa wrote what she did when she did; second, it completely obscures the valuable data these texts provide on how literary genres are embedded in material practices that do not and cannot change overnight. Reading and writing habits depend on, for instance, changes in techniques of spiritual direction; they rely as well on editorial conventions, and if there is no place for first-person narratives in the publishing institution, such places will have to be devised. Moreover, this resistance to change had non-material causes. Interest in the lives of habitually anonymous religious women encountered not only misogynist resistance (this goes without saying), but a sort of conceptual inertia as well, even among the boosters of female experience. For evidence suggests that writing one's own biography was hardly accepted by all as something perfectly normal for religious women—even exceptional ones, and even after Teresa's example—to do. In part, this is clear from the writing itself, which most often consists of fragmentary notations (via letters, or journals) of various experiences rather than full-blown retrospective narratives replete with beginnings, middles and, insofar as possible with autobiography, ends.[12] If Teresa had as many epigones as is commonly maintained, the fact that the publication of autobiographical texts as independent works was virtually unheard of in seventeenth-century France seems incongruous in the least. And yet such was the case: autobiographical texts were integrated into biographies, or on occasion appended to nonautobiographical works by the same author, but unlike Teresa's *Life*, they did not stand on their own.[13] They were dependent on publishing practices that were made to accommodate a mode of writing whose readerly recognition was only in its infancy. It is these practices, and this recognition, that is the subject of this chapter.

Nowhere is the slow encroachment of an autobiographical mode of reading more evident than in the print transmission of mystic texts of seventeenth-century religious women. These texts were generated by women, usually nuns and usually at the behest of a spiritual director, who had been blessed with a variety of divine "graces."[14] Some graces were distinctly cerebral: much of what mystics called visions ("vues") concerned intellectual and not ocular apprehension; a vision of the sacred Trinity, for instance, referred to the spontaneous, extratheological understanding of this central Christian mystery. More commonly, what contemporaries called graces fell under the category of what is now usually described as affective mysticism—tactile visions of Christ's open wounds, mystic marriage to the Beloved, and those pleasurable swoons immortalized by Bernini's famous sculpture of Teresa (1645–52). Whatever their origins or nature, however, the phenomena themselves have little to do with the present inquiry. Rather, their significance hinges on a growing association between writing and a realm of knowledge that we now know as "personal experience." The association was made in part by the autobiographers themselves, but it was theorized most explicitly by the admiring men and women who sought to present these mystics to the numerous readers of the devotional press via the burgeoning genre of religious biography. It was here, in hundreds and even thousands of *Lives*—hagiography for contemporary and uncanonized figures of exemplary piety—that the written words of nuns started to appear, slowly at first, then, especially after 1650, in larger quantities. In a sense, the confusion I have alluded to briefly between Teresa's autobiographical *Life* and the biographical *Life of Teresa* that often accompanied her works was more than mere quirk. The dissemination of Teresa's "I" within a male-authored biography was arguably more representative of autobiographical publication in the seventeenth century than her own *Life* was; it was via its incorporation into hagiographic works that the writing of religious women found a public outside of the convents. Through biography, readers learned how to appreciate the virtues and particularities of the autobiographical text — in particular, the way it opened up the subject's interior to cognition by another.

His Master's Voice: Orality and Experience

In retrospect, when Teresa's writings were first translated into French in 1601, they symbolically inaugurated a century increasingly given to discursive representations of something that was held to exist inside the individual as well as outside and just beyond language — something toward which language was turned and that, just maybe, it could capture. Contemporaries reasoned that it was from this something — personal experience — that all writing that was not mere speculation or vain ratiocination proceeded. Hence, in contrast to the Jansenists' ideal of solitary silent retreat, and to their mistrust of the ruses of *amour-propre* and its linguistic pawn, the first-person singular pronoun, seventeenth-century mysticism was all about talking about oneself and inciting others to do the same. But this experiential verbosity took some time to develop. The first half of the century certainly had its share of mystics — Madame Acarie, for instance, who introduced Teresa's Reformed Carmelites to France and who held a sort of spiritual salon that molded many influential figures (Benoît de Canfeld, or Pierre de Bérulle). Alternatively known as "la théologie mystique" (mystic theology), or "la science des saints" (the science of saints), mysticism was the object of many books; yet they were by and large the books of a spiritual elite in dialogue with various Christian mystical traditions. Measurable popular success did not come until the latter half of the century; by this time, the abstract teachings of the mystic wing of the Church hierarchy were trickling down, starting to effect changes in popular practices. Indeed, mysticism was no longer for the few who had been schooled in the theology of figures such as the pseudo-Dionysius or Tauler: as Michel de Certeau has shown so well, rather than a *knowledge* of the divine, "la mystique" as it developed in the seventeenth century was cast as an *experience*, accessible even and above all to those without knowledge of Christianity's great mystical works.[15]

This popularizing of mysticism can be observed in the mutations of two key words in seventeenth century spirituality, words that gradually lost their theological importance even as they were provoking more and more enthusiasm in devotional literature. These words were "interior" (*intérieur*), used both as a noun and an adjective, and "heart" (*coeur*).[16] Devotional literature no longer attempted to make the Augustinian distinction between exterior man (*homo exterior*—that is, the part of man also shared by animals, such as faculties of perception) and inner man (*homo interior*—a term designating faculties animals did not have, such as reason). Instead, "interior" came to designate a vague psychological space to which logic, reason, and even language were foreign, indeed, "exterior." At this point "interior" disappeared from theological discourse, to become instead a fixture of devotional literature—literature intended for consumption by a much wider audience than the clerical male readership of theology. In the first half of the century, one comes upon a few titles indicative of the trend to come, for instance, Jean-Pierre Camus's 1631 *Traité de la réformation intérieure* (why reform the Church when one can just reform one's interior?). But it is only with the 1660s that the idea of "being interior" invades the religious press. Jean de Bernières started the vogue in 1661 with his *Chrétien intérieur*, which went through fourteen editions by 1674, and sold an estimated 30,000 copies.[17] Capitalizing on the immediate success of this work, Timothée de Raynier followed suit with *L'homme intérieur ou l'idée du parfait chrétien* (1662), as did Bernardin de Paris with *Le Religieux intérieur* (1663). The next decades saw the publication of Jean Maillard's *Occupation intérieure* (1683), of Boudun's biography of Jean Chrysostome de Saint-Lô, *L'Homme intérieur* (1684), and of Nicolas Robine's *Excercices de l'homme intérieur* (1691).

A parallel shift took place with the heart. In Saint Thomas's theology, the heart had been synonymous with the will. Although the heart retained its Thomist voluntaristic character in seventeenth-century theology, devotional discourse used references to the organ quite differently. Notably, the opposition between heart and reason, rare and imprecise at the beginning of the century, soon became unavoidable. Pascal's dictum that "[l]e coeur a ses raisons que la raison ne connaît point" (the heart has reasons which reason knows not) is perhaps the best-known expression of what, at the time of the *Pensées*, was rapidly becoming a devotional commonplace.[18] According to one eminent religious scholar of the period, the heart comes to symbolize "a spontaneity of our being, not subject to logical, rational and discursive modes"; it becomes "the site par excellence of non-discursive contemplation."[19] Works on the heart multiply in the last third of the century. Vincent Contenson's

Theologia mentis et cordis is from 1668. François Querdu Le Gall first published his widely reprinted (in these years and until 1839) *L'Oratoire du coeur* in 1670. Alexandre Piny's *L'Oraison du coeur* appeared in 1683, with another volume of the same title, by N. de Montfort, following the next year. This rampant cordiality reached its paroxysm, and took for the first time a slightly sentimental turn, in Marguerite-Marie Alacoque and Jean Eudes's devotion to the Sacred Heart of Jesus.[20] By this time, then, "heart" and "interior" had become catch-all phrases, gesturing away from theological speculation towards a spontaneous and fervent spiritual life.

During the Quietist affair of the 1690s, this popular affective mysticism came under attack by spiritual conservatives such as Bossuet, who perceived its implicit threat—what becomes of the ecclesiastical establishment and its function of mediating between believers and God, once the individual is made the locus of spiritual knowledge?[21] Responding to Bossuet's challenge, François de Salignac de la Mothe-Fénelon, best known now as the author of the proto-Enlightenment fable *Télémaque*, intervened on behalf of the mystics. Arguing in his *Explication des maximes des saints sur la vie intérieure* (1696) that "[o]n peut apprendre tous les jours en étudiant les voies de Dieu sur les ignorants expérimentés" (studying the ways of God upon experienced ignorants is a daily source of learning), Fénelon echoed a line of reasoning which is now typically associated with Protestant trends in spirituality that deemphasized the mediating role of the Church or its ministers (usually in favor of a return to the Bible).[22] Knowledge of God was not doctrinal, but experiential; excessive attention to doctrine could even "dry out" the heart (as one of Augustine's translators put it), thereby precluding the experiential knowledge that was the true measure of saintliness.[23] Hence an "experienced ignorant" could be said to have much to teach those who made up what was perceived of as an increasingly bureaucratized ecclesiastical hierarchy.[24] Fénelon's line of defense was an appropriate summing-up of the century's mystic enthusiasms. The "experienced ignorants" whom all of us would do well to study came straight from a topos that was among the most seductive in seventeenth-century religious culture—what Michel de Certeau has called the topos of the "enlightened illiterate."[25] Widespread were accounts of meetings, invariably represented as moments of conversion, between knowledgeable but spiritually dead theologians and poor, unknown shepherds, servants and other lay people who had received their knowledge directly from God.

The figure of the enlightened illiterate had deep roots going all the way back to several Pauline allusions to the power of the weak.[26] During the Middle Ages, *docta ignoratia* (an ignorance that knows itself) became a major concept in mystical theology; the fourteenth-century Béguine Marguerite Porete, in her *Miroir des simples âmes*, invoked a version of the topos which Marguerite de Navarre would elaborate on in her poetry two centuries later. By the seventeenth century, the imaginative hold of enlightened illiteracy was stronger and wider still, as "ignorance" lost its qualifier "learned." In a letter dated May 1630, the Jesuit Jean-Joseph Surin told of meeting in a carriage a young man, "simple et grossier extrêmement en sa parole, sans lettres aucunes, [mais] rempli de toutes sortes de grâces et dons intérieurs" (simple and extremely crude in his speech, totally uneducated, [but] filled with every sort of grace and inner gift); Certeau has observed that this letter, circulated widely in manuscript and reprinted some twenty times over the course of the century, read like a "manifesto" for a spirituality based on experience rather than book-knowledge.[27]

Although there was nothing to prevent men from assuming the role of the enlightened illiterate—as is the case in both Surin's letter and Fénelon's *Explication*, in which the latter makes reference to Brother Laurent de la Résurrection—Linda Timmermans has noted how the poor rural illiterate object of spiritual wonder was more likely to be a woman than a man.[28] Some of the century's best-known names in spirituality were fascinated—often to the embarrassment of the Church establishment—by women who, although cowherds or peasants, were seen as being especially close to God. Jean Eudes, founder of the Congregation of Jesus and Marie and since sainted, fixated on Marie des Vallées; Charles de Condren, general of the Oratory, was devoted to Barbe de Compiègne. Women did not have to be truly "illiterate" to serve the topos; they represented intellectual simplicity by virtue of their ignorance of Latin letters. Hence Marie Rousseau, the educated widow of a wealthy wine merchant, and Jeanne Guyon, whose origins were anything but humble, played the role for Jean-Jacques Olier (founder of the Sulpicians) and Fénelon, respectively. Although Guyon wrote profusely on mystical matters, Fénelon affected little interest in the doctrinal aspects of her spirituality; as I shall detail in the following chapter, in part this was no doubt to shelter himself from accusations of heresy in the heat of the Quietist affair. The lack of interest in doctrine, however, was also perfectly congruent with the seductions of enlightened illiteracy. These "theodidacts" were sought out far and wide because they embodied a lived contemplative spirituality that was seen as the opposite of painstaking theological demonstration.

The gendering of illiteracy was consonant with the feminizing of mysticism in general, as the latter metamorphosed from a type of knowledge to be gained through study into a type of experience that would be *blocked* by study. Gendering mysticism feminine could be intended as a valorization, as when Pierre Poiret, a fervent follower of Jeanne Guyon, in a preface to a biography of an "enlightened illiterate," taunts the learned with tales of women and girls "dont les éclatantes lumières et les dons tout célestes allaient bien au-delà de tous les talents et de toutes les connaissances des Docteurs les plus habiles" (whose brilliant insights and altogether celestial gifts went far beyond all the talents and all the knowledge of the most clever Church Doctors).[29] Conversely, it could be a denigration, as when Pierre Nicole warns that "il y a beaucoup d'illusions à craindre dans ces Oraisons extraordinaires. Car il y a d'étranges ressorts dans l'imagination, et surtout dans celle des femmes" (there are many illusions to be feared in these extraordinary orisons. For there are strange forces at work in the imagination, and especially in that of women).[30] Jean-Joseph Surin sought to undo this stereotype; his use of a man as a paragon of experiential spirituality in his famous "enlightened illiterate" letter may well have been dictated by his perception that experience had to be made more gender-neutral if mysticism was to find welcome within the Church establishment.[31] But Surin was an exception: by and large, whether they denigrated it or esteemed it, men were clearly convinced that women were the locus of experience.

The enthusiasm for the figure of the enlightened illiterate enables us to understand, at least in part, why there were so many biographies of religious women in seventeenth-century France.[32] Via biography, women's experience, in all its seeming authenticity, could be made available to the public. For many men in the Church, nuns were nearly as far from the world of theological speculation as cowherds, and much closer at hand, for priests not only heard their confessions, they also met with nuns to discuss their spiritual progress. And it was thanks to the information provided by note-taking spiritual directors that the aspiring biographer could document the mystic's inner life. These notes, added to numerous other documents—eye-witness reports of superiors and fellow nuns, memoirs, and so on—produced *Lives* touted as faithful not only to the exterior actions of the biographical subject, but to her interior experience.

Spiritual direction and confession aimed to anatomize two sides of the same human coin—grace and sin.[33] For, like sin, grace had its dangers: the selfish desire for the ecstasy of divine union, for example, could lead to what John of the Cross called "spiritual avarice." Spiritual direction was nonetheless distinct from confession in several ways. Whereas confession was largely a method for regulating sexuality, spiritual direction was much closer to an erotic discourse—what Foucault has called an *ars erotica*, as opposed to the *scientia sexualis* dominant in the West: it attempted not to root out sinful impulses, but to accentuate pleasure.[34] Second, spiritual direction was narrative and accumulative in ways confession was not: unlike in confession, where the penitent erased past faults in confessing them, the directed built up an itinerary of experience.[35] Third, a friendly and interpersonal air attended the dynamic of direction, or at the very least, representations of this dynamic: when the number of treatises on direction skyrocketed in the early to mid seventeenth century, their titles often stressed the affective bond between director and directed, such as Jean-François de Reims's 1633 *Le Directeur fidèle* or Archange de Valognes's *Le Directeur pacifique des consciences* (1637–39).[36] Lastly—and most fortunately for those who were reinventing religious biography—spiritual direction was a practice, but not a sacrament, and thus the exchanges it generated came under no obligation of secrecy.

All in all, then, spiritual direction provided the best sort of documentation a biographer could ask for—an intimate narrative discourse that needed only to be carefully gathered in order to produce a *Life* which would expose the subject. In metaphorical terms, it was in spiritual direction that the subject opened up her interior—"découvrir son intérieur" is the phrase used by both biographers and aspiring mystics. Jean Maillard for instance uses the formula in referring to writings that the director of Marie Bon de l'Incarnation "lui a commandé de faire, pour lui découvrir son intérieur" (prescribed to her, in order to expose her interior to him), and Claudine Moine tells her director at the end of an exchange: "[J'ai] rendu mon âme visible à vos yeux" ([I have] made my soul visible to your eyes).[37] Biography itself seems to have been founded on this same metaphor; the biographer reenacts the exposure of interior by allowing the intimate exchanges of spiritual direction to come to light. Letters exchanged between a nun and her director are touted as giving "l'idée la plus juste que l'on puisse prendre de [son] intérieur admirable" (the most accurate idea that one might have of [her] admirable interior).[38] The indefinite "on" here allows the slippage from director to biographer to reader: all three gaze at the nun's interior from an analogous position. In another *Life*, Mathieu Bourdin tells us of Madeleine Vigneron's letters being written not for her director, but for *us*, the readers of her biography, "afin que *nous* en eussions plus de lumière, et que l'on ne pût rien désirer davantage pour son entière connaissance" (so that *we* might have more light, and so that one would need nothing more in order to know her completely). Vigneron's interior life, Bourdin says, is thus faithfully manifested, "aussi clairement que si *nous* avions lu dans la conscience de cette bonne âme" (as clearly as if *we* had read in the conscience of this fine soul).[39] Biographers put their readers in the place of the man who was first privy to the unveiling of the subject.

Besides the voyeuristic pleasure of exposing the mystic's interior, biographers made another, similar, promise—to make the oracle-like subject speak to us. Enlightened illiteracy valorized the voice of the mystic over the writing of the professional ecclesiastic; hence biographical subjects are repeatedly portrayed as *voices*—voices so authoritative that the directed takes on the role of director. "Persuadés que Dieu parlait par sa bouche" (persuaded that God spoke through her mouth), people came to consult Marie Bon de l'Incarnation as if she were an oracle.[40] Once again, as in the case of visual exposure, the biographer repeats this verbal disclosure, claiming to make audible the subject's voice, as is clear in Alexandre Piny's segue to a quotation by Marie-Madeleine de la Très-Sainte Trinité: "[O]n ne saurait mieux juger de ses sentiments intérieurs qu'en l'écoutant et l'entendant parler elle-même, selon la maxime de cet Ancien, *Loquere ut te Videam*, parle afin que je te voie" ([T]here is no better way to judge her inner feelings than by listening to her and hearing her speak herself, in accordance with the maxim of that Ancient, *Loquere ut te Videam*, speak so that I may see you).[41] Piny's sententious invocation of Socrates in order to justify the disclosure of his subject tellingly combines the verbal ("parle") and the visual ("afin que je te voie"): these oracles had become a double object of attention, as biographers both mimicked their voices and promised to reveal their most hidden interiors.

Examples of this type of rhetoric—in which women figure both the object of the penetrating directorial/readerly gaze and the object of unveiling biographical writing—could be multiplied many times over. Indeed, this objecthood would seem part and parcel of the topos of the enlightened illiterate that governed infatuation with women's spirituality. As the work of Certeau suggests, there is something distinctly ethnographic about the zeal with which male ecclesiastics canvassed the French provinces in search of an authentic spirituality, of examples of divine presence missing from the books and bureaucracy of the Church. Surin's young man, for instance, is clearly a precursor of Rousseau and Diderot's noble savages; the ecclesiastic's interest in the lay mystic prefigures as well the evocations of rural France as an object of nostalgia in the domestic ethnography of Rousseau, Rétif de la Bretonne, and Greuze. But in the name of asserting the mystic position, this oral presence needed to be "captured" by writing, and to be made assimilable, via print, to a wider audience. Thus Surin, (in his letter) and countless other men (in *Lives*) constructed an oral Other and ascribed to this Other admired but scarce values—authenticity, experience, interiority, and so on. As with most ethnography, these constructions, while clearly functioning as critiques of dominant institutions, tend fatally to reproduce the very cleavage they would denounce. Fantasies and projections of interiority and experience are ultimately referred back to their origin, to the writing subject who, unlike the spiritual savages, can bear written testimony to that experience; oral experience, in other words, is reappropriated by the religious man of letters for his own needs. As Certeau has put it, "[A]ll that remains for the lay person is to be the savage through whom the cultivated man increases his own value."[42]

It is easy to see on what side of the written/oral divide men and women came down: it was the authenticity of unlettered and illiterate women that the male biographer's pen would try to capture. Such a situation fits in with what a specialist of seventeenth-century rhetoric has recently called "the cult of the voice," but this cult should seem familiar enough to the general academic reader.[43] Indeed, because of feminist analyses dating back to the work of Simone de Beauvoir, and because of the Derridian critique of ethnographic phonologism, we have become so attuned to the role of woman-as-stimulus-for-men's-writing and so conscious of way the West has disingenuously valorized the oral Other, that the workings of religious biography might appear predictable, and in some respects this is so. Yet the insistence on experience evident in seventeenth-century religious thought made as well for intriguing ambiguities, for writing could never be only the affair of *observers* of experience; rather, it seems to be always already bound up with the experiencing subject. As even the few biographical snippets I have included above illustrate, a culture of interiority was in fact inseparable from autobiographical writing. When Claudine Moine writes to her director: "J'ai rendu mon âme visible à vos yeux" (I have made my soul visible to your eyes), this visibility is achieved precisely in the act of writing. Disclosure of the interior so that it may be read is made first by the writing subject, and only then replicated by the biographer. Behind the explosion of religious biography lay a fascination glossed over by Piny's "parle afin que je te voie"—a fascination with the writing subject. It was precisely this copious writing, born in the dynamic of spiritual direction, that fueled the explosion of "interior" *Lives*, introduced readers of the period to the virtues and functions of the autobiographical text, and, moreover, gendered that text, and the interiority it made possible, feminine.

Researching the Subject

The story of how the fetishized female interior, that repository of experiential wisdom, moved from the terrain of orality to that of writing, is only one of many told by the vast corpus of religious biography. In what follows, observations on the persistent gendering of experience and the writing it generated intertwine with other stories told by biographies — stories of the documentation of the individual, of typographical inventions, of the seductive difficulty of reading the autobiographical text.

The first story, then, involves documents. If biography came to speak the idiom of experience in ways that traditional hagiography did not, this is not to say that seventeenth-century *Lives* were any more faithful to the "facts" of individual existences than the stories of, say, Voragine's much read *Golden Legend*. But they did pretend to be: it is was in the efforts deployed to convince the reader of the biographical text's fidelity to the life whose story it told that biography broke away from earlier forms of hagiography. And these efforts crystallized around the purported factuality of the written document.

This concern for documentation was most evident in the work of the man often credited with first applying critical method to source material — Jean Bolland's *Acta sanctorum* project, of which the first two volumes were published in 1642. The *Acta sanctorum*, conceived of a half-century earlier by Bolland's mentor Heribertus Rosweyde, was intended as a sort of *summa hagiographica*, and reflected humanist interest in restoring the texts of tradition to their former grandeur: apocryphal additions would be striped away, original manuscripts would be published, reliability and provenance of sources would be discussed. Religious biographies, which first started to come on the market in significant numbers at around the same time the *Acta sanctorum* was being published, evinced a similar concern with source material, although there was a key difference. Bolland's enterprise was fundamentally textual and humanistic, in that he wanted to compare texts to each other in the hopes of finding the earliest and least contradictory versions; by contrast, seventeenth-century biographers multiplied sources because written documents — eyewitness reports, memoirs of the religious order, even miscellany such as death certificates — were seen as the material trace left by the subject in the trajectory from birth to death. Schematically speaking, if Bolland was a humanist in a library, his counterparts in the devotional press were more like anthropologists in the field, collecting as much data as possible from witnesses who had known the deceased. Such biographical research ushered in an intimate relation between the subject and certain texts — specifically, those texts which served as a metonymy for the living body that had just disappeared. To live, religious biographies seem to say, is to leave a trail of written evidence.[44]

The example of one of the most enduring works of devotional hagiography from the previous century suggests that this association between the written document and the biographical subject had not always been made as it would be in the seventeenth century. The *Life* of Catherine of Genoa (1447–1510), originally composed between 1510 and 1551 and appearing in French in three different translations over the course of the century (in 1610, 1661, and 1691), makes hardly any references to source material, apart from a passing mention of her unnamed spiritual director, who, according to an isolated remark in the text, "a mis par écrit une bonne partie des choses contenues en cette oeuvre" (put down in writing a large part of what is contained in this work).[45] Catherine of Genoa's *Life* for the most part just seems to tell itself. Yet as written biographical sources became quasi-fetishistic substitutes for the deceased, this silence around the work's origins would be broken. Two biographies of Marguerite d'Arbouze, a prominent reformer of the royal abbey of Val-de-Grâce, hint at and help to date the shift in attitudes. The first, by Jacques Ferraige, was published in 1628, and contains only one short mention (hidden in the last chapter of the first part) of the fact that he has been inserting in his narrative "quelques mémoires qu'on m'a envoyé[s]" (some memoirs sent to me).[46] In contrast, when Claude Fleury published a second *Life* of Marguerite d'Arbouze, in 1687, he used his preface to insist upon his documentation. He refers to Ferraige's *Life*, claims to have "faithfully" extracted the most important parts, adding to this material "plusieurs autres mémoires des personnes qui avaient vu cette sainte abbesse" (several other memoirs by persons who had seen this holy abbess). Of words attributed to Marguerite herself, he adds: "je ne lui fais rien dire qui ne soit rapporté par son confesseur, ou par les autres personnes qui avaient vécu avec elle" (I do not attribute to her anything that was not reported by her confessor, or by others who had lived with her).[47] Fleury's indications place his work squarely in the company of other devotional biographies of the second half of the century, whereas Ferraige's laconic "some memoirs sent to me" echoes the same pre-Bollandist disregard for the document present in Catherine of Genoa's sixteenth-century biography.

This new scrupulousness was possible precisely because the biographer's subject was not a long-dead saint whose acts had passed into the domain of myth, but contemporaries—people locally reputed as saintly who had recently passed away. Biographers were less concerned with a scientific, Bollandist approach to the past, than with the exact, chronicle-like preservation of the nearly-present. In order to best capture the existence of the deceased, for example, the biography should appear as contiguous with that existence as possible—a contiguity asserted via evocations of living witnesses and original documents: "[C]e que vous y verrez," Jean-Baptiste de Saint-Jure announces to the reader of his popular *Vie de Monsieur de Renty* (1651), "est quasi tout tiré des originaux et le reste des copies authentiques, ou il est rapporté par des témoins oculaires et irreprochables" (what you will see here is almost entirely drawn from original [documents], or has been reported by irreproachable eyewitnesses).[48] But the biographer could take other steps to reduce the distance between *Life* and life. Henri-Marie Boudun, for example, claims to have started his work on Jean Chrysostome de Saint-Lô the very day the latter died;[49] others still, whom I will cite shortly, indicated prominently that their biographical work preceded even the death of the subject. And the quicker the biography was issued, the more it seemed authentic— hence the frequent short intervals between death and the appearance of a *Life*. Jean Crasset takes pains to draw the reader's attention to the up-to-dateness of his *Vie de Madame Hélyot* by including an *achevé d'imprimé* that gives not a date, but rather "a[chevé] d'imp[rimé] un an après sa mort" (printed one year after her death).[50] Crasset links the authority of his narrative to its temporal proximity to its subject's existence.

Lives had the effect of transforming everyone whose life had been touched by the biographical subject into a historian; the rage for documentation enlisted especially the scriptural participation of religious women. Indeed, it was a topos of the biographical preface to insist on the collaborative nature involved in the production of a *Life*. In the dedication to one of his biographies, Jean-François Senault declares to the nuns who supplied him his material: "Je ne vous offre ici rien qui ne vous appartienne déjà, et le présent que je vous fais, est une faveur que j'ai reçue de vous. Je n'ai travaillé que sur les mémoires que vous m'avez fournis, et cette vie est plutôt votre ouvrage que le mien" (I offer you here nothing that does not already belong to you, and the present I am giving you is a favor that I have received from you. I have worked only with the memoirs you have provided for me, and this life is rather your work than mine).[51] Research was so in vogue that it was not only alluded to, but on occasion benefited from a veritable mise-en-scène. Antoine Boschet, after enumerating the multiple memoirs used in the composition of his *Parfait missionnaire ou la vie du R. P. Julien Maunoir*, tells of his efforts to locate a manuscript copy of Maunoir's journal so that he might compare it to the original, and narrates a trip in lower Brittany "pour m'instruire parfaitement de mon sujet" (to instruct myself perfectly in my subject).[52] Claude Martin not only enumerates the various sources of the *Life* of his mother, the Ursuline Marie de l'Incarnation, and carefully sidenotes each quote he uses; he goes so far as to narrate both his solicitation of one manuscript from his reluctant mother, and the detective work involved in locating an elusive second one, thought to be lost. Martin portrays the work of the biographer as a dogged pursuit of authentic documents.[53] As with so many seventeenth-century *nouvelles* and epistolary collections, which created the effect of authenticity by claiming to be accidentally discovered manuscripts, the biographical text is constantly turned toward a reality purported to exist outside of it.

As embodiments of this reality, sources lose their disposability as well as their invisibility. Although it may not seem unusual to the modern bibliophilic reader to conserve original manuscripts, at the time the existence of a manuscript could be seen as superfluous once a cleaned-up print version reproduced its most salient features. Claude Martin was undoubtedly acting according to contemporary norms when he destroyed, in spite of his reverence for his mother, the original manuscript of her autobiographical 1654 *Relation*. Along with the care with which biographers were indicating their sources, however, came an increasingly reverential attitude towards their very existence. In part, sources were conserved lest the veracity of the work be challenged. "Je conserve toutes ces pièces pour la justification de mon travail, et pour témoigner au public quelles précautions j'ai apportées avant de me mettre la main à l'oeuvre" (I am conserving all these papers for the justification of my work, and in order to provide public testimony to the precautions I took before starting); "Je me contente de conserver les mémoires qui m'en ont été envoyés, pour preuve que je n'avance rien de moi-même" (I am content to conserve the memoirs sent to me, as proof that I am putting forth nothing of my own); "J'ai les mémoires par-devers moi . . . de sorte que si quelqu'un voulait révoquer en doute quelques points de cette vie, j'ai par la grâce de Dieu de quoi me défendre et lui satisfaire" (I have the memoirs in my possession . . . such that if someone wished to call into doubt certain points in this life, I have, by the grace of God, the means to defend myself and to satisfy him).[54] These examples of biographical bravado may be in part a quasi-judicial move of self-protection, since at this time the mystical phenomena frequently contained in *Lives*, if quite popular in certain devotional and conventual circles, bordered on heterodoxy. The biographer, by pointing to sources — "Je n'avance rien de moi-même" — absolves him or herself of authorial responsibility. Yet judicial, defensive rhetoric may or may not reflect a real danger. In Spain, biographies did appear from time to time on the Church's Index of prohibited works.[55] In France, by contrast, in the absence of an Inquisition, *Lives* do not appear to have attracted the attention of censors; Catherine of Genoa's *Life* figured on the 1583 Spanish Index, but was frequently printed in France.[56] Behind these appeals to existing manuscript sources lies, I think, a broader concern of which the juridical rhetoric is a but variant; the stakes are elsewhere, in the strengthening bond claimed to exist between text and subject that had for a logical corollary the (at least rhetorical) conservation of original documents. Only these broader stakes can explain why, for instance, Raphaël de la Vierge Marie conserved the records of the lengthy interviews that enabled the completion of his 1680 *Vie et vertus de la soeur Jeanne Perraud*, a mystic from Marseille. Raphaël went so far as to write a preface for the documents, in which he stated that he did not want to burn them because in his opinion they captured more completely and "naïvely" (naïvement) than a biography ever would the essence of Perraud.[57]

The consequence of this interest in the biographical document was its wholesale incorporation into the published *Life*. Needless to say, these acts of transcription were rarely passed over in silence, for such obfuscation would undermine the whole point of documentation in the first place—that it be visible. The incorporation of documentary evidence was too common a phenomenon to catalog here; one example, somewhat of a limit-case, will suffice: that of the 1666 *Life* of Alix Le Clerc, founder, with Pierre Fourier, of the Congrégation de Notre Dame. For this "biography" is but a congeries of raw, unsynthesized documents. After having assembled the elements of Le Clerc's biography, her successor as superior, Angélique Milly, searched for someone to take on the task of the actual crafting of a "proper" biography that would advance the cause of Le Clerc's canonization. No one could be found, however, and Milly finally decided to publish the documents in their original state. In their dedicatory epistle, the sisters of Le Clerc's congregation make a virtue of necessity, stressing the beauty resulting from the *stylus rudus* of documentary authenticity: "[L]e sujet de ce traité a paru si riche, et si beau à tous ceux à qui nous nous [sommes] adressé[es] pour cela, qu'ils ont tous jugé que les ornements étrangers le défigureraient, plutôt que de l'embellir" (the subject of this work appeared so rich and beautiful to all those we asked about it, that they have judged that foreign ornaments would disfigure rather than embellish it). Ultimately, the biographer is seen here *not* as a guarantor of meaning and trustworthiness; his presence is superfluous, and potentially even unwelcome, in that it risks "disfiguring" the authenticity of the documents used.[58]

In the case of Le Clerc's *Life*, one of these memoirs was autobiographical and advertised as so—the title page touts it as "la relation d'icelle, écrite et signée de la même mère" (the narrative of [Le Clerc], written and signed by the mother herself). It came first in the compendium, of which it was the cornerstone. In contrast to Benoît de Canfeld's *Véritable et miraculeuse conversion*, which was reprinted numerous times yet never appreciated as somehow special, here the autobiographical text stands out. Among the many documents that can bring the reader into relation with the deceased, autobiography was privileged by biographers as a window onto the interior of the subject. First-person autobiographical testimony did no so much provide historical information as act as a relic or even fetish; going further than the many other documents that attested to the individual's passage on earth, autobiography was seen as replacing what was not (or no longer) there—the interior of the dead individual. If third-person testimony recorded acts, only autobiography could conserve experience, and permit its transmission to readers.

The Oracle Writes

The perceived primacy of the autobiographical document can be easily inferred from the place of Alix Le Clerc's own narrative in the biographical compendium which encircled her memory with texts. We do not need to rely on mere inference, however: seventeenth-century biographers could not on the whole have been more explicit about the importance of the first person to their enterprise.

The incorporation of first-person testimony into hagiography was not in itself a new phenomenon. Generally, the practice of "reproducing" occasional attributed speech (spiritually pithy comments made to fellow religious, last words, etc.) was widespread; Georg Misch, in his landmark work on autobiography, noted for instance that the *Lives* of Church Fathers often pretended to reproduce the latter's own testimony.[59] As scholars of the genre know, Misch was notoriously unselective in terms of what he judged to be autobiography—most often, any and all first-person writings he could lay his hands on would do. For at least two characteristics immediately distinguish the use of the first person in pre-modern hagiography from the practice of quotation as it would develop in seventeenth-century religious biography. First, the origins of words attributed to the saint in question were left unelucidated; there were no attempts to present such speech as verifiable. Second, these passages were not claimed to have been written; they were oral declarations.[60] Taken together, these characteristics suggest that traditional hagiography may well have made use of the first person, but that it did not attempt to associate the saint with a web of documentary evidence that bore the traces of his or her existence.

Furthermore, if we can assume that hagiographers imparted some sort of rhetorical efficacy to the use of the first person (i.e., the heightening of drama, or lyric intensity), it is surprising, at least in the light of subsequent sensitivity to things autobiographical, how little they emphasized first-person speech as a site of readerly interest and as the mark of their text's authenticity. Speech in such biographies "went without saying" in a very literal sense, in that it was incorporated without any asides to let the reader know that the hagiographer was demurring to the subject's own voice, and that the value of the work was in fact predicated on this quotation. Both the *Lives* of Catherine of Sienna (composed between 1384 and 1395, and first printed in Latin in 1553) and of Catherine of Genoa (composed between 1510 and 1551, first published 1551) are instructive here, as they do not separate, either typographically or by way of a discursive framing device, the biographer's voice from that of the subject.[61] An occasional "dit-elle" (she said) at the start of an autobiographi-cal passage, and the passage's content itself, are the only clues a reader has to mark the shift in enunciation. In these Renaissance works, the hagiographic tradition of the mystic, oral "I" had not yet been displaced by the figure who would dominate subsequent religious biographies — the writing subject.

By the seventeenth century, the indifference with which first-person speech had been incorporated was evaporating, as biographers began to look for ways to call attention to the increasingly fetishized words of their subjects and to set them apart, if necessary, from other sources. From a typographi-cal point of view, however, printerly techniques of quotation were in their infancy; not until the eighteenth century would printers start to codify typo-graphical markers in order to keep pace with the influx of quoted material and the growing acknowledgment of authorial proprietorship.[62] Seventeenth-century biographers were thus anything but consistent in their practices, which varied over time, between authors, among works by the same author, within the same work, and even on the same page. But the very inconsistency, even ingenuity, of these editorial strategies allow us to measure the import of the change involved: when the subject spoke and/or wrote, the fact had to be marked accordingly.

Early biographies tend to betray a certain sloppiness in quotation, as if the "dit-elle" of Catherine of Genoa's biographer were recognized as insuffi-cient, but the future were not yet clear. In an early *Life*, from 1621, Marie de l'Incarnation's speech is at first signaled by quotation marks. In the course of the work, however, the quotes proceed to drop off entirely; then, still later and just as unexpectedly, italics take over the role of distinguishing the sub-ject's speech.[63] Another relatively early work (1644) on Jeanne de Chantal uses quotation marks with similar imprecision. Editorial practice at the time dic-tated the repetition of the inverted commas at the start of each line of type for the duration of the quotation, but in this *Life*, the symbol commonly ends before, or continues beyond, the first-person speech of Chantal.[64] The long obituary of the Visitandine Marie-Séraphique de Gaillard, printed for circulation between the houses of the congregation, shows its concern for sources by citing first between parentheses, then between brackets.[65] By the time of this circular (1682), such typographical sloppiness was somewhat of an exception, due here no doubt to the nonprofessional publication of the circulars themselves. For in general, as the century progressed, deliberate choices were being made — sometimes implicitly, sometimes explicitly — about the typographical form first-person material should assume in the printed text.

Some of these choices seem normative, in that they vary little between individual works. The use of quotation marks for the subject's speech and italics for both biblical citation and words pronounced by Christ during the mystical visions of the subject is for example standard. Yet because of the vogue for documentation of all sorts, quotation was used for more than reported speech and Scripture. Because all documentary sources were not created equal, biographers and editors dreamed up ways to distinguish the many different voices peopling their texts. The subject's speech commonly differed from that of third parties by the sheer redundancy of typographical markers. Although the words of Marguerite du Saint-Sacrement appear rarely in Tronson de Chenevière's biography of her, when her speech is reported, it receives both quotation marks and italics. Raphaël de la Vierge Marie not only uses italics when he quotes Jeanne Perraud, but complements them as well with repeated clarifying attributions. In a single one-page long quotation, for example, he intervenes with no less than five attributions designed to draw further attention still to the miracle of first-person speech — "dit-elle," "ajoute-t-elle" (she adds), "poursuit la soeur Perraud" (Sister Perraud continues), "continue-t-elle parlant à son confesseur" (she goes on, speaking to her confessor), and finally "poursuit toujours la soeur Jeanne Perraud" (Sister Jeanne Perraud continues still).[66] In addition to distinguishing the words of the subject from those of mere witnesses, biographers also tried to impress upon their readers the difference between quotidian and affectively charged mystic speech. Pierre Poiret, in his 1704 edition of Jeanne de la Nativité's *Life* of Armelle Nicolas, theorizes — if a bit too late, as he admits — his typography:

On a virgulé en marge tous les discours de cette Sainte Fille; et quand elle les adressait à Dieu par manière de prières, de louanges, ou d'exclamations, on les a mis en lettres Italiques virgulées, mais seulement dans le second Livre, cet expédient nous étant venu trop tard en pensée pour le mettre à effet dans le premier. Les paroles que Dieu lui adressait sont mises ordinairement en simple Italique sans virgules.[67]

(We have placed quotation marks in the margins of all the speeches by this Holy Daughter; and when she addressed them to God in the form of prayer, praise or exclamation, we have printed them in Italic letters with quotation marks, but only in the second Book, for this expedient occurred to us too late to put it into effect in the first Book. The words which God addressed to her are ordinarily in simple Italics without quotation marks.)

Hence a distinction is made not only between Nicolas's speech and God's, but also between normal speech (which would bear quotation marks) and particularly emotional speech of prayer, praise, and exclamation (which would be put in italics as well).

Poiret's remark confirms the importance that quotation was assuming in religious biography: at issue here were not the haphazard or idiosyncratic decisions of a few typesetters.[68] On the contrary, when one reads typography closely, it becomes clear that a series of decisions were being made, and that they had a certain logic of their own — the logic of a speaking and writing subject who is also the subject of other discourse, such as testimony. Whereas traditional hagiography made its saints speak at critical moments, the seventeenth-century mystic was above all a locus of various forms of discourse — not only attributed speech, as in previous *Lives* of the saints, but the written testimony of others and especially autobiographical texts which could be counted on to provide a faithful picture of subjective experience. Quotation marks, italics, and the like furnished the means of signaling the presence of these authentifying texts within the biographical text; the latter acted like a frame for the former. The large corpus of religious biographies furnish a fascinating array of typographical distinctions that, in their variety, betray the lengths people were going to in order to understand and to codify different types of authority. I have already alluded to efforts to isolate the speaking subject's testimony from that of third parties; one could invoke other distinctions, such as between oral and written discourse, or between public and private writings.[69]

Ultimately, however, the general drift of interest in quotation was toward the increasingly garrulous autobiographical voice, which was, as biographers pointed out, really a text. As the practice of mystic writing spread — more on this presently — amounts of transcription grew far beyond occasional attributed speech; the inverted commas surrounding the incorporated writings of the subject could run on for several, dozens, or even hundreds of pages.[70] In limit cases, quotation marks and italics were insufficient means to cope with the new place of the autobiographical within biography. A case in point is the example of Claude Martin's *Life* of his mother, the Ursuline Marie de

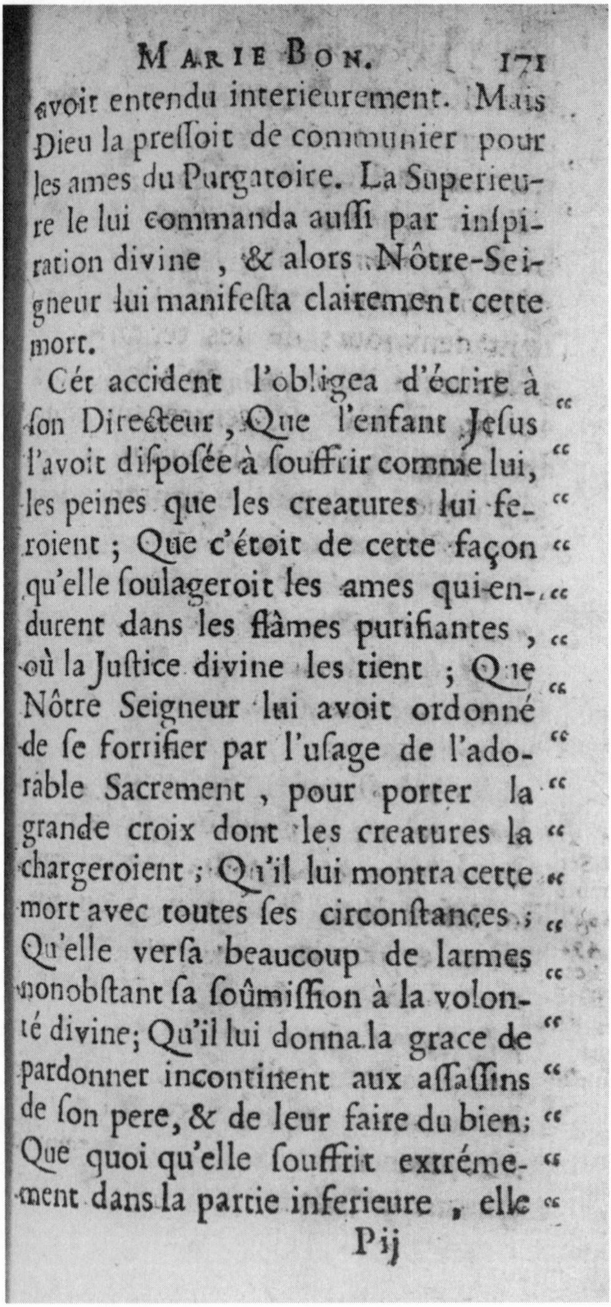

avoit entendu interieurement. Mais
Dieu la preſſoit de communier pour
les ames du Purgatoire. La Superieure le lui commanda auſſi par inſpi-
ration divine , & alors Nôtre-Seigneur lui manifeſta clairement cette
mort.

Cét accident l'obligea d'écrire à
ſon Directeur , Que l'enfant Jeſus "
l'avoit diſpoſée à ſouffrir comme lui, "
les peines que les creatures lui fe- "
roient ; Que c'étoit de cette façon "
qu'elle ſoulageroit les ames qui-en- "
durent dans les flâmes purifiantes , "
où la Juſtice divine les tient ; Que "
Nôtre Seigneur lui avoit ordonné "
de ſe fortifier par l'uſage de l'ado- "
rable Sacrement , pour porter la "
grande croix dont les creatures la "
chargeroient ; Qu'il lui montra cette "
mort avec toutes ſes circonſtances ; "
Qu'elle verſa beaucoup de larmes "
nonobſtant ſa ſoûmiſſion à la volon- "
té divine; Qu'il lui donna la grace de "
pardonner incontinent aux aſſaſſins "
de ſon pere, & de leur faire du bien; "
Que quoi qu'elle ſouffrit extréme- "
ment dans la partie inferieure , elle "

Pij

Figure 2. Varying quotational strategies in *La Vie de la Mère
Marie Bon de l'Incarnation* by Jean Maillard (1686). (Courtesy of
the Bibliothèque nationale)

„ sentoit dans la partie superieure
„ quelque plaisir de soulager cette ame
„ par ses souffrances. Et continuant,
„ *Ce qui augmente ma douleur* , dit-elle,
c'est que mon pere est mort sans Con-
fession & sans secours. Je ne me plains
pas neanmoins de ce que Dieu semble,
selon les sentimens du monde, en avoir
eu peu de soin, sçachant que le plus
grand soin qu'il prend de ceux qui
sont à lui , c'est de les faire passer
par les peines , afin qu'ils imitent Je-
sus-Christ. Au reste , ajoûte-t-elle ,
ma plus sensible douleur vient de l'in-
terest de Dieu qui a été offensé , & de
la crainte que j'ai qu'il ne le soit en-
core davantage. J'apprehende que le
point d'honneur qui est une folie de-
vant Dieu , ne porte mes freres à la
vengeance , quoi que je ne doute pas
de leur vertu. C'est pourquoi je prie
Dieu & je le faits prier pour le meur-
trier, afin que la Justice ne le fasse
pas mourir.

C'est ce que la Mere Bon fit avec
beaucoup de ferveur , & ce qu'elle
obtint de Nôtre-Seigneur. Car quoi
qu'on poursuivit le criminel avec

l'Incarnation, a mystic missionary know sometimes as "la sainte Thérèse de la France." The complexity of Martin's solution to the problem of quotation was in part dictated by his scrupulousness: he wanted not only to indicate when Marie de l'Incarnation was speaking, but from which of her many autobiographical writings he was citing. His biography is constructed around Marie de l'Incarnation's major autobiographical piece, her 1654 *Relation*, which he reproduces rather faithfully. Martin follows each chapter of the *Relation* with a commentary, labeled "Addition," in which he provides either a theological/mystical gloss of the preceding chapter, or additional biographical information culled from the Ursuline's other writings. In these commentaries, Martin's own pervasive first-person voice must be distinguished from the "je" of his mother. He does not, however, resort to quotation marks. (Given the amount of direct citation and the practice of inverted commas in the margins, they would have had been ubiquitous.) On occasion he switches over to Marie de l'Incarnation's voice first, and then only at the end of the passage indicates the source; sometimes, too, he will use a simple "dit-elle" without further explanation. Most of the time, however, he either precedes quotes with a precise indication (e.g., "Voici comme elle parle dans sa première relation" [This is how she speaks in her first narrative]), or calls attention to the change in voice via a side note ("Lettre à son fils du 1 septembre 1643" [Letter to her son of September 1, 1643]). On occasion he will both signal the transition in the text ("Elle fait une assez belle description de sa conduite en cette sorte" [She gives a quite beautiful description of her behavior in this manner]) and include a side note ("En sa première Relation" [In her first Narrative]).[71] Depending on the amount and the fragmentariness of the writings included in the "additions," the text often reads like a first-person patchwork, with these multiple indications of change in enunciation keeping apart two "je"s which, through repeated alternation, constantly threaten to collapse into one another.

Martin's volume is unique, in that no other biography I know of performs such an enunciative balancing act. But at the same time, it is perfectly representative of a moment in which the role of the biographer was not at all clear: if what was between quotation marks had such value, what would become of what was outside the marks? Briefly, the answer to the question implied in the patchwork structure of Martin's volume was that the existence of the biographical subject generated texts that the biographer would not simply "incorporate" in the digestive sense—that is, make them his own via paraphrase and occasional reference. By the autobiographical logic of the period, the best biographer would be, paradoxically, the one who interrupted as little as possible the subject's own words. The reader of these *Lives* is left with

ble ; cette perfonne étoit à deux lieuës de nous où il ne pouvoit na-
turellement fçavoir ce qui ne lui pouvoit être dit que le lendemain.
L'autre qui étoit affez proche de nôtre Monaftere, vid en efprit
comme un cercle de lumiere qui entouroit nôtre maifon & dans
cette lumiere il entendit des voix plaintives qui difoient à quelqu'un : Helas, helas n'y a-t-il pas moyen que cet accident n'arrive
point ? Hé, n'y a-t-il point de remede ? L'on répondit à cette plain-
te, non, il n'y en a point, cela fera, l'Arreft en eft donné. Il y a
de l'apparence que c'étoit l'Ange executeur de la divine Juftice qui
faifoit cette réponfe : Alors cette perfonne vid paroître une main
qui faifoit le figne fur nôtre Monaftere ; & peu aprés & quafi au
même-temps, l'on vid paroître le feu ; & entendant la cloche du
tocquefin, & les cris qui appelloient au fecours, il vid la verité de
ce qu'il venoit de penfer. Quand j'eus appris ce qui étoit arrivé à
cette fainte Ame, ce fut un nouvel aiguillon à mon cœur pour fo-
menter fon amoureufe activité & fon état de victime, prenant plaifir à me voir toute confommée & aneantie fous le bon plaifir de la
divine Juftice.

ADDITION.

COnformement à ce qu'elle vient d'écrire elle dit dans un autre lieu : Je n'ay pas voulu vous dire ouvertement dans mon
autre lettre, ce qui fe paffa dans mon interieur dans les momens de
nôtre incendie. Je l'ay refervé à celle-cy. Je vous diray donc qu'a-
prés qu'humainement j'eus fait tout ce qui fe pouvoit faire pour
empêcher la perte totale de nôtre Monaftere, foit pour appeller du
fecours, foit pour travailler avec les autres, voyant que le mal
étoit fans remede, je fis un facrifice de tout à la divine providence.
Dans toutes les courfes que je fis, j'avois une auffi grande liberté
d'efprit, & une veuë auffi tranquille à tout ce que je faifois que s'il
ne nous fût rien arrivé. Il me fembloit que j'avois dans moy-même
une voix interieure qui me difoit ce que je devois faire, où je devois aller, ce que je devois jetter par la fenêtre, & ce que je devois
laiffer perir par le feu. Je voulus jetter mon Crucifix qui étoit fur
ma table afin de le fauver, mais je me fentis arreftée, comme fi
l'on m'eut dit que cela étoit contre le refpect, & qu'il importoit
peu qu'il fût brûlé. Je vis en un moment le neant de toutes les cho-
fes de la terre, & il me fut donné une grace de denuement fi grande
que je ne puis exprimer fon effet ny de paroles ny par écrit.

Dans une let-
tre à fon
fils du -
mois de
Septem-
bre
1651.

B b b b

Figure 3. Autobiographical patchworks. Claude Martin's *La Vie de la Mère Marie de l'Incarnation* (1677). (Courtesy of the University of Pennsylvania Libraries)

the impression that the figures of institutional authority are being "squeezed out": hence, in the first translation of Teresa's *Life* published as an autonomous work—that is, not included in an edition of her *Works*—over half of the translator's preface consists of first-person citations from Teresa's autobiographical writings.[72] Many of Martin's "additions"—in principle the space of his gloss on his mother's writings—are in point of fact just such an enunciative battleground, and the reader can easily get lost in the fray.[73]

This "biographer," then, has been transformed into an editor, cutting and pasting bits of a first-person to whom he is subservient ("Elle continue son discours mais je l'interromps ici parce qu'elle le doit reprendre plus bas" [She continues her narrative, but I interrupt it at this point because she must take it up again below]), and behind which he can disappear altogether (some of "Martin's" "additions" begin directly with quotes from Marie and include only source notes).[74] *La Vie de la Mère Marie de l'Incarnation*'s structure might well be read as a symptom of the birth of the autobiographical mentality out of a biographical one: it is as if the biographer must have *some* function, must step in now and then, and yet, logically, he must efface himself, and let the subject speak (that is, write) for herself—or at least appear to do so.

Perhaps the clearest visual sign of this effacement is achieved in the *Vie et conduite spirituelle de la demoiselle Madeleine Vigneron* (1679), a biography and collected works put together by Vigneron's confessor, Mathieu Bourdin. In the biographical portion of the text, Bourdin simply puts his own interventions in smaller, indented type.[75] The impetus behind quotation—that the authority behind words depended on who wrote them—could only, therefore, if pushed to its logical limits, but drive biographers into an increasing liminal position *inside* their own works. The choice to put his words into smaller type could hardly illustrate more unequivocally his secondary enunciative status with respect to Vigneron. Furthermore, the *Life* is almost entirely of Vigneron's own composition, and Bourdin's small words become progressively rarer as the reader turns the pages. Interventions decrease from an average of 3.4 per chapter in the first quarter of the *Life*, to about one in the second quarter, to only 0.3 in the remainder. Once the "biographer" sets up the autobiographical text, his continued presence is superfluous.

Although Bourdin's strategy was exceptionally striking, the basic shift in authority underlying it can be read in the trends dictating the composition of the day's most popular biographies—though in fact only a neologism such as "(auto)biography" could really begin to describe the works. It is the biographer's apparent disappearance that is to assure the authority of the work—that is, the biographer paradoxically calls attention to his presence in order to assert his absence; his nullity is the mark of his excellence. In his preface to the biography of Marie de la Trinité, Aignan du Sendat dismisses in advance the criticism that he "[s]'érigeai[t] en faiseur de livres" (was posing as a fabricator of books), but for once this aristocratic commonplace can be read quite literally: because of the abundance of Marie de la Trinité's autobiographical works, the biographer's task is one of organization only and his "je" is entirely absent from the body of the text.[76] The preface to another biography begins:

Cet ouvrage est d'un caractère tout particulier: les personnes qui l'ont écrit ont bien moins de part que celle qui en est le sujet, ou plutôt que l'esprit de Dieu qui lui a inspiré ce qu'elle a écrit elle-même. Car sa vie n'est guère composée que de ses écrits, et on n'a fait que les arranger pour rendre l'ouvrage complet.[77]

(This work is of an altogether particular character: the persons who wrote it have much less a part in it than the woman who is its subject, or rather, than the spirit of God who inspired her with what she herself wrote. For her *Life* is composed of little more than her writings, and we have only arranged them so as to make the work complete).

Yet another reads:

[C]e n'est pas mon Ouvrage, et . . . je ne vous l'offre qu'en qualité de Secrétaire. . . . Si vous désirez savoir qui a donc fait cet écrit? Je vous dirai qu'après Notre Seigneur, ç'a été son humble servante et sa fidèle épouse la Mère Françoise des Seraphins. . . . [Comme] elle avait reçu de Dieu le don de s'exprimer d'une manière naïve, sainte et énergique, je n'ai pas ajouté un seul mot à ses redditions de compte ni aux extraits des ses lettres.[78]

(This is not my Work, and . . . I offer it to you only in the capacity of a Secretary. . . . And if you were to want to know who made this piece of writing? I would reply that after Our Lord, it was his humble and servant and faithful bride, Mother Françoise des Seraphins. . . . [Since] she had received from God the gift of expressing herself in a naive, holy and energetic manner, I have not added a single word to the her account, nor to the selections from her letters).

The need for the biographer to write a *Life* is obviated by the new cultural obsession with self-expression, what the biographer calls here, in a revealing turn of phrase, "le don de s'exprimer."

As cases such as these make clear, the written words of the biographical subject, who was by now quickly becoming an autobiographical subject, could win out over the sanctioning voice of the biographer. A ghost of its former self, that voice remains only to note sources, and to tell of how faithfully the printed volume corresponds to the original texts. If this change took place, it was because of the authority of something we now call "personal experience," and a decline in prestige of *acts*, which had previously been seen

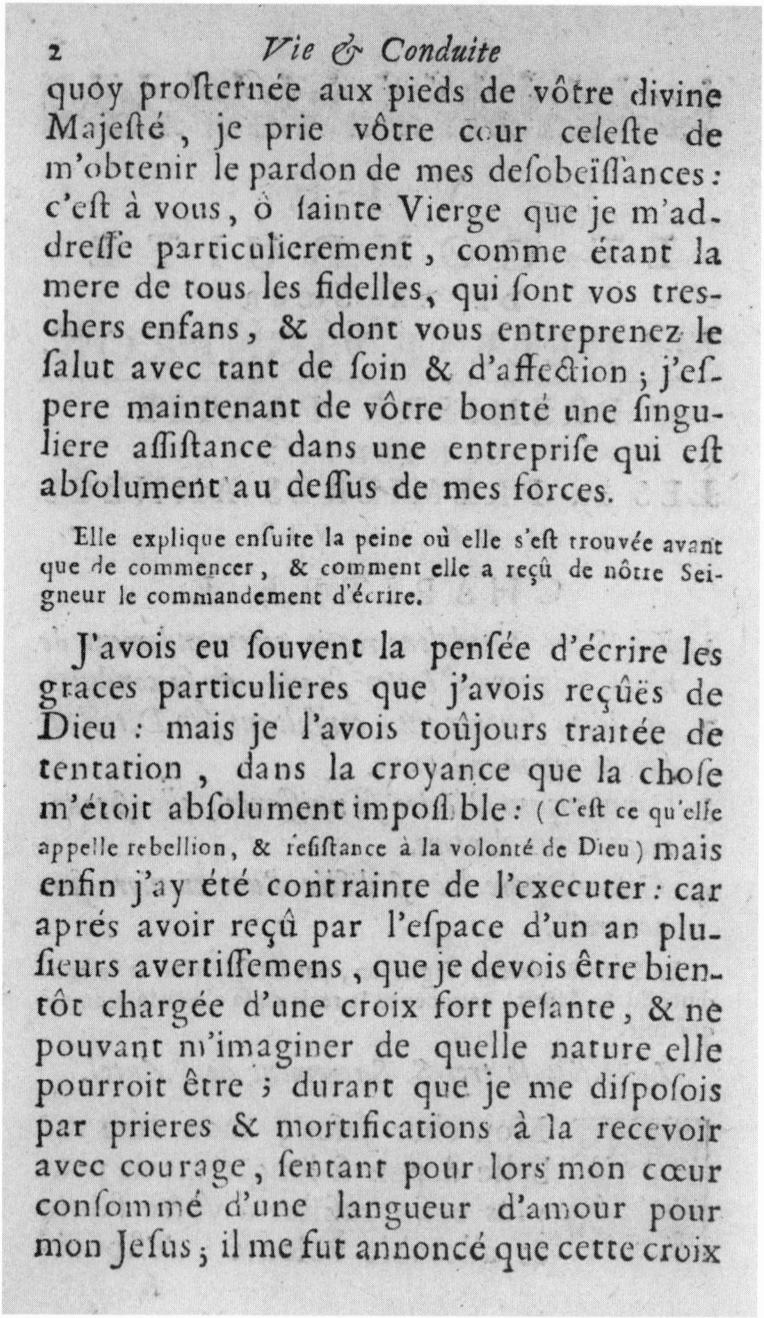

quoy proſternée aux pieds de vôtre divine
Majeſté , je prie vôtre cœur celeſte de
m'obtenir le pardon de mes deſobeïſſances :
c'eſt à vous, ô ſainte Vierge que je m'ad-
dreſſe particulierement , comme étant la
mere de tous les fidelles, qui ſont vos tres-
chers enfans, & dont vous entreprenez le
ſalut avec tant de ſoin & d'affection ; j'eſ-
pere maintenant de vôtre bonté une ſingu-
liere aſſiſtance dans une entrepriſe qui eſt
abſolument au deſſus de mes forces.

Elle explique enſuite la peine où elle s'eſt trouvée avant
que de commencer , & comment elle a reçû de nôtre Seigneur le commandement d'écrire.

J'avois eu ſouvent la penſée d'écrire les
graces particulieres que j'avois reçûës de
Dieu : mais je l'avois toûjours traitée de
tentation , dans la croyance que la choſe
m'étoit abſolument impoſſible : (C'eſt ce qu'elle
appelle rebellion, & réſiſtance à la volonté de Dieu) mais
enfin j'ay été contrainte de l'executer : car
aprés avoir reçû par l'eſpace d'un an plu-
ſieurs avertiſſemens , que je devois être bientôt chargée d'une croix fort peſante, & ne
pouvant m'imaginer de quelle nature elle
pourroit être ; durant que je me diſpoſois
par prieres & mortifications à la recevoir
avec courage, ſentant pour lors mon cœur
conſommé d'une langueur d'amour pour
mon Jeſus ; il me fut annoncé que cette croix

Figure 4. The shrinking importance of the biographer's voice: Mathieu Bourdin's *Vie et conduite spirituelle de Madeleine Vigneron*, 1679 edition. (Courtesy of
the Bibliothèque nationale)

as the visible markers of virtue. The former was deemed interior, the latter exterior; and whereas acts could be related by witnesses, experience was accessible only via the writing of the subject. As I shall now show, biographers made this dichotomy quite explicit as they explained how autobiography permitted direct access into another's subjective workings and established a virtually metonymical relationship between the subject and the autobiographical text.

Making Words Speak Louder than Actions

Medieval hagiography had been radically centered on exterior criteria of saintliness: divine virtue let itself be read on the body of the saint. The paradigmatic conversion of Saint Francis of Assisi, for instance, was representable precisely because it was accompanied by circumstances—his removal of all his clothes on a public square in front of his family and townspeople—that lent themselves to a narrative mise-en-scène; his vow of poverty was made manifest by his nakedness. Hence, also, the "superstitious" consideration given phenomena like stigmata or miracles, and the authority of spectacular ascetic practices. Even the large proportion of martyrs among the canonized reflects a predilection for an ideal of saintliness based on that which was exteriorly verifiable: every wound on Saint Sebastian's body spoke of his nearness to God; death guaranteed faith. On the other hand, a religious culture that valued interiority had less use for such spectacular acts. Claudine Moine, a lay mystic who authored four autobiographical narratives, commented on the inadequacy of a hagiography based on actions:

J'ai parfois pensé en moi-même que l'on écrit les vies des saints, et l'on n'écrit pourtant rien moins que ce qui les fait Saints. Car l'on dit leurs veilles, jeûnes, prières, pénitences, austérités, exercices de dévotion extérieurs, et choses semblables: et ce n'est pas là ce qui les fait Saints . . . puisque [ces choses] peuvent être pratiquées par des personnes très méchantes, et quelque fois avec plus d'apparence de dévotion que par des personnes véritablement vertueuses.[79]
(I have often thought to myself that people write the lives of the saints, and that what is written is in fact not at all what made them Saints. For they tell of vigils, fasts, prayers, penances, austerities, external devotional exercises, and things of such like: but this is not what made these people Saints . . . for [these things] can be practiced by persons who are very wicked, and sometimes with a greater appearance of devotion than when practiced by truly virtuous persons.)

For Moine, "what makes a saint" is God's communication with the soul, not "external exercises." As Certeau has noted, "the figure of the saint, male or female, remains, but its content changes: always extraordinary, certainly, but because of his 'states' rather than his virtues, because of what he knows rather than what he performs, because of his 'unknown language' rather than his miracles."[80] A modernized hagiography would have to come to terms with these new values and become "interior."

In her biography of Armelle Nicolas, a servant-mystic who fit clearly into the mold of the enlightened illiterate, Jeanne de la Nativité points out how the entire structure of her work is predicated on the distinction between inside and outside: the first fourteen chapters, reads her preface, are but "un simple récit historique" (a simple historical narrative); the real interest of the work is what brings us from this, "l'extérieur ou le dehors de ce Temple sacré" (the exterior or the outside of this sacred Temple), to the inner sanctum ("sanctuaire") of the subject.

[C]e qu'il y a de particulier [dans l'ouvrage], c'est qu'on y reconnaît bien mieux l'intérieur de cette grande Âme et les secrètes opérations du saint Amour, qui d'ordinaire demeurent inconnues dans la plupart de ceux dont on a écrit la vie, que l'extérieur et ce qui paraît au dehors, qui n'est toujours que de petites étincelles des flammes qui les consomment au dedans.[81]
(What is particular [in this work] is that one recognizes much better the interior of this great Soul and the secret workings of holy Love, which ordinarily remain unknown in most of those whose lives have been written, than the exterior and the outer appearance, which are always only but the little sparks from the flames that consume them inwardly.)

It is the revelation of interiority that constitutes the valuable novelty of the biographer's work. Jeanne de la Nativité hints here that she thought her "interior" enterprise unique, but if so, she was mistaken: the notion that a narration of a subject's acts could convey no real knowledge of that subject was, in fact, gaining wide currency during the second half of the seventeenth century. Claude Martin, for instance, explicitly calls attention to the secondary status of miracles and other exterior actions in Marie de l'Incarnation's *Life*, for they no longer constitute the best proof of saintliness.

[E]xcepté les miracles, qui sont plutôt des effets de la puissance de Dieu que de la vertu de la créature, il sera difficile de trouver une vie plus diversifiée en aventures singulières. . . . Mais ce que l'on y trouvera de plus admirable, c'est *l'intérieur* de cette excellente Mère, et je ne doute point que ceux qui ont lu la vie de beaucoup de saints n'avouent qu'ils n'ont encore rien vu de plus *touchant* ni de plus instructif.[82]
(Except for miracles, which are the effects of the power of God rather than of the virtue of the creature, it will be difficult to find a life more varied in singular adventures. . . . But what will be found here that is even more admirable is the *interior* of this excellent

Mother, and I cannot doubt that those who have read the lives of many saints will admit that they have never seen anything more *touching* or more instructive.)

The affective hagiographic charge—the most "touching" *Life*—comes from the interior, not the exterior, in spite of Marie de l'Incarnation's life being without parallel in terms of dramatic potential (she lived in constant interaction with the Indians of New France).

Martin, as it turns out, nuances Moine and Jeanne de la Nativité's reading of past hagiography, in that in his opinion interior concerns were not completely absent from that tradition. For he rereads the hagiographic production of the past and remarks that much material seemed to derive from something other than exterior observation; indeed, the many interior moments of hagiography can only have been realized thanks to the participation of the saint him or herself:

Saint Paul même nous a appris ce qu'il y a de plus considérable dans sa vie, et c'est de lui que nous tenons . . . ses grâces, ses vertus, ses révélations, ses tentations, ses fatigues et beaucoup d'autres choses qui nous seraient inconnues, si lui-même n'en avait donné la connaissance. Et, généralement, dans la plupart des vies des saints, nous voyons des actions et des circonstances qui leur étaient si secrètes que Dieu seul en pouvait être le témoin. Nous y trouvons même des sentiments purement intérieurs qui ne pouvaient être connus que de cet Esprit-Saint. . . . Nous les connaissons néanmoins et la connaissance que nous en avons ne peut être venue que d'eux-mêmes.[83]

(Saint Paul himself informed us of what was most important in his life, and it is from him that we learned of . . . his graces, virtues, revelations, temptations, weariness and many other things that would be unknown to us if he himself had not made them known. And, generally, in most of saints' lives, we see actions and circumstances that were so secret to them that only God could be their witness. We even find in these lives purely interior sentiments that could only be known by this Holy Spirit. . . . And yet we know of them anyway, and the knowledge we have can only have come from the saints themselves.)

Ultimately, Martin asserts the very same values as do Moine and Jeanne de la Nativité—the interior as revealed through the subject's own testimony. This passage's special significance, however, hinges on Martin's obvious desire to read past hagiography autobiographically (instead of simply declaring the need for a new autobiographical hagiography). Much in the way that Martin Lowenthal tried to piece together those bits of Montaigne that seemed to form an autobiography, or that Georg Misch collected evidence of the first person in the most generically disparate works of the classical past, Martin sought out passages of temporally and culturally remote works in which (he maintained) an autobiographical consciousness was at work. Unlike Martin,

Misch wrote at a time when the term "autobiography" had been coined, but their stance with regard to the past is homologous: in order to legitimize the link between interiority and writing that marks the modern age, they create a genealogy of autobiography that stretches back across time.

The basic theoretical move made by Martin and others was a staple of the biographies that I have been citing: the autobiographical text gives us an unprecedented window on the interior soul. Its reason for being lay in the exteriorization of an interior that would otherwise (i.e., in traditional hagiography) remain hidden. "Qui pourrait exprimer les saintes dispositions de cette âme?" (Who might express the holy dispositions of this soul?), asks one text. The answer is simple. Since "[i]l faudrait pénétrer jusques dans le sanctuaire de son coeur, pour expliquer quelque chose de la pureté de son sacrifice" (one must penetrate into the inner sanctum of her soul, if one is to explain something of the purity of her sacrifice), then one must quote: "Elle n'en dit que deux mots, mais ils peuvent bien nous en donner une grande idée" (She says only a couple of words about it, but they can indeed give us a good idea of it).[84] Another *Life* reads: "Dieu, malgré les précautions qu'une ingénieuse humilité apporte pour les cacher, en a disposé autrement, et a permis que l'on ait recouvert quantité de Lettres qu'elle avait écrites . . . où l'on voit les richesses inestimables que la Grâce avait renfermées dans son coeur" (God, despite the precautions that an ingenious humility can summon in order to hide them, has arranged it otherwise, and has allowed us to recover a quantity of Letters she had written . . . in which we see the inestimable riches that Grace had shut away in her heart).[85] Still another claims that a letter "nous donne moyen de mieux pénétrer l'état intérieur de notre précieuse défunte" (gives us the means to penetrate better into the interior state of our precious deceased) and gives thanks such a letter exists, for the biographical effort to bring to light ("mettre au jour") the secrets of the subject would have been for naught "si sa plume même ne [les] relève par ses propres expression[s]" (if her pen itself had not noted them in her own words).[86]

On the one hand, writing provided the all-around best "way in": in the above remarks biographers give thanks for those isolated letters and recovered fragments they proceed to introduce. In another sense, however, the discovery of such writing was something less than fortuitous. It had been planned all along. In their enthusiasm over interior words, biographers helped create texts where none had been before. Some of this involvement may have been of a censoring, inquisitorial kind, and the writing female mystic par excellence, Teresa of Avila, was, in this as in so much else, exemplary: she was made to generate multiple autobiographical texts precisely so that ecclesiastical authorities might put her mysticism and its growing influence on trial.[87] Many religious biographies, however, hint at circumstances considerably more ambiguous than this, if only because of the following coincidence: the spiritual director and the biographer were very often one and the same person.[88] The biographer/director was engaged in asking for mystic and autobiographical texts with the full knowledge that he would subsequently be able to put them into print circulation. In other words, autobiographical practice did not necessarily *preexist* its editorial uses; biographies did not so much come to depend on (or to assimilate, or to recuperate) autobiographical documentation as autobiographical documentation was fabricated expressly for use in biographies.

The history of directors taking dictation and subsequently working it into a biography goes back at least to Raimondo of Capua, director and biographer of Catherine of Sienna (†1380); much the same relationship governed the production of many of the seventeenth-century biographies quoted above. Needless to say, this type of practice was perfectly congruent with the power distribution I have detailed in the enlightened illiterate topos. The obsession with writing, however, was such that mere stenography would not suffice to produce the effect of interiority desired by seventeenth-century readers; the subject had to be coaxed into writing herself, in view of publication, and it is here that the question of gender comes back to the fore. Introducing his biography of Jeanne Perraud, Raphaël de la Vierge Marie first portrays the spiritual director as transcriber of Perraud's marvelous speech: "C'est donc avec ce soin, et cette circonspection qu'il écrivit de temps en temps les plus belles choses et les grâces les plus rares qu'il remarquait en cette fille, ou qu'il apprenait de sa bouche dans le Tribunal de la Confession, et dans les entretiens particulières avec elle" (It is therefore with such care and circumspection that from time to time he wrote down the most beautiful things and the rarest graces that he remarked in this girl, or that he learned from her own mouth in the Tribunal of Confession, and in private conversations with her). The "entretien" of spiritual direction is the space in which the oral treasures of the woman mystic (coming from her "bouche") are transformed with care into writing by a man ("il écrivit"). Yet Raphaël sets up the male/writing-female/orality dichotomy only to collapse it. In the following sentence, the oral authority of an enlightened illiterate gives way to her writing and even authorship: "Outre cela, quand il lui commandait d'écrire elle-même les lumières et les grâces qu'elle avait reçues, à mesure qu'elles lui étaient arrivées, il ne faisait jamais semblant que ce fut à dessein de lui faire composer sa propre vie, mais seulement comme s'il les voulait examiner" (Beyond that, when he ordered that she herself write of the insights and graces she had received as they had happened to her, he never let on that this was with the intention of having her compose her own life, but instead only as if he wanted to examine them).[89] Here, one can see how what was normally seen as the role of the examiner has been emptied of its censoring content; it remains only as an alibi for what has become the most important function of spiritual direction—a space in which women may surreptitiously be made to become authors. The director *pretends* to be an inquisitor ("comme s'il les voulait examiner") only to better permit women to take up the pen and do what had been, and indeed still seemed, an impropriety—"composer sa propre vie."

Moreover, Raphaël has been doing some pretending of his own, for he is none other than this crafty director of whom he writes, here and elsewhere, in the third person. Nowhere in the biography does he admit to this; it is only in the many Perraud manuscripts he worked from that one can read the admission that he, in fact, is the source of "la vie qu'on a imprimée" (the life that has been published).[90] Why this secrecy? Why didn't biographers identify themselves as the directors of the women they were writing about, when the fact would seem to speak for the authenticity of the information they were providing? Clearly, these overlapping roles created a classic conflict of interest. Directors, even the most sympathetic, when confronted with an aspirant claiming mystical experience, were supposed to do the work of "discerning spirits"—experience was diabolical rather than divine, for instance, if the would-be mystic was trying to attract the attention of her fellow sisters. Yet far from policing an experience that existed independently of the director/aspirant relationship, they were doing everything they could to excite more experiences, to generate texts around them, and to assure their conservation and dissemination in print.

Writing and experience were indeed becoming indissociable, as if the former were an outgrowth of the latter. Of course, at the outset the subject needed to be ordered to take up the pen, or tricked into it, as we have seen in Jeanne Perraud's case. Little by little, however, this alibi would fall away, until having a rich inner life and writing implied one another, "naturally." Hence Mathieu Bourdin downplays the role spiritual guidance played in the composition of Madeleine Vigneron's writings; in fact, he says, she wrote so that her being might become transparent to "us"—to the readers of her *Life*: "[A]fin que nous en eussions plus de lumière, et que l'on ne pût rien désirer davantage pour son entière connaissance, . . . elle se sentit obligée de lui [to her director] écrire toutes les semaines des Lettres en forme de compte de conscience, par lesquelles elle fait une continuelle expression [de ses] différents états intérieurs" (In order that we might have more light and so that one could ask for no more in order to know her entirely, . . . she felt obliged to write each week to [her director] Letters in the form of an account of conscience, by means of which she gives a continuous expression [of her] different interior states).[91] The subject, then, under cover of spiritual direction, writes for the illumination of future readers; she maintains an autobiographical play-by-play that "continually" transforms her "interior states" into writing.

Being interior brought with it the duty of self-expression because, in a sense, interiority *was* writing, and writing *was* interiority. Once we realize that this was the association these texts were ultimately aiming at, we can appreciate the significance of Bourdin's rhetoric as he continues his introduction to Vigneron's autobiographical *Life*: "j'ai cru qu'il était . . . nécessaire de vous dire de quelle façon une *vie si intérieure* est venue à notre connaissance, et comment elle nous est manifestée *aussi clairement que si nous avions lu dans la conscience de cette bonne âme*" (I thought that it was . . . necessary to tell you in what way we came to learn of a *life so interior*, and how this life became manifest to us *as clearly as if we had read in the conscience of this fine soul*).[92] There is here an intriguing and perfectly logical slippage—which other biographies confirm—between the two meanings of the word "vie": Bourdin means the *Vie de Madeleine Vigneron*, a book, as much as he means the "vie de Madeleine Vigneron," for both are seen as texts. One reads the interior life of the subject as one reads her *Interior Life*.[93] This wordplay, then, is not my own, but results from the confusion produced once the subject and the autobiographical text are conceived of as metonymically linked. When Claudine Moine, at the end of her last autobiographical relation, writes to her director in a phrase I have already cited, "C'est maintenant, mon très cher et Révérend Père, que je puis bien dire que j'ai mis mon cœur entre vos mains, et rendu mon âme visible à vos yeux" (It is now, my dear and Reverend Father, that I can indeed say that I have placed my heart in your hands, and made my soul visible to your eyes), she is playing on such a metonymy.[94] The same can be said of the obituary notice on the Visitandine Marie-Judith Gilbert, which introduces one of Gilbert's letters as "cet échantillon de l'état de son âme" (this sample of the state of her soul).[95] And if Jeanne de la Nativité, in her *Life* of Armelle Nicolas, claims that ecclesiastical dignitaries previewing her book "ont reconnu la Copie très conforme à l'Original" (recognized the Copy as quite in conformity with the Original), she makes clear that she is not referring to accurately copied documents at all: "je veux dire que ce qui est rapporté ici est autant conforme qu'il le peut être à ce qui s'est passé dans l'Ame de cette vertueuse Fille" (I mean to say that what is reported here conforms as much as possible with what happened in the Soul of this virtuous Girl).[96] Conformity lies not between two texts (i.e., an original document and its transposition into a biography), but between a text and the soul of the subject.

Jacques Le Brun has written of how seventeenth-century Visitandine sisters sometimes not only mixed François de Sales's blood with wine and drank it (not at all an unknown practice), but went as well to the lengths of ingesting pieces of paper inscribed with pieties taken from the Bible or the writings of Saints.[97] The text had the potential to serve as a relic; its uses obeyed a sort of eucharistic logic by which this written host was not only the symbol of the divine, but the divine itself. Words signified, certainly, but not only as disembodied signs: they possessed a material presence that had its own power. Similarly, the autobiographical document seemed to derive its subjective power from its materiality, from its physical connection to the life of the mystic, rather than from the descriptions it contained. Thus, in addition to quoting autobiographical sources, biographers return again and again to descriptions of them in the body of their work. They detail the circumstances under which they were composed—for example, "Notez qu'elle écrivait cette lettre les années qu'elle était dans ses plus horribles souffrances" (Note that she wrote this letter in the years when she was undergoing the most horrible sufferings)[98]—but they also display a fascination with the bits of paper themselves. At a time in which, in other mystic circumstances, Pascal was sewing his *Mémorial* into the lining of his coat, biographers too were fixating on the intimacy of the subject-text relation even as they were making supposedly private words available for all to see.[99] The biographer of the Visitandine Jeanne-Bénigne Gojoz reveals her amazement at discovering seven or eight hundred slips of paper salted away in various hiding places of Gojoz's cell. One, in the manner of the *Mémorial*'s "Pleurs, pleurs, pleurs de joie!" (Tears, tears, tears of joy!), read only: "Pouvoir, pouvoir, pouvoir!" (Power, power, power!),[100] but in a sense the actual content of these writings was of secondary importance; their value derived rather from their place in the nun's life. Where there was experience, there was also writing: it was this metonymy that proved much more captivating than any sort of *mimetic* correspondence between the words and the experience they grew out of.

As we shall see, the metonymical status of autobiography was at bottom a mysterious affair, as indeed it was supposed to be: the authenticity of autobiographical writing was predicated not on the familiar mystic topos of "automatic" (inspired) writing, but rather on its difficulty, on its inability to render the subject fully transparent to the reader's gaze. No doubt the uncertainty with regards to the precise relation of a written representation and experience (especially when the former might read only "Pouvoir, pouvoir, pouvoir!") prompted biographers to focus instead on the materiality of the signifier. Materiality guaranteed the authenticity of writing while the meaning remained inaccessible. The circuit between a subject's experience and the printed words before the reader was composed of a number of relays: experience was corporeal; the hand that writes was part of the experiencing body; the act of writing occurred on a given piece of paper; and finally those words were reproduced in print. Experience and printed words were linked not by a mimetic relation, but via this metonymical path, a series of overlaid arrows that pointed at the subject. Hence biographers insist particularly on the physical state of the paper that holds the precious writing, and conjure up before the reader the presence of the author's hand. These moments are legion in seventeenth-century *Lives*: "On trouva dans sa Chambre un morceau de papier à demi déchiré, où ses paroles étaient écrites de sa main" (We found in her Room a half-torn piece of paper on which her words were written in her own hand); "[Le discours] qui suit a été trouvé écrite de sa main parmi de vieux papiers" ([The narrative] that follows was found written out in her hand among some old papers); and so on.[101]

Tags such as these function as elements of a proto-"autobiographical pact," to use Philippe Lejeune's famous term for the sine qua non condition of autobiography. For Lejeune, the difference between autobiography and fiction does not lie in the greater "truthfulness" of the former, but in the type of contract that governs their reception. The "autobiographical pact" is made between author and reader by virtue of some passage or paratextual clue that the author, narrator, and primary character are in fact one and the same person. Biographers' insistence on the materiality of the autobiographical source had a similar function: to make it understood that the subject was speaking of himself or (more commonly) herself, to bind the printed word and the experience it claimed to be transmitting. At its most extreme, as in Marie-Madeleine de Mauroy's *Life* of Elisabeth de l'enfant Jésus, this pact was reinforced via an appeal to a very special type of materiality—the authorial signature made in blood: "Mais écoutons-la parler elle-même sur le sujet des souffrances, dans un papier écrit de sa main, et signé de son sang" (But let us listen as she herself speaks on the subject of her sufferings, on a paper written in her hand, and signed with her blood). Blood, for Mauroy, creates the most original of originals, the most subjectively tainted text: "Ceci est signé de son sang dans l'original" (This is signed with her blood in the original).[102] The link between author and text becomes so tight that the autobiographical document is, quite nearly, a piece of flesh.[103] As the concrete vehicle of interior sensibility, auto-biographical writing was a relic; the reader was brought into the vicinity of the saint not through the possession of hair, bones or coagulated blood, but via the reading of a text.

"Un Abîme à Ecrire": The Burden of Writing

The iconography of Teresa of Avila sometimes shows the saint with paper and pen in hand, looking skyward, waiting for inspiration, for the divine dicta-tion to commence. This type of association of mystic women and writing was linked to the age-old concept of *eloquentia sacra*; this was an eloquence in which discourse (written, though more often, perhaps because of the West's logocentric bent, oral) assumed the role of a kind of "immediate mediation" between man and the divine Word. *Eloquentia sacra* thus permitted some-one like the prolific mystic Jeanne Guyon to make inroads in the customarily male domain of predication because of a self-proclaimed proximity to the Word of God that was reinforced and reflected in the topos of the enlight-ened illiterate. As Philippe-Joseph Salazar has noted, figures such as Guyon and Marie de l'Incarnation insisted on the ease with which they wrote; their pens were inspired canals for the transmission of a discourse which was not their own: "The Spirit, that is, the Word, dictates to human speech; it oper-ates in its 'mode' and the writer is only a scribe, an arm, a 'stylus' put into action according to the mode of the spirit."[104] Yet one of the most important changes to which seventeenth-century biographies alert us was the replace-ment of the idea of inspired, free-flowing writing with autobiography, whose authority was derived from the difficulty, rather than the ease, with which the subject wrote. In the case of "eloquent" writing, the mystic served as a conduit between men and God; one read her words not for the insight they would provide on her subjective workings, but because God spoke through her, directly and transparently. In their mise-en-scène of the autobiographical text, however, biographers and autobiographers changed the stakes: *experi-ence* was quite different from *inspiration*, and interiority was produced the moment the mystic's transparency gave way to a certain opacity, a play of light and shadow that constituted the very mark of both the subject and the truth of her discourse. Autobiography was as far removed from representations of Teresa's divine eloquence as it was from the Classical ideals of clarity of ex-pression epitomized by Boileau's famous precept, "Ce que l'on conçoit bien s'énonce clairement" (What is well conceived can be clearly stated)[105] — a line that biographers and autobiographers would have been inclined to rewrite as, "Ce que l'on croit profond ne s'écrit qu'avec peine" (What one believes to be deep can be written only with difficulty).

Simultaneously with the emergence of Classical doctrines of clarity occurred then a converse development: writing was also something intimately linked to the subject herself, arising in the depths of her being and giving access to a unique experience. Such anti-Classicism necessitated the passage from inspiration to experiential opacity; the privileged status of the autobiographical text, according to which it functioned as a way into the mystic herself as much as or more than a path to God, depended on the rejection of the concept of the "human vessel." Certainly, at the root of all mystic writing was an attempt to communicate something beyond the mystic herself—the ineffable reality of God. In theory, readers of biographies were interested in the latter, and not in an idolatrous relationship with a person deemed saintly. And yet the impression conveyed both by biographers and by the mystics whose writings they relied on is only partially of a confidence in the transmission of the transcendent Beyond. Rather, these writers were interested in that which hinted at the Beyond yet always seemed to fall short of the mark or block it from our view. The interest of the mystic's writing derived precisely from the obstructions it placed in the way of the reader's apprehension of God. Instead of writing copiously so that all might better admire the glory of God, the autobiographical subject stubbornly hid herself from view, rejected publicity, resisted above all writing and then, when forced nonetheless to record her experience, tried to burn her papers lest they become known. This is the scenario *Lives* present the reader again and again; its reappearance is no accident, for much like the endlessly reiterated typographical distinctions that accompanied the mystic's writing, its goal was to convey that this new type of text encapsulated a precious truth.

In one respect, the resistance to publicity so ostentatiously displayed in biographies was an easy way around charges of affronts both to good Christian humility and, perhaps more importantly still, to the general invisibility demanded of women religious. One reads in Maillard's *Vie de Marie Bon de l'Incarnation*, for instance: "Mais dans des faveurs si particulières, elle avait toujours le désir d'être inconnue à tout le monde, et de cacher son intérieur. C'est pourquoi elle disait souvent à Dieu ces paroles: tant de grâces que vous voudrez, mon Dieu; mais donnez-moi, s'il-vous-plaît, la force de les porter de telle sorte qu'elles ne paraissent pas" (But in the midst of such particular favors, she always desired to be unknown to everyone and to hide her interior. This is why she often spoke to God these words: as many graces as you are willing to give, my God; but, if it please you, give me the strength to bear them so that they not be visible).[106] Out of humility, experience (described by Maillard as "particular," that is, irreducible to paradigms of comprehensibility) must remain hidden, as Jeanne de la Nativité notes: "Car notre Seigneur lui fit toujours cette grâce que toutes les faveurs qu'il lui communiqua se passèrent intérieurement; que si parfois il paraissait quelque chose au dehors, il permetait qu'on n'y prenait [*sic*] pas garde" (For our Lord always granted her this grace, that the favors he conferred on her took place internally; [and] that if at times something appeared on the outside, he allowed no one to take notice).[107] Alternately, the desire to publicize mystic favors could lead to their colonization by the forces of evil; if interiority was divine, the devil was by definition a creature of artifice and exteriority, and could corrupt mystic gifts only if those gifts first became apparent.[108]

There are, therefore, some simple reasons why writing on the part of the mystic had to be inserted into or framed by a resistance to publicity. What strikes me as more significant about these ubiquitous passages, however, is less this strategic need to cover oneself from attack than the considerable rhetorical pleasure derived from emphasizing a hide-and-seek played between writer and reader. For biography seemed to prosper best in the indeterminate space created once eloquent transparency lost out to a form of writing recognized and sought after *because* it problematized communication. Hence, autobiography may well be thought of as a map that would help to navigate a new subjective topography, but one must also recognize that if this map completely and successfully mediated between interior and exterior, then the frontier separating them would collapse, leaving the transparency of the old model, that of the eloquent oracle. In other words, the sense of interiority could only be provided if full exteriorization remained impossible; by extension, divine experience was most authentic not when the mystic spoke with prolific ease, but when the divine was tantalizingly blocked somewhere in the depths of the subject, of memory, of expressibility. We are left with a double paradox. First, even as biographers and autobiographers insisted on the desire for anonymity and secrecy, they were bent on violating that desire, on attempting to establish, via autobiographical writing, a bridge between the reader and the interior; the typographical attention given to first-person texts, for example, was just such a bridge. Second, they were just as bent on violating readerly desire for access by burning these bridges so as to protect an interior that was always stubbornly trying to withdraw itself from sight.

First among the methods for problematizing access to the interior was the initial resistance to any and all communication — a resistance that biographers and autobiographers continually bring to the fore. The subject is defined as a circumscribed space of secrecy that can only be communicated at the cost of great effort: "Il est certain que plus une âme cache son trésor; et plus il est en sûreté pour elle. [Anne-Marguerite Clément] l'a aussi toujours compris, et l'on a dû remarquer qu'elle n'en parlait jamais qu'en se faisant violence" (It is certain that the more a soul hides its treasure, the more it is in safe keeping. [Anne-Marguerite Clément] always understood this, and the reader will have noticed that she never spoke of it without doing violence to herself).[109] The allusion to the violence of communication recurs with remarkable regularity. It can, certainly, be ascribed to the circumstances in which writing took place—at the demand of a superior or director. And yet these references to repugnance toward writing, to the inherent violence of the act, had more than these material causes behind them; they were part of an immense and immensely coherent rhetoric of the autobiographical subject. Repugnance marked the words that eventually flowed (as they inevitably did) as authentic. Ease of expression was immediately suspicious: according to the maxim of Henri-Marie Boudun, "Les personnes peu intérieures se répandent facilement au dehors, et parlent beaucoup" (Persons who are not very interior easily overflow, and they speak a great deal).[110] Ordered to write, then, Anne-Marguerite Clément, being anything but "peu intérieure," resists: "elle avait une si grande peine de parler de ce qui se passait en elle, qu'elle eût fait toutes choses pour l'éviter, dans la prévoyance même de ce qu'il pourrait être manifesté un jour" (she had such great difficulty in speaking of what happened inside her that she would have done anything to avoid it, for she foresaw that it might be made manifest some day).[111] Likewise, Marguerite-Marie Alacoque "s'était fait une loi inviolable de n'écrire à qui que ce soit que dans la dernière nécessité" (made for herself an inviolable law to write to no one except in the most dire necessity).[112] The irony, of course, is that this writing is not set up to be read *in spite* of this desire for privacy; rather, its status as private makes us want to read it. Hence Alacoque's biographer continues: "on peut dire que ce grand désir d'être inconnue n'a jamais mieux paru que dans ses Lettres" (one might say that this great desire to be unknown was never so obvious as in her Letters)—letters he then goes on to cite.[113] Via autobiographical writing, invisibility *appears*: it would be hard to find a better example of how the desire for invisibility becomes itself a spectacle, of how the determination to remain in silence increases the value of words, of how, in short, the subject's self-willed opacity seems destined to capture the reader's interest more that the promise of immediate access to the word of God.

Just as secrecy is produced when the subject attempts to shield the interior from the exterior by refusing to write, the contrary can be equally true: that is, longing to speak one's interior is met by exterior incomprehension. This is an enforced or involuntary secrecy, often established via the topos of the uncomprehending spiritual director, blind to the significance of the aspirant's spiritual gifts.[114] Given seventeenth-century polemics on the proper place of mysticism within the Church, and on the reality of (usually female) mystic experience more generally, such a theme could only flourish. At the root of worry over the prescience of spiritual directors, however, lay an idea both feared and desired—that God might not speak unequivocally through the mystic, and that interior graces might at least partially be inaccessible to exterior validation.[115] The result is that a fear of misunderstanding doubles the desire for openness. Hence Jeanne Deleloë, a precursor of Alacoque in the cult of the Sacred Heart, tells of changing confessors in order to avoid reproducing the painful experience of baring one's heart to an unreceptive audience. Deleloë *does* wish to bare that heart, however: "Je disais souvent: 'Au moins, si j'avais une personne à qui je pourrais franchement découvrir mon coeur sans la mettre en peine, ce me serait un grand soulagement'" (I often said, "if only I had someone to whom I could frankly bare my heart without troubling him, it would be a great relief to me").[116] The statement can only but position the reader as that person, as the receptor of a long-deferred message from an orphaned interior.

Most biographers and autobiographers, however, are less sanguine about autobiography's ability to reach out to friends, for, inevitably, something is lost in this textual effort to translate interiority into something readable, and this loss is only partially ascribable to God's inveterate ineffability. It is no longer a question of man, in his corruption and mortality, being unable to comprehend the infinite; what occurs, rather, is that the reader is denied full comprehension of the biographical subject because these writers tend to speak of their own experience as somehow unrepresentable. Hence I would suggest that when Jeanne de La Nativité writes of Armelle Nicolas: "Elle me tint des discours si sublimes et si relevés qu'il n'est pas en mon pouvoir de les raconter. En voici seulement quelque chose de plus commun et intelligible" (She made to me such sublime and lofty speeches that it is beyond my power to recount them. All I can include here is something more common and comprehensible), something of God's incomprehensibility cannot help but rub off, so to speak, on Nicolas herself.[117] The reader is given only part of her experience so as to better leave the impression of depth, of an interior that will never be completely exposed.

If it is accurate to characterize both confession and spiritual direction as attempts to anatomize the subject, to classify exhaustively sin and ecstasy, and ultimately to put into place a subjective control as total as that in evidence in Ignatius of Loyola's *Spiritual Exercises*, autobiography is the less-than-docile instrument of this discipline. The discernment of spirits depends on the presupposition that God, who is infinite, acts upon the individual in certain finite and classifiable ways; and that writing especially can facilitate the observation of all this. The autobiographer, however, tells of the failure of observation. On the one hand, there is always something more to say: "Ce n'est pas qu'il ne se passe encore d'autres choses dans l'âme, et plusieurs! Mais il me paraît impossible de les pouvoir toutes dire" (It's not as if other things still do not occur in the soul, there are so many! But it seems to me impossible to be able to say them all).[118] At other times, the mystic looks inside only to find a swirling chaos in which none of the graduated stages of contemplation that one finds in the writings of a Saint Teresa can be discerned: "Je ne sais comment commencer, de parler d'une année entière. Je me trouve dans un labyrinthe, à n'en pouvoir pas sortir: car [comment] parler d'une chose que je ne puis comprendre? . . . Car c'est de même que si j'entrais, ou passais d'un abîme en un autre abîme: et quelque manière que j'écrive, je ne puis m'expliquer assez clairement" (I know not how to begin to speak of an entire year. I am in a labyrinth, unable to find a way out: for [how] can I speak of a thing I cannot understand? . . . For it is just as if I were entering or passing from one abyss to another, and however I write, I cannot express myself clearly).[119] The labyrinth, here, is the writer's own; she is unable to explain not God but *herself*, the year she has lived. At other times still, the subject's own hermeticism is invoked in order to create the idea of an intimate *présence à soi*, as when one biographer/director recalls being told by his charge: "Je ne puis, mon Père, vous rapporter ce qui se passe dans mon âme. Je connais que cela n'est pas pour vous: c'est un secret que Dieu ne veut pas que je révèle; ou plutôt, je suis dans l'impuissance d'en parler" (I cannot, my Father, report to you what is happening in my soul. I know that it is not for you: it is a secret that God does not want me to reveal; or rather, I am powerless to speak of it).[120] A clear limit exists to both the power of spiritual direction and of the autobiographical text; and instead of downplaying this limit, as one might expect, the biographer/director underlines it. The interior is that which escapes. So even as autobiographical writing was acquiring its status as the intimate act capable of allowing access to the interior, of revealing all to the reader/director/biographer's gaze, it also flaunted its failures.

Not coincidentally, the hide-and-seek of autobiography is perhaps most pronounced in those texts that stretch the pretext of spiritual direction to the breaking point. What differentiates most strongly the long, heavily retrospective narratives of Madeleine Vigneron or Marguerite-Marie Alacoque from the more numerous fragmentary exchanges between aspirant and director is at once a conscious address to a larger audience and a corresponding problematization of the act of writing supposed to transform inner secrecy into outward readability. Indeed, the scene of writing forms a major thematic axis of the writings of Vigneron or Alacoque, and I would like to pause briefly to take a look at the ways in which an effect of depth is created by this attention.

I have already noted how Vigneron's biographer/editor explains, in his "Avis au lecteur," how the mystic wrote not so much for the purposes of spiritual direction, but, rather, for an ambiguous and all-purpose observing "nous." Upon reading Vigneron's own writings, it becomes clear that she too was conscious of this wider audience. Leaving aside the manifest addresses to plural and anonymous readers ("mes très chers frères chrétiens" [my very dear Christian brothers], "âmes chrétiennes" [Christian souls], and so forth), she characterizes writing more generally as a sort of apostolic mission, undertaken not by order of a director but in accordance with her own "idea": "J'avais eu souvent la pensée d'écrire les grâces particulières que j'avais reçues de Dieu; mais je l'avais toujours traitée de tentation" (I had often had the idea of writing down the particular graces I had received from God; but I had always considered it a temptation). Eventually, a voice intervenes, mandating not only disclosure but, it is specified, written disclosure: "Je veux," says the voice, "[que] vous découvr[iez] les grâces que vous avez reçues [de votre Époux Jésus-Christ], et je veux même que vous les écriviez" (I want you to reveal the graces you have received [from your Bridegroom Jesus Christ], and furthermore I want you to write them down). Later, Christ himself encourages her to keep writing each and every time she would succumb to the temptation of secrecy. The struggle to write is described as a battle with the demon of silence, the devil himself. "Ce malheureux [le Démon]," she writes, "me mettait dans l'esprit que cette écriture me réduirait au lit le reste de mes jours" (this wretched [demon] put it into my mind that such writing would reduce me to lying in bed for the rest of my days). Writing is both a physical and a spiritual suffering; as such it benefits from an elaborately dramatic mis-en-scène as body and spirit converge upon the martyrdom that is autobiography: "croyant avoir les os cassés . . . , je me suis rendue pour cette fois victorieuse des ennemis conjurés de cette écriture" (thinking my bones must have been broken . . . , I finally triumphed over the sworn enemies of this writing).[121]

No doubt such colorful descriptions could be productively analyzed as metaphors for the painful "coming-to-writing" women in this milieu experienced. "Ennemis conjurés" of women's writing were not in short supply; claiming an audience beyond the male director could only be risky for those who had no authority to predicate.[122] For my purposes here, however, passages such as these serve above all to deploy a rhetoric of self-exposure *as pain*; according to this conception, autobiography is of interest because it marks the subject's resistance to and simultaneous urge for disclosure. No better example can be adduced than the autobiography of Alacoque, which stands as a veritable catalogue of all the devices writers of the period used to define the paradoxical role of the autobiographical text. First, these are the numerous references to an experience that continually proves too much for the finitude of writing: "je serais trop longue à m'en exprimer" (It would take too long for me to express myself about this), or again: "c'est un abîme à écrire, et la longueur m'a fait tout supprimer" (there is an abyss to be written, and the length led me to cut it all out).[123] The desire to remain hidden and unknown is opposed to the need to "faire éclater la dévotion du sacré Coeur" (make visible to all the devotion of the sacred heart) (103), with the result that the subject once again is defined by a painful resistance to writing overcome thanks only to the direct intervention of Christ: "je ne te demandais qu'un sacrifice secret, et maintenant je le veux public" (I used to ask of you only a secret sacrifice, and now I want it to be public), the latter tells Alacoque (84). Writing is thus a "humiliation" (84), a "martyrdom" (91); it is a task undertaken on her knees (100), and, as if it were a penitential scourge, a "violence" she does to herself (34, 42, 58, 90, 93). Once writing exists, the subject attempts to make it disappear, burning it (94) or praying that it will remain hidden to all but her confessor (90), even though, like Vigneron, Alacoque is clearly aware she has a public.

Autobiography has an iceberg effect: it attests to something massive below the surface, in the depths of the soul. Bound up with autobiography's widespread recognition in print as something special was the realization that its power is one of suggestion: it interests us less for what it says than for what it says it does not say. Out of this belief in the depths spring biographers' frequent references to the physical precarity of the autobiographical text. Perhaps the mystic, in order better to remain hidden, burnt her writings in a holocaust from which only one scrap (but how much more precious!) was salvaged.[124] Total secrecy is as impossible as total exposure, because subject and observer are caught in an endless game of cat-and-mouse. Of Elisabeth de l'enfant Jésus, we learn that her secretive "precautions" were partially thwarted by efficient surveillance: "nous nous ressouvenons encore de trois rencontres où elle n'a pu si bien se cacher, que nous n'en ayons apperçu quelque chose" (we still remember three encounters in which she was unable to conceal herself well enough for us not to have seen what was happening).[125] One might say then that the gaze of directorial scrutiny turns out to be, at best, more like a *glimpse*. Jeanne Gojoz wrote her experiences on hundreds of little pieces of paper she then hid in different parts of her cell; the strategy, according to her biographer, was that of confusing her adoring pursuers and making transparency impossible: "Elle avait fait [les billets] ainsi séparés, afin que l'on ne vît jamais ces faveurs divines avec une suite qui pût en donner une vraie connaissance" (She had thus written on separate [pieces of paper], so that we would never view her divine favors with the continuity necessary for understanding them).[126]

Earlier I spoke of how the frequent evocations of the autobiographical document's materiality made the cited text function as a kind of miraculous and powerful relic. Yet this was a power that came also from the very precariousness of that materiality. To note that something is written on an old piece of paper is to call attention to the fortuitousness of its testimony, to the limits of our knowledge. Marie-Madeleine de Mauroy presents eight pages of citation of her subject as having been found "écrits de sa main dans un vieux papier presque tout déchiré" (written in her hand on an old, almost totally torn sheet of paper); she closes the citation with the irresistible hook: "Le reste a été déchiré" (the rest has been ripped away).[127] The loss is really anything but unfortunate, of course; time and chance have converted the old scrap of paper into a monument to or representation of an experience that is always already, and by any means necessary, just out of sight. But for Mauroy, the monumentalization of autobiography is a condition of its beauty; she writes: "[P]ar le peu que nous avons, on pourra juger de ce que nous n'avons pas; de même . . . que par les tableaux et par les statues qui nous restent . . . de l'Antiquité, on juge de la perfection des ouvrages qui se sont perdus" ([B]y the little that we have, we can judge what we do not have; just as . . . by the paintings and statues remaining . . . from Antiquity, we imagine the perfection of the works that were lost).[128] If the close of the century had brought the culture of autobiography far from the early efforts of a Benoît de Canfeld, the evolution lies not only in the increased and privileged space made for the autobiographical "I"; this editorial space was now there, but Mauroy, Vigneron, Alacoque, and a host of other writers brought attention to bear on it and suggested that it was a space of shortcoming, of rips, burns, and breaks. Hence the structural ambiguity of interiority: autobiography's considerable pull does not revolve around confidence in a preexistent subject manifested in writing; autobiography from its beginnings prefers to sketch out the contours of this subject's more intriguing cousin—the preexistent subject *not* manifested in writing.

That this subject is no less a figment of the modern imagination than the subject-in-writing needs no arguing, but it is a more tenacious figment, one liable to more ingenious reappropriations over the flux of history, be- cause it is always neither here nor there—not fully present in the text, but not fully absent from the text either. If the technology of the book can accu- rately be said to have enabled the rise of a culture of interiority (by making the exteriorization of hidden truths possible via expanded literacy and access to print), and to have thereby permitted the illusion of an inner truth where none had been before, it also disabled, by that same movement of exteriori- zation, that inner truth. The paradox, in other words, is the following: like a Magritte *trompe l'oeil* sporting the caption "This is not a subject," autobi- ography gains power through the denunciation of the illusion it fosters. This explains why, for instance, at the same time a culture learned, in a almost too Foucauldian turn of events, to "document the subject," it provided a form of resistance to the all-powerful readerly gaze in the form of the torn document, through whose rip the interior receded once again safely from view. The self derived its power from never being solid at all, but, instead, slightly out of reach, repository of a truth that can never quite be uttered, visible only in text of which the most vital phrases hover just on the other side of legibility.

Gendering Autobiography

The multifaceted developments manifested in religious biographies involved many aspects of the transition to modernity: they are bound up, for instance, with the "documentation" of the modern individual, with the creation of an entirely new and foundational type of knowledge, "experience," and with the evolving science of quotation. Developments such as these attest to changes affecting a wide spectrum of practices, from law to science to book-making. But as I have occasionally pointed out, several traits of biographical produc- tion beg for analysis that takes gender into account. The question is, however, how we can take gender into account without imposing ready-made explana- tions that this material both solicits and confounds. The topos of the Enlight- ened Illiterate, for example, tellingly gendered writing masculine, inspiration feminine, and thereby invites the deployment of "recuperation" scenarios, according to which a male institutional elite appropriates female culture in order, in the words of one commentator, "to declare paternal control over an

unruly female text."[129] The insistent use of a rhetoric of visual penetration of
the female mystic indeed suggests, as Wendy Wall has argued with respect to
the cover engraving of Vesalius's *De Humani Corporis Fabrica* (1543), the usefulness of gaze theory to emphasize how women were the chosen objects of
early modern scrutiny: "Like the sonnet speaker who controls the linguistic
fragmentation of his beloved mistress, [the anatomist] Vesalius prominently
displays his own mastery vis-à-vis this inert female body. . . . Within the titil-
lating rhetoric of disclosure, the subject positions of both reader and author
became coded as male."[130] One might even insert the mania for (apparently)
making women speak into the context of a long-standing tradition of "ventriloquism": women endowed — by men — "with a potent voice figured a kind
of vocal Medusa both fascinating and fearsome";[131] yet this projected potency
"reinforced feminine silence or marginalized [women's] voices when they did
speak."[132] Hence it is tempting to read these biographies, dotted here and
there with fragments of first-person experience sutured together by the mas-
terly biographer, with something of the same eye as Janet Beizer has read
nineteenth-century hysteriological discourse, in which "[t]he silences and in-
coherencies of hysteria were perceived as an invitation to narrate: it is precisely because the hysteric cannot tell her story that this story . . . is so readily
accessible as a narrative matter."[133]

    Although the hybrid French (auto)biographies I have been dealing with
here have been almost totally unexplored by literary historians, their Spanish
counterparts have received a considerable amount of attention from American scholars in particular, and much of this scholarship has been framed to
a greater or lesser degree by arguments such as these. While acknowledging
the seeming applicability of these models, I do not think they can begin to
account for the cultural significance of the explosion of interest in (mainly)
female interiors in early modern France. Instead of rebutting these scenarios
on a point-by-point basis, I will confine myself here to three statements.

    First, if the writing mystic was overwhelmingly female, the biographer's
sex was less predictable. Many of the biographies I have been citing in order to
paint a picture of the interiorization of the subject, and the mistrust of action
which had for its counterpart the fetishization of the autobiographical document, were written by women. This fact alone confuses hypotheses as to the
"recuperation" of women's writing by men, though conceivably one might
be able to maintain that when women wrote biographies their treatment of
their subjects — and perhaps their faithfulness to the subjects' own writing —
differed from those of their male counterparts. My research has failed to convince me of such an inherent difference (leaving aside, of course, those bi-

ographies written by men mistrustful of their subjects' gifts), although I do not rule out the possibility. Rather, it seems to me that a model emphasizing collaboration, rather than one that stresses male oppression and female resistance, might better account for the phenomenon of religious biography. There was no need on the part of male ecclesiastics to find a print space for the words of women; the ones who did were invariably those who were trying to enlarge women's influence in the Counter-Reformation Church, and they met with the attacks of more orthodox biographers who preferred to ignore mystic writing when it existed.

Second, both the "ventriloquism" and "gaze" hypotheses founder on the obsession with the writing (and not merely speaking or swooning) woman, an obsession which led to those autobiographical extremes that I have documented as marginalizing the biographer. Biography itself started to take on the character of an "edition," in the sense of: an edition of so-and-so's works. Bourdin's biography, for instance, was in fact only part of a much longer work, *La Vie et conduite spirituelle de la damoiselle Madeleine Vigneron*, which consists of: (1) the *Life*, composed almost exclusively of Vigneron's own autobiographical narratives; (2) the contents of her journal; (3) Christ's instructions for Vigneron as he dictated them to her; and (4) Vigneron's letters. Much more than a biography, this is Vigneron's *Oeuvres complètes*.[134] Similarly, it is instructive that the experimental forays made into the typographical means of indicating authorial proprietorship — quotation marks, italics, and the like — did anything but occlude women's access to such status. Quotation marks, the invention of Renaissance printer Guillaume Le Bé (whence the French term "guillemets"), were from the start a response to the pressing humanist need to be faithful to the textuality of the past — to attribute sources, and, by extension, to grant authorship as a proprietary right. To quote is to mark off a space for the utterance of a specific person: X is the source of whatever lies between inverted commas; at the same time, what fell outside these marks could clearly be attributed to the commentator. But the rush to highlight women's words illustrate that this humanist invention did not serve only to isolate the text of Latin *auctoritas*; in other words, authorship was not a terrain staked out always and everywhere between men. Typography could serve to mark off a space of autobiographical authority as well, and when it did, that space was occupied chiefly by women.

Third, I would emphasize that although the phenomenon of (auto)-biography does indeed illustrate that writing *about* women ultimately elicited writing *by* women — in other words, that real women, largely through the efforts of fascinated men, gained increasing access to print — the main point

of this chapter has been to lay out the construction of an enormously powerful rhetoric of subjectivity. For this reason, it is of little concern to me, for
instance, that biographers depicted scraps of paper that may well never have
existed, or at the very least drastically altered those texts they did "reproduce." The question of whether or not biographers reproduced what women
"really wrote" is in this respect as moot as wondering if what Rousseau tells
us about his adolescence "really corresponds" to reality, for the simple reason that autobiography is, as Lejeune has suggested, a pact or a contract by
which author and reader agree to point to something "out there," rather than
the "there" itself. Even if one assumes that the endless quotations, the myriad
protestations to the effect that the female subject was writing, were a rhetorical gesture, rhetorical gestures are never empty. They operate an assignation
of value. And in this case, they assign to the autobiographical text the interrelated values of authenticity, experience, depth, and femininity, all of which
goes some way toward corroborating Nancy Armstrong's contention, based
on her study of women's conduct books and the eighteenth-century novel,
that "the modern individual was first and foremost a woman." [135]

Associations like these were made so forcefully that they have not disappeared. Indeed, the frequently asserted desire to resurrect the long-silenced
voices of "untold sisters" (as Arenal and Schlau put it in the resonant title
to their compendium of Spanish nuns' writing), and to separate their voices
from the dross of male intervention of the type that exists in religious biographies — this desire itself is a product of the autobiographical mentality whose
history I have been tracing. Indeed, if I have focused relatively little on the
content of these autobiographical writings, it is because we already know well
enough how to revisit voices of the past; what requires more scrutiny is why
retrospective reclaiming seems to possess such urgency. And understanding
this entails remembering those men and women who helped construct interiority as a locus of readerly desire. In our continued enthusiasm over the
authority of women's written personal experience, we are after all as much
the descendants of a Mathieu Bourdin, say, as a Madeleine Vigneron.

Part II
Frictions

Chapter Three
Uncomfortable Subjects
Autobiography and the Circulation of Privacy

Rousseau, to whom the French language owes a number of interesting neologisms, coined one in particular that goes some way toward elucidating a paradox of modern identity, to wit, that what we feel ourselves most deeply to be is nevertheless inseparable from what others say about us. In the eighth book of the *Confessions*, which is also the place he first begins to speak of the conspiracy supposedly mounted against him, Rousseau uses the verb "person[n]aliser."[1] The word derives from "personnalité," which, when used in the plural, could refer to calumnious personal attacks.[2] Hence "to personalize" was to engage in public slander of a private life, to bring forth the private as object of public ridicule. At the same time Rousseau was writing, however, the more familiar modern meaning of "personnalité" was already becoming well established—writers such as Condillac would commonly use it as synonymous with the *moi*. Rousseau's neologism, based on a soon-to-be archaic definition, might then scarcely rate a footnote, if it were not for the fact that these two quite different senses of the word—on the one hand, the dominant meaning we still recognize today, and on the other, its more sinister, if forgotten double—inform each other so well. To have a personality was to allow for the possibility of exposure to new modes of attack and control. Identity *was* vulnerability, for it lay not in beliefs that could be debated, but in secret behavior that could be uncovered, ridiculed, and even, in subsequent developments, criminalized.

Indeed, the *Confessions* demonstrate in exemplary fashion how any assertion of the inherent solidity of the "I" must eventually give way to anxious references to an outside whose significance is constantly denied even as it is unwittingly demonstrated. Whence the importance of Rousseau's neologism, interjected at the precise moment his autobiography was taking an increasingly paranoid turn: "personnaliser" remains as a telling trace of a time when the subject's reliance on external opposition for its existence was still vaguely recognized; only later, as the concept of the self became increasingly reified, would the second meaning be conveniently forgotten. Today, to personalize means primarily to render (somehow) a mass product authentically one's own, to leave the mark of one's indelible identity; gone is the sense that this identity depends on or is produced through a type of persecution. It bears noting, then, that one of the most familiar insights of twentieth-century thinkers such as Lacan, Foucault, or Althusser—generally put, the constitution of the subject as discourse of the Other—was in some sense written in the lexicological vagaries of the early modern period. For any investigation into the origins and nature of subjectivity, a good place to start is the dictionary.

Previous chapters have detailed how, in an emerging culture of interiority, autobiography had the dual function of both providing and blocking access to the most intimate recesses of the human soul. The dialectic of the shown and the hidden, endlessly rehearsed in the presentation of autobiographical texts to the contemporary devotional public, produced the idea of an interior and helped to define the nature and authority of the first-person discourse of experience. Yet the particular circumstances surrounding the publication of such writings were not representative of all early modern autobiographical production. Religious women of the seventeenth century wrote of their experiences for a largely approving audience (a director, usually, but also the community of the faithful); one can sense from time to time the now forgotten polemics that these writers occasionally participated in (say, the value or veracity of mystical states), but overall these were texts whose public circulation did not seem problematic. The mystic interior offered itself to adoring eyes, even if it often maintained its necessary prerogative of keeping some secrets. A great many other autobiographical acts, however, were undertaken in and defined by less friendly situations, ones in which individuals, "personalized" by forces hostile to them, replied by asserting an alternative view of their secret selves. Here, the writer appears as if on trial; the jury is the reading public; and the autobiographical text coalesces between the twin poles of desired privacy and unwanted publicity.

This precarious position is that of three autobiographers situated on the fringes of the Catholic Church—Jean de Labadie (1610–1674), Antoinette Bourignon (1610–1680), and Jeanne Guyon (1648–1717). Labadie, Bourignon, and Guyon wrote in the wavering shadow of a church whose pretensions of catholicity—in the most literal sense—had come under the attack of the Reform. Generally speaking, the splintering of the Christian faith into a multitude of churches and sects did much to promote the use of first-person testimonial: the inability of the Roman Church to sustain the fiction of its privileged relation to the Bible and to a fixed tradition of exegesis created what could be termed an "authority vacuum," into which rushed innumerable "I"s.[3] Indeed, it is to this crisis of authority, perhaps more than to some intrinsic affinity of Calvinist self-analysis and personal writing, that the flowering of seventeenth-century testimonial literature of all kinds may be ascribed. Paul Delany, for example, has described well the impression of "endemic megalomania" given off by much English sectarian autobiography.[4] Catholic France was less fertile ground for this type of competition, but the Counter-Reform climate of the continent nonetheless multiplied the peripheries from which to raise voices of protest to persecutions visited by centralized authority.

Labadie, Bourignon, and Guyon were not by any means the only figures writing in French to stake out these margins, nor were they the only ones to resort to autobiography to do so. In Jansenist and Protestant circles, for example, persecution did much to stimulate the writing of first-person chronicles—the *Relation de captivité* (1664–65) of Angélique de Saint-Jean (daughter of Robert Arnauld d'Andilly) and numerous Protestant memoirs of persecution appearing in the wake of the revocation of the Edict of Nantes all attest to this.[5] Grouping Labadie, Bourignon, and Guyon together, however, has a certain coherence, not only because their personal lives were made objects of ecclesiastical or judicial attack, but also because they were all predicators deeply enamored of the tropes of interiority. Their attempts at apology or vindication thus provide a picture of how autobiographical subjectivity may be said to be produced through the collision of interior values and exterior exigencies—through resistance to a realm seen as hostile to an experienced-based identity.

At the same time, this triptych also suggests the increasing pressures put on the autobiographical text as the century wore on. Indeed, it will become obvious that these writings are not all autobiographical in the same way or even to the same extent: compared to Guyon's massive eight-hundred-page *Life*, Labadie's hesitant and hybrid work can only appear primitive, inchoate. Nonetheless, I would emphasize from the outset that the move from Labadie, writing in 1650, to Bourignon a decade and a half later, and finally to Guyon at the century's close, is not intended to stand in for a representative evolution—as if one could pinpoint the sudden advent of interiorized subjectivity or "true" autobiography using these figures as sole guides. Still, I hope to show that the amount of attention or consciousness brought to bear on the autobiographical text does indeed intensify, and in direct proportion to the opposition and imbrication of the nascent realms of public and private. Or, put in a different way: the more the private becomes the stuff of public debate, the more autobiography becomes thinkable; but the more thinkable it becomes, the more irreducibly problematic its nature appears. Given the paradoxes of interiorized subjectivity, one could hardly expect autobiography to be any less confused, as it emerges under the double sign of integrity and slander, where the proof of one's personality becomes the matter of personalities.[6]

Jean de Labadie, Public Apology, and the Rhetoric of Privacy

Judging by its absence from most inquiries into modern subjectivity, the public nature of autobiography must seem counterintuitive, or else an impure residue of some former, pre-modern, more rhetorical form of selfhood. When historians or literary scholars set out in search of the origins of the individual, they like to look in the most out-of-the-way places — I mention once again as paradigmatic Pascal's coat-lining and the *Mémorial* it contained — as if only in the most private removes could be found the first stirrings of a "sense of self." It is of little wonder that the study of autobiographical forms such as the journal figure heavily in the monumental *Histoire de la vie privée* (1986), edited by Philippe Ariès and Georges Duby: the private, by its very nature, must be ferreted out.[7] Autobiography's association with an interior, private, and asocial subject has been slowly built up over the past three centuries, and studies such as Ariès and Duby's operate within this association: they are a product of the modern fascination with privacy, as much or more than its explanation. What bears asking, however, is how much autobiography was dependent on emerging concepts of the public — notably, a judging, critical public metaphorized as a tribunal.

The general argument of Jürgen Habermas's *Structural Transformation of the Public Sphere* has become so well known as scarcely to bear repeating. Briefly, Habermas maintains that Enlightenment in France (and in England as well, although with a slightly different time frame) was characterized by the growth of an arena of public, rational debate separate from the institutions of the state. New institutions such as coffeehouses and lodges, as well as the exponential rise of the periodical, were manifestations of this "public sphere." These advances all permitted men of quite different backgrounds and conditions to meet as "human beings," united by the least common denominator of rationality; in the public arena, private citizens came together to form judgments based on their subjective (often family) experience. Whatever the problems with Habermas's immensely influential account,[8] one aspect of it is particularly useful for understanding the contradictions embodied by the autobiographical text—to wit, that the constitution of a public sphere had as its corollary "the emancipation . . . of an inner realm."[9]

The new interiority implied and encouraged by the public sphere was manifested in the Enlightenment's cultural production. According to Habermas, the vogue for epistolary fiction and non-fiction answered the demand for an (apparently) "purely human" form of textual relations between individuals: "Through letter writing," Habermas writes, "the individual unfolded himself in his subjectivity." What is most suggestive about Habermas's discussion of the private lies precisely in this "unfolding"—the fact that the private is made for divulging, that the private individual can only but "go public." Habermas notes, for instance, how the two seemingly separate domains constantly solicit one another: "Subjectivity, as the innermost core of the private, was always already oriented towards an audience."[10] Such an observation, consonant with the mechanism of avowal described by Foucault in *The History of Sexuality*, implies a depth-structured subject, one whose public surface is determined by private experience that is constantly coming to the fore.

As much as epistolary fiction, autobiography might also be viewed as a symptom of the incessant projection of the private upon the public. With regards to the texts I will be examining, however, Habermas's argument appears to have limited applicability, if only because his pinning of causality on the rise of the bourgeoisie presents chronological difficulties. The private and public spheres evolved, according to Habermas, only in Enlightenment Europe. Pre-Enlightenment publicity, he argues, showed no private/public dialectic, and instead operated on the mode of representation. Only those in power, such as monarchical or ecclesiastical authorities, could claim access to the public realm; this "publicness" (as Habermas calls it) was "something like a status attribute."[11] According to Classical criteria of publicity, only that which was considered "high" was representable; the inferior, the plebeian, the domestic—in other words, what modern historians tend to classify as the private—all hovered below the threshold of visibility. The publicness of representation had no private as a corollary.

The paragon of publicness was the immense representational apparatus constructed by Louis XIV at Versailles. Here, the king and his court, not his subjects, constituted the public, and publicness was an attribute of power. In the words of Jean-Marie Apostolidès, "in royal representation, the privileged exchange signs of culture over which power maintains a monopoly. . . . The excluded have no access to the code of representation; . . . they make up the spectator-public [le peuple spectateur] of the new order that is being constructed against them."[12] As Apostolidès suggests, the "peuple spectateur" was far from the Enlightenment ideal of the public as tribunal, as an entity that could produce judgments and sanction political action. Whence Habermas's description of the changing connotation of the phrase "public opinion." Whereas "opinion" had been a chiefly derogatory term, the opposite of valorized "reason," it came in the course of the eighteenth century to imply "private reflection upon public affairs and . . . their public discussion."[13] The "peuple spectateur," on the other hand, was a mass to be manipulated; it had no coherence as a group, but instead, according to Roger Chartier, was "formed into a public only by the spectacle that [it was] given to see and to believe." It had no power to exercise its "opinion," or to judge; it merely "brought together all whose adherence or support were sought."[14] Hence Christian Jouhaud, in his analysis of the *mazarinades* (antimonarchical pamphlets that flourished during the revolt of the Fronde), speaks of the way the press constructed a public by offering a spectacle. The *mazarinades*, he argues, should not be confused with public political discourse; they operated not according to a mode of reason (for they contain no political ideas), but to a mode of seduction. They, like France's earliest real periodical, the *Gazette* of Renaudot (1631), offered not news that people were to debate amongst themselves, but rather "current events in the form of a spectacle."[15]

There are, however, problems with accounts of the Classical public that adopt too uncritically the Habermasian divide between the seventeenth and eighteenth centuries. As Chartier himself has pointed out, gazettes and pamphlets were inherently threatening to royal or ecclesiastical power, simply because they permitted private groups or individuals access to representation. It is no accident that Louis XIV took swift steps to counter pamphlet explosions like that of the *mazarinades*: appeal to the public was his own prerogative, the tactic by which he secured his own power.[16] Chartier concludes that access to the public via the press was in itself subversive: pamphlets were "undeniably an instrument of divulgation that broke the traditional monopoly of small minorities over political and religious knowledge."[17] Even if the seventeenth-century readership of the fledgling periodical press did not constitute a sphere of Habermasian rational-critical debate, appeal to the public via the press nonetheless provided an avenue for combating monopolies and exclusion. Such appeal is implicit proof that the king was no longer the automatic addressee of the discourse of his subjects.[18]

Was the seventeenth century, then, characterized by a true "public" in the Enlightenment sense, or was it ruled by the logic of "publicness"? The conflicting observations of commentators like Chartier and Apostolidès suggests that both could have been operative in different milieus, and in different times. Briefly, my argument here aims neither to opt for one or the other, nor to criticize Habermas's time frame. Rather, I propose to discuss how distinctions such as these were being formulated in the early seventeenth century, and specifically to situate the relation of first-person discourse to them: how do transformations in the notion of the public contribute to effects such as interiority, privacy, and, ultimately, autobiography?

One type of first-person public discourse in the seventeenth century, flourishing in the thirty-odd years following the enactment of the edict of Nantes in 1598, was the declaration of conversion.[19] The edict of Nantes did not so much calm tensions between France's Protestants and Catholics as shift the terrain of their battle from the physical to the discursive. Catholics were obliged to limit their bid for power to propaganda; as for Protestants, the edict permitted them to take part in public debate to a degree previously impossible. The first years of this relative freedom were characterized by face-to-face debates, a prolongation of the academic tradition of the *disputatio*.[20] "Dîners de controverse" were even organized. Soon, however, oral debate started to wane in favor of written exchanges; the few oral disputes that did take place started to resemble juxtaposed monologues rather than debates. The literature these controversies produced — be it declarations of conversion or the very popular interviews between a Catholic priest and a Protestant minister — would hardly qualify as a Habermasian forum of rational critical debate. It was, rather, carefully orchestrated propaganda intended mainly to impress a public whose good will was already assured. Liberty of the press was rudimentary at best — Protestants were allowed to publish only in towns and cities they held — and as a result, partisans of each side ended up representing themselves mainly to themselves.

Declarations of conversion, then, remind us of just how limited the idea of a public was at this time and in this milieu; they still conform quite well to Habermas's characterization of the seventeenth century. Declarations were made before the congregation on the Sunday following an individual's formal abjuration. Authorities keen on convincing their followers that their side was making progress then proceeded to multiply this limited audience by recourse to print. Presses of Protestant strongholds such as Montauban, Saumur, La Rochelle, and of course Geneva, churned out hundreds of first-person attestations of adherence to the Reformed church on the part of former Catholics. At the same time, Catholics, no longer engaged in physical persecution of their enemies, took up the same practice, publishing similar attestations of former Protestants as to the worthlessness of their old faith and to the veracity of their newfound one. The declarations were first printed up in octavo format at a local print shop, and often reprinted in different cities the same year.[21] The circulation of these texts outside of friendly localities was probably minimal. The convert spoke not to those he had left behind, but to those of his new faith.[22]

Given this atmosphere, it is no surprise that these declarations reveal little sense of a public capable of judgment or decision-making, little sense even of having to justify one's actions before a potentially hostile audience. The declaration of the Protestant convert Fabrice de la Bassecourt, a former priest in Orléans, makes a point of simulating a debate with his former Catholic associates, but, as the declaration was made only before Protestants and published in La Rochelle, it is doubtful that this self-justification could have been anything but a rhetorical posture.[23] Jacques Vanier precedes his declaration with an *avertissement* as to what, exactly, he expects of his audience: "Ainsi le compte que je veux rendre maintenant de mon action [est] pour en rendre grâces à mon Dieu, et faire voir à tout le monde la grandeur de ses jugements" (Thus the account I want to provide is intended to give thanks to my God, and to show to everyone the greatness of his judgments).[24] Clearly, his declaration is not a self-justification; his audience is sympathetic. It is common, however, to postulate an undecided public which might profit from the convert's example. Baptiste Bugnet writes, for instance: "Il y a des pays [où] tout homme guéri de quelque maladie vient exposer à la République les moyens et les remèdes qui ont servi à sa guérison: lesquels sont proposés en place publique, afin de pouvoir servir aux autres détenus de même maladie" (There are countries [where] every man who has been cured of some sickness comes to exhibit to the Republic the remedies that brought about his cure: and these remedies are declared in a public square, so that they might be used by others stricken with the same sickness).[25] Yet in spite of variations such as Bugnet's, none of these examples suggests a notion of public that would differ from the theatrical model used by Habermas, Chartier, and Jouhaud.

What bears emphasis, however, is that the inability to theorize a public that might be something other than the passive receptor of testimony curtails any sense of the private. Any modern reader coming upon the corpus of declarations of conversion would expect them to contain qualms of conscience, or trace out a spiritual trajectory. In point of fact, however, their general lack of any sort of autobiographical content is perhaps their most striking feature. Bugnet, for instance wants to "montrer les degrés par lesquels [il est] remonté du gouffre d'erreur" (show the steps by which [he] climbed out of the abyss of error), but for him these steps are entirely a matter of doctrine, of right-thinking, for he immediately launches into over twenty pages of teachings for which he criticizes the Catholic Church.[26] Jacques Vidouze similarly looks for the origins of his conversion, and finds only generality, not specificity: "[J]'estime que ce ne sera [pas] hors de propos que, rendant compte des sujets que j'ai eus à faire cette mienne confession et conversion à la foi catholique, je détaille brièvement les causes que les Philosophes recherchent généralement en toute action" ([I] judge that it will not be irrelevant, considering the reasons behind this confession and my conversion to the Catholic faith, if I briefly detail the causes which the Philosophers seek generally in every action).[27] Causality, here, is philosophical; and since the causes are determined to be a matter of right reason, no chronological exposition of the conversion is necessary. Conversion is not a process, nor even really an event; it is more akin to the changing of one's mind.[28]

Other declarations do give, however, some feel for conversion as a process, and manifest some sense of chronological unfolding. La Bassecourt, for example, combines a vague chronological exposition of his life with a doctrinal critique of Catholicism; he narrates, in fact, not events, but a series of reasonings, one leading to another, until it becomes impossible for him to accept the Church's "errors" any longer. The sieur de Vrillac and Gaspard Martin narrativize the conversion experience, but only as extended metaphors that harken back to biblical examples. The former tells of his battle with the temptation to remain a Catholic because of the material advantage such an adherence offered; the battle was won, he says, when "à l'exemple de l'Apôtre, j'ai secoué cette vipère" (following the example of the Apostle, I shook off that serpent).[29] The latter, after a short description of his life in the Church, tells of the Word of God, like a torch, changing his darkness into light.[30] Even with the addition of a temporal consciousness, however, there is nothing remotely "interior" about these accounts; no experience is appealed to, no public beseeched. Declarations present, at best, an allegorical drama of intention, rather than a narrative of forced individuation.[31] The production of an interiorized subject depends upon a public that has at least some characteristics of a tribunal—a judging public to which the individual can appeal for vindication.

Jean de Labadie knew during his life a far greater personal notoriety than any of the authors of the declarations I have just examined. While the conversions of these latter figures could certainly cause a stir and precipitate a flurry of dispute, Labadie's conversion to Protestantism in 1650 is notable for the amount and importance of the debate it elicited: Labadie successfully made himself the center and origin of this debate in a way that previous converts had never attempted. While most declarations of conversion were orchestrated and publicized by Protestant and Catholic propaganda machines, Labadie's declaration strategy was more or less of his own inspiration; it served less the cause of Protestantism than the cause of Jean de Labadie himself. Labadie's *Déclaration de Jean de Labadie, ci-devant prêtre, prédicateur, et chanoine d'Amiens, contenant les raisons qui l'ont obligé à quitter la Communion de l'Eglise Romaine pour se ranger à celle de l'Eglise Réformée* (1650), explicitly formulates a triangulation characteristic, I will argue, of the autobiographical mentality: that of a self-justifying subject, a judging society, and the textual exposition of the particularities of one's life story.

Labadie was born in 1610 at Bourg-en-Guyenne.[32] Both his father and his mother had at one time been Calvinists; they abjured their faith following the example of Henri IV, who had awarded Labadie's father, a military man of some distinction, the title of *gentilhomme ordinaire de la chambre du Roi*. This type of conversion, born more out of expediency than any profound religious sentiment, was far from rare at the time. The case of their son, however, would be somewhat more complicated. Early on the young Labadie showed spiritual leanings, in spite of his father's wish to direct him toward the red rather than the black. From his days at the Jesuit Collège de la Madeleine in Bordeaux (where, in the spirit of the times, there was a special *professeur de controverses*), Labadie's rise within the ranks of the Society of Jesus was rapid. He was finally ordained in 1639, after only two of the usual four years of preparation, amidst the general admiration of his superiors. Despite a weak physical appearance, his contemporaries remarked his charismatic aura: Labadie would always evoke respect, even for example as he was making moves to leave the Jesuits, which he would do the very year of his ordination.

Hints of the break with the Jesuit order that had applauded him can be discerned from his early days, as Labadie's mystical experiences (mostly visions and voices) took on an increasingly prophetic tone. Soon, he began to see the order as representative of a generalized corruption of the true spirit of primitive Christianity, and to sense the advantages of being a secular priest. More than on differences of doctrine, Labadie diverged from the Jesuits on practical issues — he found their pursuits excessively intellectual, the rules oppressive. But his break with the order was a quiet affair. The official reason given for his departure was ill health.

Upon leaving the Jesuits, he courted the Oratory, whose heavily Christocentric bent was in accordance with Labadie's own sensibilities. Settling in Amiens, where he preached, wrote, and campaigned for the reform of lax morals, Labadie enjoyed considerable popularity, among the ecclesiastical powers-that-be as much as with his parishioners. He entered into relations with Charles de Condren, general of the Oratory; and Richelieu, in Péronne in September 1641 for the signing of a treaty, was taken with his erudition and invited him to preach and dine with him each day of his sojourn. And yet hostility to Labadie was also manifest. The jilted Jesuits could not resist opportunities to libel him; and François Sublet des Noyers, Louis XIII's Secretary of State for war, denounced him as a second Calvin. (Labadie was, however, declared orthodox by Richelieu.)

Labadie's preaching, with its emphasis on the power of grace and the importance of the reading of the Bible (he had even invited a bookseller to Amiens to sell French New Testaments), became increasingly risky with the eruption of the Jansenist controversy in 1643. These were fertile times for polemic: to the binome of Catholic-Protestant antagonism was added the sticky Jesuit-Jansenist rivalry. Labadie's rapprochement with the partisans of Cornelius Jansen (there was personal contact between him and Saint-Cyran, and he would make a retreat at Port-Royal) sparked a new wave of Jesuit-sponsored opposition, attacks, and inquiries. A flurry of fake compromising letters were circulated; harangues, to be read to parishioners, were supplied to Jesuit preachers. Labadie's popular support, however, remained firm, especially among the poorer classes. Although Mazarin, never pro-Labadie, obtained a *lettre de cachet* for him and ordered him to be brought to Paris, the prime minister went no further than telling him to refrain from preaching until the division calmed.

Labadie complied; leaving Amiens, he went to Bazas, where he lay low, composing the *Traité de la solitude chrétienne* (1645). The *Traité* translated into spiritual terms his increasingly troubled relations with the world around him: Labadie here made the argument that union with God was founded on separation from the world. The break between individual and society was to become, from this point on, increasingly central to Labadie's thought. "The world" and its institutions started to appear to him a perpetual source of dissatisfaction; first it had been the Jesuits who disappointed him, and now the Jansenists, too, fell out of his favor. Ideas about election and the need for radical reform multiplied in Labadie's head. It was in Toulouse, where he stayed from 1646 to 1649, during a period of solitude he would later take great pains to cast as the spiritual "desert" that justified all the more his own election, that he made a gesture emblematic of his increasing belief in his personal mission of reform: following a vision, he decided to redesign his priest's habit.

Labadie's enemies, however, got wind of his whereabouts and sartorial excesses, and Labadie knew a break with Rome was inevitable. Leaving Toulouse, he made his way to Montauban with ecclesiastical and state authorities (the latter working at the behest of the former) hot on his tail. It was in this Protestant stronghold, where the small Catholic presence that existed was in disarray, that Labadie finally abjured on October 16, 1650. On the last day of the year his *Déclaration* appeared in print. In 1652 he would publish the *Seconde partie de la déclaration de Jean de Labadie . . . contenant le recueil des Vérités et des Maximes qu'il tenait et qu'il enseignait. . . . Pour servir de suite au Récit de son appel et de son affranchissement*, a most nonautobiographical sequel to the first declaration.

This short biographical sketch, intended to introduce this little-known figure and situate his autobiographical text in his life, indicates the extent to which Labadie was on the move, as well as in the public eye. He would establish himself in a given locality, garner popularity as a preacher, and then, inevitably, move on, from place to place, group to group. An extremely popular minister in Montauban until 1657, he eventually progressed through a series of cities, stirring up controversy in each community he joined and quit—in Orange, Geneva, Middelberg, Veere, Herford, and Altona, where he died in 1674. Labadie's relations with his followers, and with society at large, were never left to chance, but carefully mapped out. Labadie cultivated both approval and hostility; every persecution he endowed with meaning, recuperating it for his own benefit.[33]

His *Déclaration* constitutes just such an attempt at public relations. By the time of its publication in 1650, however, the genre to which Labadie's title is a clear reference had ceased to be practiced for over twenty years: the fall of La Rochelle in 1628 had signaled the end of the type of polemic that spawned the strikingly non-autobiographical declarations of conversion discussed above. Why Labadie might have chosen a title so evocative of ephemeral pamphlets surely forgotten at the time of his writing is not clear; what cannot fail to be noticed, however, is how, in adopting the anachronistic practice of the declaration of conversion, public and private would, by the mid-seventeenth century, play themselves out in much different ways than they had three or four decades earlier.

The first element of Labadie's reconfiguration of the genre involves the shift to a written mode of discourse. While practitioners of declarations of conversion early in the century pronounced their speeches before the church public, and were thus limited in terms of development by the amount of time their audience could be expected to listen, Labadie is quite clearly *writing* his life, for well over two hundred pages. Hence, he will make repeated references in the text not to an audience, but to his "reader." And the "avis au lecteur," written in the third person and explaining why the author has undertaken his project, is testimony to the fact that the shift Labadie is imparting to the genre is noticeable to the contemporary reader, for the question of whether his declaration should be written or oral is raised.[34] Labadie amends his original plans to "publier sa Déclaration de la langue et de la plume à la fois" (make the Declaration public both by tongue and pen) precisely because (reads the *avis*) an oral version would have been, of necessity, abridged, shorthand.[35]

Such shorthand—"obscure," "defective," "superficial," says the *avis*— no longer suits Labadie's purposes. Labadie does not want merely to illustrate the superiority of one church over another; in Habermasian terms, he is not interested in a representational publicness that seeks to provoke admiration or fear. Rather—and this is the *Déclaration*'s second innovation—he aims to provoke debate. In a revealing passage of his preface ("Avis aux vrais Fidèles"), Labadie argues for a form of polemic that allows the public the time to judge—time and judgment only possible for a *reading* public.

Je n'ai jamais vu qu'un cahier volant donnât connaissance de grande chose [*sic*], ou qu'il fit grande impression en courant. C'est bon à une Gazette de ne tenir pas plus d'une feuille, et à une chanson d'être lue et apprise en même moment: Un écrit de piété veut plus de temps, comme il en coûte aussi plus, et demande un lecteur aussi bien qu'un écrivain qui se donne du repos. Quand un pieux récit est trop court ou trop pressé, il ne donne ni contentement à ses amis, ni peine à ses ennemis. . . . Il est bon de donner aux uns de quoi ruminer, et se sustenter en paix, aux autres de quoi ronger, et se battre. (10–11)
(I never saw a broadsheet that provided knowledge of anything important or whose circulation made much of an impression. It is fine for a gazette not to have more than one sheet, and for a song to be read and learned in the same moment: but pious writing requires more time, just as it takes more to make it, and it demands a reader as well as a writer who grants himself leisure. When a pious story is too short or too hurried, it gives neither contentment to its friends nor pain to its enemies. . . . It is good to give to the former something to ruminate and to nourish themselves with in peace, to the latter something to gnaw on and to fight over.)

The "broadsheets" of which Labadie writes here may well be a reference to the declarations whose title he usurps even as he radically refigures their content and function. Religious polemic is no longer an exercise in admiration on the part of a theatrical public; it has become instead a matter for both individual reflection and debate (the imperatives to "ruminate" and to "fight").[36]

Although rumination leaves little trace on the historical record, there is substantial evidence of the debate provoked by Labadie's popular *Déclaration*.[37] Labadie's abjuration and declaration were certainly not the first of their kind to cause a public stir. Marco Antonio de Dominis published numerous texts on his conversions and provoked a heated polemic; and the conversion, in 1621, of François de Bonne, duc de Lesdiguières, although the object of no first person declaration, was responsible for the appearance of about a dozen texts over the following two years.[38] Yet Labadie's case stands out because he aims less to glorify his new religion than to vindicate himself before the eyes of a public that he endows with the power to hear his case. And vindication, Labadie's *Déclaration* suggests, can only come from the exposure of his own spiritual itinerary.

The shift from declaration-as-propaganda (where the convert is fully subsumed by the cause he serves) to declaration-as-personal-apology (where churches and their dogmas are exploited as an occasion to illustrate the exceptional — and no longer exemplary — trajectory of the individual) can best be perceived in Labadie's attempt to construct his public as a *tribunal* hearing personal evidence.[39] Absent from previous declarations of conversion, judicial terms appear with revealing frequency in the first pages of the "Avis aux vrais fidèles" — "tribunal" appears twice, "juge/juger/jugement" appear twelve times. Labadie inscribes a public which does not passively receive edifying discourse, but which is expected to pronounce on the case, and, moreover, to pronounce based on some sort of common experience. A public, Labadie maintains, must be qualified, possessing both the "science" (knowledge) and the "expérience" (3) that assure that his case be apprehended in its specificity: "qui est-ce qui accepte pour arbitre d'une affaire un homme qui ne l'entend pas?" (who accepts, as the arbiter of an affair, a man who does not understand it?) (4) he asks; "Je cherche un tribunal propre à mon affaire" (I seek a tribunal that is appropriate to my case) (5).

Significantly, Labadie predicates the understanding on the appeal not to general, synthetic, or doctrinal truth, but to what he calls "particularities," thereby modifying the overwhelming impersonality that characterized declarations of the first quarter of the century. Hence, any exposition of the elements of his faith must be preceded by an account of how he arrived at such positions by means of "un récit de mon Appel et de mon affranchissment" (a narrative of my Calling and of my liberation) (11). The *Déclaration* will reflect, according to the third-person "avis au lecteur," "son obligation de rendre un compte assez exact et de son coeur, et de son Appel, aussi bien que de sa doctrine et des ses sentiments" (his obligation to give a rather precise account both of his heart and of his Calling, as well as of his doctrine and his sentiments) (299). So while not discounting entirely the need for doctrinal justification, he relegates it to a subsequent, second part of the *Déclaration* (which would appear in 1652), and puts in its stead a rhetoric of divulgation. The terms he uses are staples of a culture of avowal, and the same ones that proliferated in the seventeenth century's reception of Augustine and Montaigne—"sincerity," the "heart," the "forced" exposure of the "hidden." Hence Labadie writes, for instance, "pour témoigner ma sincérité à mes vrais frères, et combien je désire marcher avec eux à coeur ouvert, n'ayant rien qui leur soit caché" (in order to prove to my true brothers my sincerity, and how much I desire to walk among them with an open heart, with nothing that is hidden from them) (53). His *Déclaration*'s sincerity, he writes elsewhere, "me for[ce] à rendre compte de la conduite que Dieu a daigné tenir sur moi" (forces me to give an account of the conduct that God has deigned to observe with me) (98)—and once again the notion of "force" accompanies the move into the autobiographical mode. Conversion, far from functioning as it had in previous declarations as transparent act or unambiguous signifier, must be authenticated through a rehearsal of its diachronic and particular causes. Only a life narrative can prove that his conversion is not, as he puts it, "l'oeuvre d'un jour" (the work of a single day): "Afin qu'il ne semble pas qu'en ne parlant qu'en général de mon affranchissement, je le veuille faire croire autre qu'il n'est, je me sens obligé d'en coucher ici des particularités" (So that it would not seem that, by speaking of my liberation in general terms, I was seeking to make it appear differently from what it is, I feel obliged to set down here some of its particularities) (51). Indeed, there is no such thing as a "general" or generic conversion.

Labadie's concern with the particular—and the very insistence with which Labadie returns to the notion of particularity seems to confirm what he thought of as its novelty—may well be an early sign of a more widespread enthusiasm that will take hold of readers in the second half of the century. Faith Beasley, for example, has traced the process by which a vogue for what was referred to as "particular history"—a history of individual people centering on secret actions and motives—would not only transform historiography but give birth to the modern, psychological novel.[40] Yet the curious thing about Labadie's text is that the rhetoric it so insistently puts into place is remarkably hollow. Perhaps the most revealing characteristic of the *Déclaration* consists of its limits, what the modern reader is even tempted to call its failures: his metatextual commentary provides the reader with a blueprint of a new kind of reading, but fails to construct a discourse commensurate with its plans. In general terms, we might observe, for instance, that if Labadie aims at "un compte assez exact de son coeur" (a rather precise account of his heart) (299) where "rien [ne] soit caché" (nothing would be hidden) (53), at the same time he constantly retreats from the exposure of particularities that he himself has prompted his reader to expect. "Je passe ici beaucoup de choses sous silence,

que la charité me fait désirer de n'être pas contraint de dire, et ensuite beaucoup de particularités, touchant les grâces que mon affranchissement doit à
Dieu, lesquelles j'ai sujet de croire que l'humilité Chrétienne, et que la bonté
de mes lecteurs, me dispensent de révéler" (I pass over in silence here many
things that charity makes me desire not to be forced to say, and many particularities as well which touch on the thanks that my liberation owes to God—
all of which I have grounds to believe that Christian humility, and the goodness of my readers, will spare me from revealing) (71). Or: "Il ne m'est pas
séant d'en dire les particularités" (it is not fitting for me to speak of its particularities) (89). And again: "je ne peux pas en dire toutes les particularités"
(I cannot tell of all these particularities) (118). He begins his account of his
break with the Jesuits, for instance, as follows: "Dieu faisant plusieurs coups
merveilleux de sa providence, pour conduire cette affaire de ce biais (lesquels
je serais trop long à déduire)" (God, through several marvelous strokes of
providence, in order to direct this affair in this way [and which it would take
too long to detail]) (120–21). Each time Labadie might choose to indicate
the exact circumstances surrounding an event, or the content of a mystical
revelation, he opts for vagueness.

A passage at the beginning of chapter 3—which commences with the
previously cited statement of intention "je me sens obligé d'en coucher ici
des particularités [i.e., of his liberation]" (I feel obliged to inscribe here some
of its particularities) (51)—furnishes a good example of how Labadie seems
to sense the imperative of autobiographical discourse and at the very same
time retreat from individuality into generality. After enumerating the benefits
of narrative exposition and several short remarks about his youth, Labadie
clearly seems to lose interest in the particular, saying of the reasons God chose
to protect him morally during his youth: "je ne [les] dirai que contraint" (I
will only tell [of them] if forced to) (57). Several pages further on, after a description of his apprenticeship in prayer, he backs off from the anecdotal particularities of his life more flagrantly still. He begins by limiting the amount
of personal anecdote he will provide his reader, "[n]'étant pas besoin que je
m'arrête à dire beaucoup de particularités qui pourraient causer de l'ennui à
un lecteur qui n'a pas besoin de les savoir" (there being no need for me to
stop to tell of many particulars that could cause boredom for a reader who
has no need to know them) (59). (One recalls the now-famous remark made
by Joseph Scaliger on Montaigne's excessive divulgations: Who cares if he
preferred white wine?) Labadie's text at once points to experience and yet
relegates it to the domain of the unsaid. Hence the particular cannot in fact be
revealed, or rather such revelation is unnecessary, for "il suffit qu'en déclarant

l'effet et la cause, sans en dire le moyen, je dis que tout se termina à m'attacher à Jésus-Christ, et me faire voir ces vérités des Ecritures" (declaring the effect and the cause, without saying the means, it suffices to say that everything ended by attaching me to Jesus Christ, and by making me see these truths of the Scriptures) (60). The "means" by which a disposition was arrived at—an individual itinerary of experience—is superfluous.

Superfluous, and yet the mere fact that Labadie might perceive the need to declare it so marks a departure from previous declarations of conversion— as if he were refusing the autobiographical logic that, perhaps unwittingly, he already obeyed. Labadie gestures toward a mode of writing that, in the man- ner editors claimed for Augustine's *Confessions*, substitutes heart for head, experience for doctrine, but ultimately turns away from using the tropes of interiority to ground his authority. In spite of brief appeals to a public that judges on the basis of shared experiences, Labadie derives his authority mainly from the concept of spiritual election, a concept that operates by pro- viding distance between writer and public. His spiritual gifts are best proved not by what he *can* say about them, but by what he *cannot*. Hence he makes a point of mentioning coming across esoteric books that taught him great mys- teries and secrets—and makes a point also of saying that the content of these books renders it impossible for him to reveal even the titles (99–100). Labadie is not tempted to voice this unsaid, to publicize it: he is in no way, he says, "obligé de découvrir tout ce que cette divine lumière me fit voir" (obliged to uncover everything this divine light made me see) (111). And unlike the dia- lectic of hiding and divulgation that characterized so much of the rhetoric of religious biographies of the day, here the unsaid is not in fact *unsayable*. Labadie might well provide more information, but he choses not to; and in that sense, his text does not present the reader with an effect of depth.

If describing a text by saying what it fails to be appears at first a bit per- verse and anachronistic, it bears keeping in mind that works such as Labadie's are flagrant hybrids, traversed by all manner of fissures which, in many cases, the authors themselves point up. Much the same might be said of most of the autobiographies considered in these pages—indeed, this is a point I shall return to in my concluding remarks. But the *Déclaration* of Labadie, half be- holden to the world of previous declarations, half participating in the im- pending order of autobiography, is a particularly intriguing case, something akin to an inconclusive mutation. One might note, for instance, that even Labadie's stated desire to separate narrative exposition from doctrinal expla- nation by publishing the *Déclaration* in two volumes is more apparent than real: out of approximately 300 pages, the first volume of the *Déclaration* contains only 110 which involve the so-called particularities of Labadie's life. (The rest are taken up by long enumerations of doctrinal points of contention and by digressions aimed at asserting the coherence of Labadie's teachings.) The autobiographies of Antoinette Bourignon and Jeanne Guyon are similarly shot through with false starts and uncertainties, but they do possess what Labadie only could hint at — the depth-creating sense of tension, maintained by the autobiographical text itself, between private and public selves.

Antoinette Bourignon's Secrets

Unlike Labadie, Antoinette Bourignon has received considerable attention — often less than flattering — from scholars of religious sects.[41] This attention is scant, however, compared to Bourignon's very successful efforts to attract the public eye during her own lifetime: even two decades after her death, she was still well-known enough to rate an article in Pierre Bayle's 1697 *Diction-naire historique*.[42] Her notoriety came mostly from her savvy manipulation of print, at a time when, virtually without exception, women depended on men for diffusion of their spiritual works. She was among the first European women to acquire a printing press for her own use (as opposed to, say, in-heriting one from a dead husband), and she put it to good use: her now ne-glected works, mostly consisting of polemical attacks against the "corrupt" Christian churches of her day, number some nineteen volumes and were widely diffused, in French and in translation, in France, Germany, Holland, and England. She even left two autobiographical narratives, so that all might know her better. Like Labadie's *Déclaration*, the *Vie intérieure (La Parole de Dieu)* (1663, published 1683) and the *Vie extérieure de Dam[oise]lle Antoinette Bourignon* (1668, published 1683) are texts written by someone who realized the power devolving from access to and mastery of the public sphere, even as her religious beliefs emphasized the importance of private experience to the exclusion of its institutional counterpart.

Antoinette Bourignon was born in 1616 to a well-off family from Lille. Her father, of Italian origin (Borignoni), was a prosperous merchant; her Flemish mother, Marguerite Becquart, came to the union with her own wealth. Both destined their daughter for a good marriage and social integra-tion, and yet from her earliest years Bourignon showed ample indications of a reclusive nature. She herself, in her *Vie extérieure*, isolated as the cause for a general sensation of ostracism and marginality a facial deformation (sub-sequently corrected by surgery) that instilled in her mother a long-lasting aversion for the third of her five children. The religious impulse served an obviously compensatory function: God would make up for the mother's lack of love. But Bourignon's piety was a solitary affair; long hours were spent reading saints' lives; and by the age of eighteen, she herself had experienced the visions, voices, and ecstasies she found in her books. In 1635, Saint Augustine appeared to her, ordering her to reestablish his order in its original purity.

When she was twenty, a marriage was arranged between Bourignon and a rich French merchant. Bourignon, who from an early age had conceived a particular aversion for the carnal state of marriage, fled from the city on Easter day 1636 dressed as a hermit. She was soon discovered, and persuaded to return to Lille on the promise that marriage would no longer be discussed. In 1640, however, her parents broke that promise and tried to get her to agree to a suitor; Bourignon again left Lille. She went to Mons, in Belgium, where the archbishop recognized her spiritual potential and granted her two unusual favors: that she be allowed to read the Gospels and to establish a small, self-sustaining community for pious women in the countryside. Meanwhile, however, staying in a Jesuit-run convent, Bourignon formed increasingly strident opinions as to the corruption of the clergy, and tried to win over some of her hosts. The archbishop got wind of her proselytizing and revoked the permission to establish the rural community of women. Already Bourignon had been caught between her desire for reclusion and her impulse to disseminate her reformist convictions.

Bourignon, forced to flee Mons, made several short sojourns in the general area, returning at least once to Lille upon the death of her mother in 1644. This period of her life was relatively low-key; she did little proselytizing, composed some pious songs while earning a living as a lace-maker, and wrote one treatise, apparently lost, *La Vie solitaire*, where she endeavored to prove that "la vie solitaire est la plus parfaite de toutes les vies" (the solitary life is the most perfect life of all).[43] Yet the solitary life was doubled by another, more engaged one. In these years, Bourignon was busy with lawsuits, attempting to secure her rights to her mother's inheritance. It was also at this time that she accepted the direction of a children's hospice in Lille, Notre-Dame-des-Sept-Douleurs, in 1653. Five years later, although still in charge of the orphanage, she took her vows in an Augustinian order, and obtained permission to live apart, as a recluse.

A case of possession at the orphanage eventually put an end to the harmony between solitude and social work. Various suspicions about her intent and abilities circulated in Lille, and a general uproar made her flee to

Flanders, where she spent the years between 1662 and 1667. From this point Bourignon would relentlessly put herself in the public eye, spurred on by the conviction that God had finally directed her to speak and to make herself known: " '*Le temps est venu de parler: déclarez-vous, et vous faites connaître. Ne tenez plus mes desseins en silence*' " (*"The time has come to speak: declare yourself and make yourself known. Hold my intentions in silence no longer"*) are the words in which she casts the divine imperative.[44] It was in Malines that she attracted her first followers, foremost among them Amatus Coriache (later vicar-general of the Oratory in Malines), Christian de Cort (superior of the Oratory), and Pierre Noëls (a scholar who had been the secretary of Cornelius Jansen). In 1663, at the behest of Coriache and Cort, she wrote her first major work, which was also her autobiography—*La Parole de Dieu, ou La Vie intérieure*.[45] During these years, her opposition to Rome, formulated in treatises with titles such as *Le Tombeau de la fausse théologie* and *L'Académie des savants théologiens*, became increasingly pronounced. Her criticisms, however, were not those of a Protestant; she was unacquainted with the teachings of the Reformed Church and later Protestants would typically charge her with being a Romanist. The followers mentioned above were all men of the Roman Church, to which Bourignon would profess a vague allegiance until her death.

Although there was a certain religious freedom in Belgium, Bourignon had to leave for Holland to secure the circulation of her writings, still in manuscript as of 1667 when she moved to Amsterdam. The years from 1667 to 1671 marked the high point of Bourignon's sway over her disciples. She earned the esteem of important figures such as the anatomist Swammerdam, Johannes Amos Comenius (the noted Moravian educationist who was later invited by a fledgling Harvard University to act as its president), and a young disciple of Descartes, Pierre Poiret;[46] even Labadie reportedly tried to secure Bourignon as an ally. She embarked on the second version of her *Life*, posthumously labeled *La Vie extérieure*.[47] And she started to publish, procuring her own printing press as well as availing herself of the services of professional publishers.

If she left Belgium in order to become more of a public figure, at the same time she aimed at increased insularity, and in the most literal sense: she wanted to establish a small community on the island of Noordstrand.[48] Amsterdam itself was planned as just a stopover. Yet from the start, her project seemed cursed. Christian de Cort, who had organized the purchase of the island under the aegis of a company in which Bourignon was a stockholder, proved to be an incompetent manager, and finally was thrown into prison. Bourignon, though a seeker of reclusion, recognized the importance of public opinion, and thus penned a vindication of Cort, *L'Innocence reconnue*, which in fact secured his release. On his way to Noordstrand, however, Cort died of an apparent poisoning, leaving his estate — which consisted mainly of debts involving the island — to Bourignon, who was now legally responsible for a piece of land looking rapidly less attractive. Wrangling with the authorities over the Noordstrand debacle would continue until her death. In the end, Bourignon never set foot on the island of her dreams.

Significantly, Bourignon again recognized that her private cause could be fueled by appeal to the public, and brought out collections of her letters and treatises, including *Le Témoignage de vérité*, a two-volume compendium of attestations by numerous personalities as to her merits and honesty. Ultimately these efforts came to naught, and she had to abandon the island project. This whole last period of her life — from 1671, when she left Amsterdam on account of conflicts (mainly financial and not doctrinal) with the clergy of the city, to 1680, when she died, emblematically, in flight from improbable calumny (she had been accused of torturing an eight-year-old) — was thus torn between the drive for solitude and a constant need for public engagement, be it legal or apostolic. When they were not confiscated by authorities worried by her proselytizing, her printing presses were in continuous use; like Labadie, Bourignon knew how to use print for her own self-defense.

Unlike Labadie, however, Bourignon did more than graft a contemporary language of avowal onto a series of doctrinal justifications; to use Rousseau's ambiguous term, she was fully "personalized." Both the *Vie intérieure* and the *Vie extérieure* tell of her belief in her own development — they retrace the history of her personality. Narrative, Bourignon takes care to explain, is necessary because her past actions are not transparent. Isolated events cannot be pronounced upon, and today's action cannot be properly evaluated without taking into account factors contained in the past. Bourignon writes, she says,

afin de donner à entendre simplement et par ordre par quelle voie [Dieu] m'a mené[e] pour arriver à ses prétentions . . . . Car si j'avais simplement dit les diverses connaissances qu'il m'a données sur la réforme de l'église seulement, l'on aurait trouvé de la contradiction en plusieurs endroits; parce que me voyant tantôt prête à me marier; tantôt hermite; lors dans un Cloître; par après retourner au monde; puis en la solitude; après dans les tracas; de là au reclusage; et après, dehors: l'on ferait de tout cela une conclusion par l'esprit humain: ce qui est pourtant une conduite divine bien particulière. (VI 126)
(so as to make known, simply and with order, the ways by which [God] led me to the

goals he set for me . . . . For if I had simply stated the various kinds of knowledge he gave me about the reform of the church alone, there would have been contradictions in several places; because in seeing me at one time ready to be married; at another a hermit; then in a Cloister; after that returning to the world; then in solitude; afterwards in difficulties; from there in a place of seclusion; and after that, out in the open: the human mind would reach its own conclusion about what was essentially a matter of singular divine guidance)

Only through the retrospective lens of autobiography can one perceive the coherence underlying what are otherwise discontinuous, contradictory, unreadable acts. The "human mind" is incapable of temporal synthesis, while autobiography is a God-like lens through which one can perceive the common thread running through an existence whose complexity overflows any exemplar. A passage such as this one takes aim at one of the prime topoi of hagiography, to wit, the essential similarity of a saint's actions, be they done as a child, youth, or adult — a similarity that perfectly reflects the atemporality of spiritual attainment.

The chronological view of her life can, as in this last passage, merely serve to highlight God's ever-present intention. As Frank Paul Bowman has written, "[a]utobiography is for her a means of using the word to create an accord between intent and event, between the will of God and the acts of man, giving the self coherence and making it inhere in the divine plan."[49] Elsewhere, however, Bourignon seems more interested in the development of her personality; autobiography consists in the perceiving of an "enchaînement," or chain of associations, as Rousseau will insist.[50] Let us take, for example, a remarkable passage on her childhood, existing only in the *Vie extérieure*, in which Bourignon attempts to locate the origin of her religious sentiment in the events of her earliest years.

Lorsque je vins au monde j'étais si défigurée que ma mère pensait d'avoir enfanté un monstre, à cause que j'avais des cheveux noirs jusques aux yeux, lesquels couvraient tout mon front, et ma lèvre d'en haut était attachée à mon nez, et par ainsi la bouche [était] ouverte . . . . [M]a mère ne pouvait oublier l'aversion qu'elle avait eue de ma difformité, et ne me pouvait aimer comme elle faisait ses autres enfants. (VE 143)
(When I came into the world I was so disfigured that my mother thought she had given birth to a monster, because I had black hair down to my eyes, covering my entire forehead, and my upper lip was attached to my nose, so that my mouth stayed open . . . . My mother could not forget the aversion she had had to my deformity, and could not love me as she did her other children.)

Few passages in pre-Rousseauian autobiography can match this one for a sense of how psychological trauma is generative of personality, and nothing here pins Bourignon's religious destiny on divine predestination. It is, rather, purely human: lack of love, which Bourignon labels a "persecution," makes her turn first to games and dolls, then, upon attaining the age of reason, to God. Later she will locate the origin of her vanity in this same rejection by her mother: "Je commençais aussi à me plaire aux louanges et estimes des hommes, parce qu'ils me disaient que j'étais belle et agréable, où ma mère m'avait toujours appelée laide" (I began thus to take pleasure in the praise and esteem of men, because they told me I was beautiful and attractive, while my mother had always called me ugly) (VE 146). This is self-analysis in the modern sense of the term.

By means of narrative unfolding, Bourignon can portray her life as a progressive liberation from blanket moral and devotional precepts. Unlike autobiographers writing in a conventual milieu, Bourignon does not dwell on her mortifications, for example. Although she admits a certain efficacy on their part, they do not liberate her, or unite her with God (VI 10); at a certain point, God reveals to her that mortification belongs to the realm of appearances (VI 44). More important, here, is her relation to charity. At first, Bourignon makes great efforts to conform to the stereotype of the *femme charitable*: she gives alms, and pushes her self-effacement to the point of sacrificing the linen intended for herself (VI 23). Later, a visit to the poor and sick leaves her feeling appropriately *dévote* (VI 29). Yet she comes to find only hypocrisy under this veneer of charity; after a year of following the rules, her disposition changes: "Je commençai . . . d'avoir un dégoût des pauvres, parce qu'ils sont trompeurs, et ne rendent point grâces à Dieu du bien qu'on leur fait; ains s'en servent souvent à des plus grands péchés" (I began . . . to feel disgust for the poor, because they are deceitful, and give no thanks to God for the good done them; indeed, they even use it for the greatest sins) (VI 30). Bourignon's reasoning on charity has been one of her character traits most mocked over the last three centuries, but it illustrates well why these texts read something like a spiritual *bildungsroman*: Bourignon learns that, if the ideal of poverty is good (in leaving her father's house she throws away her last penny, trusting entirely to God), nevertheless wealth that "befell" her, in the form of an inheritance, was not to be refused, but used (cf. VE 140) — notably for the building of a convent where undowered girls could live out their religious vocation.[51]

This education at the hands of experience leads Bourignon to conclude that her spiritual interests do *not* lie in a refusal of the secular world and its institutions. In spite of her urge to live as a recluse, to shun a corrupt world, Bourignon's autobiographies show her constantly overcoming the temptation of solitude, and insist on her competence in worldly matters. Bourignon sees no contradiction, for example, in having both a head for business and a soul devoted to God.[52] Speaking of her bedridden father, she says: "Je tenais son livre, et gouvernais son ménage à son souhait . . . . [A]u déçu de ses enfants, il se maria secrètement avec une femme qui n'était nullement de sa sorte, ni propre à aucunes de ses affaires" (I kept his registers, and governed his household as he wished. . . . To the disappointment of his children, he secretly married a woman who was in no way his type, nor fit for any of his business) (VE 179).[53] So, instead of fleeing society, Bourignon will constantly use its institutions to combat her marginalization. Indeed, for mystic autobiography, Bourignon's *Lives* contain a surprising number of references to lawsuits. First, she sues her father for her share of her recently deceased mother's estate, although her father contests and she ends up having to drop the affair (VI 62–63). Then, upon her father's death, she sues her mother-in-law for her share of the estate; after a year and a half of legal wrangling, she is finally successful (VI 67–68). Finally, when a Tartuffe-type by the name of Saint-Saulieu, rebuffed upon asking for her hand in marriage, starts stalking her and threatening to take her by violence, Bourignon again has recourse to the law to protect both her person and her reputation, much maligned by rumors circulated by her aggressor (VI 78).

Bourignon's two autobiographies both build up to the acceptance of her own authority, of her mission, of her own obligation to be in the public eye. God makes it clear to her that the cultivation of her solitude is a spiritual dead end.

Je disais: "Laissez-moi aller dans le désert, seule, pour pleurer mes péchés et ceux du monde." [Dieu] me mena dans un petit parterre, où je fus renserrée, avec lui seul comme dans une forteresse bien simple et nette, où je sentis un parfait contentement et repos. Je lui dis: "Demeurerai-je ici toujours." Il se retira de moi comme avec dédain. Et de trois mois je ne sentis plus sa présence amiable. (VI 105)
(I said: "Let me go into the desert, alone, to grieve for my sins and for those of the world." [God] led me into a courtyard, where I was closed up with him alone as in a fortress that was plain and clean, in which I felt a perfect contentment and repose. I said to him: "Would that I remain here always." He withdrew from me as though in disdain. And for three months I did not feel his amiable presence.)

After this lesson, the contradiction between engagement and solitude dissolves. "[I]l me fut dit: *Ne voyez-vous point que vous êtes dans la solitude désirée, à l'abri de vos ennemis?*" (It was said to me: *Can you not see that you are in the solitude you desired, sheltered from your enemies?*) (VI 118). The transcendent solitude she had erroneously situated outside of herself, in an endlessly elusive elsewhere, turns out to be immanent, always already there. From this moment Bourignon can no longer resist what she terms "la Vie Evang-élique" (the Evangelical Life) (VI 108). She is propulsed into the world. The *Vie intérieure* ends in a succession of commands: "*Arrête ici. Il faut parachever mon oeuvre*" (*Stop here. My work must be completed*) (VI 111); "*Faites-vous ré-tablir et justifer*" (*Reestablish and justify yourself*) (VI 113); and finally "*Ecri-vez, écrivez*" (*Write, write*) (VI 117). Diegetically Bourignon does not heed these commands; she obeys, rather, by writing the text whose genesis is its own subject—her *Lives*. It is in her access to print that Bourignon furnishes the best example of this very engagement.

There is, however, a complication in reading the *Lives* as texts of engage-ment. Given that the *Vie intérieure* and the *Vie extérieure* openly proclaim their apologetical status and recount Bourignon's move into the public eye, the paradox of their having remained unpublished during her lifetime mer-its elucidation. Why did Bourignon turn from the *Vie intérieure* in 1663 to the composition of the polemic theology that would make up most of her work? Why did she turn again to autobiography several years later, only to leave the *Vie extérieure* incomplete? Why, when her texts finally started to see the light of day in 1669, did she ignore the two *Lives*? Why, in other words, did Bourignon not become a John Bunyan, who published his phenomenally successful *Grace Abounding to the Chief of Sinners* in 1666?

The answer to this riddle is hidden in the *Lives* themselves, strewn as they are with indications of tension and conflict over the autobiographical project. The first clue is thematic, and derives from Bourignon's insistence on the ideal of rest ("repos"): with little exaggeration one could say that both these autobiographies are essentially structured around meditations on unwanted and uncontrollable publicity. Two representative examples will suffice. First, Bourignon includes in the body of the *Vie intérieure* a short "Colloque de l'âme avec Dieu" (Colloquy of the soul with God) that she had written at the behest of Father du Bois, superior of the Oratory in Maubeuge. The compo-sition of the "Colloque" is, moreover, the will of God, who tells a hesitant Bourignon: "*Déclarez-le. Je donnerai poids à vos paroles*" (*Declare it. I will give weight to your words*) (VI 45). Bourignon, however, worried over the content of a text that is, after all, highly critical of Church corruption, soon realizes that its use is distressingly out of her hands. "Je mis ce billet entre les mains du Père du Bois, croyant qu'il en userait discrètement: mais la chose fut bientôt divulguée à tous" (I placed this note in the hands of Father du Bois, believ-ing that he would make discreet use of it: but the matter was soon divulged to all). Father du Bois's indiscretion brings down upon Bourignon various threats from the clergy; yet the priest, confronted, is unrepentant: "De quoi j'avais du mécontentement contre le Père du Bois, qui avait si libéralement publié ces choses. Il me dit que cela ne me touchait" (All of which made me upset with Father du Bois, who had so liberally published these things. He answered that it was none of my business) (VI 48). Publicity, here, signals the limit of Bourignon's control of the circulation of her opinions, opinions which, once out of her hands, turn into misrepresentations.

The second example concerns the power of gossip, which again evokes the inherent uncontrollability of the public domain. Bourignon, whose chastity was a large part of her personage (Pierre Bayle joked in his *Dictionnaire* that she made such show of her sexual morals that he referred to her "virginité pénétrative," or penetrating virginity),[54] portrays numerous assaults on her virtue, most notably the case of the aforementioned Saint-Saulieu, who uses threats of calumny to secure his wants. Still another suitor takes exactly the same approach.

[V]oyant qu'il ne gagnait rien, il résolut de publier qu'il se mariait avec moi. Ce qui fut fait si dextrement, qu'en moins d'une heure toute la ville de Lille en fut servie. Un chacun en parlait avec mépris; qu'après avoir témoigné tant de dévotion, je me mariais. . . . Il fallut que les Predicateurs publiasse qu'il n'en était rien. Cependant je me tenais serrée dans ma clusette, sans savoir ce qui se disait dans la ville. (VI 65)
(Seeing that he was getting nowhere, he resolved to announce that he was going to marry me. This was done so skillfully that in less than an hour the whole city of Lille had heard of it. Everyone spoke with contempt of the fact that after showing so much devotion I was getting married. . . . Finally the Preachers had to proclaim that this was all nonsense. Meanwhile I kept myself closed up in my little cell, without knowing what was being said in the city.)

This "clusette"—an unattested word that Bourignon most likely derives from the "reclusage" (place of reclusion) where she was staying—furnishes an appropriate locus for a subject limited or hemmed in ("serrée") by uncontrollable public discourse about her person. Bourignon repeatedly shows the public domain to be a source of power, but it is a reversible, potentially hostile power that can as easily devolve to others as to herself.

Damaging rumors abound, texts circulate without authorization, and the persecution of publicity seems to dog each apostolic move Bourignon makes. It is against this backdrop—the danger publicity poses to the private subject—that Bourignon's autobiographies beg to be read, since they constitute as much a defensive response to unwanted publicity as a positive declaration of principles. For isolated rumors are not the only danger Bourignon faces. When she is arrested following the outbreak of possession at the orphanage she has been running, she finds her entire life the object of *legal* discourse: "[Les magistrats] ordonnèrent qu'information fût tenue de *toute ma vie*, et particulièrement de ma régence" ([The magistrates] ordered that information be collected about *my whole life*, and particularly about my direction [of the orphanage]) (VI 88, my emphasis). The magistrates send out their spies in Lille and to neighboring towns, collecting stories about Bourignon. The result, according to her, was positive: the court clerk reassured her, saying "n'en faites point davantage: il y en a bientôt assez pour vous canoniser" (don't worry any more about it: there will soon be enough to canonize you) (VI 89).[55] Even flattering, however, the life story thus produced is no longer the property of Bourignon, as she soon discovers. She tells of her response to the clerk: "Je croyais avoir droit là-dessus; mais l'on me dit, que je ne l'aurais point; qu'on ne me demandait rien" (I assumed I had rights over it; but I was told that I wouldn't get it back, and that they weren't asking for my opinion) (VI 89). This last phrase recalls the "cela ne me touchait" of Father du Bois: Bourignon thinks that her relation to a given text — either as its author or its subject — gives her some measure of control over it, but she is soon disabused. Hence public attention to her person is ultimately alienating; searches are made, dossiers filled, and yet this composite portrait, equated with the subject, escapes the subject.

In writing her autobiography, Bourignon is not just freely providing information about herself, "going public" about her God-given mission; she is also responding to a situation in which biographical information is systematically being collected on the part of hostile parties. The *Lives* lead the reader into a confrontation with the particular methods used by modern society — law, government, press — to control its subjects: the documentation of the individual. In *Discipline and Punish*, Foucault has explained how, starting in the seventeenth century, networks of writing were deployed (via techniques such as exams) in order to control individuals, to capture them "in a whole mass of documents."[56] This web of biographical information inevitably displaces criteria of judgment from the impersonal to the personal: it furnishes every person with an inescapable identity, grounded in the biographical, rather than a more fluid identity (if one can still call it that) based upon alliance with the proclamations of this or that authority. Hence, the question asked about the individual is no longer "How do his or her beliefs situate him or her with regard to an accepted tradition?" but rather "What do the details of this person's life tell us about who he or she really is?" So if narrative, unlike doctrinal argument, can convey a sense of change or evolution, it also has additional implications regarding how the guilt or innocence of the subject is decided.

The elaborate autobiographical apologetics of someone like Bourignon result, then, from a certain configuration of historical circumstances—the moment when law starts to colonize, as it were, biographical and narrative territory. The general judicial feel of this text continually reminds the reader that it is the product of a pseudo-legal inquiry on a par with the biographical searches of the magistrates. The judicial context is evident from the very start in a letter written by the Vicar General of Malines, Coriache, recounting how he had asked her to write the *Vie intérieure*—a letter accompanying the manuscript when the latter was sent to another follower of Bourignon's, and chosen by Pierre Poiret to serve as a preface for the *Lives*: "J'ajoute que comme j'ai été autrefois versé dans les choses du droit et du barreau, et que je me souviens encore de ses règles et de ses lois, j'ai voulu pénétrer jusque dans le fond de tout, et prendre les choses dès leur première source, désirant pour ce sujet qu'elles soient couchées par écrit" (I would add that as I used to be versed in matters of the bar, and since I still remember its rules and laws, I wanted to penetrate to the depths of everything and grasp things at their remotest source, desiring for this purpose that they be put into writing) (VI n.p.). Coriache goes on to say that the results of his inquiry leave something to be desired, "car [Bourignon] y a passé sous silence le temps de son enfance" (for [Bourignon] passed over in silence the period of her childhood).[57] In short, she has not told all, and Coriache implores his fellow reader of the *Vie intérieure* to help him uncover the whole truth: "[I]nsistez avec moi qu'elle ne nous cache pas ces choses" (Join me in insisting that she not hide these things from us).

Both parties, be they Bourignon's accusers or herself and her defenders, take essentially the same position on the judicial equation of the guilt or innocence of the subject with her life story. Bourignon, as much as the magistrates, finds that her eventual justification (or condemnation) hinges not on the debating of doctrinal points, but rather on self-exhibition. From both perspectives, doctrine and individual revelation are of secondary importance; there must be established in the life of the speaker the authoritative ground that will give meaning to what would otherwise be the empty terms of a scholastic dispute. Life and teaching enjoy a transparent relation: according to Christian de Cort, one of the followers who, with Coriache, had originally asked her to write her life: "Elle parle comme elle vit; et elle vit comme elle parle" (She speaks as she lives; and she lives as she speaks) (VI n.p.). Or as Bourignon herself says: "Si ma vie et mes actions sont contraires à mes paroles, ne tenez rien de tout ce que je dis; mais, si elles ne le sont, suivez-les" (If my life and my actions are contrary to my words, then do not believe anything I say; but if they are not, then follow them) (VI 131).

One should note that what is involved here differs greatly from a traditional hagiographic viewpoint, in which actions are manifestations of inner
virtue. With Bourignon, who one is — and this is now a function not of miracles or saintly actions, but of the systematic exposure of one's temporal life,
even in its financial aspects — determines the value of one's ideas. In religious
matters, this is hardly common sense. When, in the 1690s, Fénelon defended
Jeanne Guyon against charges of Quietism, made no appeals to Guyon's biography, but sought to show that her teachings were in line with those of mystics who had been sanctioned by the Church. This was a perfectly logical
line of defense, given that theologians had traditionally assumed that correct belief — orthodoxy — produced correct behavior — orthopraxis. Yet, as I
shall show shortly, in spite of Fénelon's efforts to cast debate over Guyon
as a question of doctrine, his tactics were distinctly rear-guard, for Guyon's
enemy Bossuet had already decided to discredit Guyon's doctrine with information culled from her autobiography. Hence, the behavior itself of the
individual was becoming the target of both ecclesiastical and secular attention, as a subtle transformation reversed traditional assumptions: orthopraxis
now guaranteed orthodoxy.

In Bourignon's writings this turn is already evident, and, as will be the
case with Guyon, it lies at the heart of the autobiographical project. Bourignon begins her second autobiography, the *Vie extérieure*, with a preamble,
stating with disgust that the human spirit has been so conquered by the devil
that "les hommes de maintenant ne se veulent rendre à la vérité par des raisons . . . convaincantes" (men nowadays do not want to accept the truth
through convincing reasoning). Instead, she laments, "il faut leur élargir des
choses grossières et matérielles, pour les faire croire à la vérité" (one must
magnify coarse and material things in order to make them believe the truth)
(VE 139). The opposition, then, is between "reasons" and "things." One might
well expect indignation at having to parade "coarse and material" proof to
be followed by accounts of miracles or stigmata, and yet this is not the issue.
Bourignon is speaking not of displaying the transparent signs of her election,
but rather her behavior itself: "[Le diable] tâche de jeter dans le[s] entende-
ments [des hommes de maintenant] quelques doutes ou arrières-pensées de
ma personne, laquelle n'est pas connue des étrangers, quoiqu'elle le soit très-
bien de ceux de ma patrie, qui ont été témoins oculaires de tous mes com-
portements" ([The devil] has been trying to put into people's minds doubts
or second thoughts about my person, which is not known by foreigners,
though it is well known by the people of my homeland, who have been
eye-witnesses to my actions) (VE 139–40). The evocation of "eye-witnesses"

underlines once again the judicial subtext of the *Lives*, as did the passage on the investigations of the court clerk of Lille, and Coriache's letter.

Both Labadie and Bourignon were messianic personalities, anointed ones, channels for God's will and words. Yet Labadie, notwithstanding a rhetorical recourse to the "particularities" of his life, ultimately derived his authority from what he would *not* say about himself. Bourignon, by contrast, almost seems to belong to a different world, one in which accusers and accused meet on the common ground of the biographical. She concludes her preamble by speaking of her detractors as follows: "[J]e leur veux bien déclarer *qui je suis, ou* [*sic*] *j'ai été, et d'où je viens*: afin qu'un chacun se puisse informer de ma personne à son apaisement" (I want indeed to declare to them *who I am, or who I have been, and where I come from*: so that anyone can be informed about my person to his satisfaction) (VE 142, emphasis in the original). One could scarcely hope for a more readable sign of the coupling of being and life narrative: when Bourignon moves from "who I am" to "or who I have been" and "where I am from" she essentially replaces the static self with a diachronic one. Related to this slippage is, as has been noted, the failure of specific beliefs or credos to define individuals or to authorize those individuals to speak. This is indeed the gist of Pierre Poiret's explanation, in his *Vie continuée*, as to why Bourignon returned to autobiography after the numerous treatises composed during between 1663 and 1668:

[E]lle remarqua que la plupart de ceux qui venaient la voir, quoique d'ailleurs ils fussent assez convaincus de la vérité des choses divines qu'elle proposait, cherchaient néanmoins à se dispenser d'y correspondre . . . par des considérations personnelles et étrangères, comme de dire que quoique cela fût bon, au reste ils ne connaissaient pas cette fille, et ne savaient qui elle était, d'où elle venait, ni ce qu'elle prétendait.[58]
(She noticed that most of those who came to see her, although in every other respect quite convinced of the truth of the divine things she proposed, were seeking nevertheless to spare themselves from conforming to them . . . out of personal and foreign considerations, saying for instance that, although this was all well and good, they nevertheless were unacquainted with this girl, and did not know who she was, where she was from, nor what her intentions were.)

Hence the operative criterion of judgment put forth by all concerned — Bourignon, her followers, *and* her enemies — is encapsulated in the question: Who is speaking? And it is this criterion that is foremost in Bourignon's mind whenever she attempts to think through the autobiographical act. Having already thought of the obvious objection to writing one's life — "que c'était un orgueil de déclarer soi-même les faveurs et les grâces qu'on reçoit de Dieu" (that is was prideful to declare for oneself the favors and graces received from

God)—she counters it by asserting that the identity of author and subject where biography is concerned is absolutely crucial: "Là-dessus j'ai pensé qu'il vaut mieux en dire soi-même la vérité, que de souffrir qu'elle soit mal rapportée [par un autre], comme il est arrivé à moi-même que les choses que j'avais dites ont été transportées tout autrement qu'elles n'étaient, et avec un sens tout contraire" (Regarding this, it occurred to me that it is much better to speak the truth of this oneself than to suffer it being wrongly reported [by another], as it happened to me when things I had said were communicated completely differently from what they were, and with the opposite meaning) (VI 126—bracketed contents in Poiret's original edition). The truth of the subject must be spoken by the subject and only by the subject, or, put differently, the biographical subject is her own best authority, so much so that she feels herself propulsed into authorship.

The paradox of Bourignon's situation, however, is that any authentic individuality is ultimately inseparable from its negative counterpart, which seems even to precede it. Deprived of the right to her own life story, and "scandalized" (VI 90) at having a judicial search made against her biographical person, Bourignon will seek, through autobiography, to resignify a legal discourse aiming at her own constitution as a subject. In other words, if Bourignon is the center of a proliferation of discourse about her person, she can master it by recourse to autobiography.[59] But the authority she claims for the first-person discourse of experience is precarious or even potentially painful: nothing guarantees that, in the manner of her purloined "Colloque de l'âme avec Dieu" and the magistrates' biographical report on her conduct, it will not be the subject of further public misunderstanding, further personalities. Whence Bourignon's bind: she finds herself having been forced to write in her own defense a private text that she cannot bring herself to diffuse, precisely because she would then consent to operating on the terrain of her adversaries.

Bourignon's treatment of a central trait of early autobiography—the topos of obedience—emerges as especially significant given an atmosphere laden with the menace and promise embodied by biographical proof. From nuns to Jansenists to secular memorialists, nearly anyone writing in the first-person in the seventeenth century justifies his or her act through reference to an originary demand. Scholars have often noted the trait, and attributed it to a fear of Christian impropriety, or to aristocratic reluctance to engage in the bourgeois task of writing. Certainly there must be some truth to the explanation, but one might hazard another one, one more historically grounded: these repeated justifications suggest that the self-authorizing nature of the

"I"—the autobiographical mentality—was not quite in place, that even as the biographical was assuming colossal importance, the "auto-" needed some sort of crutch or alibi. For even in the case of Bourignon, who broke the confessional link and admitted no superior, this basic narrative-producing structure nonetheless remains in place: she claims she had first thought it pride to write of herself, but upon solicitation from Coriache and other followers, consented (VI 126). The distinguishing feature of Bourignon's use of the topos, however, stems from the experience of publicity's uncontrollability: Bourignon refuses to relinquish control over her life story. Whereas standard practice in the Church, for autobiographical works as much as for any other, was to leave questions of use, diffusion, and publication to one's superiors, Bourignon asks not only for a promise of secrecy, but for the return of her manuscript: "sous cette promesse de secret, je vous le mets en main, ce mois d'octobre 1663, avec promesse de me le rendre après que vous en aurez vos apaisements" (under this promise of secrecy, I place it in your hands, this month of October 1663, with the promise that you will return it to me after you are satisfied with it) (VI 130).[60] At issue, then, as she terminates her first autobiography, is the control of its circulation. Bourignon decides that her "communications particulières avec Dieu" (private communications with God)—that is, the stuff of the *Vie intérieure*—should be reserved for a small circle of "amis secrets que Dieu choisira" (secret friends whom God will choose), and speaks in terms of a "treasure" that she must keep under wraps for fear of "thieves" (VI 130). Bourignon might initiate her autobiography at the behest of others, but she ends up the owner of her own work.

Moreover, she was serious enough about the threats of publicity not to publish her *Lives*. It is indeed remarkable that even a writer who so cannily made use of print for both self-promotion and self-defense shied away from publishing her autobiographies. Remarkable, but perhaps not surprising, given that the two texts in question insistently thematized the difficulties presented by the new biographical order. Yet this order was more, too, than a theme, in the sense that Bourignon's *Lives* demonstrate the extent to which autobiography might be said to have emerged as a *symptom* of public-private tension. Publicity, willed or unwanted, is present not as one narrative element among many, but rather as the trace of the originary rift that the texts attempt—unsuccessfully—to mend.

One can understand, then, Bourignon's autobiographical modesty; but even more understandable, given her attempts at secrecy, was the delectation with which the *Lives* would eventually be published. When Pierre Poiret incorporates them as the lead volume of Bourignon's collected works, he will play up their secret history, much in the way the biographers examined in Chapter 2 highlighted the fortuitous rarity of the first-person texts they brought to their readers attention. The *Lives* are, Poiret writes, composed of "precious" things she dared not write until forced to by God and man. "[E]t après qu'elle les eut écrites," he continues, "c'était la pièce secrète entre ses intimes, dont nul ne pouvait faire la lecture, et encore moins la communiquer à quelque personne de bonne volonté, sans la permission expresse, qu'elle n'accordait pas à tous" (and after she had written them, they became the secret object of her intimates, which none of them could read, never mind lend to some person of good will, without express permission, which she did not grant to everyone).[61] That the text of her autobiographies confirms her reluctance to expose herself — "se produire" (literally, producing oneself) is the revealing verb used by Poiret[62] — only makes easier still the editor's task of giving value to the works. By dint of Bourignon's irresolvable dialectic of exposure and secrecy, her *Lives* become not one text among many, but, Poiret writes, "la clef de tous ses ouvrages" (the key to all her works).[63] Antoinette Bourignon may not have published her two secret texts, but the logic and attraction of autobiography had become irresistible.

Jeanne Guyon and the Rigors of Publicity

Like Bourignon, Jeanne Bouvier de la Motte-Guyon found herself under the scrutiny of a hostile public's eye. Nothing in her early years, however, would have lead one to suspect the future celebrity which permitted, indeed solicited, the undertaking of an eight-hundred-odd page narration of the details of her existence — *La Vie de Madame Guyon écrite par elle-même*, written over a period of about thirty years and, like Bourignon's two *Lives*, finally published posthumously, in 1720.[64] Born in Montargis, in 1648, to a family of the *petite noblesse*, she might have followed so many other nearly forgotten figures into a life of quiet, conventual piety and/or mysticism. Her father, Claude Bouvier, who had been *procureur* to Louis XIII, possessed a fortune sufficient to guarantee the young girl's entry into the convent of her choice, which was the course her inclinations had dictated since before the age of ten. Her family was pious, and all the children from her father's previous marriage had taken their vows.

Guyon's desire, from as early as the age of fourteen, to enter the Visitation of Montargis was thwarted, however, by her parents, who had other ideas. Toward the end of her seventeenth year, she was married off to the wealthy Jacques Guyon, twenty-two years her elder. The marriage, which would last twelve years, was plagued by the health problems of the two partners, and apparently gave little satisfaction to Guyon, who found herself increasingly drawn down a mystic path. Unfettered, or unaided, by strong spiritual direction on the part of the ecclesiastical establishment, she read widely in authors well outside the limited canon approved for the consumption of the average nun. Ruysbroeck, the Pseudo-Dionysius, Teresa and John of the Cross all supplemented the more mainstream French offerings of François de Sales and Jeanne de Chantal. Upon her husband's death in 1676, Guyon refused the wishes of her family to remarry, preferring instead to devote herself to a life of charitable works. Guyon's charity, however—and this is perhaps the point at which her path separated from that of other pious widows, such as Madeleine Vigneron—took a remarkably apostolic turn. No doubt in imitation of her heroine Jeanne de Chantal, she soon became convinced that a future awaited her in Geneva. Although she would never spend much time in Geneva itself, for two years Guyon alternated between Gex, where she had been chosen to run the new convent of the Nouvelles-Catholiques (an order founded to convert young girls from Protestantism), and Thonon, where she wrote her first work, *Les Torrents*, as well as a substantial part of her autobiography.

Guyon's position at the head of the Nouvelles-Catholiques, however, was jeopardized in short order by her unabashed diffusion of the mystical doctrines she had been developing since her unhappy marriage. On the invitation of a well-placed friend, she left Savoy—and the troubles her apostleship had stirred up—for Turin, where again her willingness to offer spiritual instruction attracted difficulties. It was probably here in Turin that the *Moyen court et très facile pour faire l'oraison*, a soon-to-be-infamous short treatise to which I shall return, was composed. Grenoble was the next stop on Guyon's tour; here she was truly in her element, receiving from morning to night an array of the city's lay people and clergy seeking spiritual guidance. Oral teaching, however, was not Guyon's sole occupation: in the latter half of 1684 she produced the greater part of her mystical commentary on the Bible (later published in no fewer than twenty volumes between 1713 and 1715); and she allowed the *Moyen court* to be published. Again, the ecclesiastical establishment found her mystical proselytizing undesirable. By March of 1685 Guyon let herself be persuaded to leave Grenoble.

Such an apostolic calling could only but face resistance.[65] Even Teresa of Avila was being forced into a compromise with her own apostolic ambitions: in fact, her dream had been to participate in the crusades, but she had to settle for founding an order. A woman was allowed neither to preach, nor teach, nor direct consciences; instead of evangelization, all she could aspire to was "the active religious life," which meant more or less providing a stirring example of charity and self-sacrifice. Not only were Guyon's ambitions remarkable, but so was the fact that she even dared to label them "apostolic" (the word appears frequently in her *Life*) rather than cloak them in a less transgressive term.[66] It is not surprising, therefore, that Guyon's teachings came under direct attack of none other than Jacques-Bénigne Bossuet, bishop of Meaux. The story of the Quietism affair, in which Fénelon, sympathetic to the mystic wing of the Church in general, came to Guyon's defense has been well told elsewhere, and is, in any event, largely extraneous to Guyon's own life.[67] For while Fénelon and Bossuet were occupied with their theological jousting regarding Guyon's reputedly dangerous, passive brand of piety, Guyon herself sat out most of the controversy in prison.

Since her return to France in 1686, Guyon's mystical teaching had continued to make her person the center of all sorts of rumors and hostility. The alleged heresy of her teachings was often just a pretext for maneuvers motivated by pecuniary interest (her husband's death had left Guyon quite wealthy) and other such less-than-pious principles. One of her enemies, the archbishop of Paris, François de Harlay de Champvallon, perhaps irate over the mystic's refusal to allow her daughter to marry his nephew, had Guyon interned at the monastery of the Visitation on the rue Saint-Antoine in Paris. At the Visitation, her reclusion was complete, but she was, in the nine months she spent there, at least able to bring her autobiography, started during her stay in Thonon, up to date. Liberated due to the intercession of Mme de Maintenon, Guyon proceeded to be the latter's guest at her aristocratic girl's school, Saint-Cyr. By this time Guyon's apostolic zeal had been somewhat calmed, and her influence at Saint-Cyr was much less notable than that of Fénelon. Nevertheless, she did speak regularly with the nuns and the novices, and her works, both those in print (*Le Moyen court*) and in manuscript (*Les Torrents*), circulated there. Over two years would elapse before the arguably "democratic" tone of Guyon's teachings caused a certain insubordination on the part of novices who started to claim (as Guyon's detractors would have it) that sweeping the floor was detrimental to their relation with God.[68] Guyon was asked to leave Saint-Cyr in March of 1693; it would take the now hostile Mme de Maintenon and Bossuet, who was also involved, eighteen months to catch up with her once and for all. She was arrested at her home at the end of 1695, and imprisoned first at Vincennes for over two years, then at the Bastille for five more.

Upon her liberation, Guyon's health was precarious, and from then on her apostolate was largely marginal, in that she avoided all potential sources of conflict with the ecclesiastical apparatus. Given this prudence, as well as the subsiding of the anti-mystical wave that had washed across France with the Quietism controversy, Guyon was no longer troubled by Church authorities. Instead, more or less exiled to Blois after her release from the Bastille, she became the center of a circle of admirers, consisting of her many old friends from the court who had remained faithful to her cause, as well as some German Pietists and English Protestants. One of these admirers was Pierre Poiret, who, since his involvement with Bourignon, had been especially active in the publication of mystical works. To Poiret, Guyon entrusted the editing of many of her unpublished works, including her *Life*. It was here, at Blois, in 1709, that Guyon completed her autobiography, in two versions: one, which she envisioned for wider, print circulation, terminating with her imprisonment at Vincennes; and a second, intended for a more intimate audience, that included the narration of her seven-year stint in prison. It was in all probability shortly before her death in 1717 that Guyon corrected the manuscript of her circulating *Life* and ordered that it be given to Poiret for posthumous publication.[69]

Given that Guyon's life oscillated between extremes of publicity (i.e., her apostolic mission, and the open ridicule to which Bossuet subjected her during the Quietism affair) and privacy (her long years in prison, unable to see her own family), it may not be surprising that the habitually problematic relation between interior and exterior, between private and public, forms the thematic nexus upon which the eight hundred pages of her autobiography converge. What is, or what can be, the relationship between subject and society? Can autobiography heal the rent between interior and exterior, public and private? Questions such as these are similar to those posed by Bourignon's *Lives*. Guyon, however, asks them still more insistently, more consciously, and answers with even more pessimism. Faced with the near-impossibility of public vindication, a fact of which she becomes perfectly cognizant over the course of her struggle with Bossuet's judicial and carceral machine, Guyon withdraws into the liminal spaces of prison and exile, and restricts progressively her anticipated audience, until she speaks only before those who already know and trust her. Relations between public and private in Guyon's autobiography are far from stable—they shift as Guyon's own experience of being in the public eye changes. Just as it is difficult to grasp the contradictions of Rousseau's autobiographical project without following it through all the twelve books of the *Confessions, Rousseau juge de Jean-Jacques*, and finally the

Rêveries du promeneur solitaire—fourteen years and three different strategies of writing in all—one must take care to discern the different chronological strata of her autobiography, for her *Life* is a composite. Written over a period of 35 years (years encompassing the heights of her apostolate and popularity in Thonon as well as the largely silent, cautious years of her exile in Blois), like so many early autobiographies, it is far from a retrospective account of her life undertaken once and for all. Instead, it records a series of successive articulations of the subject/society relation—a relation which the act of recording is itself instrumental in producing.[70]

Discussions of Guyon's writing frequently start with its abundance. Her complete works run to forty volumes, twice that of the already remarkably productive Bourignon, who, according to Henri Bremond's slight exaggeration "wrote no less than Voltaire."[71] The works are varied, comprising a twenty-volume mystical gloss of the Bible, poetry, treatises on prayer, letters, and a compendium of passages from the mystical Church tradition intended to prove Guyon's orthodoxy. Like Bourignon, Guyon claimed to have the gift of automatic writing. In an oft-cited passage of her *Life*, she describes her first experiences with this sort of writing, in 1682, when she composed the *Torrents* and the first part of her autobiography:

Je me mis à écrire sans savoir comment, et je trouvais que cela venait avec une impétuosité étrange. Ce qui me surprenait le plus était que cela coulait comme du fond et ne passait point par ma tête. Je n'étais pas encore accoutumée à cette manière d'écrire; cependant j'écrivis un traité entier de toute la voie intérieure sous la comparaison des rivières et des fleuves.[72]
(I began to write without knowing how, and I found that it came with a strange impetuousness. What surprised me the most was that it flowed as though from the depths and did not even pass through my head. I was not yet accustomed to this manner of writing; and yet I wrote an entire treatise on the interior path by way of a comparison with rivers and streams.)

Taken on the whole, however, Guyon's *Life* does not conform to this model of automatic production. To the three main moments of composition (1682, early 1688, and 1709) must be added a series of additions, or rather updates, in the last part of 1688, and a series of corrections undertaken in Blois by Guyon, who in general did not reread her own work.[73] In addition, one must take into consideration the changes in style and flow that the different parts of the autobiography generate. Much of the 1682 version mirrors the kind of writing Guyon was doing elsewhere at the time, in her treatises or Biblical commentaries: she multiplies non-autobiographical digression (i.e., on prayer, on suffering, on mortification) to the point of often obscuring her personal trajectory, which resurfaces only momentarily so that the reader does not lose the narrative thread. She acknowledges the trouble she has keeping to her subject (what she calls, in opposition to her digressions, "mon histoire" [my story]), and seems to blame it on her automatic writing: "Je me suis beaucoup écartée de mon histoire, mais je ne suis pas maîtresse de faire autrement" (I have drifted far from my story, but I am not capable of doing otherwise) (301). Her 1682 version ends with a acknowledgment of the dispersal of her automatic narrative: "je me suis curieusement écartée" (I have curiously drifted away) (318). As we shall see, however, by 1709 Guyon will be carefully patching together a record of Bossuet's legal maneuvers against her during her imprisonment, and will only manage half a page a day.[74] What happened in the intervening three decades that so changed her writing practice?

The general impression of flow given by the 1682 version, and, to a lesser extent, by the 1688 additions, is confirmed by one of the text's major thematic axes — faith in language. Language, due to its inspired nature, can communicate a mystical teaching relatively easily, and helps to harmonize interior and exterior, the subject and the world. Although well-read in the Christian mystical tradition, Guyon employs none of the customary theological vocabulary to articulate the mystical experience; she steers away from "the science of the saints," a type of discourse based on the teachings of an illustrious line of "mystical doctors," beginning with the Pseudo-Dionysius.[75] Guyon rarely uses the phrase "les Auteurs Mystiques," invoking them only when she feels in need of an authorizing precedent. Rather than referring to an underground mystical tradition, Guyon prefers to point "inward," via the same rhetoric that characterized the presentation of both Augustine's *Confessions* and autobiographical convent writing — a rhetoric that coheres around a cluster of terms ("intérieur," "coeur," "fond," and others) whose precise theological significance had been largely lost as they gained increasing currency within devotional discourse.[76]

Guyon's experience of the interior and of the heart stems from the pivotal moment in her life at which, during a period of rather mechanical spiritual effort on her part, a passing Franciscan gives her the following advice: " 'C'est, madame, que vous cherchez au-dehors ce que vous avez au-dedans. Accoutumez-vous à chercher Dieu dans votre coeur et vous l'y trouverez' " ("The problem, madame, is that you are seeking outside what you have inside. Accustom yourself to seeking God in your heart and you will find Him there") (73).[77] With these words her interior, her heart, awaken: "O mon Seigneur, vous étiez dans mon coeur et vous ne demandiez de moi qu'un simple retour au-dedans. . . . [D]ès ce moment il me fut donnée une expérience de sa présence dans mon fond; non par pensée ou par application d'esprit, mais comme une chose qu'on possède réellement d'une manière très suave" (Oh my Lord, you are in my heart and you ask of me only a simple inward turn. . . . From this moment on an experience of his presence in my depths was granted me; it came not by thought or mental application, but like a thing one possesses truly and in a most gentle way) (73–74). "Coeur," "fond," "au-dedans"—all designate, by simple opposition to "pensée" and "esprit," the space that the "bon religieux fort intérieur" (good and very interior priest) (71) has opened to her. "Intérieur" will become, in the *Life*, the omnipresent designation for the Guyonian experience, replacing "mystical," "spiritual," "pious" and "devout." "Elle lui demanda un sermon un peu intérieur" (She asked him for a somewhat interior sermon) (276), Guyon says of a friend, an acquaintance she qualifies as "un homme fort intérieur" (a very interior man) (397). "Intérieur" is the code word for members of the mystic circle, those in the know. Regretting having written to a "homme de mérite" in the hopes he would give her spiritual advice, she says: "J'envoyai au plus vite un autre billet pour le prier de m'excuser, et comme je le croyais intérieur, je dis en moi-même: s'il est intérieur, il ne s'offensera point, s'il ne l'est pas, je serais fâchée de lui parler" (I sent with utmost haste another note begging him to forgive me, and since I believed him to be interior, I said to myself: if he is interior, he will not be offended, and if he is not interior, I would not want to speak to him anyway) (202).[78]

Although Guyon's deployment of interiority's tropes intersects with general devotional usage, she articulates their relation to her autobiographical project in specific ways. In religious biographies, for example, editors in effect "sold" first-person narration by casting it as a repository for an experience whose authenticity augmented in direct proportion to its elusiveness; autobiography let the subject's interior "speak," but the gaps in the story told were adduced to preserve some degree of inner opacity. Yet if Guyon's interiority is similarly elusive (one of her most common rhetorical moves, as we shall see, involves standard disclaimers of mystic "unsayability"), it will, in the course of its long elaboration, come to possess a charge of alienation unseen in conventual enthusiasts' use of the trope. Initially a vehicle for transmitting her inner experience to disciples, little by little her *Life* will start to explore the treacherous ambiguities of the interior/exterior binome—an exploration that will become all the more insistent as the *Life* itself is taken as a target of attacks.

As Guyon begins her project, her optimism is palpable: hers is the tale

of an apostolic calling, but a characteristically "inner" one. She herself thinks
her mission in these by now familiar terms. Normally, she writes, one imagines apostles going out and converting; her apostolate, an apostolate of spiritual direction, takes inner aim.

[Dieu] me fit comprendre qu'il ne m'appelait point... à une propagation de l'extérieur
de l'Eglise, qui consiste à gagner les hérétiques, mais à la propagation de son Esprit,
qui n'est autre que l'Esprit intérieur. Il ne me destine pas même pour la première conversion des pécheurs, mais bien pour faire entrer ceux qui sont [déjà] touchés du désir
de se convertir, *dans* la parfaite conversion, qui n'est autre que cet Esprit intérieur.
(521—emphasis in the original)
([God] made me understand that he was not calling me... to a propagation of the exterior of the Church, which consists in winning over heretics, but to the propagation
of its Spirit, which is nothing other than the inner Spirit. He does not destine me for
even the initial conversion of sinners, but rather for leading those who are [already]
touched by the desire to convert, *into* the perfect conversion, which is nothing other
than this inner Spirit.)

Conversion, emphasizes Guyon with the aid of italics, is something that must
be entered *into*, and is not to be confused with the mere propagation of the
most "exterior" aspects of Christianity (cult, baptism, confession, and so on).
The inner Spirit can only be propagated through language, however, and Guyon's autobiography, at least the parts written in 1682 and 1688, is very much
a teaching, an effort to get her interior experience into words that will make
the experience accessible to others, to those "already touched by the desire
to convert."

To do so, some adequation between experience and language must
ground the vague though insistently reiterated gesturing towards the interior
or the heart. And, in fact, Guyon takes great pains to get the most out of imperfect human language. No existing terminology, she says, does the job—
whence her complaints about the difficulty of her task: she would happily
avoid writing her experience, "tant à cause de la difficulté de m'en expliquer,
que parce qu'il y a peu d'âmes capables d'une conduite si peu connue, et si
peu comprise, *que je n'ai jamais rien lu de semblable*" (as much from the difficulty of explaining it as because there are few souls capable of actions so little
known, and so little understood, *that I have never read anything like it*) (257,
my emphasis). Yet she forges ahead, multiplying precisions, returning to her
word choice, nuancing it, highlighting what she does and does not mean by
a given term. "Ce que j'appelle *trépas*, c'est-à-dire *passage* d'une chose à une
autre" (What I call *trespass*, that is the *passage* from one thing to another)
(260); "Lorsque je parle de *pouvoir*, je ne l'entends pas d'un pouvoir absolu"

(When I speak of *power*, I do not mean an absolute power) (214); "[L]orsque je me sers du terme d'ennemis, ce n'est pas que je croie personne comme tel . . . mais c'est pour m'expliquer" (When I use the term enemies, it is not because I believe anyone to be such . . . rather it is in order to explain myself) (416); "Lorsque je dis que ces différends me causaient de la *peine*, c'est une manière de parler" (When I say that these disagreements caused me *pain*, it's a manner of speaking) (312). She rewrites metaphors that lack precision: after likening the soul's absolute obedience to "un fou qui se jette dans la mer sans crainte de s'y perdre" (a madman who throws himself into the sea without fear of being lost in it), she retreats: "ce n'est point encore cela, car se jeter dans la mer, c'est une action propre que l'âme n'a point ici" (that's not quite right either, for throwing oneself into the sea is an act unto itself that the soul in this state does not have), and goes on to make another stab at a more appropriate metaphor (307). Guyon feels language to be imprecise, but she clearly hopes that communication is nonetheless possible: the very gesture that crosses out the inadequate term expresses also, and paradoxically, the faith that a *mieux dire* can be found and that it *is* possible to be more accurately understood.[79]

Though Guyon's general lexical horizon is that of other mystics of the second half of the century, she devotes considerable energy to making her vocabulary seem improvised: the mark of inner experience is its capacity to bend received language. Thus Guyon diverts words from their traditional meanings, coining neologisms—such as the rather awkward "Paix-Dieu" (Peace-God) (208)[80]—and then doubling back to underline her inventiveness: "[C]'est un mot dont je me sers sans savoir s'il est propre" (This is a word I use without knowing whether it is proper) (260); "Je ne sais si c'est parler proprement" (I do not know if this is speaking properly) (264). And when the referentiality of language fails, Guyon tries to extract the most meaning possible from a *lack* of precision (speaking chiastically, for instance, of "une peine douce ou une douceur pénible" [a sweet pain or a painful sweetness] [263]), or from recourse to the *coincidentia oppositorum* (e.g., "j'étais abîmée et élevée" [I was abased and elevated] [260]). Behind these efforts to express her interior lies the belief that it is possible to forge a personal language (personal, because without antecedent) that will, in spite of its novelty, permit some sort of understanding between master and disciple.

All of which is relatively standard mystic fare, and feeds nicely the reader's belief in an experience existing just on the other side of a language whose weaknesses are, in fact, the best proof of that experience. Like so many mystics, Guyon thus multiplies her disclaimers of unsayability, and repeatedly laments that her linguistic efforts will be meaningless if the reader has not had an analogous experience. Yet her apostolic optimism, for the time being, keeps her writing. Even when her reader might not grasp her meaning, God will: "[I]l se fait en moi quelque chose de l'original [*sic*], qui se communique à moi d'une manière inexplicable et que la seule expérience peut faire comprendre. Cette expérience est rare. C'est donc à vous, ô mon Amour, que je rends ce que j'ai écrit pour vous" (Something original happens inside me which is communicated to me in an inexplicable manner, and which can only be understood through experience. This experience is rare. So it is to you, oh my Love, that I give back what I have written for you) (505). Guyon so ends the 1688 portion of her *Life*. Although she had started to write at the request of one of her disciples (whom she addresses from time to time as "Monsieur" in the text), a human narratee is always an uncertain guarantor of meaning, and Guyon thus prefers to ensure communication by re-routing her autobiography to God. The economy of her discourse is preserved by the certainty of divine reception.

Guyon's reflections on the imperfect but somehow serviceable relationship between language and experience are consonant with a reiterated belief in a harmony between her interior (her spiritual life) and her exterior (the way she appears to others). It thus comes as no surprise that others cannot help but take note of her inner transformations: "Je me faisais cependant violence," she writes, "pour ne rien faire paraître, sinon que l'on remarquait sur mon visage une occupation continuelle de Dieu; car, comme l'attrait était fort, il se répandait jusque sur les sens; de sorte que cela me donnait une telle douceur, modestie, et majesté, que les gens du monde s'en apercevaient" (I put up a violent struggle so that nothing would appear, yet that one could see on my face a continual occupation with God; for, as the attraction was strong, it spread even over the senses in such a way that it gave me such a sweetness, modesty, and majesty that the people of the world perceived it) (93). The Barnabite priest La Combe, for one, is immediately struck by the transparency of Guyon's inner graces.[81] "Ce père dit qu'il avait remarqué un recueillement et une présence de Dieu sur mon visage si extraordinaires, qu'il se disait à lui-même: 'Je n'ai jamais vu de femme comme celle-là' et c'est ce qui lui fit naître l'envie de me revoir" (This father said that he had noticed in my face a contemplativeness and a divine presence so extraordinary that he said to himself: "I have never seen a woman like this one" and that is what made him want to see me again) (139). Even her persecutions are lived as a perverse harmony between inner and outer worlds. Her interior poverty is figured by her exterior poverty (254); and her seven-year dark night of the soul is a time in which the latter is purified by a "double abjection" of interior and exterior ordeals: "Ce fut un renversement égal et du dehors et du dedans" (It was a total reversal of the outside and of the inside) (178, 179). Because of this spiritual transparency, Guyon can read the interiors of her disciples— she is at the height of her apostolic success.

Il venait du monde de tous les côtés, de loin et de près. . . . Rien ne m'était caché de leur état intérieur et de ce qui se passait en eux. . . . Les plus avancées de ces âmes trouvaient auprès de moi sans parole qu'il leur était communiqué une grâce qu'elles ne pouvaient ni comprendre, ni cesser d'admirer. Les autres trouvaient une onction dans mes paroles et qu'elles opéraient dans elles [i.e., les âmes] ce que je leur disais. (374–75)
(People came from everywhere, near and far. Nothing about their interior state or what was happening inside them was hidden to me. . . . The most advanced of these souls found that at my side, and without speaking, there was communicated to them a grace which they could neither understand nor cease to admire. The others found an unction in my words and felt them operate within [their souls] what I was describing.)

At best, communication is wordless—such is how Christ communicated, Guyon says ("Ce fut dans ce grand banquet que Jésus-Christ comme Verbe s'écoulait dans Jean et lui découvrait ses plus profonds secrets" [It was at this great supper that Jesus Christ as Word flowed into John and revealed to him his most profound secrets] [342]). But even with words, communication, and the interaction between interior and exterior, are unproblematic: "Pour moi, lorsque je me sers de la parole et de la plume avec les âmes, je ne le fais qu'à cause de leur faiblesse, et parce que, ou ils [*sic*] ne sont pas assez purs pour les communications intimes, ou il faut encore user de condescendance, ou pour régler les choses du dehors" (For me, when I use speech or pen with souls, I do it only because of their weakness, and because they are not pure enough for intimate communications, or because it is necessary to resort to condescension, or else in order to settle exterior matters) (341–42).

The above citations almost exclusively occur in the part of Guyon's *Life* composed in 1682; a few date from 1688. Even if, by the latter date, Guyon's first round of detention (at the convent of the Visitation) had already begun, she had not yet been broken by Bossuet's strong-arm interrogations and her years in the Bastille. More important still for my reading of the problematics of autobiographical apology, Bossuet had not yet taken her *Life* itself as his judicial target, as he would do during the Quietist controversy. Her autobiography, in these parts, still manifests the hope that she will be known as she is, both to her accusers and defenders, that her persecutions will cease, and her teachings will be received. If Guyon valorizes the subject's interior life, this in no way cuts the subject off from the community at large. Communication and teaching are possible, and the speaking subject feels an inherent confidence regarding her capacity to make herself spontaneously understood through a vocabulary of her own invention. The apostle is at home in the world, and founds the first part of her autobiography on this confidence.

At the same time, however, Guyon's *Life* cannot but figure other aspects of the interiority seized on with such singular insistence by the religious culture of the day—in particular, the dystopian rupture that this new subjective topography inscribed from the outset. It was, in fact, a topos of baroque spirituality that the exterior did *not* reflect the interior—that the latter was the only important spiritual dimension, or, rather, that all spirituality was by definition inner. The worldly manifestation of the interior soul floated free and detached, rendering the subject's interior unreadable, save to the spiritual cognoscenti. In this respect, interiority was defined negatively as much as positively; it resulted from what Michel de Certeau has described as a movement from the visible to the invisible, whereby the transparent manifestation of God in creation (notably, in institutions such as the Church) gave way to opacity.[82] In this light, the vogue for interior biographies of the type examined in the previous chapter might then be read less as proof of the overwhelming religiosity of an age not yet affected by the secularity that would characterize the Enlightenment, but an anxious or nostalgic reaction to a world already perceived as deserted by God. Just as the cosmos can no longer be read as an allegory of divine order, the saint's actions lose their unequivocal miraculousness; actions can only be interpreted by plunging inside the subject, via autobiographical testimony.

The secession of interior from exterior can be read in any number of religious phenomena of the seventeenth century, from mysticism to demonology (where authorities asked the question of whether the signs of divine or diabolical presence could be faked).[83] Even aside from these extremes, however, the invisibility of interiority was commonplace of everyday devotion. In Jean-Jacques Olier's developing cult of "l'intérieur de Jésus," for instance, the Eucharist becomes the model of interior transformation accompanied by total exterior stasis. Of the host, he notes that "l'extérieur demeure toujours le même pendant que l'intérieur et le dedans est [*sic*] tout changé et consommé en Jésus-Christ" (the exterior remains always the same while the interior and the inside are completely changed and consumed in Jesus Christ).[84] The spiritual life of the individual is similarly imperceptible to the naked eye for Olier, who describes the soul of one deacon as being "dans son corps comme dans un vaisseau vide dont elle [l'âme] ne touche jamais les bords" (in his body as in an empty vessel whose edges [the soul] never touches).[85] Guyon's *Life* furnishes abundant examples of this secession. "On se fait des idées," notes Guyon towards the very end of the section written in 1688, "et on s'imagine qu'une âme qui est à Dieu d'une certaine manière, doit être de telle et telle sorte; et lorsque l'on voit le contraire des idées qu'on s'était formées on conclut que Dieu n'est point là; et c'est souvent où il est le plus" (People imagine things, and think that a soul belonging to God in a certain way must be of this or that sort; and when one sees the contrary of the ideas one has formed, one concludes that God cannot be there; and yet this is often where He is the most) (527). She had already, in 1682, proclaimed that the apostolic path was not for those whose actions were transparent, but for those who will be fatally misread by others:

Il y a une voie de lumière, une vie sainte où la créature paraît tout admirable; comme cette vie est plus apparente, elle est aussi plus estimée des personnes qui n'ont point la plus pure lumière. Ces personnes ont des choses fort éclatantes dans leur vie, elles ont une fidélité et un courage qui étonnent, et c'est ce qui orne admirablement la vie des saints. Mais pour les âmes qui marchent cet autre sentier [i.e., the true apostolic life], elles sont très peu connues. . . . Elles n'ont rien de grand qui paraisse; de là vient que, plus leur intérieur est grand, moins elles en peuvent parler. (300–301)
(There is a way of light, a saintly life in which the creature appears altogether admirable; since this life is more apparent, it is also more highly regarded by people who do not possess the purest light. These people have very brilliant things in their lives, they have astonishing fidelity and courage, and this is what admirably adorns the lives of the saints. But as for the souls that walk this other path [i.e. the true apostolic life], they are unknown. . . . Nothing grand is visible in them; thus it is that the greater their interior has grown, the less they are able to speak of it.)

Saintliness—"mere" saintliness, Guyon implies—is based on harmony between interior and exterior; apostleship, which Guyon clearly values much more, assumes a break between the two.

While Olier's conception of an isolated interior seems mostly self-imposed, Guyon's affords her an opportunity to theorize persecution as constitutive of the subject's relation with society. Persecution is predicated on a rupture between interior and exterior in two ways. First, as the previous citation hinted, those who are gifted with a truly great interior are incapable of showing it; they can only but be misread by the public. Those who can read the paradoxical signs of interiority, on the other hand, become part of a Happy Few, the circle that forms around the otherwise unpopular apostle. Second, if the interior cannot manifest itself directly and unambiguously in the world, by the same token, the actions of the world (persecution or adversity of any sort) leave the interior person undisturbed. This neo-stoic motif appears frequently in Guyon's *Life*. The subject here experiences herself either as independent of outward distraction and pain ("cela . . . mettait quelquefois mes sens à l'agonie, mais le fond de mon âme était tranquille" [this . . . sometimes put my senses in agony, but the depth of my soul was peaceful] [304]), or, often, postulates an inverse relation between interior solidity and outward hardship ("Il me semblait que la captivité de mon corps me faisait mieux goûter la liberté de mon esprit; plus j'étais resserrée au dehors, plus j'étais large et étendue au dedans" [It seemed to me that the captivity of my body made me better appreciate the liberty of my mind; the more I was squeezed on the outside, the more I was wide and broad on the inside] [486]). Persecution is either a matter of indifference or, potentially, a source of strength: hardship lived in the body spurs the growth of a feeling of autonomy and inner integrity—something we might well want to call a self.

The idea of the acceptance of persecution, and its validation of the Christian's commitment to God is, of course, a staple of Pauline spirituality.[86] Moreover, willingness to suffer persecution had long been viewed as an integral part of the *imitatio*—the disciple must share in the destiny of the Master, carrying his own cross.[87] This theme, as well as the vogue for stoicism in the seventeenth century and a long tradition of asceticism, furnish a background for Guyon's rhetoric of persecution. Indeed, the very ubiquity of these motifs could be in and of itself an object of further inquiry. Yet it is the articulation of the theme in Guyon's *Life* that is most striking—its precise breakdown along the poles of interior and exterior, and Guyon's efforts to portray, in a tempest of worldly violence, her undisturbed inner calm. In other words, although persecution had been fully recuperated by Christian identity from the time of Paul, only with the close of the seventeenth century would it acquire the (paradoxical) virtue of opening up subjective space. Guyon not only says: "I am reviled, thus I am like Christ," but also: "When I am reviled, I go inside." The first statement indicates a purely exemplary identity; the second, subjective depth.

Guyon, while connected to the world via the mission to teach, enjoys at the same time a certain autonomy and separateness. In the world and yet simultaneously out of it, looking upon it as if from afar, she might well have appropriated Descartes's motto, *bene vixit, bene qui latuit* (he lives well, who lives hidden). Far from being a triumph, however, Guyon's inner autonomy is a kind of lesser evil. Unlike the Cartesian subject, who retreats into himself only better to understand and master the natural world, and who, in regards to the human world, adopts the nonconflictual stance of the *morale par provision*, Guyon can at best understand a select few souls, while being misunderstood by the rest. Whereas Descartes's famous *poêle*, or heated room, is a way station, a laboratory in which he has the leisure to devise the method that will be applied to the world, Guyon invokes the space of the prison as a place of self-discovery, as a metaphor for the self-sufficiency of the "interior" person—and, like Socrates, does not want to leave. "Il me semblait que, quoiqu'enfermée dans une étroite prison, mon âme était la même liberté, et plus large que toute la terre" (It seemed to me that although I was enclosed in a narrow prison, my soul was freedom itself, and larger than all the earth) (483), she says of her time at the Visitation. "[J]e ne désirais point sortir, . . . je me trouvais bien dans ma solitude" (I did not at all wish to leave, . . . I was comfortable in my solitude) (R 147). Of the ambiguous prison imagery described by Victor Brombert—prison as site of suffering and of protection— it is especially the latter pole that marks Guyon's descriptions.[88]

Guyon's paradoxical use of the prison to turn imposed suffering into autonomous pleasure ("Les pierres de ma tour me semblaient des rubis, c'est-à-dire que je les estimais plus que toutes les magnificences du siècle" [The stones of my tower seemed like rubies to me, that is, I valued them more than all worldly magnificence], she writes [618]) suggests that subjectivity is not precisely *threatened* by judicial persecution, but, on the contrary, arises alongside it. Hostility and incomprehension are the price she must pay for her total self-sufficiency, and, conversely, an exaggerated sense of self-sufficiency is a response to a world upon which the subject cannot make the hoped-for impact. Guyon, the apostolic Guyon, even feels for a moment—and thirty years before Crusoe—the temptation of the desert island, which becomes a metaphor for her feelings of isolation and otherness. "Je vous demandais, ô mon Amour, un petit trou de rocher pour m'y mettre et pour y vivre séparée de toutes les créatures. Je figurais qu'une île déserte aurait terminé toutes mes disgrâces, et m'aurait mise en état de faire infailliblement votre volonté" (O my Love, I asked you for a little hole in a rock when I could go live apart from all creatures. I imagined that a deserted island would have ended my disgrace, and would have allowed me to carry out your will infallibly) (422). Rousseau himself assumed the mantle of this most pervasive modern literary archetype by the island-worship of his fifth *Rêverie*—Rousseau whose *Emile* was heavily indebted Defoe's *Robinson Crusoe*. Guyon's desire for the desert island is closer to Rousseau's use than to Defoe's dreams of conquest and capital: the island, rather than being an allegory of colonial expansion, is the perfect locus for the uncomfortable subject.

One wonders, then, what has become of Guyon's hopes for communication, of her engagement with the world, of harmony between appearance and being. Although the independence of the interior I have just been establishing is present throughout her *Life*, it is nonetheless Guyon's experience of prison (first at the Visitation, then at Vincennes and the Bastille) that makes of this common motif of baroque spirituality an all-encompassing metaphor for the relation between subject and society. The 1709 part of Guyon's *Life* differs enormously from the sections composed in 1688 and earlier. Upon her release from the Bastille in March 1703, Guyon moved first to Suèvres, near Blois, where she lived with her son, who had promised the authorities, in return for his mother's tentative release, that she would have "aucune communication de vive voix ni par écrit avec qui que ce soit" (no communication, oral or written, with any person whatsoever).[89] Only in 1706 was she authorized to live on her own; she purchased a house in Blois where she would spend the rest of her years, welcoming followers from both France and abroad. Blois represented anything but new apostolic territory for Guyon. A relative silence enveloped her last years: forbidden to "dogmatize," Guyon drastically limited her output of writing, which now consisted mainly of pious verse and many letters to her disciples.[90]

Prior to 1688, Guyon may have made much spiritual capital off her exterior persecutions, but it cannot be denied that her behavior in Blois showed that she had clearly had enough, and hence she restricted herself to the writing of verse — perhaps the only scriptural undertaking a woman could engage in without attracting attention. And the bare fact that she no longer composed treatises that could circulate without any control, but instead communicated her teaching only by letter ("a correspondence course in prayer," is how one commentator put it) [91] indicates the extent to which Guyon had, in fact, created a sort of island for herself. Exchanges with a public unknown to Guyon herself became virtually nonexistent; even the mechanics of the correspondence with her disciples was the object of many precautions.[92] The care that she took in the exercise of her spiritual direction flirted at times with paranoia: Guyon's experiences had, by this time, made her suspicious of even her beloved daughter, not to mention the rest of her family.[93]

It was in this environment that Guyon finished her autobiography, in 1709. She prepared, in fact, two endings for her *Life*. First, she added eleven chapters to the existing manuscript, chapters treating the years from her release from the convent of the Visitation in 1688 to her imprisonment, in 1695, at Vincennes. This is the version that she would correct and give to Poiret — perhaps around 1710 — for posthumous publication. At the same time, she penned a separate text, which, chronologically speaking, represents the next installment of her autobiography. This text covers her years in prison, from

1695 to 1703. This prison narrative, however, would not be given to Poiret, being intended only for the anonymous "Monsieur" requesting it, as well as for, Guyon writes, "un petit nombre de mes amis les plus particuliers" (a small number of my most intimate friends) (R 31). As Guyon became more careful of how she spoke, and to whom, she also took evident care with the diffusion of her autobiography. From what was clearly a method of spiritual teaching to be distributed to those who wanted to learn more of the interior life, the *Life*'s audience shrinks to a chosen few, in a way reminiscent of Bourignon's circle of "amis secrets que Dieu choisira" (secret friends whom God will choose) (VI 130). And, more significantly, both parts of the *Life* of 1709 are largely devoid of spiritual instruction or content. Digressions on the interior life are strikingly rare; Guyon instead sticks to a bare enumeration of her altercations with Bossuet. Previous sections of the *Life* had discounted the importance of an exterior world that, by 1709, would overrun the text.

To a certain extent, the transformation of Guyon's fabled loquacity into sobriety can be read as the mystical goal toward which she had been steadily making progress, an illustration of the abolition of the self and the surpassing of all received discourse on experience — all in all, a happy spiritual end.[94] But the choice to document her experience of Bossuet's legal persecutions suggests that the strange turn taken by the *Life* may be more historically significant than such a hypothesis would suggest. Simply put, Guyon's prison experience forced her to reexamine the possibilities and conditions of communication that, prior to 1688, had guided her autobiographical enterprise. Previously, Guyon saw herself as having a public role to play, and subject and society, interior and exterior, were linked by means of the autobiographical text. Under resistance from orthodoxy, however, this relationship falls to pieces. Guyon abandons writing (with the exception of controlled private correspondence) as a medium for communication between interiors, and instead will consent to use it only with judicial precision. The 1709 additions to her *Life* tell the story of an apprenticeship in the worldly use of language.[95]

I have already alluded to Guyon's automatic writing which (purportedly) expresses the inner disposition of the soul without the censoring activity of the rational mind — "coula[nt] comme du fond et ne passa[nt] point par la tête" (flowing as though from the depths and not passing through my head) (323). Autobiography, for Guyon, if it were *not* automatic, would play into the trap of the *moi*, which would only too well like the chance to represent itself.[96] Her writing, in other words, is the product of neither her *moi* nor her rational mind. Quite logically, therefore, she refuses to defend what she has written, stating that the evaluation of her work lies in the hands of competent ecclesiastical authority.

This insistent disavowal of authorial responsibility could not be more at odds, though, with the tactics adopted by Bossuet during the Quietism affair. The bishop of Meaux, as Jean Orcibal has observed, abandoned quite early in the controversy a theological approach to Guyon's works, adopting instead an "inquisitorial" manner.[97] More precisely, Bossuet, indifferent to the work's *content*, aims to establish a link between the author and the work that would function reversibly: any error detected in the work would reflect on and implicate the author; and conversely, any questionable behavior on the part of the author would suffice to incriminate the work. Indeed, from the perspective of conflicting notions of authorial responsibility, the polemical swordsmanship of Bossuet and Fénelon in the summer and autumn of 1698 makes fascinating reading. In their many attacks and counter-attacks (Bossuet's *Relation sur le quiétisme*, Fénelon's *Réponse à la relation*, and the former's *Remarques sur la réponse*), innumerable permutations occur between the terms *écrits, livres* (not necessarily the same thing, as we shall see Guyon herself point out), *personne, auteur*, and last but certainly not least *intention*. A thorough look at the play of these terms in the texts of the debate would take the present study too far afield, especially given the issue's complexity: both adversaries seem unsure about the proper way to argue, let alone to resolve, the question of the relationship between author and text. Their positions were often paradoxical if not downright contradictory from one moment to the next, but what they do suggest rather clearly is that the case of Jeanne Guyon was felt to be somehow representative of an as-yet-uncertain principle which all parties intimated yet none could quite theorize—the personal responsibility of authors for their works. But this responsibility—part and parcel of Foucault's "author-function"—was of as much interest to the apostle of automatic writing as to the prelates who squabbled over her.[98]

As I have mentioned, Guyon herself did not take part in this controversy, for she was in prison. Eventually, however, she would use continuations of her *Life* as a belated and somewhat quixotic response to the storm of debate. For Guyon defends what is clearly, given what she has been through, a lost cause: that of the authorless work, whose value is determined solely by the ascertainable truth or falsity of a textual content for which she had been a mere channel. Guyon's work really isn't "hers" anyway, she argues: "J'ai encore un défaut, c'est que je dis les choses comme elles me viennent, sans savoir si je dis bien ou mal. Lorsque je les dis ou écris, elles me paraissent claires comme le jour; après cela je les vois comme des choses que je n'ai jamais sues, loin de les avoir écrites" (I have still another fault, which is that I say things as they come to me, without knowing whether I am speaking well or ill. When I speak or write them, they seem to me as clear as day; later, I see them as things I have never known, never mind having written them) (557). Both mystics and victims of possession frequently made similar assertions in order to demonstrate the veracity of their discourse, and behind this seemingly timeless Christian imperative of self-effacement lay a specific logic. By saying that one could not recall the act of writing, or that one no longer understood what one wrote, one was in fact guaranteeing meaning in a discursive economy that attributed value in inverse proportion to the amount of subjective interference tainting the message of the real speaker—the divine or diabolical Other.[99] Guyon's defense proceeds therefore by divorcing the act of writing, which implies not claims to truth but only sincerity of intent, from the act by which one becomes an author and asserts veracity—publication. Already in 1688 Guyon argued that she cannot bear responsibility for the controversial *Moyen court* on the simple grounds that she did not intend its publication:

[On] dit tout haut, que ce n'était pas [La Combe] qui avait fait le petit livre du *Moyen court et facile etc.*? Je dis que non, que je l'avais fait en son absence, sans nul dessein qu'il fût imprimé; et qu'un conseiller de Grenoble de mes amis, en ayant pris le manuscrit sur ma table, le trouva utile, et désira qu'il fût imprimé; qu'il me pria d'y faire une préface, et de le diviser par espèces de chapitres; ce que je fis en une matinée. (479) (I was asked if it was not [La Combe] who had written the little book entitled *Moyen court et facile etc.*? I replied no, that I had written it in his absence, with no intention of having it printed; and that a councilor from Grenoble who was afraid of mine, having taken the manuscript from my table, found it useful, and wanted to have it printed; that he asked me to write a preface, and to divide it into chapters; which I did in the course of one morning.)

Responsibility for a work cannot be borne by the author, whose role is strictly circumscribed: she creates (and even then, only "automatically"), but does not diffuse or propagate. Moreover, Guyon puts responsibility for the damage done by the *Moyen court* squarely on the shoulders of the ecclesiastical authorities who *approved* the work. "[Je leur déclarai] que s'il y avait quelque chose de mal il ne s'en fallait pas prendre à moi qui ne suis qu'une femme sans science, mais aux docteurs qui l'ont approuvé sans même que je les en eusse priés, ne les connaissant pas" ([I declared to them] that if there was anything bad in it, one must not put the blame on me, a mere woman without learning, but on the doctors who approved it without my even asking, for I did not even know them) (481). By dint of her being a "femme sans science" when authorial responsibility is gendered as male, Guyon deliberately seems to resist admitting she is the "author" of the *Moyen court* in any recognizable sense—say, a scriptural agent whose intention governs the production of a work, and who possesses some measure of control over its diffusion. Besides, she adds in 1709, the sloppiness of the printed version was alone enough to orphan it: "Il y avait aussi des fautes de copistes, qui rendaient les sens absolument inintelligibles" (There were also copy errors which rendered the meaning absolutely unintelligible) (558).

Nevertheless, Guyon implicitly recognizes that a defense based on the mutual incompatibility of inspiration and responsibility is looking less and less convincing: saying whatever came into her head was, she notes herself, a "fault." For her *Life* documents an increasing consciousness of the legal vulnerability of writing, and specifically of autobiography, since the latter is a genre that all too clearly poses the question of the author's relation to the text. This had already become obvious in the storm around the *Moyen court*, as Guyon came to the realization that her dissociation of author and text is useless for the very simple reason that her accusers do not seem to care about her book at all.

Il est à remarquer que l'on ne dit rien à ceux qui l'ont approuvé; que loin de condamner le livre, on l'a réimprimé de nouveau depuis que je suis prisonnière et affiché à l'archevêché et partout à Paris. . . . Le livre se vend et se débite, se réimprime, et moi je suis toujours prisonnière. On se contente dans les autres [cas], lorsqu'on trouve quelque chose de mauvais dans des livres, de condamner les livres, et on laisse les personnes en liberté, et pour moi, c'est tout le contraire; mon livre est approuvé de nouveau et l'on me retient prisonnière. (474)

(It is to be noticed that no one says anything to those who approved it; that far from being condemned, the book has been reprinted again since I became a prisoner and exhibited at the Archbishop's palace and everywhere in Paris. . . . The book is being sold, distributed and reprinted, and I am still a prisoner. Normally, when something bad is found in books, it suffices to condemn the books while letting the person remain free, and yet for me it is quite the contrary; my book is approved again and I am being held prisoner.)

Guyon could hardly be more lucid about the bankruptcy of the system of Church approval: it still nominally exists, but behind this mask hides another sort of responsibility that no one will explicitly formulate. Yet the truth can be inferred: her book is republished, ergo it can only be her person that is at stake.

Ironically, this new state of affairs should have suited Guyon well, for she had always been uncomfortable whenever the debate turned to doctrine and refutation, preferring to concentrate on the supposedly unequivocal simplicity of her actions.[100] Guyon manifests a persistent belief that her life speaks for itself, that it vindicates her cause. Hence she goes ahead and offers her life story to the infamous Gabriel Nicolas de La Reynie, chief of police under Louis XIV:

[J]e lui dis qu'il y avait une voie très sure de connaître ma vie et que je le suppliais de demander au Roi qu'on en fît l'examen, qu'il serait aisé de la connaître à fond, et qu'il lui serait ensuite assez facile de juger du fond des choses qu'il prétendait m'imputer.... Et, sur cela, j'entrai avec lui dans un détail de tous les lieux où j'avais été, de toutes les personnes qui m'avaient accompagnée, de celles chez qui j'avais logé et avec qui j'avais eu commerce, les temps, les lieux, les dates, avec de telles circonstances qu'elles renfermaient tous les temps de ma vie. (R 39–40)[101]

(I told him that there was one sure way to know my life and begged him to ask the King to have it examined; [I said] that it would be easy to know it thoroughly, and that there would then be no difficulty for him to judge the merit of the things he claimed about me. . . . Upon which I went into the details with him regarding all the places I had been, all the people who had been with me, those women who had lodged me and with whom I had conducted business, the times, the places, the dates, with such a wealth of circumstance that they encompassed all the moments of my life.)

As I have argued in the case of Bourignon, however, saying that biography can justify the individual before the law is tantamount to admitting that lives have become a legitimate object of attack. And this is indeed Guyon's situation: in cooperating so fully with La Reynie by opening up her life, she meets her adversaries on their terrain of choice; her accusers, realizing that their efforts to incriminate Guyon's teaching are coming to naught, deliberately deflect their accusations from her doctrine to her person. According to the superior of the Sulpicians, for instance, Guyon's doctrinal defense is in fact so strong that "il ne sera pas aisé de condamner la personne touchant la doctrine, à moins qu'on ne voie du déreglement dans les moeurs" (It will not be easy to condemn the person with regard to the doctrine, unless one can discern disorder in her behavior).[102]

Guyon's improvised autobiography before La Reynie (the account containing "all the moments of [her] life") fails to receive, however, a sympathetic reading, and Guyon remains in prison. As the Quietism quarrel wears on, Guyon learns that the "official," received interpretation of a life is determined by the reader with the most power — Bossuet, in this case. Guyon speaks twice of her entrusting of the manuscript of the *Life* to the bishop of Meaux — an episode that constitutes such a violation of her sense of privacy that, she says, "J'en ai encore les entrailles toutes émues lorsque j'y pense" (It still makes my blood [literally, entrails] boil whenever I think about it) (586). The expression is strong for the habitually docile Guyon. Her neo-stoic calm vaporizes when faced with biographical violation. In the first passage, she recounts a strange about-face on the part of Bossuet.

> Mr. le d[uc] de Ch... donna [à Bossuet] de mon aveu l'histoire de ma vie (afin qu'il me connût à fond), laquelle [Bossuet] trouva si bonne qu'il lui écrivit *qu'il y trouvait une onction qu'il ne trouvait point ailleurs.* . . . Ce sont, si je m'en souviens bien, les propres termes d'une de ses lettres. Ce qui paraîtra étonnant, c'est que M. de Meaux, qui avait eu de si saintes dispositions en lisant l'histoire de ma vie, et qui l'avait estimée tant qu'elle resta entre ses mains, y vit, lorsqu'il y avait près d'un an qu'il ne l'avait plus, des choses qu'il n'y avait pas vues auparavant. (550)
> (With my permission, the duke of Ch. . . gave [Bossuet] the story of my life [so that he might know me thoroughly], a story which [Bossuet] found so good that he wrote to him *that he found in it an unction he found nowhere else.* . . . These are, if I remember well, the very terms of one of his letters. What would seem to be astonishing is that M. de Meaux, who had had such a saintly disposition in reading the story of my life, and who had esteemed it so much that he held on to it, saw in it, more than a year after he no longer had it, things which he had not seen in it before.)

The things he had not seen were, of course, the propositions he would try to have declared as heretical by Rome. But what bothers Guyon is not doctrine: she repeatedly insisted that if the Church should find her teachings inaccurate she would retract them. Rather, she wants to be "conn[ue] à fond" (thoroughly known, or more literally known "to the bottom") and believes that the exposition of her life is the perfect way to achieve the manifestation of her inner self. Yet Bossuet would go on to use the manuscript of her *Life* to ridicule her. In the second passage to deal with this episode, she tells of his treachery. "Je lui avais confié [à Bossuet], comme je l'ai dit, l'histoire de ma vie sous le sceau de la confession: mes dispositions les plus secrètes y était marquées: cependant j'ai su qu'il l'avait montrée et en avait fait des railleries" (I had entrusted [to Bossuet], as I have said, the story of my life under the seal of confession: my most secret dispositions were marked in it: I found out, however, that he had shown it [to others] and had made a mockery of it) (585). This is, historically, perfectly accurate, and Guyon's anger is justified: Bossuet quoted and mocked the most confidential portions of the *Life* in the widely circulated *Relation sur le quiétisme* of June 1698.[103]

As it turns out, autobiography, instead of being transparent, becomes one more source of confusion and misrepresentation. Faced with Bossuet's public use of her private life, Guyon imposes a decisive change on her autobiography: she turns it into an indictment, into a register of a judicial wrong. Gone are the neologisms, the inadequate but somehow meaningful metaphors. After having seen clearly that "on ne m'a tourmentée jusqu'à présent que pour des termes peu exacts" (up to now I have been tormented only for imprecise terms) (R 48), Guyon starts paying attention to language and the way it can be manipulated. Already, at the close of her 1688 section, she had concluded that the language of her adversaries was not inspired and automatic, like her own, but malleable and willfully misleading.

[I]ls [her accusers] me dirent qu'il n'y avait personne qui ne fît des méprises, que cela s'appelait des erreurs. Je lui demandai s'il voulait dire *Errata*, comme l'on met dans les livres, que je le ferais volontiers, mais pour des *erreurs*, que je ne passerais jamais celui-là. (511)
([My accusers] told me that everyone made mistakes, and that that was what was called errors. I asked him if he meant *Errata*, like those placed in books, I would gladly admit it, but as for *errors*, I would never concede that word.)
Ils voulaient me faire mettre que s'il se trouvait de l'erreur dans mes livres . . . , je les détestais. Je dis que je n'avais aucun livre qui ne parût. . . . Pour s'excuser, il dit que mes écrits étaient assez gros pour passer pour livres et l'on mit *écrits* (i.e., in the written transcript of the interview). (513)
(They wanted to have me write that if there were any errors in my books . . . , I detested them. I said that I had no books that had appeared. . . . To excuse himself, [the interrogator] said that my writings were large enough to pass for books and the word *writings* was put in the record.)

Moreover, language can also be manipulated in its most material aspects — by forgery, which becomes a recurring theme of 1709. Guyon is shown a letter from La Combe (her director) denouncing her and admitting to having had immoral dealings with her, but she immediately recognizes what is behind La Combe's supposed betrayal. Guyon inspects the letter, and finds "qu'on y avait corrigé un 'V' différent de ceux du P. La Combe . . . , pour servir de modèle à l'écrivain, lequel en contrefaisant le corps de l'écriture s'était négligé sur les 'V' qu'il n'avait pas fait semblables à ceux du Père" (that someone had modified a "V" in it that was different from those of P. La Combe . . . , so as to provide a model for the copyist, who, in imitating the handwriting, had neglected the "V"s, which he had not made similar to those of the Father) (R 123). Guyon's inspection reveals the letter to be "véritablement contrefaite" (truly counterfeit) (R 123). The oxymoron is especially appropriate in this atmosphere of scriptural and linguistic trickery, where, Guyon now realizes, what is true is far less important than what can be made to seem so.[104]

Written words, then, are discovered to be servants of the realm of appearances. They are uncontrollable, fatally exterior even as they attempt to gesture toward the subject's inner "fond." The problem Guyon experiences with language is something more than its age-old inadequacy before the ineffability of God. Rather, language fails because it is always somehow *out of context*, for the printed word moves in circles the author cannot predict, read in ways the author did not intend. This is the lesson of Guyon's *Moyen court*, whose very popularity proved its author's downfall: she could no longer control her reading public. "[Je n'ai] jamais eu l'intention de donner au public ce petit livre (qui n'était proprement qu'une instruction particulière que j'avais écrite à la prière d'un de mes amis qui me l'avait demandée ensuite de quelques conversations sur cette matière, que nous avions eues ensemble)" ([I] never intended to give to the public this little book [which was in fact only a private lesson written at the request of one of my friends, who asked me for it after some conversations we had together about the subject]), Guyon says (538). A "conversation" becomes a "written private lesson" becomes a "little book": orality, haven of the communal first-person plural ("que nous avions eues ensemble") moves unstoppably toward print. The more widely a work is read, the more likely it is for it to be *mis*read, especially in the case of spiritual teaching, which must be tailored, Guyon says, to the needs of the aspirant. So she can no longer permit herself the luxury of speaking (as she had written in more optimistic times) "sans savoir si le terme est propre" (without knowing if the term is a proper one).

Language obeys not the logic of the subject, but the logic of the *public*. Guyon's 1709 *Life* marks the advent of her realization that she is a public personage—not in the sense of having disciples, of being the center of benevolent attention, but because Bossuet's accusations have thrust her before an anonymous group that will attempt to judge her. It is to this public she realizes Bossuet is appealing, and the opinion of this public that determines what will or will not be considered true. At times Guyon seems to believe she can actually make an impact upon her anonymous audience. Bossuet's machinations, she understands, are most potent when she is deprived of observers who will recognize her good conduct. Hence she breaks out in tears upon leaving Vincennes, where at least she had the comfort of being somewhat in view: "[E]n ces lieux l'on était témoin de ma conduite, mais . . . dans un lieu sans témoins il serait aisé d'en imposer au public" (In these places there were witnesses to my conduct, but . . . in a place without witnesses, it would be easy to deceive the public) (R 60). She also shows her willingness to use the public to her advantage, as when she leads her accusers to believe that she thinks "La Combe"'s forged letter to be legitimate, hoping that they will publish the letter and that she will thereupon be able to "en faire connaître la fausseté à tout le monde" (to make its falsity known to all the world) (R 124).

Guyon writes in 1709 as if before a tribunal. She starts to insert protestations of veracity where, formerly, none had been necessary. She *crafts* her text—the composition of which is now anything but automatic, proceeding at the rhythm of half a page per day—deploying the documentation that she possesses on the Bossuet affair. Letters, papers, and declarations all crowd in on Guyon's text, beginning with the last additions of 1688. They count as material proof of the inadequacy of the official version of her interrogations. "Voici la teneur des papiers que je leur avais donnés . . . dont, par la miséricorde de Dieu, j'avais gardé le double, afin que l'on voie (je veux dire ceux entre les mains de qui ces écrits tomberont) la différence qu'il y a de ceux-ci à ceux que l'on m'a supposés" (Here is the content of the papers I had given them . . . of which, by the mercy of God, I had kept duplicates, so that one might see [I mean those into whose hands these writings will fall] the difference between these papers and the ones that have been imputed to me) (513). They also indicate to what extent Guyon's attention has shifted from the exteriorization of her interior to a bare historical narrative: these formal, juridical documents are diametrically opposed in tone and content to the early sections of the *Life*.

It is odd, given the care with which she constructed and documented her prison narrative, that Guyon deemed it private, not even suitable for posthumous publication with the rest of her *Life*. Marie-Florine Bruneau, for instance, has noted the paradox of Guyon's decision, and explained it by her desire to shield her family from further attacks.[105] Perhaps the appeal to simple fear has some merit, but other reasons for keeping her indictment secret are amply inscribed, in fact, in Guyon's *Life*. For the picture Guyon gives us of the public is anything but a sphere of open debate. Although Guyon occasionally indicates that she seems to think that she can have recourse to the public tribunal, in general the public emerges as the docile audience of those in power, of those who will make their judicial moves always with a mind toward, to use Guyon's oft-repeated phrase, "en imposer au public" (deceiving the public). Bossuet cultivates this arena, which is more like a stage from which, according to Guyon, "on entretenait le public avec tant d'art et de soin" (they manipulate the public with so much art and care) (R 99–100). Guyon realizes that the accusations against her do not even need to be plausible; on the contrary, the more odious she is made to appear, the more her accusers manage to "éblouir le public" (dazzle the public) (R 96). The public is, finally, implicitly analogous to the courtiers of Versailles; Guyon paints Bossuet's judicial maneuvering as if it were a variation on Louis XIV's spectacular *fêtes* and machine plays: "Je voyais bien pourquoi l'on faisait jouer tant de ressorts, et pourquoi l'on employait tant de machines pour me faire paraître coupable et me donner dans le public comme une personne capable des plus grands crimes" (I saw indeed why they used so many ropes and pul-

leys and machines to make me appear guilty and to present me in public as a
person capable of the greatest crimes) (R 88). The *Récits de captivité* bathe in
an atmosphere of a simulacral reversal, where authenticity slips entirely over
into the domain of appearance: "Je connus bien qu'on . . . ne voulait faire ce
nouvel examen que pour imposer au public, et rendre la condamnation plus
authentique" (I well realized they . . . wanted to carry out this new examination only in order to deceive the public, and to make the condemnation
seem more authentic) (R 172). Authenticity is what can be *produced*, an effect
of truth received by a duped audience.

In such an environment it is small wonder that Guyon's interior can find
no place, nor that she does not trust her text to the public. And still she writes,
feeling she must answer the charges that "made her entrails boil." The question remains: for whom is she writing in these pages that will take nearly three
centuries to appear in print? In a sense, Guyon reverses the generic sequence
often asserted by historians of autobiographical forms, a sequence in which
historical memoirs, largely impersonal and written mainly for "posterity" or
for the "historical record" are largely supplanted by the more inward-looking
narratives of self-understanding and progress known as autobiography. Guyon starts with autobiography, realizes its contradictions and failures, and
reverts to memoirs. Sixteenth- and seventeenth-century memorialists such
as Monluc and Bassompierre, disaffected with the monarchical power that
they saw as their enemy, could only hope that their revisionary historiography
would receive a sympathetic audience sometime in the future.[106] Similarly,
Guyon resolves the dilemma of the impossible public projection of herself by
imagining an impartial tribunal before whom she argues a case her contemporaries refuse to hear.

Inserting posterity into the position of the narratee is perhaps the inevitable consequence of Guyon's long elaboration of the rupture that comes
to insinuate itself between the private, interior subject and the society this
subject seeks to minister to. Publicity would turn the text into a locus of mis-
reading, of inevitable disjunction between intention and reception. And thus
the autobiographical text cannot mediate between anything at all; at best it is
the message a marooned subject slips into a bottle in the hopes that someone
sometime will stumble upon it. Guyon's last autobiographical words, harking
back to the happy days of transparency, are a nostalgic rejection of a world
that demands authorial discipline.

Il y a certains dévots dont le langage est un bégaiement pour moi. Je ne crains point
les pièges qu'ils me tendent, je ne me précautionne sur rien, et tout va bien. On me

dit quelquefois: *"Prenez garde à ce que vous direz, à tels et tels."* Je l'oublie aussitôt, et je ne puis prendre garde. Quelquefois on me dit *"vous avez dit telle ou telle chose, ces gens-là peuvent mal interpréter, vous êtes trop simple!"* [Mais] quand il faudrait être reine en changeant de conduite, je ne le pourrais. Quand ma simplicité me causerait toutes les peines du monde je ne pourrais la quitter. (R 178)

(There are some devout souls whose language is like stuttering to me. I do not fear the traps they hold out for me, I take precautions against nothing, and everything goes well. I am told sometimes: *"Be on your guard about what you say to this person or that."* I forget it immediately, and cannot be on my guard. Sometimes I am told: *"You said such and such a thing, certain people might interpret it badly, you're too simple!"* [But] if I could be queen by changing my behavior, I could not do it. If my simplicity were to cause me all the pain in the world I still could not abandon it.)

One *can* perhaps write oneself, Guyon seems to say, but to no effect—or only to a pernicious one. So end eight hundred pages and thirty-five years of autobiography—on the assertion of the inherent, unchangeable sincerity of a subject uncomfortable within the very autobiographical order that calls that subject into being.

In the centuries following Bourignon's and Guyon's autobiographical trials we have found ways to live with the genre, perhaps by forgetting what which these figures were acutely conscious of: having something like "personal experience" is not an entirely happy state of affairs. I will discuss the history of experience in more detail in the following chapter, but at least one remark on this ambiguity is in order here. On the one hand, experience as a modern category arises as the other of institution and tradition, and therefore forms a convenient point from which to levy critiques of the social order; on the other hand, those institutions—not to mention other unsolicited parties—are only too interested in the detection and taxonomy of secrets that will serve to "identify" individuals. The paradox suggests a simple maxim: privacy exists only from the moment it can be invaded. Such would appear to be the lesson of Bourignon and Guyon, for whom the strange, half-archaic reserve of Labadie no longer seemed an option. And the dictionaries of the following century, in the two meanings that would grow up around the word "personality," point us in the same direction.

The complexities of Bourignon's and Guyon's *Lives*, however, allow us to flesh out potentially empty formulae like these, to give faces and names to the people who confronted with a good deal of lucidity the contradictions of a type of writing that did not yet feel quite "natural." Any conventional literary history might note the works of Bourignon and Guyon as two early examples of an emerging genre, but I hope to have shown something more, something subtler perhaps: that early examples of this particular genre also function, positively, as tales of their own creation, and, negatively, as critiques of the world that has made them necessary. For a moment, autobiography could be recognized as an imposition as much as an impulse. "Il me semblait . . . ," Bourignon writes at the end of her first narrative, "que je n'oserais jamais plus paraître en la présence des personnes qui auraient lu mes secrets" (It seemed to me that I would never again dare to appear in the presence of anyone who had read my secrets). And yet a mysterious voice whispers, cajoles: " '*Arrête, arrête, le temps est venu de parler, et point de fuir*' " ("*Stop, stop, the time has come to speak, and not to flee*") (VI 127). For Bourignon it was the voice of God; for her detractors it was the voice of the devil, or no voice at all; for us, now, with three centuries of remove, perhaps it would not be too far of a stretch to say that it was the voice of autobiography, burrowing its way inside our collective brain. Within and without, at once self and other, autobiography had become that shifting border on which so many moderns would nomadically wander for centuries to come.

Chapter Four
The Experience of Difference
Jean-Joseph Surin's Science expérimentale

"In this way I understood through my own experience what I had read, how 'the flesh lusts against the spirit and the spirit against the flesh' (Gal. 5:17)."[1] "Experience" is a concept so familiar that at first there may be little in Augustine's use of the word in this passage from book eight of the *Confessions* to slow the reader's eye. Indeed, it would not be unreasonable to suggest that "experience" is familiar by design, intuitive by definition, because it supposedly precedes the cultural mediations that subsequently disfigure its originary purity. As such, it ranks high in the pantheon of the West's numerous placeholders of immediacy, up next to "natural," "authentic," or, of course, "interior."[2] Yet a brief look at Augustine's use of the words "me ipso experimento" reminds us of two things: first, of the tight etymological relation between "experience" and "experiment" (a point to which I will return); and second, of the fact that the word has not always stood for some irreducible subjective immediacy. For Augustinian experience reinforces or reconfirms the lessons of an authoritative text: as in the famous scene in the garden of Milan, where Augustine's conversion is effected both through the reading and the remembering of Antony's conversion as previously recounted by Anthanasius, experience can never escape textuality. Indeed, Augustine would no doubt fail to understand why or how one might want to "escape" textuality in the first place, since his life readily organizes itself as a manifestation of the fullness of the divine Logos.

Over the years, the *Confessions* themselves would serve as an intertextual template for other writers and other experiences, and the seventeenth century had no shortage of reappropriations of the scene in the garden of Milan.[3] The following chapter does not concern the textual mediacy of experience, however, so much as the obverse of this truism: how did experience come to stand in for immediacy, anyway? What seems to me worth examining is the early modern breakdown of Augustine's ultimately reassuring textual regress, and the simultaneous construction, on the ruins of exemplarity, of the subject as that which is left over when textual authorities fail, as a sort of differential residue.

The work of seventeenth-century literature that affords the best starting point for the examination is, fittingly, sui generis. Jean-Joseph Surin's *Science expérimentale des choses de l'autre vie*, composed in the summer of 1663, was not elicited by a spiritual director, nor was it destined to function as public apology; no biographer used it as a privileged source of material, no editor wrote a preface lauding its interior virtues, and no group co-opted it as a point of sectarian cohesion. No one published it for a century and a half. Even formally, the work looks like no other: a two-part retrospective first-person narrative is bookended between two parts of a demonological treatise. But perhaps the principal oddity of the *Science expérimentale* is that saying what it is not is also saying what it is. For it is, in short, about being different. Implicitly and explicitly, the *Science expérimentale* poses a series of questions on how one might write about a type of experience that only imperfectly corresponds to things one has read. Under what form can one write about something defined as new if the codes that will assure its reception do not yet exist? Who gives the writer the authority to articulate his difference, if authority is by definition normative and normalizing, the product of a given institutional role? And how can difference grasp itself through writing, if writing (within the Church especially) has traditionally been the province of example, paradigm, and system?

The common thread running through these questions is the place of the writer in a discursive order essentially similar to the one that governed Augustine's conception of experience some thirteen centuries earlier. As we shall see, Surin is unable to live as easily as his great predecessor within the comforts of intertextuality: on the contrary, his autobiography recounts a long battle with madness resulting precisely from his inability to see any conformity at all between his experience and the teachings that an institution had provided him. He tells of a wandering, of straying into a labyrinthine, uncharted and properly *subjective* experience—for, as Michel de Certeau has remarked, "it is because he loses his place that the individual is born as a *subject*."[4] Or, rather: the modern subject has always already lost one place while simultaneously gaining another, the place of experience and difference; the subject loses its textual reference points, but finds autobiography, which is the text that needs to be invented when all others fail. Some might consider this place to be a mirage, mediacy masquerading as presence; Surin himself was not blind to the contradictions of his project. And yet the illusion of autobiographical identity enabled him to return from his painful odyssey relatively healthy, relatively optimistic, and with a manuscript that told—relatively—of what he had been through. Surin got lost, but upon his return, the literature of experience would never again be quite the same.

A word on the organization of this chapter. Because of his uncertainty regarding what and for whom he was writing, Surin took elaborate pains to "package" what most would now call an autobiography: the *Science expérimentale* has what one might term a kernel/husk structure. For reasons that will become clear, I do not believe that singling out the autobiographical kernel for analysis amounts to a betrayal of Surin's intentions, or to an anachronistic projection of modern readerly desires onto a project that possessed its own coherence. On the contrary, I argue that Surin did his utmost to encourage us to read certain parts of the *Science expérimentale* as something special, and, moreover, that *at the time he was writing* he could only craft a space now recognizable as autobiography (the kernel) by opposing it to and then rejecting something it was not (the husk). In a sense, then, it is the package itself that creates its contents: Surin invents autobiography by insistently figuring it as the "not that" of doctrinal or memorial discourse. It follows that retracing the sometimes convoluted steps Surin took to create a space for autobiography is a necessary prelude to reading the autobiography itself. Hence, after a brief look at Surin's own troubled life, this chapter will move from an analysis of the elaborate structure of the *Science expérimentale* to a close reading of the work's autobiographical portions. I will conclude with a consideration of three centuries of editorial decisions meant to bring Surin's strange hybrid in line with changing reading habits.

The Making and Unmaking of a Modern Exorcist

Temporally and geographically, Surin's life bore an emblematic relation to the history of autobiography, be it spiritual or secular. He was born in 1600, with the century that would see enormous changes in the place of the subject in the literary, philosophical, and political landscape, in a city—Bordeaux—that was home to France's first and foremost introspective author, Montaigne. Montaigne had been dead only eight years when Surin was born into a family of the *noblesse de robe*. His mother, according to Surin's testimony, was extroverted and invasive; his father, a member of the Bordeaux parliament like Montaigne, was, by contrast with his mother, drawn in the same direction as the author of the *Essais*—toward introspection.

Thirty years had passed between the death of Teresa and Surin's child-hood, but for the French public her influence was just beginning to make itself felt. Surin was still an infant when her *Life* was first translated by Jean de Bré-tigny and Guillaume de Chèvre (or du Chevre). Bordeaux in particular, due to its proximity with Spain, was a prime point of diffusion of mystical works of the Spanish Golden Age; John of the Cross, for instance, was translated first by a Bordelais. The religious revival making its way into France was repre-sented here especially by the foundation of convents and monasteries; in the first twenty years of the century, their number in the city more than doubled.

That the young Surin should, then, come under the influence of the key figures of the Spanish Counter-Reform is no surprise. This influence was dual, and to a certain extent, divided and contradictory. On the one hand, Surin was stirred by the apostolic life of Ignatius of Loyola; on the other, he was pas-sionately fond of Teresa, whose *Life* would be the principal intertextual ref-erence (with the exception of the Bible) of his own autobiographical project many years later. Contemplation was much in vogue. Certeau has described the general enthusiasm for contemplative prayer as the obverse or interior-ization of the apostolic zeal so evident especially with the Jesuits—the "re-conquista" not of foreign (or provincial) lands fallen into heresy, but of the interior domain. And so Teresa's *Life* was anything but dogmatic reading; it was, rather, "a fiery book exchanged among schoolboys." [5]

Surin's divergent enthusiasms reproduced a cleavage within the Society of Jesus, which was the site of a contradiction between two increasingly ex-clusive religious tendencies—the need for efficient worldly apostolic organi-zation and the valorization of contemplation and interiority.[6] Perhaps such a contradiction can be viewed as an inevitable extension of divergent aspects of Ignatius's own personality, formed on the one hand by his mystical experi-ence at Manresa, and on the other by an awareness of the possible excesses of mystical phenomena, phenomena that his famous *Spiritual Exercises* meant to control and channel. At any rate, the Jesuits of Bordeaux, into whose ranks Surin entered as a novice at the age of sixteen, were increasingly divided over the direction the Company of Jesus was taking. Some in the order found them-selves accused of being too attracted by the inner life, and this mystic faction soon felt itself alienated within an order it deemed disproportionately tem-poral in its concerns. Increasingly, these mystically oriented members of the Company came to define union with God as total rupture with the world. Some, like Jean de Labadie, concretized that rupture by leaving the order; others, like Surin, stayed on, attempting to reconcile their interior needs with an institution that treated as dangerous their invocation of Ignatius as a model contemplative.[7] Perhaps the psychological and/or spiritual troubles that Surin would experience arose in large part from the difficulty he had in finding a space where his interior aspirations could have free range. Coupled with the unwanted attention of his invasive mother, the atmosphere of the Company contributed to the constrictions ("serrements") he would repeatedly complain of in the *Science expérimentale*.

The *Science expérimentale* sandwiches the anecdotal account of Surin's spiritual pain and ecstasy between doctrinal ruminations on demonology. As my initial remarks have made clear, this hybridity is a particularly rich source of information regarding the evolution of the autobiographical mentality, and I will return to it in more detail presently. For the moment, I would suggest simply that the work's odd structure can be read as an attempt to achieve a tentative reconciliation between the antagonistic tendencies at work within the Society of Jesus, that is, to forge an interior space within a heavily institutional structure. In other words, Surin took an institutionally approved form (the demonological treatise) and bent it to his own needs. This penchant for the subtle deviation or detouring of the institutional toward the personal was also a particularly noteworthy aspect of what was without a doubt the most formative and determining episode in Surin's life—his role as exorcist during the famous Loudun possession of the 1630s. In exorcism Surin found a chance to combine spectacular service within the ecclesiastical order with a much more private view of the importance of interior progress and knowledge of God.

The first rumors of possession began circulating in the Ursuline convent of Loudun in September 1632.[8] The convent had been founded some seven years earlier, as part of the great religious revival of the beginning of the century. Its superior, soon to become famous throughout France, was Jeanne de Belcier, known in religion as Jeanne des Anges. She had, since her girlhood, been subject to visions; her novitiate, begun in 1622 with the Ursulines of Poitiers, was marked by the theatricality that characterized much baroque spirituality—for example, the special devotion which she lavished on those with the most repulsive sicknesses. By the time she took her permanent vows in 1623, her spiritual background resembled that of so many other women of the century, from the sainted (Marguerite-Marie Alacoque) to the shunned (Jeanne Guyon). Her destiny would be, however, quite singular.

On her own admission, Jeanne de Anges was hungry for advancement in the order; upon learning of the establishment of a new convent in Loudun, she says in the text that has come to be known as her *Autobiography*, "[j]e demandai avec grande insistance d'être une de celles qui seraient envoyées pour faire la fondation" (I insistently asked to be of the sisters sent to found [the convent]).[9] Success was soon hers: she had only been at Loudun for one year before the mother superior left and chose Jeanne des Anges as her replacement. At twenty-five, she had become the leader of a struggling convent comprising some seventeen sisters.

The years before the possession were punctuated by the scandalous activities of a priest of doubtful vocation, Urbain Grandier. A great womanizer, Grandier was the author of a *Traité du célibat des prêtres*, in which it was argued that "il vaut mieux . . . goûter de la femme que de périr d'abstinence" (it is better . . . partake of women than to perish from abstinence).[10] It was also Grandier whom Jeanne des Anges, shortly after the first symptoms of possession appeared, claimed had insinuated himself into her dreams and bewitched the women of the convent. Grandier was a convenient scapegoat, having made at least as many enemies as cuckolds in the city. Denounced first on December 11, 1632, it was another year before his arrest, upon which the interrogations and tortures began. Finally condemned for "magic, witchcraft and possession" according to the judgment handed down on August 18, 1634, Grandier was sentenced to be burned alive the same day.

The prompt execution of the sentence did nothing to stop the possession, the continued visibility of which served numerous interests.[11] Whatever the social context of the drama, however, Surin, appointed as exorcist to Jeanne des Anges in December of 1634, took his job very seriously indeed. While many, especially observers in Paris, were incredulous, Surin believed in the seven demons that Jeanne des Anges claimed were inside her. His predecessor, the Père Tranquille (ironically named, as it turned out—he was Grandier's official torturer, and died mad several years later), felt that a good exorcism was one that demanded that the devils be made to speak and answer as much as possible. But for Surin, using possession as a theater of Church power was of little importance. Physically, at any rate, he was not equipped for such a role; young, inexperienced, and frail, Surin was ill-suited for the demands of theatrical exorcism. He himself was surprised by the order to proceed to Loudun.

Yet Surin did have his own special philosophy of exorcism, one that he himself characterized as "interior." Bringing to his new job the very same affective bond that was, in these years, so in vogue in spiritual direction, Surin sought to apply the values of intimacy and interiority to a task that had been customarily undertaken only with spectacular force. Surin exposed his theory of exorcism in the *Triomphe de l'amour divin sur les puissances de l'enfer*, a memoir of his relations with Jeanne des Anges that he had begun in 1636.

Surin had initially thought himself unqualified for the role he was ordered to play—"n'ayant pas la force de se peiner comme les autres exorcistes à lutter de soi avec le Diable" (not having the strength, like the other exorcists, to exert myself in struggles with the Devil)—until he had the idea of relying on his inner vigor ("vigueur *intérieure*").[12] Loudun, then, would provide a testing ground for the power of the interior over the Devils, continually associated with artifice and exteriority. Surin, conscious of the novelty of his method ("une manière assez nouvelle," he proclaims it), as well as of the potential power deriving thereof (the "secrète vigueur . . . de cette sorte d'arme" [secret vigor . . . of this sort of weapon]), set off for Loudun thinking: "Si je ne peux autre chose, je parlerai de Dieu et de son amour aux oreilles de la possédée, et si je puis faire entrer mes propos en son coeur, je gagnerai une âme à Dieu et lui persuaderai de s'adonner à cette vie heureuse qu'on a intérieurement avec lui" (If I cannot do anything else, I will speak of God and his love into the ears of the possessed, and if I can make my words enter into her heart, I will win a soul for God and will persuade her to give herself over to this happy life that one can have inwardly with Him).[13] By using exorcism for his own interior ends, Surin was committing the first of many subtle deviations from approved practice.

Loudun, then, represented for Surin not so much a theater as a spiritual laboratory in which he would carry out his "science expérimentale," or experimental science: the possession would enable him to test the power of a cultivated interior against the exteriority of evil, perhaps thereby making his "secret vigor" manifest to all. His method made a great impression at least on Jeanne des Anges, who in her own autobiography portrays her victory over the demons as an effect of her own inner strength, as a type of spiritual growth. Quickly, however, Surin's inner vigor ebbed. Just one month after his arrival, physical symptoms of an interior disequilibrium appeared—difficulty walking, migraines, asthma attacks. Surin, by his own diagnosis, was obsessed.

To seventeenth-century demonologists, obsession was the flip side of possession. Furetière, in his 1690 dictionary, defines it as a state in which "les démons, sans entrer dans le corps d'une personne, la tourmentent et l'affligent au-dehors" (demons, without entering the body, torment and afflict the person externally). Furetière's definition is in one sense an accurate rendering of a distinction new to seventeenth-century demonology, and seems to fit the events of Loudun well. Unlike in the case of the possessed Jeanne des Anges, demons did not speak through Surin's body. But it is equally true that in Surin's own somewhat idiosyncratic view, obsession was a much more serious perturbation than possession. Devils are inside the possessed, but only in bodily terms, not in terms of spiritual interiority; the possessed is invaded, but her identity itself is not destabilized.[14] That is, Jeanne des Anges herself never doubted the truth of God; she struggled, but always knew what she was struggling for and against. Surin's physical symptoms, though, were of a different nature; they constituted manifestations of a psychological disruption that brought such certainties into question. If these distinctions seem a bit archaic, one should recall Charles Taylor's acute observation that the phenomenon of witchcraft marked the uneasy transition between two types of identity. Witchcraft took on increasing importance "just at the time and to the degree that the identity was emerging which would break our dependence on orders of ontic logos [in which the world conforms to a pattern of rational self-manifestation], and establish a self-defining subject."[15] Involving more than demonological nit-picking, distinctions between "possession" and "obsession" translated the difficulty of making the new subjective order coincide with previously dominant identity paradigms. And these efforts were of lasting importance for us: it was the term "obsession" that detached itself from its demonological origins and still survives today as a way of describing behavior, precisely because it acquired a psychological, properly subjective dimension that possession did not have. Surin's obsession—his struggle with madness and a conviction of his own damnation—would last for over twenty years.

By October 1636, Surin was exhausted; he was recalled and replaced by a proponent of spectacular exorcism. All in all the authorities, both secular and religious, were frustrated by the situation, feeling that it had gone on too long and thus implicitly brought their power and competency into question. Yet some six months after Surin's departure, one of Jeanne des Anges's seven demons, speaking through her mouth, declared that only Surin was capable of dislodging him. Surin dutifully returned to Loudun, and finally, on October 15, 1637—the feast day of Saint Teresa—the last devil, as it left the superior's body, left the name "Jesus" inscribed on the back of her left hand. Five years had elapsed since the outset of the affair, and one more would pass before things had entirely calmed down.

For a moment, Surin was famous. The Loudun affair proved enormously popular with France's devout. Interrogations with the demons were published in cheap editions; in response to the demand for first-hand information, Surin started a memoir of the affair, the *Triomphe de l'amour divin sur les puissances de l'enfer*; and Jeanne des Anges wrote a text published eventually in the nineteenth century as her *Autobiographie*.[16] In her triumph, Jeanne des Anges became in Certeau's formulation a "walking miracle,"[17] touring France, even visiting Cardinal Richelieu with a relic from Loudun destined to ease his hemorrhoids. Surin accompanied the new star on a pilgrimage to the tomb of François de Sales, in Savoy.

Surin, however, was not able to finish the *Triomphe*; his trip to Savoy was his last public activity for a long while. His obsession—or, if the modern reader prefers, whatever psychological problems awakened in Loudun—caught up with him; his psychosomatic difficulties increased to the point of incapacitation. The next eighteen years were, with intermittent exceptions, a period of near-autistic self-absorption. Unable to preach, at times even, according to his testimony, incapable of movement, Surin retreated to the Collège de la Madeleine in Bordeaux. For the years between 1639 and 1657, his usually voluminous correspondence consists of only two letters. Yet from 1654 on, Surin had been slowly recovering. Little by little he resumed his activities—first in solitude, by writing (most of his widely read spiritual works, such as his *Catéchisme spirituel* and the *Cantiques spirituels*, date from the middle of this decade); then, with increasing extroversion, by spiritual direction, correspondence, and, finally, the missionary preaching he had been doing before Loudun. But before moving on to the missionary activity that was his favorite form of service, Surin wrote in 1663 the labyrinthine *Science expérimentale des choses de l'autre vie*: in it, Surin cast a retrospective eye back upon demonology, Loudun, and the personal trauma responsible for a two-decade interruption of his true vocation. He had only two years to live.

Autobiographical Deviations

The recognition of genres such as the diary, memoirs, and autobiography amounts more or less to an institutionalization of solipsism. We moderns have learned to write for ourselves; no one need ask us to describe our experiences; we each have our own story to tell. As Philippe Lejeune has remarked, it is something of an inalienable modern right that the individual be endowed with the potential for autobiographical authorship.[18] But what would it have been like to write about oneself long before diaries were ready-made with little locks and keys, at a time when both biography and autobiography were subsumed indiscretely under the title *Life*, and when it seemed nearly impossible to say "I remember" unless so asked by some authority? Of course, many did embark upon just such a task: recent research on the genre's history has revealed vast numbers of texts—religious autobiographies, but also artisan autobiographies, and aristocratic memoirs—peopling the pre-Rousseauian subjective landscape.[19] Yet one thing that characterizes each newly discovered "cache" of autobiography is its rather clannish nature: particular institutional circumstances combined to make possible the flourishing of a micro-genre within a given population. This social dimension certainly holds true for the convent autobiographies discussed in Chapter 2, for instance, or for the sectarian apologetics of Labadie, Bourignon, and Guyon. But what of those who wrote without the stabilized reception provided by a shared class, caste, or creed? How, in that case, could one write for oneself? While many literary and cultural historians have documented the *quantity* of early modern autobiographical writing, little effort has been made to understand the conceptual difficulty that private writing presented to practitioners for whom "private writing" did not yet really exist.

Surin had written a good deal before the *Science expérimentale*, availing himself of received genres: a programmatic exposition of the spiritual life (his *Catéchisme spirituel*), a collection of poems (*Les Cantiques spirituels*), as well as several letters, were all published during his lifetime; other didactic works (*Les Dialogues spirituels*) and letters would appear in the decades following his death. All were published or circulated in manuscript for the edification of the faithful, and although the mystic content of many led to some rewriting on the part of his editors, Surin's activities as an author were implicitly sanctioned by his place in the Church hierarchy.[20] His historical memoir of the events at Loudun and his role in them—*Le Triomphe de l'amour divin sur les puissances de l'enfer*[21]—also reflected Surin's professional capacities: the *Triomphe* was a tale of spiritual direction of which Jeanne des Anges's transformation was the subject, a tale that Surin took care to present as recounting an important historical event, worthy of the invocation of heads of Church and state. While it certainly reflected Surin's own stakes in the affair—the experimentation with a new interior-style exorcism, and his insistence on documentable, historical proof of the success of this interior intervention— the *Triomphe* also fed the insatiable demand of readers for information on the Loudun possession. From both the perspective of Surin and his readers, therefore, it was a text authorized by Surin's official role as exorcist. Fittingly for such a record, it is composed primarily in the third person, Surin designating himself as "le Père"; and personal experience (if the term has any meaning in such a plainly memorial context) is evoked only to the extent that it coincides with a history to be written.[22]

Surin had more to say about the events of Loudun, however, than could be conveniently contained in the edifying tale of Jeanne des Ange's spiritual triumph: there remained the matter of his twenty-year obsession. Everything suggests that, for Surin, this would prove a far more difficult story to tell. It is surely no accident, for instance, that from the beginning Surin conceived of the *Science expérimentale* as a posthumous work. "Je ne prétends pas publier cela" — he wrote to Jeanne des Anges, with whom he corresponded until her death in 1665, just several months before his own — "mais il se trouvera dans ma chambre quand je mourrai" (I don't aspire to publish this, but it will be found in my room when I die).[23] His straightforward refusal to deal with the *Science expérimentale*'s diffusion and potential readership is a first indication of what would turn out to be an intractable problem, that of accounting for a text that seemed to lie outside the discursive practices that an ecclesiastical figure could be expected to engage in.

The best clue to the *Science expérimentale*'s unconventionality — in the strongest sense of the word — is its structure, which attempts to combine in the same work the apologetic and doctrinal lessons on demonology Surin drew from Jeanne des Anges's experiences, as well as an account of the personal upheaval provoked by his encounter with her. The *Science expérimentale* contains four parts:

— Première partie . . . où sont les arguments qui prouvent les choses de l'autre vie.
— Seconde partie . . . en laquelle le Père Surin parle des maux qui lui sont arrivés par suite de la possession des démons chassés par son ministère.
— Troisième partie . . . où le Père traite des choses en particulier qu'il a reçues à l'occasion et en suite de la possession de Loudun.
— Quatrième partie . . . contenant des réflexions sur les vérités qui ont été déduites dans la première partie.[24]
(— Part one . . . containing the arguments proving the things of the other life.
— Part two . . . in which Father Surin speaks of the pains he underwent following the possession by the demons cast out during his ministry.
— Part three . . . in which the Father treats of particular things that came to him on the occasion of, and then after, the possession of Loudun.
— Part four . . . containing reflections on the truths that were deduced in the first part.)

Parts I and IV constitute the demonstrative element of the work. Part I is in a sense a transposition of the events narrated in the *Triomphe* into the first person; these events no longer form a historical narrative, but are organized according to the specific light on demonology they provided to Surin the exorcist. The last part uses a "je" as well, one whose referent is less Surin the historical personage than Surin as articulator, in the present of writing, of a theological and demonological argument. Parts II and III, on the other hand, employ a narration alternately in the first and third persons, have little doctrinal interest, and do not concern the events of Loudun per se. These are the parts that I refer to when speaking of Surin's "autobiography"—but in so isolating them, I am, as I will show, taking my cue from Surin himself.

The four-part structure of the *Science expérimentale* may well appear odd; indeed, for nearly three centuries it would be a source of much confusion.[25] This oddity was, however, the price to be paid for attempting to make a space for autobiography: Surin creates an autobiographical "I" by opposing it to other, institutionally sanctioned uses of the first-person pronoun; he props up its still doubtful authority with the institutional guarantees afforded by demonological speculation. The *Science expérimentale* overflows with asides that remind the reader of Surin's efforts to define the type of writing he is undertaking. First, Surin constantly reiterates the distinction between memorial and personal narration, using the word *Histoire* to refer to the *Triomphe de l'amour divin*, both in his *Correspondance* and in the *Science expérimentale*.[26] The Loudun narrative becomes a kind of generic foil against which the difference of the *Science expérimentale* will be made clear. Indeed, the *Triomphe* is explicitly evoked at the beginning of both of the two middle sections of the *Science expérimentale*, as if the relation of his own troubles could not commence without a bow to Surin's official role on the theater of history (cf. 167 and 255). The private man takes over the role of speaker from the public man; these passages constitute a *prise de parole*, a deflection of the right to speak from the historical to the personal. Another chapter begins in a similar vein:

Je ne veux ici mêler les discours présents avec ce qui est déjà écrit en l'histoire [i.e., the *Triomphe*] qui a été faite de la délivrance. Dans le livre des histoires, il est dit comme quoi le Père fut envoyé [to the tomb of François de Sales], mais il faut dire ici comme quoi il tomba dans le grand mal qu'il souffrit, et qu'il eut pendant tout ce voyage. (172)
(I do not want to mix here the present discourse with what has already been written in the history [i.e. the *Triomphe*] that was told of the deliverance. In [that] book, it is explained how the Father was sent [to the tomb of François de Sales], but now it must be told how he fell into the great pain that he suffered, and that he underwent during the entire journey.)

Parts II and III are above all a distanciation from this "livre des histoires" in which Surin intends to move away from the extraordinary events that he has witnessed, toward that part of his life that has no place in an historical narration—Surin the sufferer. "Je ne veux ici mêler": Surin's sense of unity of theme (or genre) is conscious, and based on the implicit conviction that public and private do not mix. The *Triomphe* and the *Science expérimentale* represent two different forms of the autobiographical writing, for the latter, unlike the former, treats that which is invisible to history.

Within the four-part *Science expérimentale* itself a similar separation is under way, as something recognizable to us as the personal defines itself against the doctrinal and the expository. Surin so clearly isolates his proof for "les choses de l'autre vie" (part I) and his meditations on these arguments (part IV) from parts II and III that, if it were not for two passing internal allusions and an important prefatory note (existing in only one manuscript), one might suspect that the incongruous framing of the second and third parts was a later editorial choice, and not Surin's intention at all.[27] Yet all evidence points to an imbrication that was both confused and well thought through. In the prefatory note, for example, Surin both indicates the unity of the four parts and places the whole project under the sign of the *secret*. After the title, he writes:

> Ecrit à Saint-Macaire l'an 1663
> *Secretum meum mihi*
> *Secretum meum mihi*
> Combien que j'aie dit au commencement du 1er chapitre [de la première partie] que les choses ici couchées sont pour l'instruction et la consolation de plusieurs âmes, pourtant la plupart ne peuvent être communiquées, particulièrement celles de la seconde partie. La 3e partie peut être moins communiquée que la 2e, mais la 4e le peut tout à fait, si Dieu nous fait la grâce de les produire, car la 4e est une quantité de réflexions sur la vérité de l'histoire déduite en la première partie et dont on peut tirer grand profit. (129)
> (Written at Saint-Macaire in the year 1663.
> *Secretum meum mihi.*
> *Secretum meum mihi.*
> Although I have said in the beginning of the first chapter [of the first part] that the things written down here are for the instruction and consolation of many souls, most of them nevertheless cannot be communicated, particularly those of the second part. The third part is less communicable than the second, but the fourth can be communicated completely, if by God's grace they are made public, for the fourth [part] contains reflections on the truth of the history deduced in the first part, and from which one can profit greatly.)

Secretum meum mihi—"my secret for myself"—is from the Vulgate, Isaiah 24:16; repeated twice and underlined by Surin himself, it sheds light on the author's reluctance to publish his text. But if the work itself, with all its four parts, does seem to form a whole for Surin; in terms of secrecy, it is a hierarchical whole: parts I and IV are destined to be communicated for the edification of others, whereas parts II and III form the secret center of the work. The structure of the *Science expérimentale* reflects Surin's own indecision: it is an assemblage of parts which function as separate units destined for different readers (parts I and IV are communicable to others, II and III are for his eyes only).

Different sorts of discourse are juxtaposed, different readers implied, and different levels of intimacy are suggested. Within this confusion, however, one cannot fail to discern an ordering principle. For the *Science expérimentale* is depth-structured: in it, Surin hints by way of his prefatory note there can be isolated a movement from the public to the private, and from the general to the individual.

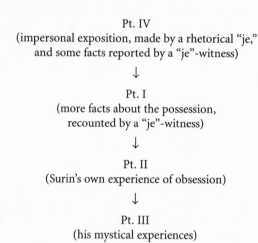

Pt. IV
(impersonal exposition, made by a rhetorical "je,"
and some facts reported by a "je"-witness)
↓
Pt. I
(more facts about the possession,
recounted by a "je"-witness)
↓
Pt. II
(Surin's own experience of obsession)
↓
Pt. III
(his mystical experiences)

Surin deviates from the model provided by another hybrid work, Augustine's *Confessions*, in which the most crucial portions are precisely the final books (X–XIII) by which the author transcends personal memory.[28] Although Surin places the most impersonal of the four parts last, thus at first glance suggesting an outgrowing, or surpassing, of personal memory similar to the one many have detected in the *Confessions*, in reality the *Science expérimentale* possesses less a linear structure than a spiral one. Impersonal meditations occupy the exterior of the autobiographical universe; the narration of the spiritual life as lived by the subject, the interior. "The diagram of the text," Francis Barker has written in reference to other writers of the period, "is as a series of concentric circles at the furtive heart of which is the secret declivity of the soul itself."[29] Surin structures his book so that the events of his life cannot be dislocated from its center.

On the most self-evident level, the purpose of all spiritual writing is edification, and the *Science expérimentale* is no exception. Yet, as Surin's preliminary note suggests ("pourtant la plupart [de ces choses] ne peuvent être communiquées" [yet most of these things cannot be communicated]), edification must be predicated on the ability of the aspirant—whence the establishment of degrees of communicability, and, by extension, of intimacy. The limiting of readership per se is nothing exceptional in the case of mystical works; not all souls, it was felt, were destined for the same spiritual direction. Hence many works (including, perhaps, the *Science expérimentale*) were intended solely for spiritual directors, as Surin notes in his *Guide spirituel*.[30] Notwithstanding such customary caveats, the limitations Surin hints at are complex enough to reflect a confusion on his own part as to the status of his writing. Surin multiplies markers intended to make up for the work's lack of codes or characteristics that would have, in effect, pre-selected readership and determined a "horizon of expectations." Even within what I have designated as the "core"—parts II and III—the attribution of secrecy varies. The readership of one specific *chapter* is limited to a prepared few, for instance.[31] Moreover, parts II and III are not equally "secret": "la plupart [des choses ici] ne peuvent être communiquées, particulièrement celles de la seconde partie. La 3e partie peut être moins communiquée que la 2e." On the whole, the *Science expérimentale* appears an elaborate system of gateways that would screen out successively more and more possible readers.

Yet even if part II falls outside the purview of accepted writing as Surin himself has defined it, it does possess a potential readership. It shares, for example, the apologetical nature of the first and last parts: Surin advances "proof"—this time taken not from the devils' work on Jeanne des Anges but on himself—in order to make others believe in demons and therefore in "celui qui les a créés et qui les a punis" (He who created and punished them) (253). More important, knowing full well that his suffering is not the result of madness as others had erroneously maintained, Surin seeks to give his own account to those who have branded him as mad.

Toutes les fois que j'avais la puissance de parler, [ce] qui était fort rare, je désirais toujours quelqu'un à qui communiquer mes angoisses, et *dire ma vie . . .* ; si bien que, comme *je ne cessais de chercher quelqu'un à qui découvrir mon coeur*, je le faisais parfois sans discernement, et tous ceux à qui je le disais me rendaient encore plus misérable, prenant pour de grands péchés *des choses qui n'étaient pas dans le fond ce qu'elles paraissaient dans la surface.* (43–44, emphasis mine)
(Each time I had the power to speak, which was very rare, I always wished for someone to whom I might communicate my anguish, and *recount my life . . .* ; so much so that, since *I did not stop searching for someone to whom I could reveal my heart*, I was sometimes imprudent, and all those I told made me even more miserable, taking for great sins *things which were not at bottom what they appeared to be on the surface.*)

In a sense, Surin's near-autistic state was only exacerbated by his inability to communicate his plight convincingly: this passage suggests that the work of the devil consists in preventing the individual from speaking, or in blocking proper reception. The *Science expérimentale* will therefore be that recovered or misinterpreted voice, and Surin is very much in need of a reader so that the harmonious textual circuit might be completed.

Part III, however, implies a more problematic readership still: the subject Surin now confronts is the work of God and not of the devil. Many a nun and lay mystic had written at length of the work of divine grace, but they had done so in the relatively codified context of spiritual direction, and always with the alibi of obedience to superiors. Surin, on the other hand, notes at the end of part II that his graces cannot be "avanc[ées] sans ordre exprès" (put forth without an explicit order), acknowledges he has not received this order (253), and yet proceeds to write down just these graces. Writing, then, in a sort of scriptural no-man's-land, with no one having asked for his text and no one to read it, protestations as to the edifying power of his experience are absent in Part III. Surin has become both the producer and the consumer of his work: "De sorte que n'ayant en vue d'écrire ceci que pour moi, je ne puis que je ne me dise à moi-même, que c'est ici vraiment le royaume de Dieu" (Such that, with the intention of writing this only for myself, I can only say to myself that this is truly the kingdom of God) (337). As narrator and narratee collapse into one, the first person proliferates ("je ne puis que je ne me dise à moi-même"). Part III of the *Science expérimentale* is the record of a mystical experience that Surin does not know quite what to do with, save perhaps repeat it to himself. He labels it unreadable ("[Ceci] est secret et ne se doit communiquer à personne" [(This) is secret and must not be communicated to anyone], reads the warning inscribed at the head of Part III [255]), carefully envelops it in more unproblematic, professional forms of discourse, and finally tries to short-circuit its reception back to its origin, himself: "n'ayant en vue d'écrire ceci que pour moi."

Sciences of Experience

Before exploring the contents of the secret space Surin labored to create outside—or rather, inside—accepted discursive practice, it remains to attend to one further paratextual detail—a title as multivalent as the contents it attempts to circumscribe.

In one sense, what is most unusual about the title of the *Science expérimentale de choses de l'autre vie* is its very existence. As I have shown elsewhere, the seventeenth century was the scene of widespread hesitation over autobiographical nomenclature among editors and biographers. With the notable exception of Antoinette Bourignon's *La Parole de Dieu* (which Pierre Poiret subsequently baptized the *Vie intérieure*), autobiographers themselves did not even bother to give their texts any title at all, and the omission is logical, given that autobiography was still an "unreceived" idea. The problematic circulation (never mind publication) of autobiographical material nullified the need for titles; a title is one of many signs used to determine a "horizon of expectations" for a given text, and the autobiographical horizon was foggy at best. Strangely, even though to all appearances he considered the *Science expérimentale* not only a posthumous work but, moreover, one that had sections that could not be read at all, Surin implicitly provided for a readership in the very act of naming his text. The question of just whom that readership might consist of is less clear: unfortunately, the sixteenth and seventeenth centuries were a time of upheaval in the semantic register of both "science" and "expérimentale."

First, "science." On the one hand, and most widely, "science" retained its etymological meaning of knowledge—knowledge not as a process or method, but rather as a simple thing known. "Je souffre peine à me feindre," writes Montaigne: "si que j'évite de prendre les secrets d'autrui en garde, n'ayant pas bien le coeur de desavouer ma science" (It is painful for me to dissemble, so much so that I avoid taking others' secrets into my keeping, not really having the heart to disavow what I know).[32] In politics, it had overtones of omniscience: a customary formula of royal edicts made reference to "notre certaine science, pleine puissance et autorité royale" (our certain knowledge, full power and royal authority). Similarly, in theology it was (and still is) used to signify God's capacity to know in different ways; his "science de vision" (science of vision), for example, designates the "connaissance par laquelle Dieu voit toutes choses comme existantes dans les différents temps" (the knowledge by which God sees all things as existing at different times) (from the *Dictionnaire* of Richelet [1679]). Alternatively, the word could refer to a domain of specialized knowledge—logic, morals, and language were all considered "sciences humaines," in opposition to natural science.

The term's dominant modern meaning, however—"a branch of study which is concerned . . . with observed facts systematically classified and more or less colligated by being brought under general laws, and which includes trustworthy methods for the discovery of new truths within its own domain" (OED)—was slowly being elaborated in the wake of the work of Renaissance thinkers like da Vinci (1452–1519) and Copernicus (1473–1543). Francis Bacon (1561–1626) was deeply distrustful of scholastic "scientific" methods in

which the acquisition of knowledge was equated with assimilation of doctrine through extensive reading and ratiocination. This scholastic sense of the
word was still Furetière's primary one in his 1690 dictionary. Bacon, however,
like his contemporary Galileo (1564–1642), lay stress on the necessity of experimental research. Closer to Surin, both Descartes and Pascal railed against
book knowledge in favor of experimental method of one sort or another. For
Pascal, for example, nature's secrets were hidden, and experimentation was
necessary in order to bring them to light.[33] Proof, he contended in his programmatic *Préface pour le traité du vide* (1647), could be furnished by experiments, but not by rational demonstrations. "Dans la physique," he writes, "les
expériences ont bien plus de force pour persuader que les raisonnements" (In
physics, experiments have much more persuasive force than rational arguments).[34]

On the religious front, "science" had a life of its own. An analogy between the spiritual and medical realms contributed one connotation to the
term. In *L'Anatomie de l'âme*, Mino Bergamo has shown how spiritual literature adopted an "anatomizing" discourse, whose practitioners came to portray themselves as "doctors of the soul" — significantly, a soul not conceived
of as one, but as containing constituent parts.[35] In a similar vein, "la science
mystique" or "la science des saints" could refer less to a secret knowledge of
the divine than to a method of orison: when Bartolommeo Ricci's *Instrut-
tione di meditare* (1600) were translated into French in 1609, it was under the
title *Science des saints contenant une très excellente méthode pour familière-
ment converser avec Dieu*. However, the term "science," too compromised by
connotations of sterile cerebral stimulation, eventually dropped out of mystic use altogether. The once-popular terms "science des saints" and "science
mystique" would eventually become simply "la mystique" (mysticism) and
finally "la piété" (piety).[36] This series of lexical shifts took place as an experiential type of knowledge detached itself from and opposed itself to both traditional speculative (scholastic) theology and positive theology—the latter
being a new entity that humanistically sought to recover an original teaching
that had been altered or corrupted through the ages. Already in 1616, François
de Sales, elaborating on the topos of the enlightened illiterate examined in
Chapter 2, shows the signs of a hardening opposition between science and
experience:

Qui aima plus Dieu, je vous prie, ou le théologien Occam, que quelques-uns ont
nommé le plus subtil des mortels, ou sainte Catherine de Gênes, femme idiote? Celui-
là le connut mieux par *science*, celle-ci par *expérience*, et *l'expérience* de celle-ci la con-

duisit bien avant en l'amour séraphique, tandis que celui-là, avec sa *science*, demeura
bien éloigné de cette si excellente perfection.[37]
(Who loved God more, I ask you, the theologian Ockham, whom some have called
the most subtle of mortals, or Saint Catherine of Genoa, an ignorant woman? The
former knew him more by *science*, the latter by *experience*, and her *experience* led
her much sooner to seraphic love, whereas the theologian, with his *science*, remained
quite far from such excellent perfection.)

In the wake of the vogue for the experiential values of the interior, "science"
soon became the enemy.

The semantic field of "science," is, consequently, treacherous territory.
Even within the Church, the term was used in quite different ways. So when
Surin uses the term "science expérimentale," to what is he referring—to an
unknown law that can be uncovered and demonstrated through experimentation? To an anatomical charting of experience? Or to a knowledge that can
only be established by the subject who experiences it? Part of the difficulty
here lies not only in the first term, but in the second, in the words "expérience"
and "expérimental." The frontier between the concept of "experiment" and
"experience" is a shifting one, as is suggested by the fact that, in France, these
two senses of the word "expérience" never separated out into two signifiers,
as happened in English: "experiment" is preserved in the verb form ("expéri-
menter" means both to experience and to perform an experiment), "experience" in the noun (meaning both experience and experiment).[38] The title of
the *Science expérimentale*—a hybrid of dogma and diary—points therefore
in both ways at once, suggesting an experimental knowledge of the divine
(and the diabolical) that can be communicated, and an experiential knowledge that, as Surin says, "est secret et ne se doit communiquer à personne" (is
secret and must not be communicated to anyone) (255). Rather than having
a single clear meaning, Surin's title inscribes the tension between rapidly di-
verging concepts of knowledge, one universalizing and objective, the other
particularizing and subjective.

Demonology is the domain in which the methodological overtones of
the title apply. Surin presents his text as a testimony to the *perceptible* irrup-
tion of the other world into this one: "Dieu ayant permis une célèbre possession en ce siècle et *à nos yeux, au milieu de la France*, nous pouvons dire
que des choses de l'autre vie, et qui sont cachées à nos lumières ordinaires et
communes, sont venues jusqu'à nos sens" (Since God permitted a well-know
possession in this century and *before our very eyes, in the middle of France*, we
can say that the things of the other life, which are hidden from our ordinary
and common perception, made their way to our senses) (127–28, my empha-

sis). Writing offers the possibility of "explaining" these experiences, thereby permitting certain deductions as to the reality of the other world. Especially in parts I and IV, Surin insists on the physicality of possession, on the way it brings proof of the existence of demons (and, by extension, of the God of the Catholic Church) to the privileged organ of knowledge that is sight.[39] "[L]'expérience nous a fait *voir* que . . ." (experience has made us *see* that . . .) (365); "l'expérience des choses qui se *voient*" (the experience of things that are *seen*) (359)—Loudun was a laboratory, and Surin its indefatigable scientist: "[J]e puis prouver la vérité [of Loudun], ayant eu tout le temps de l'examen, et mieux que ceux qui, tout bottés, ont voulu en juger pour avoir été une matinée sur le lieu, et sur les premières apparences ont voulu porter des décisions définitives sur une matière de cette conséquence" (Having had much time to examine it, I can prove the truth [of Loudun] better than those who, with their fancy boots, wanted to pronounce judgment after spending one morning in the place, and, based on superficial appearances, to make definitive decisions on a matter of such consequence) (140). Surin's testimony is trustworthy because he took the time to go beyond appearances, to examine. In this, he behaved in a way consonant with the primacy of vision in the sciences.[40]

What distinguishes demonology—the science of the diabolical—from mystical science, however, is precisely the former's visibility, its exteriority. The autobiographical portion of the *Science expérimentale*, by contrast, entertains a much more problematic relation to knowledge and communication, for here Surin seeks to tell of an experience that has gone underground, so to speak: after the events recounted in the *Triomphe*, he writes, "le Père [i.e., Surin himself] sortit . . . de la manifeste obsession, qui lui rendait la présence de l'Esprit malin sensible sur sa personne et passa dans un travail intérieur du tout extrême" (Father [Surin] came out . . . of the manifest obsession, which made the presence of the evil spirit sensible on his person, and passed into a most extreme interior travail) (167). The passage from the *Triomphe* to parts II and III of the *Science expérimentale* are, therefore, a movement from the outwardly perceptible ("sensible sur sa personne") to the purely subjective domain ("un travail intérieur"). It follows that such inner experience cannot be the object of an experimental science, to the extent that it cannot be *shown*.

Nevertheless, the interiority of experience does not necessarily *preclude* the establishment of an experiential science—understanding science here to mean a systematic way of describing empirical data. Mystic writing in general insists on the need for the subject to experience directly the effects of divine union, and, as I have mentioned, it normally propounds a method for achieving this union. Unlike demonology, mystical science may not be visible and experimental, but it *is* systematizable, theorizable. The concept of mystical science presupposes the identity of experience: knowledge, and its communication, are possible because we are all basically put together in the same way. Teresa, in moving from the first version of her *Life* to the second, final, version, takes the random notation of isolated experiences and adds the didactic metaphor of the four waters. Her experiences are organized into a pattern, a map; as much as a chronology of *her* life, she provides a topology of *the* spiritual life.

By insisting on the notion of *degrees* of prayer that govern spiritual life, Teresa was putting an emphasis on time and method that differed notably from medieval mysticism; as one scholar of the subject has explained: "For the medieval masters, the life of the soul is commanded by a theologico-metaphysical view of the relation of the soul to the divine essence and the Trinity. [In the works of Saint Teresa], it is a *succession of states of consciousness* in which the soul has the sensation of undergoing the empirical experience of its union with God." [41] The notion of a succession of states implies necessarily a chronology, and opposes itself to the predominant medieval view in which separate states have no temporal articulation among themselves. [42] Yet in another sense, insisting on the development or chronological unfolding of the subject's identity did not ultimately upset the position of the individual within the authoritative circuits of equivalence described by Augustine when he claimed that he experienced what he had previously read. Teresa's map was still based on a knowledge that proceeded from exemplarity and purported to be in some sense transmissible through writing. Of course, Teresa did routinely discount book knowledge (though with somewhat less vehemence than Surin would), predicating her readers' assimilation of her words on their prior experience. [43] But her mystical theology (the term she uses) left the epistemological underpinnings of scholastic and positive theology unscathed. Her autobiographical project — indeed, her whole oeuvre — reflects a belief that her experience is a model for that of others. Teresa constructed, out of the elements of her experience, Foundations (*The Book of Foundations* [1573–76]) and Castles (*The Interior Castle* [1577]), elaborate architectures of the interior, intended to facilitate the access of other aspirants to divine union.

The title of the *Science expérimentale* alone might lead us to expect a similar emphasis on method and system, both of which are undergirded by a confidence in the analogic and metaphoric capacity of language to organize and communicate an experience that existed precisely because it was endlessly replicable. But if Surin's expository commentary on Loudun, unhesitantly dogmatic, fits well with the title, the autobiographical center of the text requires that we read its title in yet another way: as designating an experiential knowledge that refused all attempts at systematization. The new subject of experience was one whose likeness to others was always in question.

Surin's Secret Knot

The paradox at the heart of Surin's notion of a "science expérimentale" can be summed up in simple terms: Surin agonizes whether he should try to be just like everyone else, chalking up feelings of difference to mere pride or fancy, or whether he must, in fact, accept this difference in order to achieve mental equilibrium. On the one hand, Surin longs to situate himself both as the follower of the exemplary figures of the Christian mystical tradition, and, in turn, as an example in his own right of the profound effects of God's compassion. Here, he seeks to anchor his identity in a communicable, systematic, and imitable knowledge. On the other hand, this type of knowledge is at odds with another sort, an experiential knowledge based not on precedent but on irreducible singularity. By way of this struggle, Surin explores the limits of exemplarity, and ends up articulating a new type of knowledge, situated at the core of the subject and inaccessible through reference to tradition.[44]

Surin's principal difficulty following Loudun was the belief that he was damned; others thought him mad, he says, but in his estimation his ills were distinctly spiritual. Madness, he writes in terms reminiscent of Descartes, consists in mere mental error: "[D]ès qu'un homme dit qu'il est damné, les autres ne jugent de cela que comme d'une folie, mais ordinairement la folie est dans les idées qu'on a conçues. . . . [L]'un dit qu'il est une cruche, l'autre dit qu'il est cardinal, et ces idées sont légitimement tenues pour folies" (When a man says he is damned, others judge it as madness, but ordinarily madness is in the ideas one has conceived. . . . One man says he is a pitcher, another that he is a cardinal, and these ideas are legitimately considered mad) (178). By contrast, the idea of damnation implies pain: what he and other mystics have suffered "ne sont point folies, mais peines extrêmes d'esprit" (not madness at all, but extreme pains of the spirit) (179). Most of Surin's self-justification in this second part of the *Science expérimentale* turns around just this invocation of other mystics who have suffered from an analogous sense of damnation. Surin proceeds to defuse accusations of madness by arguing that the strangeness that constitutes the mark of madness (according to received opinion) is only apparent. In fact, he argues, the feeling of being damned is not unusual—

and perhaps exemplary—and quite compatible not only with sanity, but also with saintliness. "[C]roire que l'on est damné, est une chose que plusieurs fort sages ont cru" (Believing oneself damned is something that many very wise men have believed) (179), he notes, and invokes in his favor the examples of Suso, Ignatius, Teresa, Louis de Blois, and John of the Cross. Whenever he was told he was mad "il alléguait toujours les exemples que j'ai dits" (he always put forth the examples I have mentioned) (180).

The ability to view oneself as a follower of such exemplary figures accompanies the subject's return to normality; Surin suggests that mental health can be found in conformity with traditional paradigms of religious experience. Recourse to example is the strongest possible proof of one's self-possession. As Surin indicates, one source of his error in thinking himself damned (for, according to Catholic dogma this *must* be an error—damnation during this life is never a *fait accompli*) lies precisely in his incapacity to garner consolation from spiritual authorities. He lives a divorce between what he reads and hears about the spiritual life—which should have assured him that great psychic and physical pain was in no way a sign of damnation ("on lui disait cela mais rien ne pouvait lui faire impression" [they told him so, but nothing could make an impression on him] [175–76])—and his own experience. A great breakthrough for him comes when one of the few compassionate souls he encounters during his long ordeal tells him of an "impression" he has had: "Notre-Seigneur vous fera la grâce de voir que vous vous trompez et que vous viendrez enfin à *faire comme les autres hommes*" (Our Lord will grant you the grace to see that you are in error and that in the end you will come *to do as other men do*). Upon which Surin asks himself "s'il était bien possible que Notre-Seigneur me fît miséricorde, et que je puisse vivre avec espérance *comme les autres hommes* et fidèles chrétiens" (if it were really possible that Our Lord would have mercy, and that I might live with hope *like other men* and faithful Christians) (227, my emphasis). The thought of being, in the end, just like everyone else, is what shakes him out of his torpor; he describes the affirmative answer he hears to this question as waking him out of a deep sleep ("profond sommeil"). Thus he ends the first part of his narrative—the part dealing with his "descent into hell"—with the happy declaration of his rediscovery of the human community of sameness: "ainsi donc ce me fut une grande nouveauté et merveilleux contentement que de pouvoir être réduit à la forme des autres" (in this way it was therefore a great novelty and a marvelous contentment to be able to be reduced to the form of others) (252).

Once he is able to persuade himself of the commonality linking him to others, the contemplative path, and its ecstasies, opens before him. This path consists of *topoi* that, while not necessarily fixed in an immutable hierarchy, guarantee, in the manner of examples, the authenticity and the orthodoxy of Surin's experience. Thus those parts of the autobiography that appear to the modern reader the least "original" are also the ones that indicated, to Surin's contemporary readership, the authenticity of the mystical graces received. Surin's entire ordeal, after all, was quite in the tradition of John of the Cross's "dark night of the soul," very much in vogue in seventeenth-century spiritual autobiography and hagiography.[45] In religious biography in particular, long periods of spiritual aridity were frequently advanced as proof of saintliness, for they figured Christ's days in the desert. In addition, Surin goes through periods of infantile simplicity, during which he can only address Jesus and Mary as "papa" and "maman." This too is a *topos* of the period — as Surin himself is proud to point out: "Et afin que la sagesse naturelle ne s'étonne point de cela, il y a des exemples de plusieurs âmes que Notre-Seigneur a réduit[es] à cet état" (And so that natural wisdom not be astonished at this, there are examples of several souls which Our Lord reduced to this state) (300). The need to anchor his experience in example is so imperious that Surin even adopts a commonplace of female spirituality, speaking of feeling wedded to Jesus, "le divin époux de l'âme" (the divine bridegroom of the soul) (330–31).

So the existence of these *topoi* and examples, of this common "form" to which Surin is reduced, ultimately founds the very possibility of spiritual knowledge, and does so by gesturing outside of the discourse of the speaker or writer, "toward support in a commonly accepted textual or referential world." [46] The ultimate such referential gesture is perhaps the *imitatio Christi*, one of the most powerful exemplary forces shaping Christian identity: the ideal Christian, in order to "follow" Christ, as the New Testament enjoins, imitates him. Although what constitutes imitation has varied immensely over the past two millennia, baroque spirituality in particular emphasized especially the reproduction of Jesus's character traits and life experiences, notably his suffering. Not surprisingly for the period, then, Surin often narrates his past experiences as an imitation of Christ. Of the many mystical graces visited upon him by God following his eighteen-odd-year struggle with the idea of being damned, some are plainly inspired by the Ignatian spiritual exercises. On the day of the Invention of the Holy Cross, for example, Surin describes an experience of crucifixion as an inner inscription of Christ's example:

Alors donc comme j'étais assis il me vint une impression de Jésus-Christ souffrant, et je fus lié sur mon siège intérieurement, et me trouvai comme si j'eusse été en croix, je fus trois heures là. La première heure je fus dans une agonie si extrême, que je n'en pouvais plus . . . , comme si j'eusse été cloué . . . ; la seconde heure, j'eus une peine en l'esprit, avec le travail d'aridité d'esprit et délaissement, et il me fut dit au haut de l'âme: *pure souffrance* [;] et à la troisième . . . , j'eus l'idée des douleurs de Jésus-Christ avec goût de sa douleur; mais j'eus la pensée que je n'avais pas comme lui le fiel et le vinaigre. (271–72)

(So then, seated, there came to me the impression of Jesus Christ in his suffering, and I was bound to my chair inwardly, and felt as if I were on the cross[;] I remained there for three hours. The first hour I was in such extreme agony that I could take no more . . . , as if I had been nailed down . . . ; the second hour, I felt a pain in my spirit, together with the travail of spiritual aridity and abandonment, and it was said to me in the upper part of the soul: *pure suffering*[;] and in the third hour . . . , I conceived of the sufferings of Jesus Christ and tasted his pain; but I had the thought that I had not had, like him, the gall and the vinegar.)

This Ignatian *mise en scène* is faithful right down to the sharp partitioning of time. Roland Barthes has commented on the extent to which Ignatius's *Spiritual Exercises* are founded on the principle of what Barthes calls articulation — notably, the temporal articulation we see here. Barthes defines articulation as the breaking up of experience into units through language, but takes care to note that strictly speaking, in the Ignatian text there is in fact no "experience" to come before this breaking up.[47] For the imitative or exemplary individual, nothing lies *outside* of the articulation of language; personal identity exists only within a shared language.

The key term in the above passage, however, is "impression" ("il me vint une impression de Jésus-Christ souffrant"). The exemplary self is a wax tablet, palimpsestically receiving impressions from the ideal model of which he is, or would be, a copy. Indeed, this copying process for Surin is lived intensely from within: more than an exterior imitation based on mere resemblance — a manipulation of signifiers such as stigmata — Surin speaks of an imitation that borders on the metonymical. Imitation is possible not through the subject's miming of the actions or physical characteristics of Christ, but because there is an inherent inner correspondence between the two. Another episode is described with the help of the recurrent metaphor of impression:

Il semblait vraiment que Jésus-Christ possédait l'âme et *gravait* en elle ses mystères. . . . Cela *imprimait* en l'âme fort vivement et fort délicieusement l'agonie de Notre-Seigneur au jardin des Olives. . . . Elle [l'agonie du Christ] était . . . *imprimée* en mon âme . . . comme si Jésus-Christ souffrant se fût *imprimé* lui-même sur l'esprit, et comme j'ai raconté ci-dessus que les démons *s'imprimaient* dans les âmes en leur communiquant leurs malices, . . . de même ici Jésus-Christ *s'imprimait* en l'âme, s'y communiquait soi-même comme un *caractère* divin . . . et cela fut *imprimé* d'une façon qui ne se peut dire. . . . J'eus en ce temps-là plusieurs pareilles *impressions*. (259–60, my emphasis)

(It seemed truly that Jesus Christ possessed the soul and *engraved* in it his mysteries. . . . This *impressed* very vividly and deliciously in the soul the agony of Our Lord on the Mount of Olives. . . . [The agony of Christ] was . . . *impressed* in my soul . . . as if Jesus Christ in his suffering had *impressed* himself on the mind, and as I have re- counted above that the demons were *impressed* into the souls by communicating their evil to them, . . . likewise did Jesus Christ here *impress* himself into the soul, commu- nicating himself to it like a divine *character* . . . and this was *impressed* in a way that cannot be said. . . . I had at this time several similar *impressions*.)

Like other mystical autobiographers of the period, Surin frequently resorts to this vocabulary which is, in the end, scriptural: God impresses/prints (*im- primer*), engraves (*graver*) or writes (*écrire*) his characters (*caractères*) in the mystic; and the devil uses the same tools to insinuate himself into victims of possession. Imitation is intimately tied up with a language grounded in di- rect, metonymic relation to the real; language is the physical link between imitator and model.[48]

But if the essential sameness of the spiritual path authorizes recourse to biblical citation as validation of individual experience, it follows that indi- vidual experience that somehow exceeds (or falls short of) the replication of an experience previously described in Scripture or patristic gloss lies out- side the scope of mystical science. That is, Surin's *idée fixe* of damnation is the exact contrary of all this healthy referentiality; at the root of his "identity crisis" lies a feeling of being outside of language and all that it guarantees. Mentally acknowledging the authority of an example brings no comfort to the subject, who can no longer *identify* with the text of tradition — a text that alone not only validates, but, as Barthes says, *creates* experience. Damnation, on the other hand, implies a subject that has fallen into the hell of differ- ence. It is, points out Certeau, "the exile of the speaker from the plausible [du vraisemblable], from the system of enunciations received as true (or false)."[49] Whether Surin was "really" in the grips of paranormal phenomena follow- ing the Loudun possession is doubtful for most of us, but it is also ultimately unrelated to the real difficulty raised by his autobiography: how is knowl- edge of the world, and by extension, of oneself, possible once the individual feels himself alienated from the authority of exemplars, from a commonly accepted structure which alone decides the truth, falsity, or verisimilitude of experience?

This question has no easy answer, and notwithstanding the relief evident in Surin's realization that he will indeed be able to "faire comme les autres hommes" (do as other men do), the journey back to sameness, to imitation, to exemplarity, is in fact less than certain. While Surin often equates both physical and spiritual health with exemplarity, at the same time he reveals the extent to which the authority of example has been shaken by his experience of singularity. One of Surin's spiritual directors, for instance, appeals to the authority of Saint John of the Cross in order to convince Surin that he must detach himself from, and even refuse, the graces visited upon him. Surin tries to obey, but finds that the doctrine cited simply does not fit his case. In theory John of the Cross may be correct; however, Surin writes, "dans la pratique, je trouvais que cela portait un grand mal à l'âme. . . . Cet exercice de rejeter ainsi les grâces . . . me tournait à si grand dommage et à si grande peine, que je ne savais que devenir" (in practice, I found that this brought great pain to the soul. . . . This technique of rejecting graces . . . led me into such great harm and such great pain that I did not know what to do with myself) (317). Hence submission to authority, far from being a cure, constitutes one more ordeal — an ordeal that leaves Surin's soul "détrui[te]" (destroyed) and "accabl[ée] entièrement" (completely overwhelmed) (317). Another well meaning priest attempts to show Surin how he has demonstrated in his writings that one cannot be damned in this life, again to no avail; scholastic knowledge is declared impotent — "cela me semblait de la paille" (this seemed like straw to me) (207). In spite of the "notion ordinaire de la grandeur et majesté de Dieu" (ordinary notion of the greatness and majesty of God) constantly before him, in spite of feeling like the Bible tells us Job felt, "je ne pouvais m'appliquer cela" (I could not apply this to myself).[50] Appeals to Church doctrine, be they anchored in names Surin respects in the highest, are useless before the immediacy of his experience; theological "notions" no longer *apply* to the subject.

So Surin is exiled from a comforting exemplarity, and alienated from a tradition that fails completely to make sense of — and thus to normalize — his relation to the visible Church and more generally to the world. Yet Surin was by no means the first to have to make sense of a world in which modes of knowledge tottered in the balance and whose history no longer seemed fixed by the glue of exemplarity. Generally, these are problems that characterize the Renaissance,[51] and Surin's observations might seem to come a bit late, as a kind of religious footnote to a text such as Montaigne's *Essais*, which deals, from a humanist perspective, with just these questions. As I have already suggested, part of Surin's distinctiveness arises from his invention of autobiography *qua* experiential space of difference as a response to the disintegration of the exemplary cosmos. Moreover, what sets Surin apart, and what pushed him to the autobiographical solution, was the degree to which the oft-noted epistemological crisis of the early modern period undermined the very health of his personality. Perhaps it is no accident that such an extreme reaction occurred within the Church, where daily existence was regulated by ritual, and whose community was founded on sameness. For if individual experience is, in fact, singular, how can the flock be united? How can even that most basic tool of religious community, obedience, be exercised?[52]

Surin's discussion of obedience—its necessity, but also its impossibility —reveals best the dilemma of reconciling a singular interior and the demands of organized community. Certainly, Surin cannot help but recognize that the feeling of exceptionality lies at the root of all disobedience, fanaticism, and heresy. In this he was a man of his time, a time when feeling different was a vice: as Jean Auvray warns the reader of his biography of Jeanne Absolu, one must never "tombe[r] dans le vice de singularité" (fall into the vice of singularity).[53] It was precisely because a description of Surin's ordeal might appear strange and singular that people would be tempted to call him mad—reason enough to keep quiet about what he had been through: "ce sont des choses si étranges et si peu croyables, que ceux qui les verront écrites les prendront pour des vraies fantaisies et imaginations d'un esprit égaré" (these things are so strange and so incredible that those who see them in writing will take them for the simple fantasies and imaginings of a wayward mind), Surin speculates at the outset of the *Science expérimentale* (165). Portraying his experience as a mystic commonplace both effects a return to normalcy, as we have seen, and defuses accusations like these.

Surin takes his turn leveling charges of singularity, however. He spends the better part of one chapter of the *Science expérimentale* analyzing the spiritual character of his fellow Jesuit, Jean de Labadie. Labadie would eventually traverse a series of orders and churches in search of a space that would allow the unhindered transmission of the graces he claimed to have received from God.[54] The Jesuit Labadie was in short order an ex-Jesuit, then an ex-Jansenist, an ex-Catholic, and, finally, an ex-Protestant. In Surin's autobiography, he plays the role of a vaguely evil double: owing to what Surin calls Labadie's "esprit de singularité et d'erreur" (spirit of singularity and error) (304) (note the telling association between the two terms), the latter has allowed his very real spiritual aptitude to be corrupted. Whereas Surin is always ready to submit his experiences to the judgment of his director, Labadie claims that Surin's exaltation of obedience's virtues is tantamount to allowing one's spiritual wings to be clipped: "Il me dit . . . que l'obéissance me retiendrait toujours bas et me lierait les ailes" (He told me . . . that obedience would always hold me down and would bind my wings) (308). The difference of opinion is irresolvable, and the two separate for good. In response to Surin's parting assertion that he would never fail in obedience, Labadie delivers the ultimate individualistic retort: "Cela est bon pour vous" (That is good for you) (308).

But Labadie's parting remark overstates the case for Surin's happy conventionality. For, as Surin knows only too well, if one is sure one's superiors are in error, and their commands cause one pain, the question of obedience becomes more problematic. This is why Surin devotes the longest chapter of his autobiography to theorizing obedience. He proceeds by dividing it into two types—obedience to one's superiors and obedience to one's director of conscience. He resolves the first problem, which concerns purely external conduct, by allowing for a space of inner dissent: yes, one must obey, but one does not need to give any truth-value to what is commanded. The authority of one's superior is exclusively *formal*, organizational; it is not, in fact, grounded in any claim to knowledge. Hence Surin, in a quasi-Cartesian gesture, places the subject in the position of arbiter of truth, stripping authority of its pretense of "knowing better." Nevertheless, by a sort of "morale provisoire" that safeguards the subject's link to society, Surin still considers it expedient to go through the motions of an obedience that has ceased to be anchored in truth.

This is only the case, however, "quand la chose ordonnée ne contient aucun mal" (when what is ordained contains no *mal*) (387), and it is Surin's definition of "mal" that creates a loophole in the dictates of obedience. "Mal" in parts II and III of the *Science expérimentale* refers to bad things, and to the subject's *pain* in particular, rather than to evil in general.[55] Obedience to one's director of conscience differs from obedience to one's superior, in that errors here create pain that the subject cannot simply ignore. "Quant aux directeurs de ma conscience, j'ai eu d'autres extrêmes *peines*, et je les nomme extrêmes, car ce sont les plus grandes de celles que j'ai eues. Je veux déduire ce qui s'est passé en cette manière, et combien j'y ai souffert de *maux*" (As for my directors of conscience, I had other extreme *pains*, and I call them extreme for they are the greatest of all those I have had. I want to describe what happened in this way, and how much *pain* I suffered thus) (311, my emphasis). Specifically, the root of this pain ("La racine de tout ce mal" [311]) arises from the antagonism between the singularity of the individual and traditional Church teachings: "[C]omme j'ai une conduite pour mon intérieur du tout extraordinaire, comme on le pourra juger par les choses que j'ai décrites ici, il est aussi arrivé que j'ai eu de terribles oppositions par ceux qui étaient les directeurs de mon âme" (Since I have a method of conducting my interior that is altogether extraordinary, as one might judge from things I have described here, it has also happened that I have encountered terrible oppositions from those who were the directors of my soul) (311).

The saga of inept spiritual direction runs through much early modern spiritual writing. Teresa made it a leitmotif of her *Life*, and Surin explicitly identifies with her description of the pains suffered at the hands of uncomprehending directors (315). Religious biography frequently took up the theme of incompetent direction. Maupas du Tours's 1642 biography of Jeanne de Chantal, for instance, tells of her great scruples in leaving her director. What is significant in the *Science expérimentale* is that the demands of the institution come to constitute a *problem* for the subject. If Teresa accepts the errors of her directors as a trial, as a sort of martyrdom (which, like obedience, is another subspecies of imitation), Surin ends up *contesting* misplaced authority. Similarly, while Jeanne de Chantal eventually leaves her director, her choice has no psychological drama; Surin, on the other hand, agonizes over the issue, refusing to play the misunderstood servant of God suffering upon the cross of spiritual (mis)direction.

Certainly, at the outset of his analysis, caught between the contradictory dictates of interior and exterior, Surin claims that in spite of very good reasons, he never wanted to "secouer le joug" — to shake off the yoke of obedience (311). Yet if we trace the recurrence of this crucial expression, and its eventual negation, we can start to gauge the import of Surin's struggle. Surin again evokes the individualistic specter of Labadie, who succumbed to the temptations of self-direction. Labadie forgot that both God and the devil are at work in each of us, and that, having only one's own dangerous subjectivism to go by, one cannot always tell one from the other. This is why, Surin says, "je n'ai jamais osé me hasarder à secouer comme lui le joug de l'obéissance, et m'abandonner pleinement à l'esprit qui me guidait" (I never dared, like him, to shake off the yoke of obedience and to abandon myself fully to the spirit that was guiding me) (313). Surin returns compulsively to the same overdetermined protestations of fealty and submission. "[J]e ne voulais pas me départir de l'obéissance" (I did not want renounce obedience) (318); "je lui [à Labadie] répondis que . . . je ne me départirais jamais de l'obéissance" (I answered him [Labadie] that . . . I would never renounce obedience) (308); "comme je m'étais résolu à l'obéissance, je ne voulais pas me départir de [l']idée [de mon directeur]" (as I was resolved to obedience, I did not want to renounce the idea [of my director]) (317).

The proliferation of these protestations betrays Surin's longing for a conformity between interior and exterior, between individual experience and systematic doctrine. Yet this prayer cannot be answered, because, in contrast to the case of obedience to one's superiors, here the subject cannot partition off a space of inner truth, for the commands of the director violate that inner space. And so Surin comes to the end of the longest chapter of his autobiography, deferring again and again, through these repetitions, the avowal that, in reality, he *did* "shake off the yoke." After pages of hedging, he finally declares the dilemma of subjective conscience and obedience to be irresolvable, "unbearable," and admits he could only opt for freedom: "je conclus que pour me mettre au large, et pour ne pas succomber sous le poids d'une si rude conduite, il fallait que je secouasse le joug de cette obéissance, changeant de directeur" (I concluded that in order to set out on the open sea, and in order not to succumb to the weight of such harsh conduct, I had to shake off the yoke of this obedience and change directors) (318). The expression occurs yet again several pages later, as a state of peace descends upon a liberated Surin: "[J]e demeurai en paix, secouant le sentiment de ce Père directeur et ce joug qui m'était insupportable" (I remained in peace, shaking off the advice of this director and this yoke that was unbearable to me) (321). "Pour me mettre au large": overthrowing obedience permits he who had complained repeatedly of constrictions ("serrements") to gain the open sea.

This is not the first occurrence of the dilemma of obedience; some twenty years earlier, another well-meaning superior had tried to get Surin out of his troubles just by ordering him, "en vertu de sainte obéissance" (by virtue of holy obedience), to "get over it" (passer outre) (213). The experience was similarly painful (again he uses the words "accablé" and "détruit" to describe his state). The basic problem here lies in the ecclesiastical belief in continuity and correspondence between the outer (the Church and its doctrines) and the inner—that which Surin calls "le noeud secret qu'il fallait défaire avec paix et avec le temps" (the secret knot that peace and time [alone] could untie) (213). This secret knot at the heart of the subject is what no scholastic knowledge can untie and no ecclesiastical order can break. If Surin's invocations of precedents and accepted teachings, and the common-place stages he passes through, often make of him an exemplary individual, his autobiography also, and more importantly, charts the growth of his conviction in the irreducibility of the individual, in the knot of subjectivity.

Apophasis and the Failure of Science

Since exemplarity and its discontents were of concern to the early modern world in general, Surin's tale of obedience betrayed has larger stakes than one man's personal religious practice. Indeed, the overturning of example in favor of some type of singularity appears in authors as opposed to the claims of Surinian mysticism as La Bruyère, who would write in a quite different context of the need for cultivating a cautious "esprit de singularité" (spirit of singularity), given that the examples at our disposal are so corrupt:

"Il faut faire comme les autres": maxime suspecte, qui signifie presque toujours: "il faut mal faire," dès qu'on l'étend au delà de ces choses purement extérieures, qui n'ont point de suite, qui dépendent de l'usage, de la mode, ou des bienséances.[56]
("One must do as others do": a suspect maxim, which almost always means: "one must do poorly," once one extends it beyond those purely exterior things of no consequence, which depend on habit, custom or propriety.)

La Bruyère here is speculating on the same division Surin tries to come to terms with by theorizing two kinds of obedience, interior and exterior. Yet for Surin, the divorce is of quite vital consequence to the whole uncertain project of the *Science expérimentale*, for the failure of exemplarity undermines the very project of a "science" of experience that the title promises, and casts doubt on the extent to which Surin shares Teresa's faith in the analogic, metaphorical, and communicative capacity of language. Once the "esprit de singularité" loses (as it will with La Bruyère) its association with madness, sin and error, and is instead embraced by the subject as the chief source of truth in a hollow world, the didactic possibilities of religious writing itself are called into question.

Teresa may have had reiterated the mystical topos of unsayability, of the inadequacy of language, but always within the constraints of method and the possibility of some sort of instruction. She writes *as if* language had some metaphorical power; to use Certeau's paraphrase of Teresa's oddly confident rhetoric of unsayability, her writing seems to say: "ce n'est pas ça, mais vous me comprenez" (that's not it, but you understand me).[57] The metaphor of the Four Waters in the *Life* is presumably analogous to the workings of the divine in man; this analogy makes instruction possible. Surin too appears to trust in the analogic power of language—he will, now and then, systematize his experiential knowledge, his subjective impressions, as if they somehow constituted objective descriptions of the working of God in the human body and soul. But what is most intriguing about the moments when experience seems to solidify into doctrine is that Surin tends to subvert these very systems of classification as he writes—as if he were attempting to imitate the didacticism of Teresa's autobiography, only to fail, and by this failure, to demonstrate once again the singularity of the subject's experience.

An example of this subversion of Teresian didacticism can be found in Surin's description of the four kinds of breaths ("respirs") that a mysterious voice explains to him and makes him experience.[58] Each type of breath has its own characteristics, and serves to render the spiritual corporeal. Surin catalogs these effects, explicitly invoking similar descriptions in Teresa's *Life*. Soon, however, he starts to unravel the very mystical science he has been building up. He quickly notes, for example, that while he has re-experienced these four breaths since receiving the angel's lessons, he has been unable actually to "engager en des réflexions fort particulières de leurs effets" (engage in any very precise reflections on their effects) (269). He adds patiently: "ce sera quand il plaira à Dieu" (this will be for whenever it pleases God). All in all, he says, "[i]l m'est seulement resté une notion de ces différences" (I have only been left with a notion of these differences) (270). Of the best of the breaths, glory ("gloire"), which he felt for two whole months, Surin can only say that he has not yet been able to figure out ("débrouiller") just what he experienced. He then proceeds to evacuate the very possibility—even desirability—of Teresian mystical theology, giving up all hopes of systematizing his experience: "Je ne sais ce que Dieu me réserve, je vois aussi qu'il n'y a rien de tel que de marcher en foi sans avoir aucune attache à ces différences, car une attache cause de grands embrouillements et travaux d'esprit, quand on s'y amuse" (I know not what God reserves for me, but I do see that there is nothing but to continue in faith without any attachment to these differences, for attachment can cause great difficulties and travails of spirit if it is a source of mere diversion) (270). Surin seems to say: Yes, something most definitely happened, but no, there is no use in my trying to think my way through it. The possibility of providing a potential disciple with a model is thereby eliminated.

This passage contains what might be termed an apophatic breakdown of representational language.[59] Apophasis is a term first encountered in Dionysius the Areopagite's *Theologica Mystica* (c. 500). By opposition to kataphasis, a discourse that speaks of God by saying what He is *like*, apophasis tells us only what God is *not* like—the logic being that God is beyond all representations or comparisons. Etymologically an "un-saying" or a "speaking-away," apophasis is not an exposition of doctrine, but rather a mode of discourse that refuses to reify the transcendent by the deployment of a never-ending series of negations of previous statements—or, as Michael Sells defines it, "a propositionally unstable and dynamic discourse in which no single statement can rest on its own as true or false, or even meaningful."[60] Apophatic discourse has many features, but no hard and fast rules. In respect to traditional, "positive" theology, it has always been a marginal type of discourse, relatively rarely used. Two of its most noted practitioners ran into considerable trouble with the Church: Marguerite Porete, the thirteenth-century Beguine, was burnt at the stake; the Dominican Meister Eckhart may have been headed for a similar fate when his natural death made it unnecessary. Indeed, apophasis is a type of discourse threatening to any order in that, as Jacques Derrida says, its essential trait is one of *going too far*—"passing to the limit, then crossing a frontier, including that of a community, thus of a socio-political, institutional, ecclesial reason or *raison d'être*."[61]

Eckhart and Porete use apophasis in a manner similar to Surin: they posit hierarchies of mystical states while simultaneously retracting or collapsing them. A hierarchy of states—say Surin's breaths, or the Four Waters of Teresa's *Life*—presupposes progress, direction; it provides a framework against which the aspirant can measure his or her moral, spiritual or intellectual distinction. Apophasis is the method by which an author both asserts the possibility of such progress, and ultimately, of experience of God, but simultaneously denies the absolute truth of a hierarchy which is at best heuristic, and at worse, the source of auto-suggestion, theatricality, and spiritual pride.

Surin's use of apophasis, however, emerges as almost unintentional, rather than calculatedly subversive—as if his efforts to be expository were constantly hitting up against the unsystematizable wall of this new entity called experience. Another example is in order. I quote the following passage in full, for it shows well how experience continually slips through Surin's scientific fingers:

Je voudrais faire connaître que tout cela vient à l'âme par l'union avec Jésus-Christ, laquelle est la source de tous les biens qui lui adviennent, et tandis qu'elle sent ainsi Jésus-Christ en soi, elle a quatre ou cinq effets qui lui sont ordinaires; le premier est une élévation aux choses célestes, et une impression continuelle des biens de l'autre vie, avec un dédain de la vie présente. Le second est une force et vigueur pour agir et entreprendre toutes choses qui se présentent, et tandis que l'âme le sent ainsi en soi, en la façon que j'ai dite, elle a comme un continuel tempérament de gloire, qui fait que, dans les affaiblissements comme ceux qui arrivaient au Père [Surin], parfois extrêmes, au lieu de succomber, il rejaillissait du dedans des choses qui étonnaient tout à fait l'âme par leur grandeur, car il se faisait comme une saillie de l'esprit intérieur, qui mettait tous les sens comme s'ils eussent été en gloire. Cela arriva trois ou quatre fois, principalement que l'âme était réduite aux plus grands affaiblissements, et lors elle se trouva environnée de biens qu'on ne saurait décrire. Et même à présent, je ne saurais les mettre en avant, tant ils sont difficiles à représenter. Mais cela venait à l'âme par l'assistance de ce qu'elle sentait en soi, qu'il lui semblait être comme si Jésus-Christ l'eût remplie et pénétrée du tout. Voilà pourquoi il lui semblait voir sortir de ses yeux comme des rejaillissements de gloire, si doux, et si élevants que je n'ai jamais rien éprouvé de si étrange. (332–33)
(I would like to make it known that all this comes to the soul through union with Jesus Christ, a union which is the source of all the soul's blessings[.] While the soul feels Jesus Christ within, four or five effects are typical[.] The first is an elevation toward celestial things, and a continual impression of the blessings of the other life, together with a disdain for the present life. The second is the strength and vigor to act and undertake whatever presents itself[;] and while the soul feels this way inside, in the

manner I have described, it has so to speak a constant sensation of glory, making it so that even in the weak and often extreme moments, like those that came over the Father [Surin], instead of his succumbing, things astonishing to the soul burst forth[;] for it was like the inner spirit was shooting out, putting all the senses as though in a state of glory. This happened three or four times, usually when the soul was weakest, and from that moment it was surrounded by good things that cannot be described. And even at present, I am unable to explain them, so difficult are they to represent. But this came to the soul through the assistance of what it felt in itself, namely that it seemed to him as though Jesus Christ had completely filled and penetrated him. This is why he thought he saw something like reverberations of glory flowing from his eyes, so gentle and so uplifting that I have never experienced anything so strange.)

The passage commences with a desire—"faire connaître." This phrase can be translated as "to make known," "to tell," but also as "to make *understood*," as his efforts to be methodical and expository suggest: the soul "a quatre ou cinq effets qui lui sont ordinaires." Surin moves away from anecdotal or narrative description as a way of making known; he wants his experience to be understood by its dissection into parts. Hence he starts to enumerate *characteristics* of this type of experience—the first is, the second is, and so on. But there is, in fact, no "so on" at all: the classification gives way entirely, as he alludes to his own case ("comme ceux qui arrivaient au Père"), and from that moment on is returned to the particulars of his own past ("Cela arriva trois ou quatre fois"), leaving his enumeration hanging. Once face to face with his experience, Surin invokes the topos of unsayability (his soul "se trouva environnée de biens qu'on ne saura décrire"). The topos functions doubly, however, like the originating desire to "faire connaître." The experience, he suggests, is not only indescribable, but moreover, *incomprehensible*: "Et même à présent, je ne saurais les mettre en avant, tant ils sont difficiles à représenter." This is a recurrent theme with Surin: temporal distance *should* make things clearer to the mind, but it does not ("même à présent"). The passage finishes on a word that stresses this failure of the intellect—what he experiences is "si doux" and "si élevant," but above all, "si étrange."

Porete, Eckhart, and others may well have advanced the unknowability of the divine, and used apophatic language to evoke the inadequacy of language before the majesty of God's grace. The crucial difference, however, between Surin and earlier "mystics of unsaying" (to paraphrase Michael Sells), lies in the notion of the interiority of the divine.[62] The inexpressibility and unknowability of God are now situated inside, and not beyond, the subject; and with Surin, these qualities are transferred to the subject's own past. And at that moment, in that very transfer and not before, a term like "personal experience" begins to have meaning. It is not God that undoes or surpasses all systems, articulations, or paradigms, but the subject's infinitely receding interior—the secret knot, as Surin writes, of his past experience.

The failure of the intellect, however, deprives autobiographical writing of its biggest spiritual alibi. When an aspirant wrote her experiences for her director, the text's most direct purpose was the "discernment of spirits"— via autobiographical writing, the director could (so the theory held) verify whether visions and other such phenomena were divine inspiration or devilish temptation (they might be an effect of the desire to appear extraordinary, for instance).[63] In Surin's case, autobiography is the space where he himself can undertake such analysis, since he writes for no director. One of the chief functions of the *Science expérimentale* lies in the clarification for himself of what he has lived, and thus what he is living. Whereas the author of a spiritual treatise writes from the position of one who *knows*, and whose mastery of his or her knowledge is proved by the organization of the teaching (Surin's own methodical *Guide spirituel* is an example—but so is part IV of the *Science expérimentale*), autobiography can help disentangle the strands of an existence whose meaning and direction are far from clear for the author. One day, Surin writes, "je fus surpris en telle sorte, qu'il se fit un mélange des opérations de Dieu et du Diable, se faisant toutes deux, non seulement ensemble, mais aussi en une même heure, tantôt l'une et tantôt l'autre, en sorte qu'on avait peine à les discerner" (I was overtaken by a mixture of the operations of God and of the Devil, both carried out not only together, but also at the same time, first one and then the other, such that it was difficult to discern them) (267). The *Science expérimentale* provides him the occasion to distinguish these various operations, and he is able to conclude several pages later that those of the devil seem to come from outside, whereas God's seem to come "par instinct comme naturel" (as though by natural instinct) (275). He will later try to extricate these operations in the case of Jean Labadie (cf. 303ff).

Yet as we have seen, what Surin depicts most forcefully is his inability to know, to understand why, to theorize, in spite of his efforts. His invocations of unsayability, therefore, run contrary to the standard protestation of poetic modesty. Whereas a poet such as Dante claims at the outset of a description the inadequacy of language, only to go on to describe that which he has just claimed to be indescribable, Surin tries to describe, only to arrive at a point where the description collapses. In chapter 6 of book III, for instance, Surin deploys a whole spectrum of descriptive techniques (straightforward description of divine voices, analytical discussions of the nature of "visions," comparisons with Augustine and the Bible) that terminate in a typically Surinian metaphor which likens experiencing God's love to eating jam: "Et ce Père ... le contraint de manger ses confitures, qui sont les tendresses délicieuses de son amour" (And this Father ... forces him to eat his jam, which is the delicious tenderness of his love) (287). Upon which Surin remarks the insignificance of language — and therefore, of understanding — before the immediacy of experience: "Qui le pourrait dire, qui le pourrait comprendre, sinon celui que l'expérimente? [C]ela mettait le coeur en une extrémité que l'on ne peut décrire, et je ne sais comment le faire entendre" (Who could say it, who could comprehend it, if not he who experienced it? All this pushed the heart to an extreme that cannot be described, and I do not know how to make it understood). The next, and last, sentence of the chapter is a testimony to the elusiveness of language's object: "Il faut que je laisse cela, que je l'abandonne pour aller ailleurs" (I must leave this behind, abandon it in order to go elsewhere) (287). And so Surin bounces from one experience to another, touching on each only a moment, long enough to come face to face with the futility of description, and to retreat into temporary silence.[64] Totality and system are beyond Surin's grasp.[65]

Why, then, does Surin write, if his descriptions fade off into silence, if discernment of spirits is uncertain, if experience always lies outside of language and communication? The uniqueness of the *Science expérimentale* lies in the epigraph from Isaiah 24:16 that Surin gives his work: it is, after all, "his secret for himself." Autobiographical writing emerges on the ruins of pedagogy and the latter's futile hopes of continuity between master and disciple, author and reader. The *Science expérimentale* substitutes for confident communication the goal of self-inspiration. In itself, the place of writing in personal spiritual practice is not new, nor need it imply autobiography at all: Michel Foucault, for instance, has done much to exhume the Stoic tradition of writing as *askèsis*, in which meditation and writing were part of an infinite loop outside of which there was nothing.[66] Foucault's description of ascetic writing meshes with Barthes's characterization of Ignatius's exercises: language constitutes the experience of the subject; it is the sole reality of the self. Part III of the *Science expérimentale* functions differently, however, for it is quite important to Surin that his floundering descriptions point to something pre-existing, something lived. At one point for instance Surin appears to play on the relationship (the antonymical relationship, as it turns out) between the words *expérience* and *expression*: he alludes to that which "ne se peut exprimer, mais qui se peut bien sentir, par cette vue d'expériences que j'ai dites ci-dessus, et dont les paroles ne peuvent faire l'expression" (cannot be expressed, but which can indeed be felt, through this perception of experiences related above, and which cannot find expression in words) (332). The importance of Surin's text is there, in the convoluted creation of something that for centuries to come could be taken for granted: "experience" by Surin's own definition is that which *cannot* be "expressed" or exteriorized by language.

And yet the difference that inheres to autobiography does not only cleave self and other, author and reader, master and disciple, as if to create thereby an integral and autonomous subject. For Surin, experience is not self-evident even to the one who has "experienced": difference itself is introjected within the subject. Autobiography memorializes an irretrievable origin, an experience he has left behind; this new type of text becomes necessary because his past experience eludes reproduction, not only in another but even within himself. The dilemma of Surin is this: he knows the extreme joy he has felt to be at an end, that he has passed as if to the other side of mystic union (in his case, among other unions, he has felt the manifest presence of Christ's body in his own), and that he is now in what he calls "l'état de la foi" (the state of faith). Unfortunately, the state of faith is not one of total certainty ("vraiment l'âme dans cet état ne sait que devenir" [truly the soul in this state knows not what will become of it] [339]), nor is it free of temptation ("Les tentations l'assaillent [l'âme], au moins quelques-unes, les autres la heurtent et la molestent" [Some temptations assail [the soul], [while] others jostle and accost it] [336]). The soul in this state "est heureuse et misérable tout à la fois" (is happy and miserable all at once) (339). Although the state of faith is less ecstatic than the experience of mystic union, Surin feels nevertheless that this union is not to be recaptured, repeated, relived. The memories contained in part III of the *Science expérimentale* are something of a record of this unrelivable past, a souvenir of his true home that comforts him in the exile that is human temporality.

Dans cet état [de la foi], [l'âme] se sent, ce lui semble, délaissée et tellement faible, qu'elle a besoin, pour se soutenir, de remémorer en son idée, les choses que je viens de décrire; et le plus grand motif que j'ai eu de mettre ceci par écrit, c'est pour animer cette foi et me mettre dans la foi qui nous est nécessaire pour persévérer. (336)
(In this state [of faith], [the soul] has the impression of being abandoned and so weak that for support it needs to recall the things I have just described; and the greatest motive I had to put this into writing is to enliven this faith and to place myself in the faith that is necessary for us to persevere.)

Autobiography comforts the mind ("ces idées relèvent extrêmement le courage, et confortent l'esprit" [these ideas greatly uplift one's courage, and comfort the mind]), Surin goes on to say. Unlike Augustine, Surin does not distance himself from these memories by acceding to impersonal meditation; he writes precisely because he does not want to forget what cannot be found in any book. There is nothing remotely ascetic, therefore, about the *Science expérimentale*, for ascesis posits the blank slate of a remakable self; nor is it precisely a "hagiographic" text, if the hagiographic lens makes us see even in the tale of radical conversion the triumph of an institutionally and communally sanctioned master narrative. Surinian experience makes possible, rather, a historicized subject.[67]

Writing enables Surin to continue by a turning back. But perhaps it is because the retrospective moment always fails that the *Science expérimentale* is no narcissistic mirror. This is not to make a judgment on Surin's moral integrity, but simply to point out what we have already seen in the examples of Bourignon and Guyon: even as autobiography promises to function as "a secret for oneself," it returns the subject, by virtue of its own existence, to the same community whose insufficiencies had made it necessary in the first place. Surin does not retreat into solitude with his intimate, very unscientific knowledge: he goes forth into the world. The metaphor Surin uses to express the relationship of his private writing to his public life is one of his most beautiful, and merits being quoted in full:

Et cette comparaison me vient de certaines gens que l'on m'a dit qui, pêchant les perles et allant jusqu'au fond de la mer pour les prendre, ont un tuyau qui va jusqu'au haut, et qui est soutenu par du liège, au bout d'en haut, et par là ils respirent et sont effectivement au fond de la mer. Je ne sais si cela se fait, mais ce que je veux dire est bien exprimé par là, car l'âme a un tuyau qui va jusqu'au ciel, et sainte Catherine de Gênes disait qu'il y avait un canal qui allait jusqu'au coeur de Dieu. . . . De là elle respire la sagesse et l'amour, et s'en soutient. Tandis qu'elle est ici au fond de la terre où elle pêche les perles, elle parle aux âmes, elle prêche les peuples, elle négocie pour Dieu, mais cependant il y a un tuyau qui va jusqu'au ciel pour tirer de Dieu vie et consolation éternelle. Et c'est ce que dit saint Paul. (338–39)

(And there occurs to me this comparison with certain people whom I was told about who, fishing for pearls and going to the bottom of the sea to find them, have a tube that goes to the surface, supported by cork on its upper end, and through it they breathe while being nevertheless at the bottom of the sea. I do not know if this is true, but it expresses well what I mean, for the soul has a tube that goes all the way to heaven, and Saint Catherine of Genoa said that there is a channel that reaches to the heart of God. . . . From there it breathes wisdom and love, and lives off of this. Here at the bottom of the earth fishing for pearls, it speaks to [other] souls, it preaches to the masses, it negotiates for God, but at the same time there is a tube going up to heaven, drawing life and eternal consolation from God. And that is what Saint Paul says.)

If experience cannot be reduced to science, and if autobiography is incapable of defining intellectually the four kinds of *respirs*, it can itself be, like the tube of the pearl-gatherers, that which permits the soul, bound anew to an always hostile environment, to breathe. The examples of Catherine of Genoa and Paul are carefully chosen: Surin situates himself in a tradition of mystics-turned-apostles. Memory of one's past—however imprecise—is the condition of this return to history.

There is, of course, an irony here, in that example always returns to haunt the subject who seems to constitute himself through its rejection: "[C]'est ce que dit saint Paul." Rather than propose, then, that subjectivity and exemplarity are inimical, or that one can only come into existence after the historical passing of the other, it would seem that the two are caught in a pas de deux: the crisis of exemplarity is never-ending. Although the notion of experience that Surin tries to elaborate does differ greatly from that of Augustine, in which the life lived confirms the life read, here too books and received authority always return, however Surin might try to conceive of a life without them. The intimacy of his experiential knowledge can only be achieved, it seems, through a simultaneous denunciation of a different kind of knowledge—hence the virulent diatribes against those whose "trade" (métier [327]) is religion, "ces docteurs arides et secs comme des rochers" (these learned men as dry and arid as rocks) who "n'ont que leur science, leurs arguments, et leur scolastique" (have only their knowledge, their arguments, their scholasticism) (326). And yet even experiential knowledge can never break free from the text of tradition: "[C]eci de quoi je parle," Surin contends, "sont des expériences, comme saint Paul disait en expérimentant: *Quaeritis qui in me loquitur Christus*" (What I am speaking of are experiences, as Saint Paul said while experiencing: *Quaeritis qui in me loquitur Christus*) (326).

If Surin sketches out the improbable but seductive position of being outside of exemplarity, the descent into solipsism (which Surin has learned spells madness) is checked by a confidence in a community of the different, of those who just might experience as he does. Hence his course does not lead to a Rousseauian effort to produce ever more intimate, unreadable texts (such as the *Rêveries*), nor to the flight from any and all representation that is Lafayette's solution to the dangers of exemplarity in *La Princesse de Clèves*.[68] Refusing to be the object of any scripts provided for women by her society, the Princess of Clèves opts for silence and retreat, leaving behind only "exemples . . . inimitables" (inimitable examples) that signal the impossibility of continued narrative given a logic of total difference.[69] But then, the Princess of Clèves is a limit case for modern subjectivity—a subjectivity so ferociously interiorized that it makes literature (not to mention autobiography) impossible. Private and public in the *Science expérimentale* are not pitted against one another as irreconcilably as with the Princess of Clèves, first, because autobiography exists, and second, because Surin labored hard to conciliate the personal and the professional. Autobiography is a symptom of his alienation—as his diatribes against Church incomprehension show—but it also articulates the relationship between Surin's interior experiences and his exterior duties, allows him to circumscribe an interior textual space that is his own and that sustains his action in the world.

Autobiography's Vanishing Point

There is a coda to Surin's orchestration of public and private, difference and sameness—the story of the reception of Surin's autobiographical deviations. In an age when the autobiographical document was fetishized by biographers eager to lend the cachet of authenticity and interiority to their subjects' writings, what was made of Surin's attempts at writing privacy and difference? The *Science expérimentale* aimed to serve a divergent group: his anticipated readers ranged from the dabbler in exorcism, to the mystic, to the author himself, writing and rereading the textual souvenir that maintained his public self. Did all these autobiographical practices find their mark? How did Surin's contemporaries read the *Science expérimentale*? Did they perceive his manipulation of their horizon of expectation? Specifically, if Surin has achieved, in parts II and III, a rhetorical distancing of his institutional identity, is the private space thus created by the rent in his public personage readily readable in seventeenth-century clerical France? To attempt to answer this question, I would like to look through the only window that exists into the reception of Surin's autobiographical writing—the mass of manuscripts in which the *Science expérimentale* circulated from the second half of the seventeenth century until the first print edition of 1828.

All Surin's manuscripts, including those of his poetic or didactic works, were subjected to dispersion and general reworking. One text published during his lifetime, the *Catéchisme spirituel* (1657), when finally printed, surprised the author himself: in the odyssey from author to publisher, the manuscript had been significantly altered by its readers—"quelques personnes de piété" (some pious persons), as Surin generously put it.[70] For a second edition, in 1661–63, the original four volumes were condensed into two through massive cuts. Perhaps because of these episodes, and especially after the completion of the *Science expérimentale*, Surin apparently took pains to control the diffusion of his works.[71] Upon his death in 1665, however, the last bulwark of authorial intention was lifted. The first posthumous publication was the *Fondements de la vie spirituelle* (1667), and the modification of his work — this time sanctioned by print — continued: "the work is in reality an anthology of texts which Surin had conceived neither in this form nor in this order," Certeau has written.[72]

The fate of the *Triomphe* and the *Science expérimentale* was similar: as in the case of the *Fondements* and the *Catéchisme*, their form and order would be drastically altered. Here the method of transmission was not print, but manuscripts, of which the copies proliferated. Twenty-seven were mentioned by Louis Michel, co-editor, with Ferdinand Cavallera, of an edition of Surin's correspondence.[73] However, only three give the *Triomphe* in its original form, and none of the twenty-seven reproduces the *Science expérimentale* as Cavallera has hypothesized it had been written — the four-part structure I have been commenting on. What this body of manuscripts represents is a series of attempts to rework the *Science expérimentale*, less on the level of its literary expression (though there were of course alterations there too), but rather on the level of its structure. As it turns out, Surin's editors were constantly dislocating the space of difference he had labored to create.

There are five distinct editorial responses to the material provided by Surin — points at which the *Triomphe* and the *Science expérimentale* underwent major changes. I will refer to each of these responses as a manuscript transformation; each transformation altered both stylistic points and the general shape the text took. Sometime in the years between Surin's death in 1665 and the turn of the seventeenth century, three separate transformations attempted to deal with the mixture of memorial, doctrinal, and personal prose contained in the original works. The first transformation consisted of a uniting of all the narratives concerning Loudun and its aftermath: parts II and III of the *Science expérimentale* were grafted on to the *Triomphe*, thus producing a chronological account of the years 1632 to 1663. A second transformation, complementing the first, involved the copying of parts I and IV of the *Science expérimentale* together — thus producing a uniformly expository text on demonology. A third transformation isolated parts II and III of the *Science expérimentale* — the parts I have been calling Surin's "autobiography."

Following this, two related attempts were made to unite the entire contents of both the *Triomphe* and the *Science expérimentale* under a single title. Toward the turn of the century, an unidentified scribe calling himself simply "une personne solitaire" came into possession of examples of transformations one to three.[74] In his "Avertissement," the Solitaire states that the manuscripts had proven popular and edifying, but obviously of flawed composition: they suffered from repetition and confusion owing to the fact that the work was "composé à plusieurs reprises pendant l'espace de vingt-cinq ans" (composed at different times over a space of twenty-five years).[75] The Solitaire does say the "work" and not the "works"—he assumes these parts all go together, and proceeds to amalgamate them under the title

Abrégé de la vraie histoire de la Possession des religieuses ursulines de la ville de Loudun . . . arrivée en l'an 1632 et qui a duré plusieurs années, écrite par le R.P. Jean-Joseph Seurin [*sic*] de la Compagnie de Jésus, exorciste pendant trois ans des dites religieuses. Rédigée en ordre et divisée en trois parties par une personne solitaire.

(A short history of the true events of the Possession of the Ursuline nuns of the town of Loudun . . . occurring in the year 1632 and lasting several years, written by the Reverend Father Jean-Joseph Seurin [*sic*], S.J., exorcist of said nuns for three years. Put in order and divided into three parts by a solitary person.)

As the title hints, the Solitaire underlines especially Loudun and the memorial dimensions of the work; in his paratexts he speaks of the importance of Surin's "témoi[gnage] oculaire" (eyewitness testimony) and his professional responsibility in the affair, as well as of the steps the Solitaire has taken to verify the authenticity of the manuscripts (he claims to have undertaken a stylistic analysis). The Solitaire also takes pains to extend the demonological import of the work, adding information from previous works printed on Loudun. He emphasizes that his changes took aim only at overly long or potentially delicate passages—"mais," he assures, "cela ne regarde point le fond de l'histoire ni les faits de la possession" (but this does not affect the basic story or the facts of the possession).

The last transformation was also the most successful in terms of circulation—eleven copies are known, and it ultimately furnished the published text of 1828.[76] Probably not long after the Solitaire, another scribe, calling himself "un ecclésiastique," imparted yet again a new order. Creating four parts where the Solitaire had put three, and accentuating still further the demonological dimension of the text, he gave the work a telling new title:

La Science expérimentale ou l'histoire véritable de la possession des religieuses ursulines de Loudun au diocèse de Poitiers, arrivée à l'année 1632 jusqu'en 1638, par le Révérend Père Surin de la Compagnie de Jésus exorciste de ces mêmes religieuses—ouvrage divisé en trois parties par un solitaire, et réduit en un meilleur ordre par un ecclésiastique lequel pour appuyer la vérité de cette histoire y a ajouté plusieurs faits remarquables, tirés de ses expériences ayant lui-même pris soin de plusieurs possédés secrets et de l'ordre exprès de son prélat durant plus de 20 ans, en forme d'annotation sur les deux livres.

(The experimental science, or the true history of the possession of the Ursuline nuns of Loudun in the diocese of Poitiers, occurring in the year 1632 until 1638, by the Reverend Father Surin of the Society of Jesus, exorcist of the said nuns—a work divided into three parts by a solitary person, and put in better order by an ecclesiastic, who in order to support the truth of this history added to it several remarkable facts drawn from his experiences—himself having secretly taken care of several possession cases over more than 20 years by order of his prelate—in the form of annotations to the two books.)

Obviously familiar, then, with the Solitaire's transformation, the Ecclésiastique nonetheless complains in his "Avis" of lack of order (the manuscripts were "sans presque aucun ordre" [almost without any order]) and undertakes to make of the mess "un vrai corps d'histoire" (a true work of history).[77] And whereas the Solitaire limited himself to quoting material regarding Loudun, the Ecclésiastique adds demonological readings having nothing to do with Loudun at all.

What, if anything, can be deduced from these transformations? What horizon of expectations do they bring to a text—the *Science expérimentale*— that seems at once to appeal to and to deviate from an accepted type of writing? In the first series of transformations (I–III) there appear to have been two distinct responses. On the one hand, transformations I and II—the most numerous, with six examples total—eliminate the strange hybridity of the original *Science expérimentale*. There was a tendency to collapse Surin's reiterated distinction between the subject matter of the *Triomphe* and the secret center of the *Science expérimentale* (parts II and III). Surin's attempts at private writing were thus assimilated with the memorial function of the *Triomphe*; unlike the practice of religious biographers who did everything in their power to draw readers' attention to the writings of their subjects, contemporaries here forewent the possibility of heightening the effect of intimacy that Surin himself had done so much to create. Loudun, more than Surin's fight with madness, furnished the organizing principle. On the other hand, two manuscripts (transformation III) *do* seem to recognize Surin's private space as something altogether different—they reproduce only parts II and III of the *Science expérimentale*.[78] These, however, were relatively rare responses, and ultimately seem to have had little effect on the way Surin was read: one was sufficiently out of circulation as to have escaped Cavallera's research; the second was eventually (probably toward the beginning of the eighteenth century) bound with a truncated version of the Ecclésiastique's transformation, so as to produce the overarching Loudun narrative that was becoming increasingly popular. In this way, Surin's private space was again recuperated by his public record. Eighteenth-century responses were much less ambiguous than transformations I–III, in that *diablerie* became the manifest interest of editors. The Ecclésiastique, for example, retains the title *La Science expérimentale* while imparting to the words a very limited meaning—the science, here, is demonology, a science at which the Ecclésiastique was, like Surin before him, adept ("ayant lui-même pris soin de plusieurs possédés," notes the new title).

Given the editorial norms of the time, one would hardly expect the *Triomphe* or the *Science expérimentale* to have been transmitted with critical care, neither stylistically nor in terms of content. As I have mentioned, even Surin's nonautobiographical texts were routinely altered. Yet the sheer number of alterations undergone by the *Science expérimentale* speaks to the idiosyncrasies of Surin's attempted negotiation of the readerly and authoritative horizons of his day. And in the end, the negotiation was unsuccessful. Much like Benoît de Canfeld's autobiographical narrative, whose path to oblivion I mentioned in Chapter 2, the *Science expérimentale* never received the paratextual hymns to the glories of the autobiographical voice that were becoming increasingly common coin in the devotional press of the last third of the seventeenth century. The Solitaire's "Introduction au récit de cette possession" (Introduction to the story of this possession), which contains a brief allusion to the fact that Surin had not thought it wise to make the story of his pains and graces known to a wide audience, certainly sketches out a rhetoric of secrecy and divulgation ("C'est ce qui nous en a dérobé la connaissance jusqu'à présent" [That is what has kept knowledge of it concealed from us up to now]),[79] but it is a rhetoric that pales in comparison with the surrounding emphasis on the "truth" of the possession. Ironically, contemporaries accentuated what for moderns readers is no doubt the *Science expérimentale*'s most unreadable part. Surin's private narrative was even ignored by Henri-Marie Boudun in his 1683 biography of Surin.[80]

Given the vogue for interiority in the devotional press, what explains such a muted reaction to a text that underlines compulsively its own interior status? As in the case of Montaigne, who was less and less read at the very moment Augustine was provoking increasingly vehement readerly identification, the failure of Surin to attract the same editorial attention heaped upon women's writing might well be explained by the nature of his audience. Surin's texts most likely circulated primarily among Jesuits who had more interest in Loudun than in the predominantly female mystical topoi that were virtually synonymous with the autobiographical interiority; Augustine's *Confessions* became associated with this readership, while the *Essais* and the *Science expérimentale* did not. The latter work certainly contains many of the same topoi couched in a similarly interiorizing rhetoric, but as Surin's efforts to invent a frame for this contents suggest, the problem was one of authority and readership: how was it possible to find a generic context for the interiority of a male ecclesiastic? And who would possibly look toward a man to provide such reading? In addition, the context of the *Science expérimentale*'s production cut it off from the affective discourse of spiritual direction, a discourse that had its own markers and followed its own patterns. Because of Surin's role in history, his reader came to the text with certain expectations, those of reading either an eyewitness account of Loudun or a treatise on the theological lessons of possession. Thus, both in terms of composition and reception, and as Surin's own hesitations suggest, the *Science expérimentale* was a text not easily assimilable within the devotional paradigms of the time.

Once Surin's efforts to write differently had become thoroughly integrated into the context of the Loudun affair, it took a long time to disengage them. Parts II and III of the *Science expérimentale* needed to await a more tenacious version of the literary mentality that was, ironically, starting to be elaborated in precisely the time and the milieu in which Surin wrote. This would happen only in 1928, when, after his archival research, Cavallera published a critical edition of parts II and III, under a title that will surprise no one—*L'Autobiographie du Père Surin*.[81] In other words, readerly horizons needed to expand in order for these parts to assume publicly the importance that Surin had attributed to them two and a half centuries earlier. According to Hans Robert Jauss:

> The distance between the actual first perception of a work and its virtual significance, or, put another way, the resistance that the new work poses to the expectations of its first audience, can be so great that it requires a long process of reception to gather in that which was unexpected and unusable within the first horizon. It can thereby happen that a virtual significance of the work remains long unrecognized until the "literary evolution" through the actualization of a newer form reaches the horizon that now for the first time allows one to find access to the understanding of the misunderstood older form.[82]

Certainly, there is much in the long history of the *Science expérimentale* that supports Jauss's notion of literary expectation and evolution. Yet one might well wonder if there is ever such a harmony of intent and expectation that the "virtual significance" of a "misunderstood" form can at any point be accessed without the mediation of hundreds of years of reading habits and subjective change. Cavallera was a product of the autobiographical mentality, a man whose horizon of expectations was quite the opposite of that of the anonymous Solitaire and Ecclésiastique; he too, however, picked and chose among

Surin's experiments, just as Marvin Lowenthal sorted through Montaigne's *Essais*. It seems doubtful that the recent publication of largely complete texts of both the *Triomphe* and the *Science expérimentale* will open a substantially new horizon, one that might lead to the apparition of the "virtual significance" of Surin's original work(s), because we always read what interests us, what retains applicability. In this, the literary scholar shares the historian's dilemma: as Certeau has argued, the very condition of the discipline lies in sorting out "what can be '*understood*' and what should be *forgotten* in order to represent what is presently intelligible." [83] Cavallera wanted to minimize the importance of the Surin of Loudun, the Surin who believed in Jeanne des Anges's demons and stigmata, and retain rather a good, "modern" Surin, mystic and autobiographer.

Nonetheless, Surin hardly invites such pessimistic view of the reading process, and it would be a mistake to argue that in isolating the secret center of Surin's work, we indulge in pure anachronism. No, we do not quite share a seventeenth-century horizon of expectations, but, then again, neither did Surin: the *Science expérimentale* from its inception was never anything but a hybrid, a willed mutation of received discourses, but a mutation willed by Surin only because the culture of autobiographical interiority was already taking hold of his contemporaries. Already, but imperfectly: it so happened that the many devotional readers who might have responded in some way to Surin's efforts never got the chance, for Surin's copyists were somewhat less open to a text whose sole authority was interior. Early modern horizons were multiple. By now, the authoritative space of first-person experience looms a good deal larger, as Cavallera's edition of the "*Autobiographie*," and indeed my treatment here, suggest. Like the *Essais* and the *Confessions*, the *Science expérimentale* has, with the passing of centuries, unavoidably "become" an autobiography, but with even better reason, for Surin himself explicitly engaged that process of becoming, thereby revealing why we might be curious about an early example of autobiography in the first place. Few other texts furnish us such an uncannily vivid history of our own desire to read them. The story of Surin's obsession has indeed become that of our own.

Conclusion
The Future of Experience

"Quelle est, demandai-je à Platon, cette figure gigantesque qui
vient à nous?
"Reconnaissez l'Expérience, me répondit-il; c'est elle-même."
("What," I asked Plato, "is this giant figure coming toward us?"
"Behold Experience," he answered; "this is he.")

In Diderot's *Les Bijoux indiscrets* (1748), after too much ratiocination and reasoning the day before, Prince Mangogul's usually tranquil sleep is disturbed
by a dream. He is in the land of Hypothesis; milling about what used to
be Socrates's temple of Philosophy are lost souls called "Systematics," who
spend their existence chasing soap bubbles, those fragile creations of their
own minds. While speaking with Plato about the sad fate of wisdom in this
strange land, Mangogul sees in the distance a child approaching, a child
who at first seems weak but whose appearance is transformed as he advances
toward the temple, stronger, bigger, soon a colossus. Plato identifies the giant
child, and Mangogul awakes as Experience lays waste to the edifice of the
Systematics.

By Diderot's time, the cultural visibility of the phenomena that Surin
and others were groping to define would be such that an allegory like this
one would be easy enough to write, and just as easy to interpret: far too big
to ignore, experience had become a thing, with its own capital E. Before long
autobiography would be reified as well, terminologically speaking: the first
uses of the word date to the end of the eighteenth century.[1] The ensuing self-
evidence of the categories thus established has provided an easy target, as I
mentioned at this study's outset, for a wave of critiques of many of the concepts and practices I have been dealing with here—autobiography, self and
subject, interiority. But do such critiques mark a victory of present lucidity
over the naïveté of the past? The prehistory I have proposed here has sought
not only to show the rise of specific ways of thinking and writing, but also
to unearth the many conflicts that hide behind the keywords of modernity.

Even if temporal distance brings many things into sharper focus, beginnings (of a genre, of a technology, of a regime) are moments when the promises and dangers of the new are assessed with much urgency and even lucidity: witness the wary enthusiasm of early practitioners of autobiography. And it is precisely because of the inconclusive, hesitant manner with which these men and women went about characterizing what they were doing that we can learn so much about where these terms came from, what forces they translated and resisted, and why — in spite of the capital letters they now sport — they are more slippery and multifaceted than they might appear. In the century preceding Diderot and Rousseau and in the shadows of the great thinkers immortalized by intellectual history, in works their authors could barely conceive of as works, the imprint of modernity's contradictions is preserved, fossil-like.

The fossil metaphor, however, should not blind us to the endlessly labile nature of experience and autobiography — elements of modernity that exist never as solids but always in suspension. The solidification of terminology evident in a text such as Diderot's in no way amounts to the birth of a stable "thing": the robust vitality of the signifier "experience" over the past three centuries hides many idiosyncratic uses and complicated families of meaning. Thus Diderot's Experience was not identical to the moments of mystic interiority that escaped the strictures of a bureaucratic institution and the irrelevance of book learning: the passage of *Les Bijoux indiscrets* is clearly based on a scientific model of progress, rather than on irreducible first-person certitude. And yet there are undeniable filiations: Diderot's allegory is not without resemblance to, say, Surin's construction of system and experience as mutually exclusive — Surin who, after all, also reminds us of the imbrication of science and subjectivity via his shifting play of experience and experiment.

So if something like solidification will occur in the century following Surin, I do not suggest that experience will mean only one thing, or that its meanings do not continue to change over time. Rather, it is the category itself that has established itself in our minds, while the signifier itself has colonized the tips of our tongues. Certainly the modern age has written many kinds of autobiography, and has advocated, theorized, attacked, and even felt many different experiences. But umbrella terms like these have meaning, and have become ubiquitous, not because they designate something precise — rather the contrary. This is why my discussion of autobiography has of necessity unraveled into many component threads — experience, but also the interior, the private, the personal — and why the threads themselves can be unraveled further still. The elasticity of the phenomena that make up an equally elastic "modernity" should not cause us to shrug them off, as if because they meant many things they meant nothing. Modernity is not a single thing, and it never simply took place, in some year, or in some man's book—Descartes's, Kant's, even Surin's. For not only does it consist of both ideas *and* their contraries; more important, it is embedded in a material culture that took time to develop, in practices that had many sources—none of which can be easily dismissed through a heroic effort to think differently. Perhaps the only way to use the terms that have fallen within the scope of this study is to remember to hold them under the type of erasure displayed with virtuosity by a Steven Shapin ("There was no such thing as the Scientific Revolution, and this is a book about it," opens one of his studies) or a Bruno Latour (modernity exists—but we have never been modern).[2] For these mirages have oriented centuries of walking, and our cultural wanderings, present and past, are incomprehensible without them.[3]

Returning to the colossus announced by Diderot, it bears pointing out that the fundamental opposition between inner experience on the one hand and dogma and institution on the other continues to play itself out in many of the same terms used by seventeenth-century autobiographers. This is true within everyday language (witness the omnipresent distinction, in casual conversation, between "spirituality" and "organized religion"), but also in the work of thinkers as central to current academic debates as Bataille or Foucault. More than a lexical echo links Bataille's 1943 *Expérience intérieure* to Surin's *Science expérimentale* of three centuries earlier. Bataille too proposes a knowledge—what Surin still called a science—that refuses any exterior determinations, being based instead on "une expérience nue, libre d'attache, même d'origine" (a naked experience, free of attachments and even of origins): "Les présuppositions dogmatiques ont donné des limites indues à l'expérience: celui qui sait déjà ne peut aller au-delà d'un horizon connu" (Dogmatic preconceptions have imposed unwarranted limits on experience: the person who already understands cannot go beyond a known horizon).[4] Like Surin's, Bataille's inner experience is negative, apophatic; it breaks down the positivities of tradition. And both men cite the Pseudo-Dionysius. I underline these commonalties not so as to dress Surin up in Bataille's prestige, nor to assert (for Bataille says it himself) that his notion of "limit-experience" updates old mystic tropes. Rather, what seems important to me is that, beyond questions of origins, beyond the specificity of the "ideas" put forth by this or that thinker, a remarkable continuity exists in the terms that enable us to articulate our local variations—the terms of inner versus outer, experience versus received discourse. So when in *La Nausée* (1938) Sartre writes that, sometime in their middle age, the numbed inhabitants of Bouville "baptisent leurs petites obstinations et quelques proverbes du nom d'expérience" (baptize their little obstinacies and a few proverbs under the name experience), it is only to reassert a true experience, one that, ever corrosive, has not yet ossified into sententious discourse.[5]

Unsurprisingly, the built-in contradictions of experience have not been navigated any better in our time than in Surin's. They are glaringly obvious in Foucault's appropriation of Bataillian limit-experience, for instance: "An experience is, of course, something one has alone; but it cannot have its full impact unless the individual manages to escape from pure subjectivity in such a way that others can—I won't say re-experience exactly—but at least cross paths with it or retrace it." Foucault's hesitation ("I won't say . . . but") points to the very impossibility which, I have argued, lies at the heart of the autobiographical mentality. This sentence of Foucault's could very well serve as an epigraph to Surin's *Science expérimentale*, a text that takes something experienced as "purely subjective" and puts it back into language and communal circulation—in the hopes of a subsequent "crossing of paths" that the original definition of experience would appear to preclude. Martin Jay, who has commented this very passage and looked at Foucault's concept of experience in some detail, sums up the problematic formulation as follows: "What Foucault seems to mean by limit-experience, then, is a curiously contradictory mixture of self-expansion and self-annihilation, immediate, proactive spontaneity and fictional retrospection, personal inwardness and communal interaction." Curiously contradictory, indeed, but also, as Jay goes on to point out, somehow inescapable: "[C]ontrary to the dominant Anglo-American reception of poststructuralist thought, experience is a term that cannot be effortlessly dissolved in a network of discursive relations."[6] Whatever their precise configurations, the terms of the debate are circumscribed; while we wait for others to take their place, we might at least avoid congratulating ourselves for problematizing that which has always been problematic.

Bataille did not fail to evoke, albeit in a depoliticized way, another important reason why a term like experience continues to resonate: "L'expérience, son autorité, sa méthode ne se distinguent pas de la contestation" (Experience—its authority, its method—is indistinguishable from contestation).[7] In a sense, experience is an always-otherness that not only tears down shaky scientific hypotheses but undermines procrustean structures of oppression; and perhaps the most important of the many functions of autobiography is to transmit the voice of experiences that (by definition) lie outside of official representation. For quite some time now, many feminist critics have been reclaiming a forgotten tradition of autobiographical production and showing how our view of the history and nature of the genre changes when texts by women are taken into account.[8] And indeed, studying early modern autobiography in any depth without the category of gender is a self-defeating task, so much were women instrumental in creating a culture of autobiography. But beyond assigning priority in autobiography to one or another sex (or creed, or class), one of my main concerns here has been to understand the history of our desire to recall to the center marginalized texts and experiences. Is the writing and reading of autobiography a contestatory and subversive act? Perhaps, but the subversion is scripted: there is nothing as fully consonant with Western culture as the infinite attraction of hunting after voices of the people, listening to the experience of women, and retracing the struggle for self-expression of those without access to the main knowledge-producing institutions of their time.

Looking at trends in historiography and literary studies over the past three decades it is, in fact, hard not to be reminded of the work done by seventeenth-century figures such as Mathieu Bourdin, Claude Martin, or Marie-Madeleine de Mauroy, who with a combination of naïveté and eloquence imagined organizing new and more vibrant communities around the voice of experience, and wrote of what we now call the need to let the Other speak. Take for instance the fetishizing of verbatim quotation in historical scholarship, which rivals (or reenacts) the obsessions of biographers like these. Whereas the nineteenth-century historian organized his material into a seamless narrative in which, as Barthes has written, it seemed as if History itself was speaking,[9] many historians of the twentieth century have been concerned with letting the past speak rather more polyphonously, via quotation. Annales historians especially have used citation as a means to allow the reader direct access to bygone mentalities. Witness, say, Emmanuel Le Roy Ladurie's *Montaillou*, which integrates source material verbatim by way of italics; or the entire "Archives" collection, edited by Pierre Nora and Jacques Revel, whose format italicizes the historian's narration while furnishing ample quantities of source material in Roman type. Here what intrudes into the normality of Roman type is the historian's italicized voice, and not vice versa; the voice of the past takes center stage, and the historian only fills in its silences.[10]

Needless to say, lending an ear to the Other is not an inherently progressive act: the reclaiming of the "everyday" can and does function as a way of obfuscating the real violence wrought by governmental policies and military directives.[11] Moreover, many have underlined the problematic nature of the historical or sociological "evidence" that these resurrected voices might provide. Certainly Foucault, in archival studies such as *Moi, Pierre Rivière*, did not just propose to make heard the repressed murmur of history's excluded, but to problematize the relation of such voices to a historical real, and to show how they constitute, from their very origin, "offensive and defensive weapons within relations of power and knowledge."[12] In the domain of feminism and postcolonialism, Gayatri Spivak has consistently attempted to expose the appropriation by first-world feminists of the voice of the third-world Other. Warning of the "new orientalism" hidden under well-intentioned efforts to let the silenced speak, Spivak argues that "we are now involved in the construction of a new object of investigation — 'the third world,' 'the marginal' — for institutional validation and certification."[13] And Lejeune, dealing directly with contemporary uses of autobiography, has addressed the power dynamic implied by the massive processing of the oral testimony of the lower classes for public consumption: "We let them speak, but so that we may take that speech in order to turn it into writing."[14] If no such caveats can fully blunt the powerful attraction exercised by the nearly messianic promise of an authentic voice, this might not be entirely a bad thing. Autobiography and experience are no panaceas for a corrupt and oppressive world, and yet, in spite of the power relations built into them, they continue to provide an indispensable way of attracting attention when needed most. Perhaps this has recently become most clear in the Latin American *testimonio* — as demonstrated, for example, when in the early 1980s *I, Rigoberta Menchú* galvanized world opinion concerning army massacres in Guatemala, precisely by playing to first-world desire to let the Other speak.[15]

Just battles can no doubt be waged and identities asserted without the help of these specific tools and terms inherited from the early modern period. We have others as well at our disposal, ones that at first appear so diametrically opposed to the world of deep subjective experience that one might hasten to conclude that we have as of late broken definitively with the modern reign of interiority. I am thinking particularly of the virtues ascribed to the "performative" self — a type of non- or post-subjectivity that eschews reduction to biographical determination or some sort of inner essence. Once again, however, it appears as if modernity has always been big enough to include the mutually informing opposites of the deep and the superficial. For alongside the interiorized subject, perhaps in response to it or perhaps just as its inevitable counterpart, a depth-less non-subject of pure appearance has intermittently asserted its power. The Dandy is one such creature of the shallows, opposing his artifice and stoic insensibility to the vulgar dictates of Nature. His heyday in the mid-nineteenth century corresponds well to a new obsession with feminized depth in the natural sciences. By affirming his resolutely *anti-natural* superficiality, the Dandy reacted to the threatening interiority and animality of life described by the discourse of biology—a life characterized, in the words of Foucault, by "its hidden framework, its enveloped organs, innumerable invisible functions, and, at the bottom of everything, that far away force which keeps it alive."[16]

Yet well before the Dandy's reactions to the new "life sciences" of the nineteenth century, the promise of self-fashioning had already been working its magic on people for whom medieval sociocosmic masterplots no longer anchored identities.[17] Numerous writers from Machiavelli to La Bruyère articulated, with approval or fear, a new state of affairs in which socially unmoored individuals could supposedly transform themselves, chameleon-like, into whatever they wanted to be. Yet the possibility of self-fashioning, although not without resemblance to the stoic "care of the self" discussed earlier, took on a particular character and urgency given the gradual formulation of an interiorized subjectivity. Once again, it is Diderot who would be able, from his position in the mid-eighteenth century, to make the stakes explicit, and his examination of these two paradigms of identity was, unsurprisingly, coincident with the mainstream popularization of interiority and autobiography in the work of Rousseau. *Le Paradoxe sur le comédien*, from 1769, deals with the built-in limits of interiority, to the unfortunate lack of transparency which forever disadvantages *l'homme sensible*, who will never be able to appear as such on stage. In contrast to actors who rely on their hearts, who act through the interior and emotional resemblance between themselves and the character on stage, Diderot posits a protean actor who, by study and reflection, mimics interiority through the sole manipulation of the exterior: "Qu'est-ce donc que le vrai talent? Celui de bien connaître les symptômes extérieurs de l'âme d'emprunt, de s'adresser à la sensation de ceux qui nous entendent, qui nous voient, et de les tromper par une imitation de ces symptômes . . . ; car il leur est impossible d'apprécier autrement ce qui se passe au-dedans de nous" (So what does true [acting] talent consist of? Of mastering the exterior symptoms of the soul one is trying to be, of making an appeal to the senses of those who listen to us, who see us, and of fooling them by an imitation of these symptoms . . . ; for it is impossible for them to grasp by any other means what happens inside us).[18] Diderot, of course, is making an argument about the theater, one that continues to separate acting schools and philosophies to this day. But the stage, after all, is a place for asking questions about identity, and Diderot's commentary on acting can also be read as a comparative reflection on the ongoing modern struggle between flat and deep selves.

Our culture as a whole has found it hard to choose between these twin and complementary responses to the problems of identity peculiar to the modern age. Interiority had its protective virtues, but it could also be a prison —not the prison that Guyon lauded for separating her from a hostile world, but one that impinged upon the individual's freedom to transform endlessly him or herself, and through such transformations, to escape determinations and oppressions of all kinds. It is therefore no wonder that the power of artifice over essence continues to fascinate, and even to furnish a platform from which political action may be launched.[19] On the other hand, as I hope to have shown in these pages, interiority too could serve—indeed was invented to serve—as a quasi-political tool, a mode of resistance. And, on a more abstract level, it must be admitted that neither model for identity is any more or less of a "construct" than the other; in choosing between them we hardly effectuate a theoretical "advance" over some outmoded world view. For whatever choice we make, the terms in which we make it are so familiar, so dependent on tropes and expressions handed down to us over the centuries, and so tied up in still-useful practices that a break from the modern past seems unlikely. Given this, I suspect autobiography will still be with us for some time to come, at least until we find a substitute for a category as central as "experience," one commensurate with the colossal task of pushing us, once and for all, out of our depth.

Notes

Introduction

1. Louis XIV, *Mémoires pour l'instruction du dauphin*, ed. Pierre Goubert (Paris: Imprimerie nationale, 1992), 83

2. Jean-Joseph Surin, *Correspondance*, ed. Michel de Certeau (Paris: Desclée de Brouwer, 1966), 178.

3. On Scudéry's gendered mapping of "Tendre" in her 1654 novel *Clélie*, see Joan DeJean, *Tender Geographies: Women and the Origins of the Novel in France* (New York: Columbia University Press, 1991), 43–70.

4. Surin, *Correspondance*, 185. The manuscript of the aborted project still exists (*Abrégé de la vie de Mad. Du Verger*, in Jean-Joseph Surin, *Recueil de lettres*, Bibliothèque nationale ms. f.f. 24,809, 242–395). (Marie Baron was Madame Du Verger's maiden name.)

5. Mino Bergamo, *L'Anatomie de l'âme: De François de Sales à Fénelon*, trans. Marc Bonneval (Grenoble: Jérôme Millon, 1994), 9–12.

6. Hence commentators from Heidegger to Bruno Latour have stressed that modernity is not dependent on atheism, but on a God who "could descend into men's heart of hearts without intervening in any way in their external affairs" (Bruno Latour, *We Have Never Been Modern*, trans. Catherine Porter [Cambridge, Mass.: Harvard University Press, 1993], 33). Or, as Heidegger puts it: "[T]he loss of the gods is so far from excluding religiosity that rather only through that loss is the relation to the gods changed into mere 'religious experience'" (Martin Heidegger, "The Age of the World Picture," in *The Question Concerning Technology and Other Essays* [New York: Harper and Row, 1977], 117).

7. Oblivious to potential contradictions, Jean-Jacques Rousseau for example will describe his idyllic retreat on the island of Saint-Pierre as a type of positive imprisonment: "[J]'aurais voulu qu'on m'eût fait de cet asile une prison perpétuelle, qu'on m'y eût confiné pour toute ma vie" (I would have liked to have had this asylum made a perpetual prison, to have been confined there for my whole life) (*Rêveries d'un promeneur solitaire*, in Jean-Jacques Rousseau, *Oeuvres complètes*, ed. Bernard Gagnebin and Marcel Raymond, vol. 1 [Paris: Gallimard, 1959], 1041).

8. Judith Butler, *The Psychic Life of Power: Theories in Subjection* (Stanford, Calif.: Stanford University Press, 1997), 10.

9. A paradigmatic example of the deconstructive "attack" on autobiographical naïveté has been provided by Candice Lang, "Autobiography in the Aftermath of Romanticism," *Diacritics* 12 (1982), 1–16; for a prognosis of autobiography's "end," see Michael Sprinker, "Fictions of the Self: The End of Autobiography," in *Autobiography: Essays Theoretical and Critical*, ed. James Olney (Princeton: Princeton University Press, 1980), 321–42. For an appraisal of "what's left" for autobiography as a referen-

tial genre after deconstruction, see Paul John Eakin, *Touching the World: Reference in Autobiography* (Princeton: Princeton University Press, 1992).

10. The phenomenological vogue for interior spaces can be found in such works as Gaston Bachelard, *La Poétique de l'espace* (Paris: Presses universitaires de France, 1974), Jean Rousset, *L'Intérieur et l'extérieur: Essais sur la poésie et sur le théâtre au XVIIe siècle* (Paris: José Corti, 1976), and Jean Starobinski, *L'Oeil vivant* (Paris: Gallimard, 1961). In what was by all accounts the first important critical reflection on autobiography, Georges Gusdorf elaborated the relation of the genre to an individual who thinks itself from the inside out; see Georges Gusdorf, "Conditions et limites de l'autobiographie," in *Formen der Selbstdarstellung: Festgabe für Fritz Neubert*, ed. Maurice Boucher (Berlin: Duncker and Humblot, 1956), 105–23. For a phenomenological reading of autobiography as a play between interior and exterior, see Janet Varner Gunn, *Autobiography: Toward a Poetics of Experience* (Philadelphia: University of Pennsylvania Press, 1982). Michel Foucault, *Discipline and Punish: The Birth of the Prison*, trans. Alan Sheridan (New York: Vintage, 1995) and Foucault, *The History of Sexuality*, vol. I, *An Introduction*, trans. Robert Hurley (New York: Random House, 1978), both contained within them the means to equate autobiography with the oppression visited by the modern "will to know"; for condemnations of the interiorized sense of bourgeois selfhood that follow from this work of Foucault's, see Francis Barker, *The Tremulous Private Body: Essays on Subjection* (Ann Arbor: University of Michigan Press, 1995), and Jeremy Tambling, *Confession: Sexuality, Sin, the Subject* (Manchester: Manchester University Press, 1990).

11. Katharine Eisaman Maus, *Inwardness and Theater in the English Renaissance* (Chicago: University of Chicago Press, 1995), 2–3.

12. "Autobiography is a human right," observes Philippe Lejeune, with a mixture of irony and approval (Philippe Lejeune, *Moi aussi* [Paris: Seuil, 1986], 213). Lejeune's multifaceted archival work has been especially useful in getting a picture of how autobiographical practice has come to assume this cultural role; see for instance Philippe Lejeune, *Je est un autre: L'Autobiographie de la littérature aux médias* (Paris: Seuil, 1980), and Lejeune, *Le Moi des demoiselles: Enquête sur le journal de jeune fille* (Paris: Seuil, 1993). Current American interest in the sociology of autobiography is running high as well; see for instance Vered Vinitzky-Seroussi, *After Pomp and Circumstance: High School Reunion as an Autobiographical Occasion* (Chicago: University of Chicago Press, 1998), who argues that autobiography qua device for creating a centered identity is far from outmoded.

13. In a classic response to Foucault, Nancy Hartsock has written: "Why is it that just at the moment when so many of us who have been silenced begin to demand the right to name ourselves, to act as subjects rather than objects of history, that just then the concept of subjecthood becomes problematic?" (Nancy Hartsock, "Foucault on Power: A Theory for Women?" in *Feminism/Postmodernism*, ed. Linda J. Nicholson [New York: Routledge, 1990], 163). Foucault's use of Beckett is from Michel Foucault, "What Is an Author?" in *Language, Counter-Memory, Practice*, ed. D. Bouchard (Ithaca: Cornell University Press, 1977), 138.

14. To cite but one example for the moment—I will return to the point in Chapter 2—see Electa Arenal and Stacey Schlau, *Untold Sisters: Hispanic Nuns in Their Own Works* (Albuquerque: University of New Mexico Press, 1989).

15. Whence a recent *PMLA* forum on "the place of the personal in scholarship" (111.5 [October 1996], 1063–1079). The political usefulness of the autobiographical mode in criticism has become a point of much scholarly interest; see for example Nancy K. Miller, *Getting Personal: Feminist Occasions and Other Autobiographical Acts* (New York: Routledge, 1991), Michael Awkward, *Negotiating Difference: Race, Gender, and the Politics of Positionality* (Chicago: University of Chicago Press, 1995), and the collection edited by Judith Roof and Robyn Wiegman, *Who Can Speak? Authority and Critical Identity* (Urbana: University of Illinois Press, 1995). On how it might still be possible to make strategic use of the concept of the self even if the latter is always already "constructed," see George Lewis Levine, "Introduction: Constructionism and the Reemergent Self," in *Constructions of the Self*, ed. George Lewis Levine (New Brunswick, N.J.: Rutgers University Press, 1992), 1–13.

16. For representatives of this encyclopedic approach, see Georg Misch, *Geschichte der Autobiographie*, 4 vols. (Bern: A. Francke, 1949), as well as Georges Gusdorf, *Les Ecritures du moi* (Paris: O. Jacob, 1991), and Gusdorf, *Auto-bio-graphie* (Paris: O. Jacob, 1991).

17. This — from Augustine to Malraux, via Montaigne and Descartes — is the trajectory established in Robert Elbaz, *The Changing Nature of the Self: A Critical Study of the Autobiographic Discourse* (Iowa City: University of Iowa Press, 1987). A basically similar tack has been taken in John N. Morris, *Versions of the Self: Studies in English Autobiography from John Bunyan to John Stuart Mill* (New York: Basic Books, 1966), James Olney, *Metaphors of Self: The Meaning of Autobiography* (Princeton: Princeton University Press, 1972), Karl Joachim Weintraub, *The Value of the Individual: Self and Circumstance in Autobiography* (Chicago: University of Chicago Press, 1978), William C. Spengemann, *The Forms of Autobiography: Episodes in the History of a Literary Genre* (New Haven: Yale University Press, 1980) and Paul Jay, *Being in the Text: Self-Representation from Wordsworth to Roland Barthes* (Ithaca: Cornell University Press, 1984).

18. Georges Duby, "Histoire des mentalités," in *L'Histoire et ses méthodes*, ed. Charles Samaran (Paris: Gallimard, 1961), 938. For a valuable synthetic account of the *histoire des mentalités* and its relation to related currents such as the history of ideas and intellectual history, see Roger Chartier, "Intellectual History or Sociocultural History? The French Trajectories," in *Modern European Intellectual History: Reappraisals and New Perspectives*, ed. Dominick LaCapra and Steven L. Kaplan (Ithaca: Cornell University Press, 1982), 13–46. Philippe Carrard, *Poetics of the New History: French Historical Discourse from Braudel to Chartier* (Baltimore: Johns Hopkins University Press, 1992), provides a more detailed look at trends in the *Annales* school.

19. Anthony Cascardi has written of the impoverishment often visited on notions of the modern by those who define it as the sole and coherent system of thought we purportedly owe to Descartes: "[W]hereas existing analyses of the relationship between subjectivity and modernity accept the Cartesian model of self-consciousness as the dominant one even where they argue against it, the modern subject is in fact positioned within a field of conflicting discourses, such that modern culture can best be imagined as a 'detotalized totality' (Sartre's phrase)" (Anthony J. Cascardi, *The Subject of Modernity* [Cambridge: Cambridge University Press, 1992], 2). I would simply hasten to append "practices" to "discourses."

20. See Roger Chartier, "Les Pratiques de l'écrit," in *Histoire de la vie privée*, ed. Philippe Ariès and Georges Duby, vol. 3 (Paris: Seuil, 1985), 113–61. Already, for Duby, a history of reading had been an integral part of the *mentalités* approach: "The book is both a vehicle and a repository. It endures—and it is in contact with it, in taking it in our hands and leafing through it that we can best adopt the psychological attitude of men of the past" ("Histoire des mentalités," 960). For an example of this type of approach applied to early modern conceptions of authorship, see Roger Chartier, *L'Ordre des livres: Lecteurs, auteurs, bibliothèques en Europe entre XIVe et XVIIIe siècle* (Aix-en-Provence: Alinéa, 1992).

21. Philippe Lejeune, *Le Pacte autobiographique* (Paris: Seuil, 1975).

22. For further meditations on the way, in Walter J. Ong's formulation, "writing is a technology that structures thought," see his essay of the same title in *The Written Word: Literacy in Transition*, ed. Gerd Baumann (Oxford: Clarendon Press, 1986), 23–50. A thorough discussion of the importance of such considerations for a history of autobiography is provided by Michael Mascuch, *Origins of the Individualist Self: Autobiography and Self-Identity in England, 1591–1791* (Stanford, Calif.: Stanford University Press, 1996). Mascuch's invaluable and exhaustive study intersects with my own on many points, envisaging a "prehistory" (23) of autobiography, the latter conceived less as a genre than as a broad-based cultural practice rooted in changes in printing, authorship, and so on. With regard to the periodization of these cultural changes, I reach similar conclusions to those of Mascuch—in both England and France they are principally an invention of the second half of the seventeenth century. (Compare, for instance, Mascuch's discussion of the shift from speech to writing to print as vehicles for Protestant piety [55–131] to my own discussion of French Catholic analogues in Chapter 2.)

23. See, e.g., Nancy Armstrong, *Desire and Domestic Fiction: A Political History of the Novel* (New York: Oxford University Press, 1987), and Barbara M. Benedict, *Making the Modern Reader: Cultural Mediation in Early Modern Literary Anthologies* (Princeton: Princeton University Press, 1996).

24. Cf. Ian P. Watt, *The Rise of the Novel: Studies in Defoe, Richardson, and Fielding* (Berkeley: University of California Press, 1957), and Jürgen Habermas, *The Structural Transformation of the Public Sphere: An Inquiry into a Category of Bourgeois Society*, trans. Thomas Burger (Cambridge, Mass.: MIT Press, 1989). Two suggestive recent explorations of the practice of English autobiography are Felicity Nussbaum, *The Autobiographical Subject: Gender and Ideology in Eighteenth-Century England* (Baltimore: Johns Hopkins University Press, 1989), and Michael Mascuch, *Origins of the Individualist Self*. The fact that France has inspired few similar studies is indicative of the persistent association of autobiography and Protestantism. Already in Montaigne one can read: "En faveur des Huguenots, qui accusent nostre confession privée et auriculaire, je me confesse en publicq, religieusement et purement" (Michel de Montaigne, *Les Essais*, ed. V.-L. Saulnier [Paris: Presses universitaires de France, 1924], 846) (In honor of the Huguenots, who condemn our private and auricular confession, I confess myself in public, religiously and purely [Michel de Montaigne, *The Complete Essays of Montaigne*, trans. Donald Frame [Stanford, Calif.: Stanford University Press, 1958], 643]). Goethe was perhaps the first to wonder whether or not Protestants might be more inclined to autobiography than Catholics: since Protestants did not confess

orally, he speculated in 1826, perhaps they had to do it in writing (Johann Wolfgang von Goethe, *Goethes Briefe*, vol. 4 [Hamburg: Christian Wegner Verlag, 1967], 187). Georges Gusdorf has been one of the most vocal proponents of this thesis, arguing that Rousseauian autobiography was an outgrowth of Pietism, a sort of self-confession; see especially Georges Gusdorf, "De l'autobiographie initiatique à l'autobiographie genre littéraire," *Revue d'histoire littéraire de la France* (1975), 957–94. For ample proof, however, that even in Britain autobiographical practice transcended both denomination and class, not to mention the Enlightenment, see Paul Delany, *British Autobiography in the Seventeenth Century* (London: Routledge & K. Paul, 1969).

25. See for instance Lejeune's more or less structuralist generic separations (*Pacte* 14). Working within the precepts of traditional literary history, however, Georges May has attempted to distinguish autobiography from other neighboring genres, only to conclude that it is the nature of autobiography to "absorb and assimilate the most heterogeneous materials" (Georges May, *L'Autobiographie* [Paris: Presses universitaires de France, 1979], 200).

26. James S. Amelang, *The Flight of Icarus: Artisan Autobiography in Early Modern Europe* (Stanford, Calif.: Stanford University Press, 1998), 48.

27. Amelang, *Flight of Icarus*, 44; Jonathan Dewald, *Aristocratic Experience and the Origins of Modern Culture: France, 1570–1715* (Berkeley: University of California Press, 1993), shows how concerns commonly associated with the bourgeoisie—e.g., individualism, ambition, personal worth, skepticism—could be found as well within the aristocratic military culture the bourgeoisie eventually overthrew. Belief in the importance of the culture of pre-Enlightenment France when considering a history of personal writing is of course nothing new; historical memoirs, for instance, have long received considerable attention from the French themselves. See (among many) Marc Fumaroli, "Les Mémoires du XVIIe siècle au carrefour des genres en prose," *Dix-septième siècle* 94–95 (1972), 7–37; Marie-Thérèse Hipp, *Mythes et réalités: Enquête sur le roman et les mémoires, 1660–1700* (Paris: C. Klincksieck, 1976); and Frédéric Briot, *Usage du monde, usage de soi: Enquête sur les mémorialistes d'Ancien Régime* (Paris: Seuil, 1994).

28. Here, I follow on the work of Frank Bowman, who has pointed out the importance of religious autobiography for a more general history of the genre through close readings of some of the texts examined in the present study; see Frank Paul Bowman, "Suffering, Madness and Literary Creation in Seventeenth-Century Spiritual Autobiography," *French Forum* 1 (1976), 24–48, and Bowman, "Le Statut littéraire de l'autobiographie spirituelle," in *Le Statut de la littérature: Mélanges offerts à Paul Bénichou*, ed. Marc Fumaroli (Geneva: Droz, 1982), 313–34. More recently, Marie-Florine Bruneau, *Women Mystics Confront the Modern World: Marie de l'Incarnation (1599–1672) and Madame Guyon (1648–1717)* (Albany: State University of New York Press, 1998), has used the autobiographies of two of the figures I will study, Marie de l'Incarnation and Jeanne Guyon, though more to examine the links between gender and modernity than to flesh out the history of autobiographical practice. I am also much indebted to the rich work on seventeenth-century spiritual writing by Jacques Le Brun and Michel de Certeau, whose concerns, like Bruneau's, nevertheless stop short of the subject that I pursue here.

29. For an example of just such an unmasking, see Robert C. Solomon, *Continen-*

tal Philosophy Since 1750: The Rise and Fall of the Self (Oxford: Oxford University Press, 1988). This caricature forms the backdrop for a virtual subgenre of autobiographical criticism, in which such-and-such an author is shown to contest—through attention to the collective rather than the individual, to the circular rather than the linear, and so on—traditional paradigms of Western identity, the latter being inevitably very narrowly defined. Excessively rigid characterizations of both autobiography and modern subjectivity detract as well from Mascuch's otherwise fascinating study of the practice: "The modern autobiographer is . . . the prototype of the individualist self, and the modern autobiography is the ideal medium of individualist self-identity" (Mascuch, *Origins of the Individualist Self,* 23). I would thus echo Paul Smith's objection, formulated as part of his effort to theorize the possibility of the subject's resistance to ideological constitution, to the tendency of academic discourse "to abstract the 'subject'": "My project," he writes, "[is] to argue that the human agent *exceeds* the 'subject' as it is constructed in and by much poststructuralist theory as well as by those discourses against which poststructuralist theory claims to pose itself" (Paul Smith, *Discerning the Subject* [Minneapolis: University of Minnesota Press, 1988], xxx).

30. Foremost among these arguments has been Charles Taylor, *Sources of the Self: The Making of the Modern Identity* (Cambridge, Mass.: Harvard University Press, 1989), who backtracks to classical times in order to understand the modern philosophical localization of truth at the center of the subject. Other scholars have thrown light on the importance of the interior in domains other than philosophical, revealing interiority as not only a "concept" but a rhetoric that underwrites a host of different practices. Such accounts take us from the dissecting table (Jonathan Sawday, *The Body Emblazoned: Dissection and the Human Body in Renaissance Culture* [New York: Routledge, 1995]) and the stage (Maus, *Inwardness and Theater in the English Renaissance*) to the pulpit (Bergamo, *L'Anatomie de l'âme*), the prison (John B. Bender, *Imagining the Penitentiary: Fiction and the Architecture of Mind in Eighteenth-Century England* [Chicago: University of Chicago Press, 1987]), and the halls of the Académie française (Joan DeJean, *Ancients Against Moderns: Culture Wars and the Making of a Fin de Siècle* [Chicago: University of Chicago Press, 1997]). One can add to these recent studies the classic work of Norbert Elias, *The Civilizing Process,* trans. Edmund Jephcott (Oxford: Blackwell, 1994), which has documented the "civilizing process" through which modern man has internalized social norms, and Hans Blumenberg, *The Legitimacy of the Modern Age,* trans. Robert M. Wallace (Cambridge, Mass.: MIT Press, 1983), whose account of the history of theoretical curiosity provides a detailed picture of how the withdrawal/death of God gave rise to the interior-exterior dyad. Although this is not the place for a (or another) critique of the idea of epistemic rupture, one might note in passing that almost all of the above work belies Foucault's claim that depth was strictly nineteenth-century phenomenon, resulting from a break with the "classical *episteme*;" see Michel Foucault, *Les Mots et les choses: Une Archéologie des sciences humaines* (Paris: Gallimard, 1966), especially chapters 7 and 8. Last, constructive comparisons can be drawn between modern concepts of interiority and those of the Greeks—mostly because the latter are so different from our own; see Ruth Padel, *In and Out of the Mind: Greek Images of the Tragic Self* (Princeton: Princeton University Press, 1992).

31. Philippe Lejeune, *L'Autobiographie en France* (Paris: Armand Colin, 1971), 59, his emphasis.

32. On the many uses of Augustine's *Confessions*, see Pierre Paul Courcelle, *Les Confessions de Saint Augustin dans la tradition littéraire: Antécédents et posterité* (Paris: Etudes Augustiniennes, 1963).

33. This proportion fluctuated over the course of the century; by the last few decades, it was at its high point, having reached fifty percent of the total print production. This figure reflects the percentage of volumes in the Bibliothèque nationale for the period 1670–1700 (Henri-Jean Martin, *Livre, pouvoirs et société à Paris au 17e siècle (1598–1701)*, 2 vols. [Geneva: Droz, 1969], 1:89). Statistics such as these are not easy to interpret—to what degree is the Bibliothèque nationale collection representative of total output in France?—but they do give an idea of the preponderance of the religious press. Moreover, one must add to this group of printed books the numerous circulating manuscripts that furnished a way of reaching readers without official Church or state approbation.

34. Jeanne-Marie Bouvier de La Motte Guyon, *La Vie de Madame Guyon* (Paris: Dervy-Livres, 1983), 397.

35. On the differences between seventeenth-century concepts of interiority and those of earlier times, see Bergamo, *L'Anatomie de l'âme*. I will examine Augustine's metaphors of interiority, and the ways in which they were transformed in the seventeenth century, in Chapter 1.

36. One could cite as key early modern French demystifications of the sign Cyrano's *L'Autre monde* (partial pub. 1657), La Bruyère's *Caractères* (1688), as well as Arnauld and Nicole's *Logique de Port-Royal* (1662) and the work of Pascal. Of course, the sign's arbitrariness is something that nearly every age seems to be aware of, but it can be argued that this awareness becomes modern only when it is promoted as a historical "discovery," lived both as a liberation from tradition and as a fall from previous wholeness—something that is arguably not quite the case in Montaigne, for instance, nor in the medieval quarrel that had long opposed realists and nominalists. "Strictly speaking, there is neither a temporal nor absolute break [between the traditional and the modern], only what amounts to the consciousness of such a break," notes Anthony Cascardi (*The Subject of Modernity*, 69).

37. See Jean-Marie Apostolidès, *Le Roi-machine: Spectacle et politique au temps de Louis XIV* (Paris: Editions de Minuit, 1981), and Peter Burke, *The Fabrication of Louis XIV* (New Haven: Yale University Press, 1992).

38. See Louis Marin, *La Parole mangée et autres essais théologico-politiques* (Paris: Méridiens Klincksieck, 1986), 11–35, and Frank Lestringant, *Une Sainte horreur, ou, Le Voyage en eucharistie: XVIe–XVIIIe siècle* (Paris: Presses universitaires de France, 1996).

39. To give but one example, the doctrine of *ex opere operato* declared that the efficacy of liturgical acts was unaffected by the potential corruption of the priest carrying out those acts. First formulated by Peter of Poitiers in the twelfth century, *ex opere operato* was subject to a barrage of criticism during the Reform, and, though upheld by the Council of Trent (1545–63), was as much as the Eucharist a continuous topic of controversy.

40. See Daniel Roche, *La Culture des apparences: Une Histoire du vêtement (XVIIe–XVIIIe siècle)* (Paris: Fayard, 1989), and Stephen Greenblatt, *Renaissance Self-Fashioning: From More to Shakespeare* (Chicago: University of Chicago Press, 1980).

41. Augustine, *Les Confessions*, trans. Philippe Goibaud du Bois (Paris: Jean-Baptiste Coignard, 1686), "Epître au Roi," n.p.

42. Jean Starobinski, *Jean-Jacques Rousseau: La Transparence et l'obstacle* (Paris: Gallimard, 1971).

43. Foucault's theories of governmentality are developed in Michel Foucault, *Résumé des cours, 1970–1982* (Paris: Julliard, 1989), and in "Governmentality," in Michel Foucault, *The Foucault Effect: Studies in Governmentality, with Two Lectures by and an Interview with Michel Foucault*, ed. Graham Burchell, Peter Miller, and Colin Gordon (Chicago: University of Chicago Press, 1991), 87–104.

44. As Bruno Latour has memorably put it (in a somewhat different context), "[m]odern discipline has reassembled, hooked together, systematized [a] cohort of contemporary elements to hold it together and thus to eliminate those that do not belong to the system. This attempt has failed; it has always failed. There are no longer — there have never been — anything but elements that elude the system" (*We Have Never Been Modern*, 74–75).

45. Foucault, *Discipline and Punish*, 200.

46. See Paul De Man, "Autobiography as De-Facement," *Modern Language Notes* 94 (1979), 919–30. For more or less deconstructive appreciations of how, via autobiography, Rousseau and Augustine unseat the self's historical stability instead of demonstrating it, see, respectively, Michael Sheringham, *French Autobiography: Devices and Desires* (Oxford: Clarendon Press, 1993), 31–66; and Eugene Vance, "Augustine's *Confessions* and the Grammar of Selfhood," *Genre* 6 (1973), 1–28.

47. Blumenberg notes in this context Georg Agricola's *Bermannus sive de re metalica* (1528), for instance (*The Legitimacy of the Modern Age*, 639n3).

Chapter 1. The History of an Anachronism

1. Michel de Montaigne, *The Autobiography of Michel de Montaigne*, ed. Marvin Lowenthal (Boston: Houghton Mifflin, 1935), xvii–xviii.

2. See, for example, Michel Beaujour, *Miroirs d'encre: Rhétorique de l'autoportrait* (Paris: Seuil, 1980), and Craig Brush, "A Self-Portrait Is Not an Autobiography," in Craig Brush, *From the Perspective of the Self: Montaigne's Self-Portrait* (New York: Fordham University Press, 1994), 23–35.

3. All references to the *Essais* are taken from Michel de Montaigne, *Les Essais*, ed. V.-L. Saulnier (Paris: Presses universitaires de France, 1924). English translations are from Michel de Montaigne, *The Complete Essays of Montaigne*, trans. Donald Frame (Stanford, Calif.: Stanford University Press, 1958). Pagination of both will be given parenthetically in the text: (book, chapter: French page; English page).

4. See Antoine Compagnon, *Nous, Michel de Montaigne* (Paris: Seuil, 1980); Claude Blum, "Ecrire le 'moi': 'J'adjouste, mais je ne corrige pas,'" in *Montaigne 1580–1980: Actes du colloque international*, ed. Marcel Tetel (Paris: Nizet, 1983), 36–53; André Tournon, *Montaigne: La Glose et l'essai* (Lyon: Presses Universitaires de Lyon, 1983); and Timothy Hampton, *Writing from History: The Rhetoric of Exemplarity in Renais-*

sance Literature (Ithaca: Cornell University Press, 1990). These arguments are many and varied; I will be referring to others in the pages that follow.

5. One might note that this type of warning has been frequently issued by scholars of the middle ages regarding anachronistically autobiographical readings of lyric poets such as Rutebeuf or Villon; see, for example, Leo Spitzer, "Note on the Poetic and the Emprical 'I' in Medieval Authors," *Traditio* 4 (1946), 414–22; and Paul Zumthor, "Autobiographie au Moyen Age?" in *Langue, texte, énigme* (Paris: Seuil, 1975), 165–80.

6. Montaigne's thought was mainly disseminated in the seventeenth century via Charron's text, which went through some 49 editions before 1672. The three collections, which had much less success, are *Esprit des Essais* (1677), *Pensées de Montaigne* (1700), and *Esprit de Montaigne* (1753). A fourth collection was published by Christophe Kormart in Germany under the barely recognizable title, *Abrégé des mémoires illustres contenant les plus remarquables affaires d'état enrichi d'un sommaire des Essais de Montaigne* (1689). See Mathurin Dréano, *La Renommée de Montaigne en France au XVIIIe siècle, 1677–1802* (Angers: Editions de l'Ouest, 1952) for information on the contents of these collections, which I will return to later.

7. See, for instance, Nicolas Boileau, *Bolaeana, ou les bons mots de M. Boileau*, ed. Monchesnay (Amsterdam: Lhonoré, 1742).

8. Catherine Magnien-Simonin, *Une Vie de Montaigne, ou Le Sommaire discours sur la vie de Michel Seigneur de Montaigne (1608)* (Paris: Honoré Champion, 1992), 38, 53. As a point of comparison, Montaigne's contemporary Cardano's *The Book of My Life* (1575) consisted of fragmentary chapters with no chronological articulation between them — "Stature and Appearance," "Customs, Vices and Errors," "Testimony of Illustrious Men Concerning Me," etc.

9. Cf. Francis Goyet, "A propos de 'Ces pastissages de lieux communs' (Le Rôle des notes de lecture dans la genèse des *Essais*)," *Bulletin de la Société des Amis de Montaigne* 7ème série, no. 5 (1986), 11–26.

10. Examples abound, but witness Gérard Defaux, who, in the introduction and notes to his recent edition of Clément Marot's works, argues for an autobiographical understanding of Marot's poetry through recourse to this metaphor, in spite of the fact that the concept of interior, subjective space — never mind the word "interior" itself — is completely absent from Marot's work: "[Etienne Dolet], for his part, understood that Marot's poetry was . . . a poetry of interiority, and that it was in the self, and not in the poetic conventions exterior to this self, that it had its roots" (Clément Marot, *Oeuvres poétiques de Clément Marot*, ed. Gérard Defaux, 2 vols. [Paris: Garnier, 1993], 2:xxix).

11. On the discovery and publication history of the *Journal*, see François Rigolot's critical edition (Michel de Montaigne, *Journal de voyage*, ed. François Rigolot [Paris: Presses universitaires de France, 1992]), which reproduces the prefaces quoted here.

12. Montaigne, *Journal de voyage*, 305n22.

13. Michel Foucault, "What Is an Author?" in *Language, Counter-Memory, Practice*, ed. D. Bouchard (Ithaca: Cornell University Press, 1977), 127; translation slightly modified.

14. Montaigne, *Journal de voyage*, 303.

15. Montaigne, *Journal de voyage*, 315–16.

16. Montaigne, *Journal de voyage*, 316.

17. *Correspondance littéraire, philosophique et critique par Grimm, Diderot, Raynal, Meister, Etc.* . . . , ed. Maurice Tourneux, vol. 10 (Paris: Garnier Frères, 1879), 430.

18. *Correspondance littéraire*, 431. By the eighteenth century, notes Dréano, Montaigne's much-discussed vanity had become a virtue (*La Renommée de Montaigne*, 163). The motif of the fireside chat is recurrent in accounts of the time, as is an emphasis on the *Essais* as the space of the secret heart's divulgation: "Comme c'est le portrait du coeur humain qu'il [Montaigne] fait, en faisant le sien, les lecteurs ne pensent qu'à eux-mêmes, en lisant Montaigne, ils se recherchent, et ils s'étudient en lui. La plupart même se flattent dans la comparaison secrète qu'ils font de leurs idées, de leurs moeurs, et de leurs sentiments, avec du plus naïf, du plus profond, et du plus singulier Ecrivain que nous ayons" (Since it is the portrait of the human heart that he [Montaigne] is drawing, in drawing his own, readers think only of themselves while reading Montaigne, they look for themselves and they study themselves in him. Most even flatter themselves with the secret comparison they make between their ideas, their mores and their feelings and those of the most naive, most profound, and most singular Writer we have) ("Observations sur le *Huetiana*," *Mercure de France*, 1744, 5, 946–47).

19. Richard L. Regosin, *The Matter of My Book: Montaigne's "Essais" as the Book of the Self* (Berkeley: University of California Press, 1977), 200. Note that recently the question of Montaigne's interiority has come under closer scrutiny by scholars who wish to situate him in a subjective evolution while maintaining his historical specificity. See Charles Taylor, *Sources of the Self: The Making of the Modern Identity* (Cambridge, Mass.: Harvard University Press, 1989), 177–84; Eva Kushner, "Intériorité, altérité, spatialité chez Montaigne," in *Le Lecteur, l'auteur et l'écrivain: Montaigne 1492–1592–1992*, ed. Ilana Zinguer (Paris: Honoré Champion, 1993), 31–40; and Fausta Garavini, "Voyage du 'je' au pays de l'écriture," in *Montaigne: Espace, voyage, écriture*, ed. Zoé Samaras (Paris: Honoré Champion, 1995), 237–42.

20. Glossing this very passage, Lawrence Kritzman writes: "The work is created at the same time as it creates [Montaigne] . . . The authority of the text depends on its being erected as the monument of a self analyzing itself and offered to the world in the movement of its own production" (Lawrence D. Kritzman, *Destruction/Découverte: Le fonctionnement de la rhétorique dans les Essais de Montaigne* [Lexington, Ky.: French Forum, 1980], 124). See also Terence Cave, *The Cornucopian Text: Problems of Writing in the French Renaissance* (Oxford: Clarendon Press, 1979), 273: "In that the *Essais* aim to project the image of a self which conforms to the book, they are neither memoirs nor autobiography, but rather a surrogate self, an auto-performance which cannot but displace the 'real' Montaigne."

21. Michel Foucault, *Technologies of the Self*, ed. L. Martin, H. Gutman and P. H. Hutton (Amherst: University of Massachusetts Press, 1988), 46, 33 (translation modified).

22. Michel Foucault, *The History of Sexuality*, Volume I: *An Introduction*, trans. Robert Hurley (New York: Random House, 1978), 59.

23. It has long been observed that the Renaissance owed much to the rediscov-

ery of Stoic thought (e.g., Léontine Zanta, *La Renaissance du stoïcisme au XVIe siècle* [Paris: Honoré Champion, 1914]); regarding Montaigne specifically, it was Pierre Villey who initially traced Stoic motifs and theorized their gradual disappearance over the fifteen or so years the *Essais* were composed. According to Villey, an initial Stoic phase, in which Montaigne meditated on heroic exemplarity, gave way, after an intervening bout with skepticism, to a somewhat hedonistic Epicurianism that rejected ascetic effort as useless if not downright perverse. See Pierre Villey, *Les Sources et l'évolution des Essais de Montaigne*, 2 vols. (Paris: Hachette, 1908). For a sample critique of Villey's now-discredited thesis, see Hugo Friedrich, *Montaigne*, trans. Dawn Eng, ed. Philippe Desan (Berkeley: University of California Press, 1991), 66–70 and 322–24.

24. Hampton, *Writing from History*, 153.

25. As an aside, it comes as no surprise that "introspection" has seventeenth-century roots. In English, its first appearances date from the last quarter of the century (OED); the word, unlisted in Furetière's dictionary, only enters the French language much later, in the early nineteenth century.

26. Jean-Jacques Rousseau, *Les Confessions*, in Jean-Jacques Rousseau, *Oeuvres complètes*, ed. Bernard Gagnebin and Marcel Raymond, vol. 1 (Paris: Gallimard, 1959), 234–35.

27. Jean-Jacques Rousseau, *Les Rêveries du promeneur solitaire*, 5, in Rousseau, *Oeuvres complètes*, 1047. It is no accident that Rousseau conflates retreat with imprisonment, both being manifestations of what John Bender calls the "penitentiary idea"—"an ideal of confinement as the story of isolated self-consciousness shaped over time" (John B. Bender, *Imagining the Penitentiary: Fiction and the Architecture of Mind in Eighteenth-Century England* [Chicago: University of Chicago Press, 1987], 44).

28. On retreat in the early modern period, see Bernard Beugnot, *Le Discours de la retraite au XVIIe siècle: Loin du monde et du bruit* (Paris: Presses Universitaires de France, 1996).

29. As Hampton demonstrates, even Cato's example provokes problems of readability (cf. *Writing from History*, 159–66).

30. On "the hermeneutical illusion of personality, of hidden intentions and individuality" in relation to the Cartesian text, see Dalia Judovitz, *Subjectivity and Representation in Descartes: The Origins of Modernity* (Cambridge: Cambridge University Press, 1988). On the prominence of reflexive verbs in the *Essais*, see also Jean Starobinski, *Montaigne en mouvement* (Paris: Gallimard, 1982), 27.

31. Antoine Compagnon, *La Seconde main, ou le travail de la citation* (Paris: Seuil, 1979), 235

32. Cf. Cave, *The Cornucopian Text*, 307: "invasion by alien authors is countered by a withdrawal into his own property, an imaginary *rus* where, alone, the writer fabricates a book which is exactly his."

33. Compagnon, *La Seconde main*, 311.

34. For similar readings see, for instance, Anthony Cascardi, who maintains that although Montaigne is not yet "modern," his strange and somewhat unhinged use of the first person is indicative of a crisis to which the modern subject à la Descartes will be a response (Anthony J. Cascardi, *The Subject of Modernity* [Cambridge: Cambridge

University Press, 1992], 65). See also Timothy J. Reiss, "Montaigne and the Subject of Polity," in *Literary Theory/Renaissance Texts*, ed. Patricia Parker and David Quint (Baltimore: Johns Hopkins University Press, 1986), 115–49: "I am tempted indeed to suggest that in the *Essays*, the 'subject' is glimpsed only by these signs of its *absence*. In Descartes, the subject is *there* by the certainty of its *presence*" (134).

35. Starobinski, *Montaigne en mouvement*, 272–73.

36. Regosin, *The Matter of My Book*, 200.

37. Qtd. by Cave, *The Cornucopian Text*, 42, 65. Cave has more recently proposed the beginnings of what he calls the philological history of the self, tracing notably the first uses of the substantive "le moi." See Terence Cave, *Pré-histoires: Textes troublés au seuil de la modernité* (Geneva: Droz, 1999).

38. Cf. Foucault, *History of Sexuality*: "[Confession] had to be exacted, by force, since it involved something that tried to stay hidden" (66).

39. Here I follow Katharine Eisaman Maus, *Inwardness and Theater in the English Renaissance* (Chicago: University of Chicago Press, 1995), 28, who details how the reign of what she calls "inwardness" is productive of two interdependent fantasies: that selves are obscure, hidden and ineffable, and that they are fully manifest or capable of being made manifest.

40. E.g., "Certes, c'est un sujet merveilleusement vain, divers et ondoyant, que l'homme" (Truly man is a marvelously vain, diverse, and undulating object [I, 1: 9; 5]); "Si on ne les [les esprits] occupe à certain sujet, qui les bride et contreigne, ils se jettent desreiglez, par-cy par-là, dans le vague champ des imaginations" (Unless you keep them [minds] busy with some definite subject that will bridle and control them, they throw themselves in disorder hither and yon in the vague field of imagination [I, 8: 32; 21]); "Je ne peints pas l'estre. Je peints le passage" (I do not portray being: I portray passing [III, 2: 805; 611]), etc. On movement in the *Essais*, see Starobinski, *Montaigne en mouvement*; and Michel Jeanneret, *Perpetuum mobile: Métamorphoses des corps et des oeuvres, de Vinci à Montaigne* (Paris: Macula, 1997).

41. On the Baroque fold as that which harmonizes interior and exterior, see Gilles Deleuze, "The Fold," *Yale French Studies* 80 (1991), 227–47. On Montaigne's "Baroqueness" more generally, see Richard A. Sayce, "Baroque Elements in Montaigne," *French Studies* 8 (1954), 1–16.

42. Hence Richard Regosin's gloss of the passage leads him to generalize: "Montaigne's journey toward the self takes place in the figurative space of interiority" (Regosin, *The Matter of My Book*, 166). This may, however, be overstating the case, in that references to psychological depths are not exactly common in the *Essais*. Invoking the same passage, another critic comments: "There are indeed a few passages in the *Essais* in which Montaigne refers to those depths in himself whose secret ferment he sometimes feels and which he is attempting to explore in writing. These passages are not numerous" (Garavini, "Voyage du 'je,' " 237). The metaphor of interiority does not organize all of Montaigne's reflections on himself; rather, it is a concept he hits upon from time to time.

43. "Ideas and events of the outside world, and the writer's own life there, become a function of interiority" (Regosin, *The Matter of My Book*, 171).

44. For a theory of how power creates a psyche metaphorized in terms of interiority, see Judith Butler, *The Psychic Life of Power: Theories in Subjection* (Stanford,

Calif.: Stanford University Press, 1997), esp. chap. 6: "[Conscience] is the vanishing point of the state's authority, its psychic idealization, and, in that sense, its disappearance as an external object. The process of forming the subject is a process of rendering the terrorizing power of the state invisible — and effective — as the ideality of conscience" (191). Butler here is elaborating on Althusserian "interpellation" and especially on Foucault's contention that a disciplinary society ultimately relies on the subject's own participation in the maintenance of power: "He who is subjected to a field of visibility, and who knows it, assumes responsibility for the constraints of power; he makes them play spontaneously upon himself; he inscribes in himself the power relation in which he simultaneously plays both roles" (Michel Foucault, *Discipline and Punish: The Birth of the Prison*, trans. Alan Sheridan [New York: Vintage, 1995], 202–3). In Montaigne, of course, the power that is internalized is not state power, but rather that of the *exemplum*.

45. Rousseau as well will put his autobiographical project under the sign of anatomy — "intus, et in cute," reads his epigraph — but by that time the ubiquity of the medical gaze, as well as human interiority, will have become givens. See, for example, Rétif de la Bretonne, who in his 1794–97 autobiography repeatedly makes reference to his writing as a sort of "dissection morale" (Nicolas Rétif de La Bretonne, *Monsieur Nicolas, ou le coeur humain dévoilé*, vol. 1 [Paris: J.-J. Pauvert, 1959], xxxvii).

46. Michel Foucault, *Naissance de la clinique: Une Archéologie du regard médical* (Paris: Presses universitaires de France, 1963), 123. For a detailed discussion of the relation between the sense of human interiority and anatomy in the Renaissance, see Jonathan Sawday, *The Body Emblazoned: Dissection and the Human Body in Renaissance Culture* (New York: Routledge, 1995); his work extends the "archeology of the medical gaze" Foucault undertook in *Naissance de la clinique*, which is limited to the nineteenth century. On the anatomical gaze and seventeenth-century subjection, see Barker, *The Tremulous Private Body*, 65–102. On the growing late-medieval interest in innards — such as the "opening virgin" statues of the fifteenth century which combined anatomical curiosity and Marial piety — see Marie-Christine Pouchelle, *The Body and Surgery in the Middle Ages*, trans. Rosemary Morris (New Brunswick, N.J.: Rutgers University Press, 1990).

47. On the heart as a symbolic organ from the Greeks to the seventeenth century, when its precise anatomical function was discovered, see Milad Doueihi, *A Perverse History of the Human Heart* (Cambridge, Mass.: Harvard University Press, 1997). For an account of the heart's role in the developing cultural politics of the emotions during the transition from Classicism to the Enlightenment, see Joan DeJean, *Ancients Against Moderns: Culture Wars and the Making of a Fin de Siècle* (Chicago: University of Chicago Press, 1997), 78–123. The link between Enlightenment *sensibilité* and medicine is explored by Anne C. Vila, *Enlightenment and Pathology: Sensibility in the Literature and Medicine of Eighteenth-Century France* (Baltimore: Johns Hopkins University Press, 1998).

48. Blaise Pascal, *Pensées*, ed. Philippe Sellier (Paris: Mercure de France, 1976), 322.

49. As the anonymous reviewer of the *Pensées de Montaigne* put it, "La principale fin qu'eut Montaigne en écrivant ses Essais, fut de tracer son Portrait, et de se faire connaître. Quel besoin le public avait-il de cette connaissance? Quelle nécessité qu'il

fût informé des travers de son esprit, de ses pensées vaines, de ses idées fausses, de ses opinions dangereuses, de ses passions folles et insensées?" (Montaigne's principal aim in writing his essays was to trace his Portrait, and to make himself known. What need had the public for this knowledge? What necessity was there to be informed of the errors of his mind, his vain thoughts, his false ideas, his dangerous opinions, his mad and insane passions?) (*Journal des savants pour l'année MDCCI*, tome 29 [Amsterdam: Chez Waesberge, Boom et Goethals, 1702], 437).

50. For studies of Montaigne's reception, see Alan M. Boase, *The Fortunes of Montaigne: A History of the Essays in France, 1580–1669* (1935; New York: Octogon, 1970); Pierre Villey, *Montaigne devant la postérité* (Paris: Boivin, 1935); Donald Frame, *Montaigne in France, 1812–1852* (New York: Columbia University Press, 1940); Dréano, *La Renommée de Montaigne*; Ian Winter, *Montaigne's Self-Portrait and Its Influence in France, 1580–1630* (Lexington, Ky.: French Forum, 1976); Jules Brody, *Lectures de Montaigne* (Lexington, Ky.: French Forum, 1982), 13–27; Olivier Millet, *La Première réception des Essais de Montaigne (1580–1640)* (Paris: Honoré Champion, 1995).

51. François Grude La Croix du Maine, *Les Bibliothèques françaises de La Croix du Maine et de Du Verdier* (1584; Paris: Saillant et Nyon, 1772), 130.

52. Estienne Pasquier, *Choix de lettres sur la littérature, la langue, et la traduction*, ed. D. Thickett (Geneva: Droz, 1956), 47.

53. On the many readings of Montaigne as moral philosophy, see especially Villey, *Montaigne devant la postérité* and Millet, *La Première réception des Essais*, 28–33. Huet's statement that "A peine trouverez-vous un gentilhomme de campagne qui veuille se distinguer des preneurs de lièvres, sans un Montaigne sur sa cheminée" (Hardly will you find a country gentleman who, wishing to distinguish himself from the local rabbit catchers, does not have a copy of Montaigne on his mantelpiece) (qtd. in Villey, *Montaigne devant la postérité*, 310–11), indicates to what extent this care of the self, like the doctrine of *honnêteté* that continued it, was coded as an aristocratic concern.

54. La Croix du Maine, *Les Bibliothèques françaises*, 130.

55. Pasquier, *Choix de lettres*, 46.

56. Marie de Gournay, "Préface de 1635," *Montaigne Studies* 2.2 (1990), 93.

57. Dominique Baudier, qtd. in Villey, *Montaigne devant la postérité*, 303.

58. " 'Private' designated the exclusion from the sphere of the state apparatus. . . . The authorities were contrasted with the subjects excluded from them; the former served, so it was said, the public welfare, while the latter pursued their private interests" (Jürgen Habermas, *The Structural Transformation of the Public Sphere: An Inquiry into a Category of Bourgeois Society*, trans. Thomas Burger [Cambridge, Mass.: MIT Press, 1989], 11). Montaigne's typical use of private is in line with Habermas's characterization: "On attache aussi bien toute la philosophie morale à une vie populaire et privée que à une vie de plus riche estoffe" (You can tie up all moral philosophy with a common and private life just as well as with a life of richer stuff) (III, 2: 805; 611). On how the concept of the private in Montaigne fails to produce a modern subject, see Reiss, "Montaigne and the Subject of Polity."

59. Jean-Louis Guez de Balzac, *Oeuvres*, vol. 2 (Geneva: Slatkine, 1971), 659.

60. These are not the only moments in which Montaigne's text reflects a change in usage of the term—"descouvrir ses humeurs privées" (discover his personal hu-

mors) (II, 10: 414; 302) and "Il n'est action si privée et secrette" (There is no action so private and secret) (I, 30: 198; 147) are two other examples.

61. Pasquier, *Choix de lettres*, 49.

62. Jean-Pierre Camus, *Les Diversités*, reproduced in Millet, *La Première réception des Essais*, 189, 169, 190.

63. Marie de Gournay, "Préface à l'édition des *Essais* de Montaigne," *Montaigne Studies* 1.1 (1989), 34, 43. Millet has noted Gournay's instrumentality in eliminating the aristocratic reading of Montaigne (*La Première réception des Essais*, 14).

64. For a description of the varying paratextual accompaniments of the various editions of the *Essais*, see R. A. Sayce and David Maskell, *A Descriptive Bibliography of Montaigne's Essais, 1580–1700* (London: Bibliographical Society, 1983).

65. François Rigolot, "Introduction [à la préface de 1595]," *Montaigne Studies* 1.1 (1989), 11.

66. On this, see Catherine M. Bauchatz, "Marie de Gournay's 'Préface de 1595,'" *Bulletin de la Société des Amis de Montaigne* 3–4 (1986), 73–82, and Richard L. Regosin, *Montaigne's Unruly Brood: Textual Engendering and the Challenge to Paternal Authority* (Berkeley: University of California Press, 1996), 48–79.

67. Gournay, "1595," 34.

68. Foucault, "What Is an Author?" 115.

69. Gournay, "1595," 45–46.

70. Regosin, *Montaigne's Unruly Brood*, 69.

71. See, respectively, Maurice Laugaa, *Lectures de Mme de Lafayette* (Paris: Armand Colin, 1971) and Robert Darnton, "Readers Respond to Rousseau: The Fabrication of Romantic Sensitivity," in *The Great Cat Massacre and Other Episodes in French Cultural History* (New York: Vintage Books, 1984), 215–56.

72. Gournay, "1595," 24.

73. Gournay, "1595," 43; Gournay, "1635," 85.

74. Gournay, "1595," 43.

75. "En faveur des Huguenots, qui accusent nostre confession privée et auriculaire, je me confesse en publicq, religieusement et purement. S. Augustin, Origene et Hippocrates ont publié les erreurs de leurs opinions; moy, encore, de mes meurs" (In honor of the Huguenots, who condemn our private and auricular confession, I confess myself in public, religiously and purely. Saint Augustin, Origen, and Hippocrates have published the errors of their opinions; I, besides, those of my conduct) (III, 5: 846–47; 643).

76. Gournay, "1635," 87.

77. Gournay, "1635," 92, 80.

78. Gournay, "1635," 88.

79. Taylor, *Sources of the Self*, 178. Cf. also Foucault's contention that modern avowal takes as its subject not only what the subjects *wants* to hide, but more importantly, "what [is] hidden from himself" (*History of Sexuality*, 66).

80. Gournay, "1635," 88.

81. Gournay, "1635," 92.

82. Cf. Sayce and Maskell, *A Descriptive Bibliography*.

83. Montaigne, *Esprit des Essais*, "Préface," n.p. An account of all the changes imparted by these editions would be fastidious; suffice it to say that they both more or

less do away with the book-self relationship, cutting, for example, the "livre consubstantiel" of II, 18. In the context of confessional discourse, an additional example is telling: the passage at the beginning of "De la praesumption," from "nous ne sommes que ceremonie" (we are nothing but ceremony) to "quant aux branles de l'ame, je veux icy confesser ce que j'en sens" (as for the movements of my soul, I want to confess here what I am aware of) (II, 17: 632–33; 478–80), in which Montaigne writes of Lucilius, "[qui] commettoit à son papier ses actions et ses pensées, et s'y peignoit tel qu'il se sentoit estre" ([who] committed to his paper his actions and thoughts, and portrayed himself there as he felt he was), is totally eliminated from both editions.

84. Antoine Arnauld and Pierre Nicole, *La Logique ou L'Art de penser*, ed. Pierre Clair and François Girbal (Paris: Vrin, 1981), 268; 266–67.

85. Arnauld and Nicole, *La Logique*, 266–69.

86. To give just one example: Antoine Arnauld's *De la fréquente communion* (1643) contains 38 uses of variants of "secret," 21 of "intérieur," 12 of "caché," 10 of "profond," and 7 of "invisible."

87. Nigel Abercrombie discusses the question of Montaigne's knowledge of the *Confessions*, and concludes on the side of unfamiliarity (Nigel Abercrombie, *Saint Augustine and French Classical Thought* [1938; Oxford: Oxford University Press, 1972], 40). Friedrich establishes a comparison between Augustine and Montaigne while nonetheless following more or less Abercrombie's assertion (*Montaigne*, 217). For a recent *mise au point* on the question, see Cave, *Pré-histoires*, 123n37.

88. For more general assessments of the influence of Augustine's thought on the century, see L. Barbedette, "L'Influence augustinienne au XVIIe siècle," *Revue de l'histoire des religions* 93 (1926), 279–93, Abercrombie, *Saint Augustine*, the April–June 1982 special issue of *Dix-septième siècle* devoted to "Le Siècle de Saint Augustin," and Bruno Neveu, *Erudition et religion aux XVIIe et XVIIIe siècles* (Paris: Albin Michel, 1994), 451–90. The question of the seventeenth-century dissemination of Augustinian *topoi* such as his conversion scene has been analyzed by Pierre Paul Courcelle, *Les Confessions de Saint Augustin dans la tradition littéraire: Antécédents et posterité* (Paris: Etudes Augustiniennes, 1963), chap. 7.

89. See Pierre Blanchard, "L'Espace intérieur chez saint Augustin d'après le Livre X des 'Confessions,'" *Augustinus Magister*, no. 1 (1954), 535–42; Gareth B. Matthews, "The Inner Man," *American Philosophical Quarterly* 4, no. 2 (1967), 166–72; Boghos L. Zekiyan, "Interiorismo agostiniano e l'autoconscienza del soggetto," *Augustinianum* 16 (1976), 399–410; Karl Joachim Weintraub, *The Value of the Individual: Self and Circumstance in Autobiography* (Chicago: University of Chicago Press, 1978), chap. 2; Maria Daraki, "L'Emergence du sujet singulier dans les Confessions d'Augustin," *Esprit* (Feb. 1981), 95–115. Taylor (*Sources of the Self*, 126–42) inserts Augustine's concept of the interior into the unfolding narrative of the modern self, as does Jeremy Tambling, *Confession: Sexuality, Sin, the Subject* (Manchester: Manchester University Press, 1990), though from a considerably more critical position. For a good overview of evolving theological conceptions of the inner man from the Old Testament to recent times, see André Derville and Aimé Solignac, "Homme intérieur," in *Dictionnaire de spiritualité ascétique et mystique*, ed. Marcel Viller, vol. 7 (Paris: Beauchesne, 1939–94), col. 650–74.

90. Rom. 7:22–23, translation modified: the Revised Standard Version glosses

over the theological specificity of the words *interiorem hominem* in favor of "inmost self," a term that projects back onto the Epistles precisely the depth-structured subjectivity whose history I am trying to trace. The original Greek, clearer still, reads "kata ton eso anthropon" (according to the inner man) — there is no "my" whatsoever. (Thanks to Jeff Fort for bringing this last detail to my attention.) Additional references to the *homo interior* can be found at 2 Cor. 4:16 and Eph. 3: 16.

91. Matthews, "Inner Man," 166.

92. For a brief discussion of the Augustinian concept of memory, see Taylor, *Sources of the Self*, 134–36. All citations from the *Confessions* indicate the book and chapter, followed by the page from Henry Chadwick's recent translation (Augustine, *Confessions*, trans. Henry Chadwick [Oxford: Oxford University Press, 1991]), which is especially useful because of its refusal to subsume Augustine's prose in modern metaphors. (On two occasions I have modified Chadwick's word choice.) The original Latin, given in parentheses, is taken from the text of the Loeb Classical Library edition (Cambridge, Mass.: Harvard University Press, 1977–79).

93. Augustine uses the term only once more, again speaking of memory — "into remote recesses" (in remotiora penetralia) (X, 11, 189). He may well have got this use from his much-admired Ambrosius, who had written of "penetralia animi."

94. Cf. also "See the broad plains and caves and caverns of my memory" (ecce in memoriae meae campis et antris et cavernis innumerabilibus) (X, 17, 194). Elsewhere Augustine refers to an allegorical "inner house" (interioris domus meae) (VIII, 8, 146), the "intimate chamber" of which is the human heart (in cubiculo nostro, corde meo).

95. "[I]n interiore homine habitat veritas," *De vera religione* XXXIX.72 (qtd. in Taylor, *Sources of the Self*, 129).

96. Qtd. in Taylor, *Sources of the Self*, 136.

97. John Freccero, "The Fig Tree and the Laurel: Petrarch's Poetics," in *Literary Theory/Renaissance Texts*, ed. Patricia Parker and David Quint (Baltimore: Johns Hopkins University Press, 1986), 22–23.

98. Commentators have frequently adduced this final impersonality in order to differentiate Augustine's text from modern autobiography. See for example Blanchard's account of how Augustine's metaphor of inner space eventually gives way to an abolition of the notion of that space ("L'Espace intérieur"). Similar views of how Augustine abolishes the speaking subject can be found in Eugene Vance, "Augustine's *Confessions* and the Grammar of Selfhood," *Genre* 6 (1973), 1–28, and Beaujour, *Miroirs d'encre* (42–53).

99. An additional example is provided by the reference to the infant who has no means of communicating inner desires to the outside, adult world: "For my desires were internal" (illae [voluntates] intus erant) (I, 6, 7).

100. The text of Arnauld d'Andilly's edition, minus its important preface, has recently been made accessible by Philippe Sellier's edition (Augustine, *Confessions*, trans. Arnauld d'Andilly, ed. Philippe Sellier [Paris: Folio/Gallimard, 1993]). One can easily see from Sellier's own presentation of the work that its interiority continues to be trumpeted in much the same terms as it was three centuries ago.

101. Augustine, *Les Confessions*, trans. Arnauld d'Andilly, 133.

102. Augustine, *Les Confessions*, trans. Arnauld d'Andilly, 286.

103. Augustine, *Les Confessions*, trans. Arnauld d'Andilly, 82. Another word com-

monly used by Arnauld d'Andilly to translate (and extend) Augustine's metaphoric subjective depths, "replis," has a similar tendency to appear where little in the original seems to warrant it. Whereas Augustine writes, "But you, Lord, know everything about [man]; for you made [him]" (tu autem, domine, scis ejus omnia, qui fecisti eum) (X, 5, 182), seventeenth-century readers found the following: "Mais vous, Seigneur, pénétrez dans les replis les plus cachés de son âme, parce que vous le connaissez comme l'ouvrier connaît son ouvrage" (But you, Lord, penetrate into the most hidden recesses of his soul, for you know him as the artisan knows his work) (338).

104. Augustine, *Les Confessions*, trans. Philippe Goibaud du Bois (Paris: Jean-Baptiste Coignard, 1686), 84.

105. Augustine, *Les Confessions . . .* , trans. Aemar Hennequin (1582; Lyon: Pierre Rigaud, 1609), 40v.

106. Augustine, *Les Confessions*, trans. René de Cérisiers (1638; Paris: Compagnie des marchands libraires du palais, 1665), 55.

107. In the early modern period, writes Certeau, "the difference (considered intolerable) between the religious *consciousness* of Christians and the ideological or institutional *representations* of their faith becomes sharper. Is this truly anything new? What is in any case especially striking in the texts is less the *fact* of this difference . . . than the explicit *feeling* of a gulf between beliefs and doctrines, or between experience and institutions" (Michel de Certeau, *L'Ecriture de l'histoire* [Paris: Gallimard, 1975], 135, italics in original). Much of Certeau's work has been an elaboration of this gulf, which I will explore in greater detail in subsequent chapters. It should be stated from the outset, however, that although the incompatibility between experience and institutions may have been more perceived than real, the perception of divorce resulted in two very separate reading publics, the devotional and the theological; their libraries, in fact, did not mix. On the multiple readerships of religious works, see Henri-Jean Martin, *Livre, pouvoirs et société à Paris au dix-septième siècle (1598–1701)*, 2 vols (Geneva: Droz, 1969), 2:776–90.

108. The Library of Congress contains a copy of this edition, indicated as the first by Remi Ceillier, *Histoire générale des auteurs sacrés et ecclésiastiques*, vol. 9 (Paris: Louis Vivès, 1858), 813; note, however, that Ceillier's dates are often quite wide of the mark. The earliest copy in the Bibliothèque nationale, which possesses several editions dating to 1633, is from 1609.

109. Augustine, *Les Confessions*, trans. Hennequin, 5r. In ecclesiastical Latin, *confessio* could refer to avowal (as a penitential discipline), to praise of God, or to the confession of faith pronounced by martyrs before the tribunal. The first two meanings are interdependent, as in the Hebrew term *jada*—the avowal of sin is at the same time praise for the God who pardons.

110. Augustine, *Les Confessions*, trans. Hennequin, 12v.

111. Augustine, *Les Confessions*, trans. Cérisiers, "Eclaircissement," n.p.

112. Foucault, *History of Sexuality*, vol. I, 61.

113. On the tendency of the interior to be alternately, in the formulation of one religious author of the time, a muddy well and a font of pure water, see Mino Bergamo, *L'Anatomie de l'âme: De François de Sales à Fénelon*, trans. Marc Bonneval (Grenoble: Jérôme Millon, 1994), 17–19. As I shall explore in more depth in Chapter 4, "la science expérimentale" needs to be read also as "experimental knowledge": both of its

terms had dual meanings. Foucault, it should be pointed out, did not overlook the mystic science of experience. On the contrary, he assimilated Christian mysticism to the Classical legacy of the *ars erotica*, which made of pleasure the source of any and all truth. See *History of Sexuality*, vol. I, 70–71.

114. I quote Arnauld d'Andilly's (unpaginated) "Avis au lecteur" from the second edition (Paris: Chez la veuve Camusat et Pierre le Petit, 1649).

115. Cf. also the Church approbation, which confirms the splitting off of the *Confessions* from Augustine's theological contributions: "Quoique toute l'Eglise ait toujours été dans de très grands sentiments d'amour et de respect pour la doctrine de s. Augustin, il faut avouer néanmoins que les livres de ses Confessions ont emporté l'estime et l'approbation de tout le monde par dessus tous ses autres écrits, parce que cet ouvrage était encore plus une production de sa piété . . . que sa doctrine" (Although the Church has always had great feelings of love and respect for the doctrine of Saint Augustine, it must be admitted nevertheless that the books of his *Confessions* have won every one's esteem and approbation more than all his other writings, because this work was even more a production of his piety . . . than his doctrine).

116. Goibaud du Bois, for instance, urges readers to follow Augustine's example and "work on their hearts" ("travailler sur [leur] coeur"). Goibaud du Bois had formulated elsewhere a theory of spontaneous eloquence in order to account for the devotional appeal of Augustine's work, an eloquence that came not from study but from a "disposition intérieure" (inner disposition): "[I]l n'appartient qu'à un coeur touché de la vérité d'en passer le sentiment dans les coeurs des autres" (Only a heart touched by truth can impart its feeling to the hearts of others) (Philippe Goibaud du Bois, *Avertissement en tête de sa traduction des sermons de saint Augustin*, ed. Thomas M. Carr, Jr. [1694; Geneva: Droz, 1992], 109).

117. Augustine, *Les Confessions*, trans. Goibaud du Bois, xiv.

118. Augustine, *Les Confessions de saint Augustin abrégées, où l'on n'a mis que ce qui est le plus touchant et le plus à la portée de tout le monde*, trans. Simon Michel Treuvé (Paris: Charles Robustel, 1703).

119. A few years before Treuvé's edition, François Paris had also remarked in his *Prières et élévations à Dieu extraites des livres des Confessions de s. Augustin* (Paris: Edme Couterot, 1698) that these last four books were full of abstractions that left them "hors la portée du commun des fidèles" (beyond the reach of the average person of faith). Paris's book differed from the translations of the *Confessions* discussed above, for his goal was to create a text in which Augustine's "I" could be assimilated by the "I" of the reader. He therefore eliminates historical specificity, and even goes so far as to move Augustine's narration into the present tense. This type of devotional use of the text was also quite popular (similar volumes include *Les Plus tendres sentiments d'un coeur envers Dieu, tirés exactement du livre des Confessions de s. Augustin* [1688]), and led to the repeated publication of another "accessible" work of Augustine's, the *Soliloquies*, for those readers seeking "l'intelligence de ce gémissement intérieur" (knowledge of this inner moaning) (*Les Soliloques, le manuel et les méditations de saint Augustin* [Paris: Chez Charles Savreux], "Avis," n.p.). Devotional thirst for interiority, then, took many forms, some autobiographical, some aiming at the reproduction in the reader of Augustine's own state of mystic grace.

120. It reminds one as well of the fact that college courses of the "Great Books"

type often assign only the first nine or ten books of Augustine's classic. Significantly, some of the most interesting modern literary analysis of the *Confessions* has concerned itself precisely with trying to uncover the logic of a text that to modern eyes can only appear as fractured. According to Beaujour, for example, Augustine sets up an autobiographical "I" only to abolish it: "The tenth book retraces the process by which one comes to forget oneself by emptying the memory of all temporal residue" (*Miroirs d'encre*, 44). Vance ("Augustine's *Confessions*") reaches similar conclusions.

121. The second volume (1679) completed the first by adding Possidius's well-known biographical piece, and by cutting and pasting passages from Augustine's other works. Translations of only the first nine or ten books of the *Confessions* would be popular in England until the beginning of the twentieth century.

122. On sensibility as the grounds for scientific and literary exploration of the human subject, see Vila, *Enlightenment and Pathology*. Some time ago and in passing, Lionel Gossman pointed to Treuvé's title as an indication of the changing readerly tastes that would eventually culminate in Rousseau's own autobiographical work; see his "The Innocent Art of Confession and Reverie" (*Daedalus* 107.3 [1978]), 75n7.

123. See Petrarch, *Epistolae de rebus familiaribus* IV, 1.

124. The historian's goal, Foucault writes, is to "examine both the difference that keeps us at a remove from a way of thinking in which we recognize the origin of our own, and the proximity that remains in spite of that distance which we never cease to widen" (Michel Foucault, *The History of Sexuality*, Volume II: *The Use of Pleasure*, trans. Robert Hurley [New York: Vintage, 1980], 7n [translation slightly modified]).

125. Eugene Vance, "Le moi comme langage: Saint Augustin et l'autobiographie," *Poétique* 14 (1973), 165.

126. Augustine, *Les Confessions*, trans. Arnauld d'Andilly, "Avis," n.p.

127. Augustine, *Instruction tirée de S. Augustin sur le gémissement intérieur, où nous devons être durant tout le cours de notre vie* (Paris, 1653), 5, 7.

Chapter 2. Verbatim

1. Benoît de Canfeld, *Règle de perfection . . .* , ed. Nantilly (1614; Paris: Chez la veuve Charles Chastellain, 1622), 42.

2. Benoît's *Life* can be found in Jacques Brousse, *La Vie du R. P. Ange de Joyeuse, . . . ensemble les vies des RR. PP. P. Benoît Anglais, et P. Archange Ecossais . . .* (Paris: Adrian Taupinart, 1621).

3. Benoît de Canfeld, *Règle de perfection . . .* (Paris: Gilles André, 1666).

4. Benoît de Canfeld, *Véritable et miraculeuse conversion*, in *Règle de perfection . . .* , ed. Nantilly, 42.

5. Augustine, *Les Confessions . . .* , trans. Aemar Hennequin (1582. Lyon: Pierre Rigaud, 1609).

6. By "independent works," I mean those published on their own and not as part of an author's collected works. The earliest French examples are Jeanne Guyon, *La Vie de Madame Guyon écrite par elle-même* (1720) and Jean Hamon, *Relation de plusieurs circonstances de la vie de Monsieur Hamon, faite par lui-même, sur le modèle des Confessions de S. Augustin* (1734), both of which had been composed in the seventeenth century.

7. On the confusion of Teresa's autobiography and biography, I follow the hypotheses of Alphonse Vermeylen, *Sainte Thérèse en France au XVIIe siècle, 1600–1660* (Louvain: Publications Universitaires de Louvain, 1958), 54–57.

8. Marie de Gournay, "Préface de 1635," *Montaigne Studies* 2.2 (1990), 69, 92. On Gournay's feminism, see Domna Stanton, "Woman as Object and Subject of Exchange: Marie de Gournay's Le Proumenoir (1594)," *L'Esprit créateur* 23, no. 2 (1983), 9–25, and Elyane Dezon-Jones, *Fragments d'un discours féminin* (Paris: José Corti, 1989).

9. Augustine, *Les Confessions*, trans. René de Cérisiers (1638. Paris: Compagnie des marchands libraires du palais, 1665), "Eclaircissement," n.p.

10. Augustine, *Les Soliloques et méditations de S. Augustin*, trans. René de Cérisiers (Paris: Compagnie des marchands libraires du palais, 1664), n.p.

11. Sonja Herpoel, "Sainte Thérèse et le Libro de Recreaciones (1585)," in *Écrire sur soi en Espagne: Modèles et écarts. Actes du IIIe colloque international d'Aix en Provence (1986)* (Aix-en Provence: Université de Provence, 1988), 46.

12. Indeed, commentators on early modern convent writing tend to imply great numbers of Teresa-like *Lives*, when in fact this "vogue" consisted mainly of autobiographical fragments. Referring to Spain, Arenal and Schlau write that "[i]n a huge revival of the hagiographic tradition, thousands of men and women deemed saintly were urged to record their lives" (Electa Arenal and Stacey Schlau, *Untold Sisters: Hispanic Nuns in Their Own Works* [Albuquerque: University of New Mexico Press, 1989], 7). More generally, Orest Ranum claims that "[the narratives] of Catherine of Sienna and of Teresa of Avila led thousands of nuns to follow their example" (Orest Ranum, "Les Refuges de l'intimité," in *Histoire de la vie privée*, ed. Philippe Ariès and Georges Duby, vol. 3 [Paris: Seuil, 1986], 241). Such assertions are both impressionistic and misleading, as they suggest vast numbers of full-scale imitations of Teresa's work. A more well-documented researcher, Isabelle Poutrin, puts the number of autobiographical texts by Spanish nuns at over one hundred for the late sixteenth to mid-eighteenth centuries; out of these, only about twenty narrated something of their author's childhood (Isabelle Poutrin, *Le Voile et la plume: Autobiographie et sainteté féminine dans l'Espagne moderne* (Madrid: Casa de Velásquez, 1995), esp. 34ff). Poutrin's work on the Spanish analogues of the texts I will be dealing with in this chapter confirms many of my factual contentions regarding the production of autobiography in French convents.

13. The same is generally true in Spain, although with a few exceptions. See Poutrin, *Le Voile et la plume*, 251.

14. I say "generated," for the question of who actually wrote the works varies from case to case, as will become clear. Some mystics gave dictation to an amanuensis, others wrote themselves.

15. See Michel de Certeau, *La Fable mystique, XVIe–XVIIe siècle* (Paris: Gallimard, 1982), esp. 107–55, for an excellent overview of the early modern permutations of the word "mystique" and the theological evolution underpinning them. Similar conclusions are reached by Jacques Le Brun ("Expérience religieuse et expérience littéraire," in *La Pensée religieuse dans la littérature et la civilisation du XVIIe siècle en France*, ed. Manfred Tietz and Volker Kapp [Paris: Biblio 17/PFSCL, 1984], 123–44), who studies the concept of experience in early modern theology.

16. Historians of Catholicism have long noted the enthusiasm surrounding these notions during the seventeenth century. See especially Mino Bergamo, *L'Anatomie de l'âme: De François de Sales à Fénelon*, trans. Marc Bonneval (Grenoble: Jérôme Millon, 1994), 7–21, as well as three articles in Marcel Viller, ed., *Dictionnaire de spiritualité ascétique et mystique*, 17 vols. (Paris: Beauchesne, 1937–94); Louis Cognet, "Le Coeur chez les spirituels du XVIIe siècle" (11: col. 2300–2307); Michel Dupuy, "Intérieur de Jésus" (7: col. 1870–77); and André Derville and Aimé Solignac, "Homme intérieur" (7: col. 650–74). The latter provides a good overview of evolving representations of interiority from the Old Testament to recent times.

17. Henri-Jean Martin, *Livre, pouvoirs et société à Paris au 17e siècle (1598–1701)*, 2 vols. (Geneva: Droz, 1969), 2:785. Bernières's book was sufficiently well-known to have attracted the attention of La Bruyère: in his *Caractères*, Onuphre, a *faux dévot* more subtile than Tartuffe, leaves a copy of the volume lying around his bedroom (Jean de La Bruyère, *Les Caractères* [Paris: Livre de Poche, 1973], 375 [De la mode, ¶24]).

18. Blaise Pascal, *Oeuvres complètes*, ed. Jacques Chevalier (Paris: Gallimard/Pléiade, 1954), 1221 (Brunschvig 277).

19. Cognet, "Le coeur," 2302, 2305.

20. Alacoque's vision of the Sacred Heart dates from June 1675, although in the decades preceding many of the mystics discussed here had articulated visions of Jesus's heart as striking as Alacoque's. On the Sacred Heart, see Jacques Le Brun, "Politique et spiritualité: La Dévotion au sacré coeur à l'époque moderne," *Concilium* 69 (1971), 25–36.

21. For a detailed account of the Quietism affair, see Louis Cognet, *Crépuscule des mystiques* (Tournai, Belgium: Desclée, 1958). On Bossuet's changing views of mystic experience, which culminated in outright hostility, see Jacques Le Brun, *La Spiritualité de Bossuet* (Paris: Klincksieck, 1972).

22. François de Salignac de la Mothe-Fénelon, *Oeuvres*, ed. Jacques Le Brun (Paris: Gallimard/Pléiade, 1983), 1109. On the "Protestant turn" in spirituality, see François Lebrun, "Les Réformes: Dévotions communautaires et piété personnelle," in *Histoire de la vie privée*, ed. Philippe Ariès and Georges Duby, vol. 3 (Paris: Seuil, 1985), 70–111.

23. Augustine, *Les Confessions de saint Augustin abrégées, où l'on n'a mis que ce qui est le plus touchant et le plus à la portée de tout le monde*, trans. Simon Michel Treuvé (Paris: Charles Robustel, 1703), "Avertissement," n.p.

24. On the perceived bureaucratization of the Church at this time, see Michel de Certeau, *L'Ecriture de l'histoire* (Paris: Gallimard, 1975), 131–212.

25. The following gendered reading of enlightened illiteracy would not have been possible without Certeau's brilliant treatment of the topos; see the chapter "L'Illettré éclairé" in Certeau, *Fable Mystique*, 280–329. "Illettré" has the double valence of "illiterate" and "uncultured"—I play most on the first, but in either case, the *illettré* refers to a person whose knowledge of God cannot have come from books.

26. 1 Cor. 1:27 reads: "But God chose the foolish in the world to shame the wise; God chose what is weak in the world to shame the strong." Cf. also 2 Cor. 12:8–10 and 13:3–4.

27. Jean-Joseph Surin, *Correspondance*, ed. Michel de Certeau (Paris: Desclée De Brouwer, 1966), 140; Certeau, *Fable Mystique*, 280.

28. Linda Timmermans, *L'Accès des femmes à la culture (1598–1715)* (Paris: Honoré Champion, 1993), 615–17.

29. Jeanne de la Nativité, *L'Ecole du pur amour de Dieu ouverte aux savants et aux ignorants dans la vie merveilleuse d'une pauvre fille idiote . . . Armelle Nicolas*, ed. Pierre Poiret (Cologne: Jean de La Pierre, 1704), 34.

30. Pierre Nicole, *Traité de l'oraison* (1679), qtd. in Timmermans, *L'Accès des femmes*, 623. Timmermans furnishes many other examples of both positive and negative appraisals of feminized mysticism (502–15; 621–59).

31. In his autobiographical *Science expérimentale des choses de l'autre vie* (written 1663, published 1829), Surin takes pains to convince his presumably male reader that, contrary to received opinion, mystical experiences are not just a product of the sensitive female imagination. Of his own experiences, Surin writes: "Ce ne sont pas des goûts ou sentiments de femmelettes; plusieurs hommes spéculatifs et savants font mépris de cela, et le comparent aux larmes et tendresses qu'ont certaines femmes. . . . [I]ls prennent toutes ces expériences surnaturelles pour des rêveries de femme" (These are not the tastes and feelings of weak-minded little women; many speculative and learned men [nevertheless] show contempt for these things, and compare them to the tears and tender emotions that certain women display. . . . They take all these supernatural experiences for feminine daydreaming) (Jean-Joseph Surin, *Triomphe de l'amour divin sur les puissances de l'enfer . . . et Science expérimentale des choses de l'autre vie* [Grenoble: J. Millon, 1990], 325–26). Similar examples can be found elsewhere in his work, which I will analyze separately in Chapter 4.

32. There were other types of biography besides those that arose out of the fascination for women's experience: most men's *Lives*, for example, served the cause of the Counter-Reformation by emphasizing apostolic service to an embattled/victorious Church; *Lives* of women, in addition to stressing mystic gifts, frequently immortalized the founders of the many new congregations popping up across France since the beginning of the century, or held nuns up to readers as imitable models of feminine virtue (chastity, obedience, selflessness, and so on). The "interiorizing" biographies I deal with here are but a distinctive part of a much larger production.

33. The history of spiritual direction is long; its beginnings are to be found in the nascent monastic practices of the fourth century. In the Middle Ages, the last part of the confession was theoretically reserved for discussion of what the confessant should strive for, as opposed to what he or she had done wrong. But the vogue for spiritual direction that accompanied the creation of sixteenth-century texts as important (and different) as Teresa's *Life* and Ignatius's *Spiritual Exercises* was for all intents and purposes a new phenomenon, reaching out beyond monastic walls to the lives of everyday Catholics. See Irénée Noye, "Notes pour une histoire de la direction spirituelle," *Supplément de la Vie spirituelle* 34 (15 Sept. 1955): 251–76.

34. "In the Christian Confession, but especially in the direction and examination of conscience, in the search for spiritual union and the love of God, there was a whole series of methods that had much in common with an erotic art: guidance by the master along a path of initiation, the intensification of experiences extending down to

their physical components, the optimization of effects by the discourse that accompanied them" (Michel Foucault, *The History of Sexuality*, Volume I, *An Introduction*, trans. Robert Hurley [New York: Random House, 1978], 70).

35. Autobiographical accounts furnished by an aspirant to his or her director were often made weekly, or sometimes only at those times of the year when the director was out of town and could not converse with the aspirant directly. They were frequently demanded when an aspirant changed confessors; in these cases, the directed would then give an account of the main moments of his or her life, starting from childhood, up to the present. It was common, moreover, to continue such accounts through supplementary relations, often to the point of blurring any distinction between retrospective autobiographical narration and the journal. On this, see Poutrin, *Le Voile et la plume*, esp. 121.

36. This bond explains one of La Bruyère's barbs against what had become, by his time, a social type, the *femme à directeur*: "Si une femme pouvait dire à son confesseur, avec ses autres faiblesses, celles qu'elle a pour son directeur, et le temps qu'elle perd dans son entretien, peut-être lui serait-il donné pour pénitence d'y renoncer" (If a woman could tell her confessor, along with her other weaknesses, those she has for her director, and the time she wastes in conversation with him, perhaps the penance given to her would be to renounce him) (La Bruyère, *Les Caractères*, 82 [Des Femmes, ¶39]). The vogue for spiritual direction continued into the eighteenth century (Jacques Bertot's [†1681] *Directeur mystique* was first published in 1726), by which time the *femme à directeur* had become a popular object of literary satire — in Marivaux's *Paysan parvenu*, for instance.

37. Jean Maillard, *La Vie de la Mère Marie Bon de l'Incarnation, religieuse ursuline de Saint Marcelin, en Dauphiné. Où l'on trouve les profonds secrets de la conduite de Jésus-Christ sur les âmes, et de la vie intérieure* (Paris: Jean Couterot et Louis Guerin, 1686), 20; Claudine Moine, *Ma Vie secrète* (Paris: Desclée de Brouwer, 1968), 452.

38. *La Vie de la Vénérable Mère Anne-Marguerite Clément...* (Paris: Jean-Baptiste Coignard, 1686), 122.

39. Mathieu Bourdin, *Vie et conduite spirituelle de la damoiselle Madeleine Vigneron, soeur du tiers-ordre de saint François de Paule. Suivant les mémoires qu'elle en a laissés par l'ordre de son directeur. Le tout recueilli par les soins d'un religieux minime* (Paris: Bonaventure Le Brun, 1679), n.p., my emphasis. The prefaces I will often be citing were rarely paginated, and I will henceforth omit mentioning the fact.

40. Maillard, *Vie de Marie Bon*, 245, 249. Women taking on the authority of a director was a commonplace of the time; see Timmermans, *L'Accès des femmes*, 539–67.

41. Alexandre Piny, *La Vie de la Vénérable Mère Marie Madeleine de la très-sainte Trinité...* (Annecy, 1679), 401.

42. Certeau, *Fable mystique*, 323. For additional speculations on the place of orality within an early modern culture increasingly dominated by print, see Certeau, *L'Ecriture de l'histoire*, 213–88, where he highlights the homologous functioning of ethnographic and hagiographic discourse, and Michel de Certeau, *L'Invention du quotidien, I: Arts de faire*, ed. Luce Giard (Paris: Gallimard, 1990), 195–238.

43. Philippe-Joseph Salazar, *Le Culte de la voix au XVIIe siècle: Formes esthétiques de la parole à l'âge de l'imprimé* (Paris: Honoré Champion, 1995).

44. The antecedent of religious biography of the time is to be found less in the Bollandist enterprise than in Protestant martyrology of the preceding century. Both Jean Crespin, in his *Histoire des martyrs* (1554), and John Foxe, in the *Acts and Monuments* (1563), strove to include eyewitness reports and even papers left behind by the martyrs themselves in their accounts. Foucault has devoted several vivid pages to the concern for documenting the subject—for constituting the subject *through* documentation—that Foxe, Crespin, and religious biographers all put into practice. See Michel Foucault, *Discipline and Punish: The Birth of the Prison*, trans. Alan Sheridan (New York: Vintage, 1995): "These small techniques of notation, of registration, of constituting files, of arranging facts in columns and tables that are so familiar to us now, were of decisive importance in the epistemological 'thaw' of the sciences of the individual" (190–91). As will become clear, I believe that the corpus under examination in the present chapter nuances the rather one-way account of the interest in writing remarked by Foucault: far from being only the tool of disciplinary institutions, documentation emerged as well as a means by which women gained the status of authors.

45. Cataneo Marabetto, *La Vie et les oeuvres de sainte Catherine de Gênes. Nouvelle édition . . .*, ed. Jean Desmarests (Paris: Florentin Lambert, 1661), 225. It appears that this director—Cataneo Marabetto—was in fact the author of the work. On the particularly tenebrous circumstances surrounding the attribution of authorship, see Umile Bonzi da Genova, "L'Opus catharinianum et ses auteurs: Etude critique sur la biographie et les écrits de sainte Catherine de Gênes," *Revue d'ascétique et de mystique* 16 (Oct. 1935), 351–80.

46. Jacques Ferraige, *La Vie admirable et digne d'une fidèle imitation de la b. Mère Marguerite d'Arbouze . . .* (Paris: Fiacre Dehors et Jean Moreau, 1628), 516.

47. Claude Fleury, *La Vie de la Ven. Mère Marguerite d'Arbouze . . .* (Paris: Veuve Clouzier, 1687), 2, 3.

48. Jean-Baptiste de Saint-Jure, *La Vie de Monsieur de Renty* (Paris: Pierre le Petit, 1651). Other writers go beyond mere mention of sources and enumerate by name the respectable figures who have provided information on the subject; see, e.g., Charles-Louis de Lantages, *La Vie de la vénérable Mère Agnès de Jésus. . . . Avec l'abrégé de la vie de la Mère Françoise des Séraphins . . .* (Puy: André et Pierre de Lagarde, 1665).

49. Henri-Marie Boudun, *L'Homme intérieur ou la vie du vénérable Jean Chrysostome . . .* (Paris: Estienne Michalet, 1684), 3–4.

50. Jean Crasset, *La Vie de Madame Hélyot* (Paris: Estienne Michalet, 1683).

51. Qtd. in Marie-C. Guedré, "La Femme et la vie spirituelle," *Dix-septième siècle* 62–63 (1964), 48–49.

52. Antoine Boschet, *Le Parfait missionnaire ou la vie du R.P. Julien Maunoir . . .* (Paris: Jean Anisson, 1697).

53. Claude Martin, *La Vie de la vénérable Mère Marie de l'Incarnation, première supérieure des ursulines de la nouvelle France, tirée des ses lettres et de ses écrits* (1677; Paris: Chez Pierre de Bats, Martine Jouvencel, et Antoine Vuarin, 1684). The story of how a manuscript made it into the hands of the biographer is a frequently recurring motif; see, e.g., Tronson de Chenevière, *La Vie de la vénérable Marguerite Acarie . . .* (Paris: Loüis Sevestre, 1689).

54. Denis Amelotte, *La Vie de la soeur Marguerite du Saint-Sacrement . . .* (Paris: Pierre le Petit, 1655); Crasset, *Vie de Madame Hélyot*; André Duval, *La Vie admirable*

de soeur Marie de l'Incarnation (1621; Paris: Adrian Taupinart, 1625). Duval's concern for his source material is unusual for the time in which he was writing.

55. A 1679 scandal surrounding the biography of Juana de Jesús María, for example, had an effect on subsequent *Lives*; see Poutrin, *Le Voile et la plume*, 241–50.

56. Even an author's appearance on the Index was hardly sufficient grounds for pursuit or punishment of the author; a work (say, Fénelon's mystic apology *Explication des maximes des saints*, with its invocations of the enlightened illiterate) was condemned for its errors, but the author was free, if humiliated.

57. Marseille, Bibliothèque municipale, ms. 1250, n.p.

58. Alix Le Clerc, *La Vie de la vénérable Alix Le Clerc* (Nancy: Antoine, Claude et Charles les Charlots, 1666), 9–10. The sisters of the congregation narrate at some length their efforts to find a real biographer; all maintain "qu'il ne pouvait rien faire de mieux que ce que nous avions, et que nos préparatifs valaient mieux que le Bâtiment qu'ils en feraient" (that it would be impossible to do better than what we had, and that our preparations were worth more than the Building they would make of it) (21–22). This type of argument became in this period an ubiquitous biographical topos, one which suggests that memoirs, formerly the stuff of biography ("Matériaux" is the word used by Le Clerc's sisters), have been deemed worthy in themselves of the reader's attention and admiration. The (purportedly) unmanipulated documents seeping into these biographies are no doubt reflective of a broader trend in the seventeenth century, a trend that saw historical memoirs gradually assume the status of texts readable in their own right. In general memoirs were most often considered not history, but a source for an "official" history yet to be written. For the seventeenth century, writes Marc Fumaroli in his seminal study of the genre, "[m]emoirs . . . are only imperfect sketches of an ideal History remaining to be written. . . . [They are] opposed to History as the rough draft is opposed to the definitive work, the note file to the thesis, an element of analysis to a synthesis" (Marc Fumaroli, "Les Mémoires du XVIIe siècle au carrefour des genres en prose," *Dix-septième siècle* 94–95 [1972], 10–11). As with religious biography, however, a change was underway: memorialists too, Fumaroli notes, were starting to manifest a desire to present the reader with unmediated documents.

59. Georg Misch, *Geschichte der Autobiographie*, 4 vols. (Bern: A. Francke, 1949), 2: 310–59. I owe this reference to Michel Zink, *La Subjectivité littéraire autour du siècle de saint Louis* (Paris: Presses universitaires de France, 1985), 172n2.

60. The life of the martyr Perpetua (†203) is an exception, since it reproduces a diary she purportedly kept while in prison. However, even in this case the verifiability of the information is not stressed; the hagiographer merely mentions that Perpetua left her own account of what happened to her. As I have noted, Protestant martyrologies present an exception to this; Crespin, for instance, specifically exhorts his readers not to look to relics of saints for comfort (as do Catholics), but instead to examine "leurs dits et écrits, leurs réponses, la confession de leur foi, leur paroles et adhortations dernières" (their words and writings, their responses, their confessions of faith, their last words and exhortations) (Jean Crespin, *Histoire de martyrs . . .*, vol. 1 [1554; Toulouse: Société des livres religieux, 1885], xxxv).

61. Seventeenth-century French translations of these texts follow the original practice.

62. See for example C. J. Mitchell, "Quotation Marks, National Compositorial

Habits and False Imprints," *The Library, 6th series* (1983), 358–84. On the relationship between these typographical innovations and changing conceptions of authorship, see Joseph F. Loewenstein, "Idem: Italics and the Genetics of Authorship," *Journal of Medieval and Renaissance Studies* 20, no. 2 (1990), 205–24.

63. Duval, *Vie de Marie de l'Incarnation.*

64. Henri Cauchon de Maupas du Tour, *Vie de la vénérable Mère Jeanne-Françoise de Frémiot* . . . (1644; Paris: Simon Piget, 1646). The whole concept of quotation in this period was inseparable from printing practice: "Seventeenth-century dictionaries defined *quote* as to 'marke in the margent, to note by the way,' Randle Cotgrave, *A Dictionarie of the French and English Tongues* (London, 1611)" (Margreta De Grazia, "Shakespeare in Quotation Marks," in *The Appropriation of Shakespeare: Post Renaissance Reconstructions of the Works and the Myth,* ed. Jean I. Marsden [New York: St. Martin's Press, 1993], 69n6).

65. *Lettres circulaires des religieuses de la Visitation de Sainte Marie* (Aix, 1678–1757); *circulaire* dated 14 March, 1682, n.p.

66. Raphael de la Vièrge Marie, *Vie et vertus de la soeur Jeanne Perraud* . . . (Marseille: Claude Garcin, 1680), 74–75; similar examples can be found on 93 and 96–97.

67. Jeanne de la Nativité, *L'Ecole du pur amour,* 49. The original edition of this text had indiscriminately employed quotes for all three types of speech; see Jeanne de la Nativité, *Le Triomphe de l'amour divin dans la vie d'une grande servante de Dieu nommée Armelle Nicolas* . . . (Vennes: Jean Galles, 1676).

68. The question of just *who* was paying so much attention to typographical form—was it the biographer? the typesetter?—is probably moot as far as an inquiry into a mentality is concerned, for what is of issue are broad, evolving practices rather than a story of individual innovation. For the record, however, other prefaces echo Poiret's explicit interest in the technology of quotation. In Arnauld d'Andilly's translation of Teresa of Avila's works, the translator himself writes: "J'ai fait marquer ces paroles de la Sainte à Dieu avec des doubles virgules à la marge afin qu'on les puisse trouver sans peine; et j'ai fait mettre en italique celles que Dieu lui disait" (I have had these words of the Saint to God marked with double commas in the margins so that they can be easily located; and I have had placed in italics the words God spoke to her) (Saint Teresa of Avila, *Les Oeuvres de sainte Thérèse* . . . , trans. Arnauld d'Andilly [Paris: Pierre le Petit, 1670]). The *faire causatif* here ("j'ai fait marquer") suggests that if differences appeared in the printed text, they were there on order of Arnauld d'Andilly himself.

69. See, e.g., Boschet, *Le Parfait missionnaire,* who uses italics for speech (both dialogue and interior voices), quotation marks for written citations; or Marie-Madeleine de Mauroy, *La Vie de la vénérable Mère Elisabeth de l'enfant Jésus* . . . (Paris: Sebastien Mabre-Cramoisy, 1680), where the author places attributed oral speech and letters in italics, reserving quotation marks for notes or writings that Elisabeth de l'enfant Jésus, her subject, addressed to her director. In this last case, the distinction made is between public and private. Letters at the time—especially in a religious milieu—were widely circulated; they constituted a semi-public form of discourse. Communications with one's director, however, were of a different sort—it was there, as I have mentioned, that the subject really "uncovered her interior"—and were flagged with distinctive typography.

70. For an example of quotational extremes, see Chevalier d'Espoy, *La Vie de Madame du Houx, surnommée l'épouse de la croix* (Paris: François Babuty, 1713), which contains thousands of inverted commas running down the sides of the hundreds of pages of citation from du Houx's ample manuscripts. It bears pointing out that the practice of verbatim transcription in religious biography was strikingly similar in England. For some examples, see Michael Mascuch, *Origins of the Individualist Self: Autobiography and Self-Identity in England, 1591–1791* (Stanford, Calif.: Stanford University Press, 1996), 67–69.

71. Martin, *La Vie de Marie de l'Incarnation*, 50, 19, 55.

72. Teresa of Avila, *La Vie de sainte Thérèse, écrite par elle-même en Espagnol* . . . (Paris: Frederic Leonard, 1664).

73. An example of the many enunciative curiosities of this volume can be found in the following passage, Marie's "je" is without warning interrupted by Martin's, which in turn gives way to Marie's: "Enfin étant actuellement en oraison, je me sentais saisie par l'amour, et [Dieu] me tenait collée à lui d'une telle manière que je n'étais plus à moi, sinon que de fois à autres il me laissait respirer quelques paroles d'amour, qui bien loin de me donner la liberté, l'engageaient à renforcer l'union où il me tenait. Je ne dirai rien davantage d'une matière dont l'occasion se présentera incessamment de parler. J'ajouterai seulement un emportement d'amour surprenant qui fera voir jusqu'à quel point allait sa privauté, et l'accès que notre Seigneur lui donnait. Dans les entretiens, dit-elle, et dans les familiarités que j'ai avec lui" [etc.] (117) (Finally, being presently in the act of prayer, I felt myself seized by love, and [God] held me rapt in such a way that I was no longer myself, except that from time to time he let me breathe a few words of love, which, far from granting me liberty, moved him to reinforce the union in which he held me. I will say nothing more of a matter of which there will be constant occasion to speak. I will add only a surprising transport of love which will show how far her intimacy went, and the access the Lord gave her. In conversations, she says, and in the familiarities I have with him [etc.]). The sentence beginning "Je ne dirai rien davantage" is, of course, Martin's, but this is not clear to the reader until the possessive "sa" (her) in the following sentence.

74. E.g., Martin, *La Vie de Marie de l'Incarnation*, 234.

75. In the second (1689) edition, this device disappears—there will be no typographical distinction at all between Vigneron's words and Bourdin's. This may have been because Bourdin had exposed himself to criticism that he had given too much importance to the teachings of a woman. He tries to refute such accusations in his preface to the second edition.

76. Etienne d'Aignan du Sendat, *"Mère sainte": Fondatrice du Carmel d'Auch, 1570–1656. Vie et écrits* (Paris: P. Lethielleux, 1930), 20.

77. Mauroy, *Vie de la Mère Elisabeth de Jésus*, "Avertissement."

78. Charles-Louis de Lantages, *La Vie de la vénérable Mère Françoise des Seraphins* . . . (Clermont: N. Jacquard, 1669), "Préface."

79. Moine, *Ma Vie secrète*, 441.

80. Certeau, *Fable mystique*, 139.

81. Jeanne de la Nativité, *Triomphe de l'amour*, "Préface."

82. Martin, *La Vie de Marie de l'Incarnation*, "Préface," my emphasis.

83. Martin, *La Vie de Marie de l'Incarnation*, "Préface."

84. *Vie d'Anne Marguerite Clément*, 37, 78.

85. *La Vie de la Mère Antoinette de Jésus . . . avec un abrégé de ses lettres recueillies par les religieuses du même monastère* (Paris: Jean Villette, 1685).

86. *Lettres circulaires des religieuses de la Visitation*; *Circulaire* for Marie-Séraphique de Gaillard dated 14 March 1682.

87. Such is, at any rate, the theory of the relation between Teresa's *Life* and the Inquisition to be found in Carol Slade, *St. Teresa of Avila: Author of a Heroic Life* (Berkeley: University of California Press, 1995). For other commentators who have similarly emphasized the inquisitorial nature of the male/female confessional relationship, see Kathleen A. Myers, "The Addressee Determines the Discourse: The Role of the Confessor in the Spiritual Autobiography of Madre María de San Joseph (1656–1719)," *Bulletin of Hispanic Studies* 69 (1992), 39–47, and Electa Arenal and Stacey Schlau, "Stratagems of the Strong, Stratagems of the Weak: Autobiographical Prose of the Seventeenth-Century Hispanic Convent," *Tulsa Studies in Women's Literature* 9 (1990), 25–42. More recently, however, Isabelle Poutrin has contested outright the inquisitorial motivation behind the solicitation of Teresa's writings; she maintains that—in Teresa's case and more generally—since the demand for writing was made most often not when the mystic graces were seen as dubious, but when the director already had faith in them, the relationship was essentially "cooperative" rather than adversarial (Poutrin, *Le Voile et la plume*, 115). Poutrin's claim, which is based on a broad empirical study, is more in line with France's analogous autobiographical production.

88. Approximately one quarter of Spanish book-length biographies were authored by the subject's director (Poutrin, *Le Voile et la plume*, 218); a thorough statistical approach to their French counterparts (which is not my aim here) would no doubt reveal a similar proportion.

89. Raphaël de la Vierge Marie, *Vie et vertus de la soeur Jeanne Perraud*, "Avertissement."

90. Marseille, Bibliothèque municipale, ms. 1250, n.p.

91. Bourdin, *Vie et conduite spirituelle de Madeleine Vigneron*, "Préface."

92. My emphasis.

93. *La Vie intérieure* was, in fact, the suggestive title of Antoinette Bourignon's autobiography, to be discussed in the following chapter.

94. Moine, *Ma Vie secrète*, 452.

95. *Lettres circulaires des religieuses de la Visitation de Sainte Marie* (Annecy, 1675–1764); *Circulaire* dated 30 Sept. 1675, 21.

96. Jeanne de La Nativité, *Triomphe de l'amour*, "Préface."

97. Jacques Le Brun, "L'Institution et le corps, lieux de la mémoire," *Corps écrit* 11 (1984), 116–17.

98. Paul Ragueneau, *Vie de la Mère Catherine de Saint-Augustin . . .* (Paris: Florentin Lambert, 1671), 60.

99. If the *Mémorial*—a sheet of paper on which Pascal recorded a mystic illumination and that was discovered in his coat only after his death—has so captured the imagination of modern commentators on the author of the *Pensées*, this is clearly because the act can be read as an effort to circumscribe a private (as opposed to apologetic or public) space for writing.

100. Marie-Elisabeth Gertrude de Provane de Leyni, *Le Charme du divin amour*,

ou la vie de Jeanne-Bénigne Gojoz . . ., ed. F. Petetin (Besançon: Paul Jacquin, 1901), 10, 77.

101. Piny, *La Vie de Marie Madeleine de la très-sainte Trinité*, 219; Jean-Marie de Vernon, *Vie de Marguerite de Saint-Xavier . . .* (Paris: G. Josse, 1665), 210.

102. Mauroy, *Vie d'Elisabeth de l'enfant Jésus*, 174, 232.

103. One might situate this rhetoric as a particular variation on poetic images of the English Renaissance, for instance Spenser's first sonnet of the *Amoretti*, "written with teares in harts close bleeding book." On the creation of the "interior" poetic text in England, see Wendy Wall, *The Imprint of Gender: Authorship and Publication in the English Renaissance* (Ithaca: Cornell University Press, 1993), 169–226.

104. Philippe-Joseph Salazar, "Voix d'oraison féminine: Sur le style de l'éloquence d'extase," *Littératures Classiques* 28 (1996), 164. This idea resurfaces from time to time in the many religious biographies I have been examining, for instance, in the frequent claims of nuns not to be able to recall what they have just written.

105. Nicolas Boileau, *L'Art poétique* (1674), v. 153.

106. Maillard, *Vie de Marie Bon de l'Incarnation*, 30–31.

107. Jeanne de la Nativité, *Triomphe de l'amour*, 28.

108. Cf. the warning given to Marie Bon by her director that she must not "témoigner extérieurement ce qui se passait dans l'intérieur, de peur qu'elle ne donnât prise au démon sur elle, cet esprit ne connaissant notre intérieur que par des signes extérieurs" (testify externally to what occurs inwardly, lest she place herself in the grasp of the demon, a spirit which knows our interior only by external signs) (Maillard, *Vie de Marie Bon de l'Incarnation*, 98).

109. *Vie d'Anne-Marguerite Clément*, 188–89.

110. Boudun, *L'Homme intérieur*, 28.

111. *Vie d'Anne-Marguerite Clément*, 120–21.

112. Jean Croisset, "Abrégé de la vie de la soeur M.-M. Alacoque," in *La Dévotion au Sacré-Coeur de N. S. Jésus-Christ*, ed. Jean Croisset, vol. 2 (Lyon, 1696), 42–43.

113. Croisset, "Abrégé de la vie de M.-M. Alacoque," 44.

114. Teresa of Avila had made this theme—which I will explore the theme in more depth with regard to Jean-Joseph Surin, in Chapter 4—one of the principal organizing axes of her *Life*.

115. The problem of the reliability of mystic "signs" has as its complement the doubt that arose in demonology as to the readability of the possessed body and as to the limits of vision qua instrument of truth. See Michel de Certeau, *La Possession de Loudun* (1970; Paris: Gallimard/Julliard, 1990), esp. chaps. 8 and 9: "The stubbornness with which a surer vision and more ample observation are sought suggests an anxiety. The need for certainty reveals also the fear of losing it. What does one *really* see? Illusion insinuates itself into perception. A suspicion undermines the ambitions of the eye. There is a worm in the beautiful fruit of vision" (168).

116. Jeanne Deleloë, *Vie, correspondance et communications spirituelles*, ed. B. Sodar (Lille: Desclée de Brouwer, 1925), 41.

117. Jeanne de la Nativité, *Triomphe de l'amour*, 337.

118. Moine, *Ma Vie secrète*, 452.

119. Jeanne Perraud, *Les Oeuvres spirituelles de la soeur Jeanne Perraud . . .*, ed. Raphaël de la Vierge Marie (Marseille: Claude Marchy, 1682), 197.

120. Raphaël de la Vierge Marie, *Vie et vertus de la soeur Jeanne Perraud*, 317.

121. Bourdin, *Vie et conduite spirituelle*, 5, 66, 2, 3, 8, 9.

122. For more on the risks and rewards of female apostleship, see Chapter 3. One might note that insisting too heavily on gendering the anti-writing conspiracy male ignores the documented fact that often a mystic's enemies were jealous women within her own convent; see Poutrin, *Le Voile et la plume*, 159.

123. Marguerite-Marie Alacoque, *Vie et oeuvres de la bienheureuse Marguerite-Marie Alacoque*, ed. Gauthey, 2 vols. (Paris: Ancienne Librairie Poussielgue, 1915), 2: 63, 66. Following references in the paragraph will be included in the text. On the rhetoric of experience as that which eludes writing in Alacoque, see Jacques Le Brun, "Une Lecture historique des écrits de Marguerite-Marie Alacoque," *Nouvelles de l'Institut Catholique de Paris* (Feb. 1977), 38–53.

124. See, e.g., Mauroy, *Vie d'Elisabeth de l'enfant Jésus*, 2–4; *La Vie d'Antoinette de Jésus*, "Préface"; and Marguerite-Marie Alacoque and Joseph de Galliffet, *L'Excellence de la dévotion au coeur adorable de Jésus Christ avec le mémoire qu'a laissé de sa Vie la V. M. Marguerite Alacoque, Religieuse de la Visitation* (Lyon: Pierre Valfray, 1733), ii.

125. Mauroy, *Vie d'Elisabeth de l'enfant Jésus*, 108.

126. Provane de Leyni, *Le Charme du divin amour*, 10.

127. Mauroy, *Vie d'Elisabeth de l'enfant Jésus*, 33, 41.

128. Mauroy, *Vie d'Elisabeth de l'enfant Jésus*, 3–4. One is reminded of the passage early in Rousseau's *Confessions*, where he reproduces the only words he can remember of a ditty of his youth, deliberately leaving a dotted line in place of the forgotten fragments: the irreducibility of his own past would be contested were he to fill them in. See Jean-Jacques Rousseau, *Oeuvres complètes*, ed. Bernard Gagnebin and Marcel Raymond, vol. 1 (Paris: Gallimard, 1959), 11–12.

129. Kathleen Ross, *The Baroque Narrative of Carlos de Sigüenza y Góngora: A New World Paradise* (Cambridge: Cambridge University Press, 1993), 128.

130. Wall, *The Imprint of Gender*, 202, 221.

131. Claire Kahane, *Passions of the Voice: Hysteria, Narrative, and the Figure of the Speaking Woman, 1850–1915* (Baltimore: Johns Hopkins University Press, 1995), x.

132. Elizabeth D. Harvey, *Ventriolquized Voices: Feminist Theory and English Renaissance Texts* (New York: Routledge, 1992), 5. See also Janet Beizer, *Ventriloquized Bodies: Narratives of Hysteria in Nineteenth-Century France* (Ithaca: Cornell University Press, 1994), who defines ventriloquism as "the narrative process whereby women's speech is repressed in order to be expressed as inarticulate body language, which must then be dubbed by a male narrator" (9).

133. Beizer, *Ventriloquized Bodies*, 8.

134. For further examples of subject-authored material (letters, treatises, and so on) coming into print on the coattails of biography, see *La Vie de la vénérable Mère Anne Marie Clément* and *La Vie de la Mère Antoinette de Jésus*.

135. Nancy Armstrong, *Desire and Domestic Fiction: A Political History of the Novel* (New York: Oxford University Press, 1987), 8. By this somewhat sweeping statement, Armstrong means that "[d]uring the eighteenth century, one author after another discovered that the customary way of understanding social experience actually misrepresented human values. In place of the intricate status system that had long dominated British thinking, these authors began to represent an individual's value in

terms of his, but more often *her*, essential qualities of mind" (3–4). One could easily plug in here the terms of the religious trends of the previous century, replacing for instance "essential qualities of mind" (i.e., love, compassion) with "interior experience."

Chapter 3. Uncomfortable Subjects

1. Jean-Jacques Rousseau, *Oeuvres complètes*, ed. Bernard Gagnebin and Marcel Raymond, vol. 1 (Paris: Gallimard, 1959), 399. Littré gives this passage, where Rousseau defends an honorable friend, Palissot, "[qui] fut indigné qu'on osât ainsi person[n]aliser en sa présence" ([who] was indignant that someone would dare to personalize in his presence), as the word's first use.

2. This meaning, which still subsists in English, is now archaic in French.

3. The relation between the autobiographical "I" and the breakdown of the authority of tradition will be treated at length in Chapter 4.

4. Paul Delany, *British Autobiography in the Seventeenth Century* (London: Routledge and K. Paul, 1969), 84.

5. Similarly, Delany has noted in England the extent to which suffering at the hands of the law provided substantial subject matter for early autobiography: "It would seem that Catholic, Calvinist, or other ideas did not usually find expression in autobiographical form until the shock of some external stimulus, such as persecution, had moved men to testify concerning their beliefs" (*British Autobiography*, 38).

6. I am aware that there are variables other than temporal that might be responsible for the gap separating Labadie and earlier converts from Bourignon and Guyon, notably that of gender. As Chapter 2 has made clear, the mystic zone of inner authenticity was repeatedly cast as feminine, and the fact that Labadie did not have at his disposal the tropes relating interiority to writing is indeed only partly due to his writing in 1650 according to the (bent) conventions of the decades-old genre of the declaration of conversion — the rest was due to his being a man. (For an example of male autobiographical interiority, however, see the case of Jean-Joseph Surin, discussed in Chapter 4.) It may also be that the persecution he endured as a male heretic was of a different nature than the insistently personalizing attention directed at Bourignon and Guyon. These qualifications are pertinent and convincing. Nonetheless, I would add (1) that the diachronic hypothesis seems to me to explain best the dramatic difference in subjective "feel" between the three texts, and (2) that, even more than causal explanations (temporal change, gender), what has concerned me is the ways in which this feel is produced — that is, the textual building blocks of selfhood, so present in Guyon, and tantalizingly absent from Labadie. What are the signs of a recognizably modern form of first-person writing? What are the stylistics of subjectivity?

7. Philippe Ariès, and Georges Duby, eds., *Histoire de la vie privée*, 5 vols. (Paris: Seuil, 1985). See, regarding the early modern period, the following articles in volume 3: Madeleine Foisil, "L'Ecriture du for privé"; Orest Ranum, "Les Refuges de l'intimité"; and Jean-Marie Goulemot, "Les Pratiques littéraires ou la publicité du privé." The latter, in spite of his title, does not consider how privacy depends on publicity for its definition. Other scholars have paid somewhat more attention to the relation between apologetic and/or judicial defense and autobiography. See especially

Gisèle Mathieu-Castellani, *La Scène judiciaire de l'autobiographie* (Paris: Presses universitaires de France, 1996), who traces (without, however, historicizing) the judicial theme in autobiography since Job; and Arnaldo Momigliano, *The Development of Greek Biography* (1971; Cambridge, Mass.: Harvard University Press, 1993), who points to the apologetical speech as an early source of autobiography in the Classical world (58–62).

8. Many critiques have been leveled at Habermas's idealistic, indeed nostalgic, view of the Enlightenment as a time of rational communication; others still have taken aim at his somewhat rigid caricature of pre-Enlightenment publics. For a succinct appraisal of the biases and blind spots of Habermas's theory, see Anthony J. La Volpa, "Conceiving a Public: Ideas and Society in Eighteenth-Century Europe," *Journal of Modern History* 64 (1992), 79–116.

9. Jürgen Habermas, *The Structural Transformation of the Public Sphere: An Inquiry into a Category of Bourgeois Society*, trans. Thomas Burger (Cambridge, Mass.: MIT Press, 1989), 47. Habermas's insistence on the political importance of privacy—on the fact that the modern political sphere *needs* the private—has been emphasized by Dena Goodman, "Public Sphere and Private Life: Toward a Synthesis of Current Historiographical Approaches to the Old Regime," *History and Theory* 31 (1992), 1–20, and has provided a point of departure for important recent works of cultural history. The relation between the sudden Enlightenment interest in the private lives of public figures and the French Revolution, for instance, has been explored by Sarah Maza, *Private Lives and Public Affairs: The Causes Célèbres of Prerevolutionary France* (Berkeley: University of California Press, 1993); an account of how enthusiasm over the heart as basis for aesthetic judgment became a political issue as the Enlightenment was beginning is offered in Joan DeJean, *Ancients Against Moderns: Culture Wars and the Making of a Fin de Siècle* (Chicago: University of Chicago Press, 1997).

10. Habermas, *Structural Transformation*, 48, 49.

11. Habermas, *Structural Transformation*, 7.

12. Jean-Marie Apostolidès, *Le Roi-machine: Spectacle et politique au temps de Louis XIV* (Paris: Editions de Minuit, 1981), 8. In parallel fashion, Foucault notes that in pre-disciplinary societies, maximum individuation occurred in the superior echelons of power: "The more one possesses power or privilege, the more one is marked as an individual" (Michel Foucault, *Discipline and Punish: The Birth of the Prison*, trans. Alan Sheridan [New York: Vintage, 1995], 192).

13. Habermas, *Structural Transformation*, 94.

14. Roger Chartier, *The Cultural Origins of the French Revolution*, trans. Lydia G. Cochrane (Durham, N.C.: Duke University Press, 1991), 33

15. Christian Jouhaud, *Mazarinades: La Fronde des mots* (Paris: Aubier, 1985), 240.

16. A first *arrêt* against pamphlets published without due royal approbation was made in 1656 (i.e., soon after the Fronde), with other acts to follow.

17. Roger Chartier, "Pamphlets et gazettes," in *Histoire de l'édition française*, ed. H.-J. Martin (Paris: Promodis, 1982), 423.

18. Compare this situation with that of, say, the autobiographical pardon tales analyzed by Natalie Davis; these were never published as pamphlets, but were addressed to the king who alone had power of pardon. See Natalie Zemon Davis, *Fiction*

in the Archives: Pardon Tales and Their Tellers in Sixteenth-Century France (Stanford, Calif.: Stanford University Press, 1987), 14, 64. Marc Fumaroli has rightly pointed to the flourishing of memoirs in the seventeenth century as an indication that the king had lost his status as sole arbiter of historical truth. In the previous century, someone like Blaise de Monluc, feeling his contributions to the crown had been slighted by official historiographers, nonetheless addressed his memoirs to the king, Charles IX. Later memorialists, however, bypassed the king entirely, appealing instead to "the tribunal of posterity." "As far as high nobility was concerned, the plots against Richelieu, and the Fronde, are based largely on the feeling that the pact of justice has been broken and that the sacrifice of blood no longer finds at Court the compensations it rightly expects" (Marc Fumaroli, "Les Mémoires du dix-septième siècle au carrefour des genres en prose," *Dix-septième siècle* 94–95 [1972], 17).

19. The term "conversion narrative" (récit de conversion) is the one used by Louis Desgraves, who has done much bibliographical work on these numerous texts (Louis Desgraves, "Un Aspect des controverses entre catholiques et protestants: Les Récits de conversion [1598–1628]," in *La Conversion au XVIIe. Actes du XIIe colloque de Marseille* [Marseille: CMR 17, 1983], 89–110). It is, however, somewhat of a misnomer, for the texts are rarely, as we shall see, narrative. In addition, the translated term is unfortunately the same as the one used to refer to widespread Quaker and Puritan autobiographical practices in seventeenth- and eighteenth-century America. Given these grounds for confusion, I prefer to refer to these texts as simply "declarations," the generic designation that appears more often than not in their titles.

20. In 1600, for example, Henri IV, eager to prove his orthodoxy, organized a debate at Fontainebleau between the bishop of Evreux and the Protestant governor of Saumur, Du Plessis-Mornay. (Not surprisingly, the former emerged victorious.) On the cultural transformations following the Revocation, see Jean Quéniart, *La Révocation de l'Edit de Nantes: Protestants et catholiques en France de 1598 à 1685* (Paris: Desclée de Brouwer, 1985).

21. The declaration of Gaspard Martin, which I will mention shortly, was published in four cities in the same year: Die, Geneva, Montpellier, and Orange (Desgraves, "Un Aspect des controverses," 103).

22. The masculine here is intentional: in the declarations I have been able to consult, the convert is invariably male. Women of course did convert, but apparently did not declare their conversion before the congregation, or, at the very least, these declarations were not published. Aside from the obvious hypothesis of sexism (especially in the Protestant Church, where, in accordance with Pauline precepts, women did not have the right to speak), I have no explanation for this silence.

23. Fabrice de La Bassecourt, *Déclaration de Fabrice de La Bassecourt . . . par laquelle il expose les raisons qui l'ont mu à quitter la religious romaine pour embrasser la vérité de l'évangile* (La Rochelle, 1603).

24. Jacques Vanier, *Déclaration de maître Jacques Vanier, . . . naguère converti à la religion réformée . . .* (Saumur: Thomas Partav, 1620), 2.

25. Baptiste Bugnet, *Déclaration de Baptiste Bugnet, . . . pour laquelle il déduit les raisons qui l'ont mu à quitter la religion romaine . . .* (Geneva, 1604), 3.

26. Bugnet, *Déclaration*, 4.

27. Jacques Vidouze, *La Conversion de Jacques Vidouze, ministre de la religion pré-*

tendue réformée, rangé sous l'Eglise catholique, apostolique et romaine . . . (Lyon: Léon Savine, 1608), 10.

28. This conception of conversion is in keeping with standard hagiographic practice, where the typical conversion of an adult involves reason; see Donald Weinstein and Rudolph M. Bell, *Saints and Society: The Two Worlds of Western Christendom, 1000–1700* (Chicago: University of Chicago Press, 1982), 105.

29. [Sieur] de Vrillac, *Epître envoyée par le sieur de Vrillac . . . au sieur de Vrillac son père sur le sujet de sa conversion* (n.p.: n.p., n.d.), 18.

30. Gaspard Martin, *La Conversion de Gaspard Martin . . . Suivant la déclaration faite en l'église réformée de la ville d'Orange* (Montpellier: Jean Gillet, 1615), 4–5.

31. Certain texts do seem to see in life narrative a potential not only for rhetorical efficacy, but also for psychological specificity. Marco Antonio de Dominis, archbishop of Spalato, one of the most notorious converts of the time (he converted to Protestantism then back to Catholicism, and published numerous texts each time), comes the closest to producing a text one might classify as autobiography—his *Déclaration de Marc-Antoine de Dominis . . . sur les raisons qui l'ont mu à se départir de l'Église romaine* (Saumur: Thomas Purtav, 1616). He uses a rhetoric of simplicity ("je m'en vais vous dire franchement, sans fard, et sans fraude, ce que ç'a été" [I've set out to tell you frankly, without covering up and without deceit, how it really was] [6]), and embarks on a quest for the origins of his conversion, tracing his predisposition to Protestantism back to his youth. His text, obviously the product of a man of high learning (it was, in fact, originally written in Latin), contains passages on his interior strife that translate his struggle with his conscience.

32. For information on Labadie's biography, see Trevor J. Saxby, *The Quest for the New Jerusalem: Jean de Labadie and the Labadists, 1610–1744* (Dordrecht: M. Nijhoff, 1987), a reliable, well-documented history of his life as well as the posterity of the Labadist movement, and upon which my account here relies. See also the suggestive chapter on Labadie in Michel de Certeau, *La Fable mystique, XVIe–XVIIe siècle* (Paris: Gallimard, 1982).

33. Labadie's ample movements and oppositional stance were, it is true, dictated in large part by very real persecutions. His estranged Catholic brethren, for example, chased him from one town to the next, and Louis XIV's clampdown on Protestant liberties starting in 1657 was largely responsible for his departure from Montauban. In addition, outlandish rumors constantly circulated about his sexual and religious practices (one maintained that he forced nuns under his direction to strip naked in order to reproduce the state of original innocence), and an attempted poisoning seriously sickened his entire household for weeks.

34. Although there is nothing in this *avis* to suggest that Labadie could *not* be its author, the attribution of authorship here is in fact of little importance: the *avis*'s very presence reveals that Labadie's shift to a written form of declaration was a sufficiently obvious and significant change as to be in need of explanation.

35. Jean de Labadie, *Déclaration de Jean de Labadie, . . . contenant les raisons qui l'ont obligé à quitter la Communion de l'Eglise Romaine pour se ranger à celle de l'Eglise Réformée* (Montauban: Philippe Braconier, 1650), 298. Future references will be included parenthetically in the text.

36. This emphasis on private rumination informing public debate can perhaps

be understood as a typically Protestant contribution in the evolution of the public sphere. For an extension of Habermas's paradigm to the religious milieu of seventeenth-century England—one that invokes positions analogous to Labadie's in support of this hypothesis—see David Zaret, "Religion, Science, and Printing in the Public Spheres in Seventeenth-Century England," in *Habermas and the Public Sphere*, ed. Calhoun (Cambridge, Mass.: MIT Press, 1992), 212–35. Zaret critiques Habermas for assigning to economic considerations a preponderant role in the development of the public sphere, and attributes causation instead to technological developments (i.e., experimental science, printing), and to religion. However, it might be pointed out that in the case of France at least the insistence on writing as an instrument of reflection and debate does not follow automatically from Protestant doctrine, for in the early part of the century the publicity embraced by both Catholic and Protestant propaganda machines was substantially the same.

37. Quantification of the actual readership, unfortunately, is impossible. The *Déclaration*'s reprintings may be indicative of a substantial continuing readership—or only of Labadie's own flair for self-publicity. Circumstances suggest the latter. The reprints followed his movements, and thus were probably orchestrated by Labadie himself: a second edition in 1666, just before leaving Geneva, a third the same year, upon his arrival in Middelburg, and a fourth in Amsterdam in 1670. At any rate, Labadie took pains to widen his audience as much as possible, writing in February of 1651 a *Lettre à ses amis de la Communion Romaine touchant sa déclaration*, designed to supplement the original *Déclaration*, which had been written only for the Protestant fold. Response on the part of Labadie's adversaries was quick. Within weeks of the publication of Labadie's work, the anonymous *Le Grand chemin du jansénisme au calvinisme enseigné par . . . Labadie* appeared in Paris, distributed by a Jesuit bookseller, only to be countered by Antoine Arnauld in his anonymously published *Lettre d'un docteur en théologie . . . sur l'apostasie de Labadie*. Other tracts appeared in the same year.

38. Desgraves, "Un Aspect des controverses," 97–98, 100.

39. The importance of the notion of the tribunal—through which the individual appeals to the judgment of his or her peers—to public autobiographical discourse in pre-revolutionary France is discussed in Sarah Maza, "Le Tribunal de la nation: Les Mémoires judiciaires et l'opinion publique à la fin de l'ancien régime," *Annales E.S.C.* 42 (1987), 73–90. By the Enlightenment, the type of appeal that Labadie hesitantly makes will become commonplace: judicial memoirs, Maza maintains, had been clearly influenced by Rousseau's *Confessions*.

40. Faith E. Beasley, *Revising Memory: Women's Fiction and Memoirs in Seventeenth-Century France* (New Brunswick, N.J.: Rutgers University Press, 1990); see especially chapter 1.

41. Leszek Kolakowski, who devotes a chapter of his study of seventeenth-century heterodoxy to her, asserts: "It is indeed the utter mediocrity of this person that renders her interesting" (Leszek Kolakowski, *Chrétiens sans église: La Conscience religieuse et le lien confessionnel au XVIIe siècle* [Paris: Gallimard, 1969], 663). Bourignon receives a few pages in Ronald Knox's *Enthusiasm*, and the tone is similar: "The chief interest about her . . . is how she came to interest anybody" (Ronald A. Knox, *Enthusiasm: A Chapter in the History of Religion* [Oxford: Clarendon Press, 1950], 352). An exception to this dismissal can be found in Paul Hazard, *La Crise de*

la conscience européenne (Paris: Boivin, 1935), who closes his monumental study with her example. Serious sociological and doctrinal treatment of Bourignon is limited to Joyce Irwin, "Anna Marie van Schurman and Antoinette Bourignon: Contrasting Examples of Seventeenth-Century Pietism," *Church History* 60, no. 3 (1991), 301–15; and literary analysis to Frank Paul Bowman, "Suffering, Madness and Literary Creation in Seventeenth-Century Spiritual Autobiography," *French Forum* 1 (1976), 24–48. Biographical studies, however, are relatively numerous, and afford us quite a bit of information on the last twenty years of her life especially. (Details on her early life are more or less limited to what she provides in her *Lives*.) Pierre Poiret's rewriting and continuation of Bourignon's autobiographies, *La Vie continuée* (vol. 2 of Antoinette Bourignon, *La Vie de Dam[oise]lle Antoinette Bourignon, écrite partie par elle-même, partie par une personne de sa connaissance . . .* , 2 vols. [Amsterdam: Jean Riewerts & Pierre Arents, 1683]), is highly hagiographic. An old, but highly readable, detailed, and even-handed monograph is Alex R. Macewen, *Antoinette Bourignon, Quietist* (London: Hodder and Stoughton, 1910). For a more recent attempt at the rehabilitation of Bourignon's memory, see Marthe van der Does, *Antoinette Bourignon, 1616–1680: La Vie et l'oeuvre d'une mystique chrétienne* (Amsterdam: Holland University Press, 1974); Does's synthetic treatment contains a complete contemporary bibliography of her works, both in French and in translation. These sources repeat much of the same information; my biographical account here is indebted particularly to both Macewen and Does.

42. Bayle's article is under Bourignon's own name; he also refers to her in the article "Adam." On Bayle's assessment, see Joy Charnley, "La Vie et l'oeuvre d'Antoinette Bourignon jugées par Bayle," *Papers on French Seventeenth-Century Literature* 21, no. 41 (1994), 443–52.

43. Poiret, *Vie continuée*, 125. Both she and Labadie thus shared the need to theorize solitude as part of their spiritual education (the latter's *Traité de la solitude chrétienne* dates from about the same time).

44. Bourignon, *La Parole de Dieu, ou La Vie intérieure*, in volume 1 of Bourignon, *Vie*, 103; italics in the original. References to the *Vie intérieure* and the *Vie extérieure* will be indicated by VI and VE, respectively, parenthetically in the text.

45. She herself referred to this work as her "grand écrit" (Poiret, *Préface apologétique*, in Bourignon, *Vie*, vol. 1, 221). The subtitles of *Vie intérieure*, and of *Vie extérieure* for the second autobiography, are probably ascribable to Poiret, who by the time he published the work was already more influenced than Bourignon herself by the interiorizing lexicon of French devotion. For the sake of symmetry, I refer to *La Parole de Dieu* under the title of *Vie intérieure*. Unfortunately, no conclusive information exists as to why Bourignon undertook two separate autobiographies, or as to why she broke them off. Poiret's title choice is simply a device to make them seem complementary, when in fact the perspective of both volumes is similar.

46. Poiret, although he himself wrote nothing devotional, was, as his intermittent appearance in these pages will suggest, an important presence in seventeenth-century mysticism. By publishing autobiographies—of Bourignon, of Guyon—and by reprinting the most "interior" (i.e., autobiographical) *Lives* he could find—Jeanne de la Nativité's biography of Armelle Nicolas, for instance (see Chapter 2)—he provided the print infrastructure that allowed for the dissemination and deepening of

the autobiographical mind-set. A full-length study has recently been devoted to this instrumental figure; see Marjolaine Chevallier, *Pierre Poiret (1646–1719): Du Protestantisme à la mystique* (Geneva: Labor et Fides, 1994), esp. 41–62, which treat his relationship with Bourignon.

47. The question of whether Bourignon had read Labadie's *Déclaration* before writing her autobiographies can only be a matter of speculation; we do know that her dealings with Labadie date from around 1665, that is, after her *Vie intérieure* and before her *Vie extérieure*.

48. "Le but principal pourquoi je suis venue en Hollande a été . . . le dessein que j'ai de me retirer en Noordstrand avec quantité de personnes pour y vivre à la façon des Chrétiens en la primitive Église: parce que ce lieu est fort retiré, solitaire, et propre à abandonner entièrement le monde, pour mieux vaquer à Dieu" (The main goal for which I came to Holland was . . . my plan to withdraw to Noordstrand with a number of people and to live there in the manner of the Christians of the early Church: because this place is very isolated, solitary, and suitable for entirely abandoning the world, in order better to attend to God) (qtd. in Does, *Bourignon*, 88).

49. Bowman, "Suffering," 38.

50. "Pour bien connaître un caractère il y faudrait distinguer l'aquis d'avec la nature, voir comment il s'est formé, quelles occasions l'ont développé, quel enchaînement d'affections secrètes l'a rendu tel, et comment il se modifie, pour produire quelquefois les effets les plus contradictoires et les plus inattendus" (To know someone's character well one must distinguish the acquired from the natural, see how it has been formed, what events led to its development, what chain of secret affections made it that way, and how it is modified, as to produce at times the most contradictory and unexpected effects) (Rousseau, *Oeuvres* 1149). On the idea of "the chains of narrative" in Rousseau, see Michael Sheringham, *French Autobiography: Devices and Desires* (Oxford: Clarendon Press, 1993), 31–66.

51. One of the deceptions of her youth was the discovery that no convent would accept her if she was not able to bring a dowry with her (VI 6). (Although her family was wealthy, they would not consent to underwriting, by means of a dowry, Bourignon's vocation.)

52. Such competence has been a trait of many female mystics, such as Teresa of Avila or Jeanne Guyon.

53. See also the corresponding scene in the *Vie intérieure*, where the inaptitude of her step-mother in business matters again furnishes Bourignon the means to juxtapose the dual dictates of solitude and engagement (VI 62).

54. Pierre Bayle, *Dictionnaire historique et critique*, vol. 1 (1697; Basel: Jean-Louis Brandmuller, 1738), 646.

55. The clerk's comment was an allusion to the thorough and often multiple biographical searches made before, and as evidence to be presented during, any canonization procedure.

56. Foucault, *Discipline and Punish*, 189. Similarly, Foucault speaks of each individual becoming a "case," but a case quite unlike that of casuistics or jurisprudence: "The case is no longer . . . a set of circumstances defining an act and capable of modifying the application of a rule; it is the individual as he may be described, judged, measured, compared to others, *in his very individuality*" (191, my emphasis). This distinction lies at the root of the opposition made, in *The History of Sexuality*, between

sex viewed as an act and as an identity (the latter constituting "sexuality" proper). For an examination of the stakes of this much-discussed opposition, see David M. Halperin, "Forgetting Foucault: Acts, Identities, and the History of Sexuality," *Representations* 63 (1998), 93–120.

57. Coriache may simply have in mind traditional hagiographic practice, in which brief depiction of childhood was necessary in order to prove the continuity of the saint's vocation. Or his comment may speak to the increasing importance of childhood first traced in Philippe Ariès, *L'Enfant et la vie familiale sous l'Ancien Régime* (Paris: Plon, 1960). In either event, however, his demand is couched in the rhetoric of legal inquiry.

58. Poiret, *Vie continuée*, 313–14.

59. And by other means: many of the volumes of her *Works* (especially the two-volume *Témoignage de vérité*) are less treatises than a massive deployment of justificative documents about her person.

60. One might compare Bourignon's request with others. Teresa of Avila asks her confessor to tear up anything he finds in error; Jeanne Guyon demands of those who have asked for the accounts to incinerate them; Marie de l'Incarnation specifies that "papiers de conscience" be inscribed on the cover of her manuscript, and orders her son Claude Martin to burn it if he is near death.

61. Poiret, *Préface apologétique*, 221.

62. "Sa pudeur et son humilité naturelles lui faisaient sentir une horrible aversion de se produire" (Her modesty and her natural humility made her feel a horrible aversion to showing herself) (Poiret, *Préface apologétique*, 56). The expression "se produire" still retains this sense in French.

63. Poiret, *Préface apologétique*, 221.

64. There are two easily accessible full-length biographies of Guyon, perhaps the best known of all the seventeenth-century figures examined in the present study. Françoise Mallet-Joris's *Jeanne Guyon* (Paris: Flammarion, 1978) is narrative and intended for a general audience, while Marie-Louise Gondal's *Madame Guyon (1648–1717): Un Nouveau visage* (Paris: Beauchesne, 1989) is analytical and scholarly. For the biographical details in the following section, I have followed mostly Louis Cognet, "Guyon," in *Dictionnaire de spiritualité ascétique et mystique*, ed. Marcel Viller, vol. 6 (Paris: Beauchesne, 1937–94), col. 1306–36. Further treatment, both biographical and literary, has recently been provided by Marie-Florine Bruneau, *Women Mystics Confront the Modern World: Marie de l'Incarnation (1599–1672) and Madame Guyon (1648–1717)* (Albany: State University of New York Press, 1998), who studies Guyon as representative of the precarious position occupied by women within Catholicism. Guyon's *Life* in particular, Bruneau advances, is "the account of the difficult and dangerous voyage of a woman seeking official recognition of her mystical calling" (204). As my pairing of Guyon with Bourignon suggests, I fully agree with the precarity Bruneau points to. However, the latter's failure to historicize categories such as experience, interiority, and autobiography itself blunts somewhat the very specific tensions that Guyon's *Life* both points to and embodies, and that form the subject of the pages that follow.

65. On the question of women and apostolic mission, see Linda Timmermans, *L'Accès des femmes à la culture (1598–1715)* (Paris: Honoré Champion, 1993), 501–37.

66. Cf. Timmermans, *L'Accès des femmes*, 529.

67. For clear presentations of the interventions of the two main players, Fénelon and Bossuet, see Louis Cognet, *Crépuscule des mystiques* (Tournai, Belgium: Desclée, 1958). See also Bruneau's situating of Guyon's place within the quarrel, especially with regard to the gendering of mystical experience (*Women Mystics*, 167–96).

68. Like many mystical writers of the century, Guyon insisted that union with God knew no hierarchies: "Tous sont appelés. Tous peuvent faire oraison" (All are called. All can pray) begins the *Moyen court* (Jeanne Guyon, *Moyen court et très facile pour l'oraison: Approches du Quiétisme*, ed. Patrick D. Laude [Paris: PFSCL [Biblio 17], 1991], 99). This type of declaration is consonant with a perceived gulf between a bureaucratized institution and its followers. Jean-Joseph Surin's work, especially his autobiography, returns obsessively to institutional inadequacy; see Chapter 4.

69. Marie-Louise Gondal, "L'Autobiographie de Madame Guyon: La Découverte et l'apport de deux nouveaux manuscrits," *Dix-septième siècle* 164 (1989), 316–17.

70. The thrust of my reading of Guyon depends to large degree on her autobiography's multiple dates of composition. To recap: in 1682, in Thonon, a primitive version of the *Life* was written, but then discarded, apparently because it concentrated too much on Guyon's supposed sins (cf. Jeanne-Marie Bouvier de La Motte Guyon, *La Vie de Madame Guyon* [Paris: Dervy-Livres, 1983], 562); Guyon then wrote, in 1682 or 1683, the version we now possess, up to Part II, chapter 10. In 1688, jailed in the Visitation, she composed up to Part III, chapter 9. The rest of her *Life*, including the prison narrative which was never published by Poiret, was written at Blois in 1709. (This chronology, which differs somewhat from the one proposed by Louis Cognet ["Guyon," 1328], is confirmed by manuscript notes; see Gondal, "L'Autobiographie," 310 and 316.) In what follows, the date of any particular citation will be made clear in the surrounding commentary.

71. Henri Bremond, *Histoire littéraire du sentiment religieux en France*, 12 vols. (1916; Paris: A. Colin, 1971), 6:139.

72. Guyon, *Vie*, 323; she is alluding here to the *Torrents*. Future references will be given parenthetically in the text. On Guyon's loquacious brand of eloquence, see Philippe-Joseph Salazar, "Voix d'oraison féminine: Sur le style de l'éloquence d'extase," *Littératures Classiques* 28 (1996), 159–69.

73. This last point is made by Gondal, "L'Autobiographie," 316. Based on Gondal's work, Bruneau has contested the spontaneity of Guyon's *Life*—without, however, noting the varying methods of composition over time (*Women Mystics*, 138).

74. Jeanne Guyon, *Récits de captivité*, ed. Marie-Louise Gondal (Grenoble: Jérôme Millon, 1992), 96. Future references to this volume, which includes the parts of the 1709 version that were not published by Poiret in 1720, will be indicated by an "R" followed by the page number.

75. I will return to the question of mystical science in my discussion of Jean-Joseph Surin (see Chapter 4). For a brief presentation of the historical development of the term "la science des saints," see Certeau, *Fable Mystique*, 138–43.

76. See Chapter 2.

77. Guyon makes explicit here her reference to Luke 17:21 ("The kingdom of God is within you").

78. In her commentary on the Bible, Guyon emphasizes even further the somewhat clannish nature of interiority: one's "intérieur," she reasons, can be persecuted

mainly by "anciens intérieurs" (formerly interior people) whom God has allowed to defect from the cause (qtd. in Ernest Seillière, *Mme Guyon and Fénelon: Précurseurs de Rousseau* [Paris: Félix Alcan, 1918], 131).

79. Cf. Certeau's comments on Teresa's style, which, "streaked with gaps and ruptures, punctuated by moments of impatience," seems to say "'that's not it, but anyway you see what I mean'" (Certeau, *Fable mystique*, 263). For an analysis of the metadiscursive implications of "repair terms" such as *c'est-à-dire*, see Gerald Prince, *Narrative as Theme: Studies in French Fiction* (Lincoln: University of Nebraska Press, 1992), 113–20.

80. "Paix-Dieu" may be an attempt to render the Latin *Pax Dei*, usually translated as "paix intérieure" (by Fénelon, for instance) or "paix de l'âme" (by Surin and Jacques Vignier, author of a 1635 volume bearing the term for its title).

81. La Combe was Guyon's spiritual director, although, like the many male spiritual directors discussed in Chapter 2, he often behaved more like her disciple. He was later imprisoned for his allegedly Quietist teachings, but unlike Guyon, he was never released, and, half-mad, died in prison.

82. For Certeau, early modern mysticism was in large part a reaction to such disenchantment. See Michel de Certeau, "La Pensée religieuse," in *Histoire littéraire de la France*, ed. Anne Ubersfeld and Roland Desné, vol. 2 (Paris: Editions sociales, 1975), 149–69: "The reading of divine signs becomes more complex. . . . At first readable, [God's] presence becomes more and more 'mystical,' that is, hidden. . . . The 'Manifestation' is made richer, more technical, and opaque" (162).

83. On the issue of faked sanctity, see for instance Sophie Houdard, "Des Fausses saintes aux spirituelles à la mode: Les Signes suspects de la mystique," *Dix-septième siècle* 200 (1998), 417–32; on the increasing difficulty, both in and out of the Church, of understanding what possession meant, see Michel de Certeau, *La Possession de Loudun* (1970; Paris: Gallimard/Julliard, 1990), esp. chapter 9.

84. Qtd. in Michel Dupuy, "Intérieur de Jésus," in *Dictionnaire de spiritualité ascétique et mystique*, ed. Marcel Viller, 7 (Paris: Beauchesne, 1937–94), col. 1874.

85. Qtd. in Maurice Nédoncelle, "Intériorité et vie spirituelle," in *Dictionnaire de spiritualité ascétique et mystique*, ed. Marcel Viller, 7 (Paris: Beauchesne, 1937–94), col. 1900.

86. "When reviled, we bless; when persecuted, we endure" (1 Cor. 4, 12); "Indeed, all who desire to live a godly life in Christ Jesus will be persecuted" (2 Tim. 3, 12). Paul's apostolic mission and persecution go hand in hand (cf. 2 Tim. 3, 11); in this he fulfills Jesus's prophecy: "But before all this they will lay their hand on you and persecute you, . . . and you will be brought before kings and governors for my name's sake" (Luke 21, 12).

87. Cf. Mark 8, 34; Mt. 10, 38; Luke 14, 27. Guyon will constantly reiterate this. "[Dieu] n'avait garde de laisser la fin de ma vie sans une plus grande conformité avec Jésus-Christ. Il a été traduit devant toutes sortes de tribunaux: il m'a fait la grâce de l'être de même" ([God] took good care not to leave the end of my life without a greater conformity with Jesus Christ. [Christ] was brought before all sorts of tribunals: [God] granted me the same favor) (615).

88. "The walls of the cell sequester the guilty and make the innocent suffer; they also protect poetic meditation and religious fervor," writes Brombert, who notes in

particular that the Romantic prison is represented as accentuating the possibilities for introspection (Victor Brombert, *La Prison romantique: Essai sur l'imaginaire* [Paris: José Corti, 1975], 11). More recently, John Bender has argued that it is confinement itself—both as representation (in the novel) and as reality (in the prison)—that produces modern subjectivity through the promotion of introspection. Of Daniel Defoe's carceral fiction and the way it constructs subjectivity out of sense impressions, Bender writes: "[Defoe] delineates the subjective order—the structure of feeling—that [prisons] institutionalize and discloses to that order the power latent in the minutely sequential representations of realist narration" (John B. Bender, *Imagining the Penitentiary: Fiction and the Architecture of Mind in Eighteenth-Century England* [Chicago: University of Chicago Press, 1987], 45).

89. Qtd. in Cognet, "Guyon," 1325.

90. On the other hand, most of Guyon's previously composed works saw publication at this time, due to the efforts of Pierre Poiret. They appeared, however, in Amsterdam, and although they attained an international and very receptive audience (William Cowper translated her poems into English), they probably did little to bolster the fading memory of Guyon in France.

91. Agnès de La Gorce, "Mme Guyon à Blois, d'après des documents inédits," *Etudes* 310 (1961), 186.

92. Cf. Gondal, *Guyon*, 47–48.

93. La Gorce, "Mme Guyon," 192. Furthermore, the tone of the advice she offered to her corespondents was increasingly conciliatory with regard to conventional religious practice. She advised one woman hesitant over conversion to Catholicism not to neglect the exterior duties of her current faith: "Pour le sermon," Guyon writes, "allez-y quelques fois pour ne point faire de peine aux autres et pour ne point attirer la persécution" (As for the sermon, go from time to time so as not to pain others and in order not to attract persecution) (qtd. in La Gorce, "Mme Guyon," 188).

94. Such is the argument of Bruneau: "The autobiography, which established a place for [Guyon] in the eternal, in the temporal, and in the future, exits into nothingness" (*Women Mystics*, 218).

95. Unless otherwise noted, all of the following citations are from the 1709 additions to the *Life*.

96. "Il est vrai que notre nature est si rusée, qu'elle se fourre partout, et que l'âme n'est pas impeccable; mais ses plus grandes fautes sont ses réflexions, qui lui sont alors très dommageables, voulant se regarder sous prétexte même de dire ses états" (It is true that our nature is so cunning that it pokes into everything, and that no soul is without sin; but its greatest fault lies in its own reflections, so damaging to the soul who seeks to observe itself under the pretext of telling of its states) (293). Guyon's caution repeats—perhaps only better to diffuse—that of the conservative ecclesiastical establishment, perennially suspicious of the journals and accounts solicited by the less perspicacious spiritual directors/biographers discussed in Chapter 2.

97. Jean Orcibal, "Madame Guyon devant ses juges," in *Mélanges de littérature française offerts à René Pintard*, ed. N. Hepp, R. Mauzi, and C. Pichois (Strasbourg: Klincksieck, 1975), 422.

98. Foucault has noted that one of the salient characteristics of modern authorship is precisely judicial responsibility: "Speeches and books were assigned real au-

thors . . . when the author became subject to punishment" (Michel Foucault, "What Is an Author?" in *Language, Counter-Memory, Practice*, ed. D. Bouchard (Ithaca: Cornell University Press, 1977), 124). More generally, the author-function refers to the way works are ascribed to a writer in a given society.

99. As Michel de Certeau explains, "what makes possible the discourse of possession, what in the end authorizes it, is that the nun does not remember it, that no personal admixture compromises the autonomous functioning of diabolical grammar" (Certeau, *La Possession de Loudun*, 63). Obviously, this logic flies in the face of the emerging order of autobiography, according to which even the religious public was learning to take subjective interference as a *positive* standard of value: we read with the most interest precisely when the writing has been difficult, as if the pages had been excised at great cost from one's most secret being (cf. Chapter 2). These two radically opposed standards of value met especially in first-person possession narratives; see Nicholas Paige, "Je, l'Autre et la possession; ou pourquoi l'autobiographie démoniaque n'a jamais constitué un genre," in *L'Autre au dix-septième siècle: Actes de Miami* (Tübingen: Gunther Narr Verlag/Biblio 17, 1999), 385–92.

100. Cf. Gondal, *Guyon*, 130.

101. For a similar passage, see also *Récits*, 69–70.

102. Qtd. in Orcibal, "Mme Guyon devant ses juges," 413 n21.

103. Bossuet will single out for ridicule Guyon's accounts of her sensorial mystical experiences. See Bruneau, *Women Mystics*, 181–90.

104. A related incident occurs a bit earlier (R 114). Already in 1688, Guyon had reported a dream in which she and La Combe were denounced by a counterfeit letter (450). The prophecy seems almost too good to be true: Guyon may well have inserted the dream when she was revising her text in Blois.

105. Bruneau, *Women Mystics*, 202.

106. Fumaroli has characterized the explosion of memoirs in this period as a practice of oppositional historiography: "History is a trial that posterity alone can bring to a conclusion. While awaiting the arrival of the ideal Historian, . . . testimony must be multiplied, archives accumulated, memoirs prepared so that each person will not have to show up unarmed at the hour of judgment" ("Les Mémoires du dix-septième siècle," 12). On the battle over who could tell history and how, see also Beasley, *Revising Memory*, and Erica Harth, *Ideology and Culture in Seventeenth-Century France* (Ithaca: Cornell University Press, 1983). It should be noted, however, that memoirs of the Fronde found a large contemporary readership in the aristocracy. Widely circulated, either in print (Bassompierre's memoirs were a best-seller of the 1660s, reprinted almost yearly) or in manuscript, they were not nearly as jealously guarded as Guyon's *Life*.

Chapter 4. The Experience of Difference

1. Augustine, *Confessions*, trans. Henry Chadwick (Oxford: Oxford University Press, 1991), 140.

2. I take the expression "placeholders of immediacy" from Martin Jay, *Cultural Semantics: Keywords of Our Time* (Amherst: University of Massachusetts Press, 1998), 46, to whose discussion of experience I will return in the Conclusion. In the pages

that follow, I will drop the quotes around "experience" (and around another key term "difference"): by this point in the present study, it should be sufficiently obvious that for me these are not transhistorical entities but rather local constructions, and that what is at issue is (among other things) the process by which a culture invents and then naturalizes the terms.

3. See Pierre Paul Courcelle, *Les Confessions de Saint Augustin dans la tradition littéraire: Antécédents et posterité* (Paris: Etudes Augustiniennes, 1963).

4. Michel de Certeau, *L'Invention du quotidien, I: Arts de faire*, ed. Luce Giard (Paris: Gallimard, 1990), 204, his emphasis.

5. Jean-Joseph Surin, *Correspondance*, ed. Michel de Certeau (Paris: Desclée de Brouwer, 1966), 38n1. Certeau's copiously annotated edition of Surin's letters is a mine of information on Surin's life and times. I have drawn on it here for Surin's biography, as well as on Michel Dupuy, "Surin," in *Dictionnaire de spiritualité ascétique et mystique*, ed. Marcel Viller, vol. 14 (Paris: Beauchesne, 1937–94), col. 1311–25. A detail regarding Surin's familiarity with Teresa's *Life*: as I have pointed out in Chapter 2, during these years two texts went by the name of the *Life* of Teresa—the one Teresa herself wrote, and Ribera's biography of her, translated in 1602; Certeau asserts that the version read by the young Surin was the latter, not the former (Michel de Certeau, *La Fable mystique, XVIe–XVIIe siècle* [Paris: Gallimard, 1982], 349). Because of oddities such as this, explaining away Surin's (or anybody's) autobiography as an "imitation" of a predecessor is an unfortunate simplification.

6. On this contradiction, which Certeau calls "a schism between the God of the heart and the God of a society at work," see *Fable mystique*, 330–73. For the purposes of my discussion of Surin, I accept Certeau's characterization while recognizing that this particular historian's perspective is more than a little colored by his own concerns: Surin provided Certeau with a means of voicing his own unease within the Jesuit order of which he too was a member. Nevertheless, Surin's work more than bears out Certeau's contention, whatever its applicability to the broader religious milieu of the time.

7. Cf. Certeau, *Fable mystique*, 331.

8. I have only sketched out the events of the possession here. For a full account, see, among numerous studies, Aldous Huxley, *The Devils of Loudun* (New York: Harper & Row, 1952) and Michel de Certeau, *La Possession de Loudun* (1970; Paris: Gallimard/Julliard, 1990).

9. Jeanne des Anges, *Autobiographie*, ed. Gabriel Legué and Gilles de la Tourette (Grenoble: J. Millon, 1990), 67.

10. Urbain Grandier, *Traité du célibat* (Paris: Editions Hors Commerce, 1995), 52.

11. First, Loudun, chiefly Protestant, was the target of Catholic expansionism following the fall of La Rochelle in 1628. The spectacle of Church power provided by the exorcism allowed the Catholics to consolidate their hold on the population's imagination. Second, control over the exorcism was soon ceded to the *intendant du Roy* Jean-Martin de Laubardemont, and the battle against the devils became very much the manifestation of the political struggle between centralized royal power and provincial resistance. See, on both points, Certeau, *La Possession de Loudun*.

12. Jean-Joseph Surin, *Triomphe de l'amour divin sur les puissances de l'enfer . . . et Science expérimentale des choses de l'autre vie* (Grenoble: J. Millon, 1990), 28, my

emphasis. On Surin's idea of exorcism and its link to an interiorized subjectivity, see Sophie Houdard, "De l'exorcisme à la communication spirituelle: Le Sujet et ses démons," *Littératures Classiques* 25 (1995), 187–99. Surin's methods were no doubt an extension of a "therapeutic" exorcism evolving since Bérulle; cf. Robert Mandrou, *Magistrats et sorciers en France au XVIIe siècle: Une Analyse de psychologie historique* (Paris: Seuil, 1968), 191.

13. Surin, *Le Triomphe de l'amour divin*, 28, 19.

14. One version of the manuscript of the *Science expérimentale*, dating from the beginning of the eighteenth century, makes this important distinction quite clear. "L'obsession est bien plus pénible à l'âme que la possession. Le démon se sert du corps de la possédée, pour faire beaucoup d'actions déréglées, et de sa langue pour dire des blasphèmes et des horreurs; et pendant qu'il se comporte de la sorte, l'âme est le plus souvent unie à Dieu, [et] le goûte et le possède dans une profonde paix. . . . Dans l'obsession le démon agit sur les puissances de l'âme dans l'esprit, dans l'imagination, et dans toutes les facultés, par mille tentations, et fait tous ses efforts pour engager l'âme dans le péché" (Obsession is much more damaging to the soul than possession. The demon makes use of the body of the possessed in order to carry out many unruly actions, and of her tongue in order to utter blasphemies and horrors; and [yet] while he carries on in this way, the soul is most often united with God, [and] enjoys and possesses him in a profound peace . . . . In obsession the demon acts on the powers of the soul through the mind, the imagination, and all the faculties, using a thousand temptations, and makes every effort to lead the soul into sin) (Bibliothèque nationale f.f. 25253, fol. 99v.). Thus, if the possessed's body is a docile instrument, her mind remains steady, and her interiority intact, whereas obsession qualifies as a true spiritual crisis. From a gendered perspective, such a distinction is important, for the possessed woman is denied agency; her body is the theater on which male exorcists prove their power, and the privileges of successful spiritual combat do not accrue to her. The obsessed man, on the other hand, engages in precisely the valiant inner combat denied to the possessed woman. Note, however, that Surin, in promoting the conception of interior exorcism, sought ultimately to make Jeanne des Anges the agent of her own cure — so successfully that it is in this light that she casts herself in her *Autobiographie*.

15. Charles Taylor, *Sources of the Self: The Making of the Modern Identity* (Cambridge, Mass.: Harvard University Press, 1989), 192.

16. On this proliferation of documentation, printed and manuscript, about Loudun, see Surin, *Correspondance*, 417.

17. Surin, *Correspondance*, 421.

18. Philippe Lejeune, *Moi aussi* (Paris: Seuil, 1986), 213.

19. See most recently Jonathan Dewald, *Aristocratic Experience and the Origins of Modern Culture: France, 1570–1715* (Berkeley: University of California Press, 1993); Isabelle Poutrin, *Le Voile et la plume: Autobiographie et sainteté féminine dans l'Espagne moderne* (Madrid: Casa de Velásquez, 1995); Michael Mascuch, *Origins of the Individualist Self: Autobiography and Self-Identity in England, 1591–1791* (Stanford, Calif.: Stanford University Press, 1996); and James S. Amelang, *The Flight of Icarus: Artisan Autobiography in Early Modern Europe* (Stanford, Calif.: Stanford University Press, 1998). Pioneering accounts of early modern autobiographical writing could be every bit as comprehensive as this later work; see Paul Delany, *British Autobiography in the*

Seventeenth Century (London: Routledge and K. Paul, 1969). See also the Annales-inspired syntheses of Pierre Pachet, *Les Baromètres de l'âme: Naissance du journal intime* (Paris: Hatier, 1990), Orest Ranum, "Les Refuges de l'intimité," in *Histoire de la vie privée*, ed. Philippe Ariès and Georges Duby, vol. 3 (Paris: Seuil, 1986), 210–65, and Madeleine Foisil, "L'Ecriture du for privé," also in *Histoire de la vie privée*, vol. 3, 331–69; much of this latter type of work tends to view the rise of private forms of writing as a triumphant march toward the victory of the personal over the general, as a change in writing practice that encountered no substantial internal resistance—my subject here.

20. In his study of writerly authority in the seventeenth century, Alain Viala points out that in Surin's milieu during the seventeenth century, "the role of author was an integral part of ecclesiastical status" (Alain Viala, *Naissance de l'écrivain: Sociologie de la littérature à l'âge classique* [Paris: Minuit, 1985], 242).

21. Because of Surin's illness, the *Triomphe* would not be completed until 1660.

22. Surin wrote certain sections of the *Triomphe* (70–79) in the first person, sections which may be drafts he intended to intercalate with the main text. As I shall show, the *Science expérimentale* contains a much more unstable oscillation between the first and third persons.

23. Surin, *Correspondance*, 1472.

24. Page references are to the recent edition of the *Science expérimentale* and the *Triomphe de l'amour divin* (see note 12), and will appear in the text.

25. That Surin's amalgamation of the personal and the doctrinal appeared as counterintuitive at the time as it does today finds confirmation in the convoluted transformations the *Science expérimentale* underwent after Surin's death and before its initial publication in 1828. Indeed, the work was widely circulated in manuscript form, but with each recopying it resembled a little less what Surin had actually written. In fact, deducing the original contents of the *Science expérimentale* (as given above) required considerable archival effort on the part of Ferdinand Cavallera, a Jesuit who, alongside of Henri Bremond (author of the encyclopedic *Histoire littéraire du sentiment religieux en France* [1916–36]), strove to rehabilitate the image of a man tainted by his involvement with Jeanne des Anges and her demons. I will save the story of the work's many transformations for the conclusion of the present chapter.

26. This is the abbreviation of what appears to have been the primitive title of the *Triomphe*—the *Histoire de la délivrance de la mère des Anges*. See Surin, *Correspondance*, 1563. For a complete list of references to the *Histoire* as they appear in all the manuscripts, see Ferdinand Cavallera, "L'Autobiographie du P. Surin," *Revue d'ascétique et de mystique* 6 (April 1925), 150–51.

27. These mentions occur at the end of part II (253) and the beginning of part III (255). Against this internal evidence, and Cavallera's hypothesis as to the original four-part structure of the *Science expérimentale*, Certeau has written: "These two parts [i.e., parts II and III] form a whole [and] it was, I believe, much later that they were placed between parts one and four on Loudun and demonology" (Michel de Certeau, "Voyage et prison: La Folie de J.-J. Surin," in *Voyages: Récits et imaginaire*, ed. Bernard Beugnot [Paris: PFSCL, 1984], 62n3). This judgment contradicts a previous statement of Certeau's in which he seems to underline the unity of the four parts (Surin, *Correspondance*, 1470).

28. The break occurring after book IX of the *Confessions* has been the subject of much speculation, in the twentieth century as well as in Surin's day; see Chapter 1.

29. Francis Barker, *The Tremulous Private Body: Essays on Subjection* (Ann Arbor: University of Michigan Press, 1995), 7.

30. Jean-Joseph Surin, *Guide spirituel pour la perfection*, ed. Michel de Certeau (Paris: Desclée de Brouwer, 1963), 182.

31. "Ce que je dois dire dans ce chapitre ne se peut pas bien communiquer à d'autres qu'aux religieux de notre Compagnie, à cause qu'il passa des choses fort étranges, dont d'autres qu'eux ne seraient pas capables" (What I have to say in this chapter cannot be communicated to anyone other than the religious men of our Company, because very strange things happened, which others would be incapable [of understanding]) (192–93).

32. Michel de Montaigne, *Les Essais*, ed. V.-L. Saulnier (Paris: Presses universitaires de France, 1924), 846; Michel de Montaigne, *The Complete Essays of Montaigne*, trans. Donald Frame (Stanford, Calif.: Stanford University Press, 1958), 642.

33. "Les secrets de la nature sont cachés. . . . Les expériences en donne l'intelligence" (The secrets of nature are hidden. . . . Experiments provide knowledge of them) (Blaise Pascal, *Oeuvres complètes*, ed. Jacques Chevalier [Paris: Gallimard/Pléiade, 1954], 532).

34. Pascal, *Oeuvres*, 430–31. On the developing rhetoric of scientific observation, see Christian Licoppe, *La Formation de la pratique scientifique: Le Discours de l'expérience en France et en Angleterre* (Paris: Editions de la Découverte, 1996).

35. Mino Bergamo, *L'Anatomie de l'âme: De François de Sales à Fénelon*, trans. Marc Bonneval (Grenoble: Jérôme Millon, 1994), 26–7. The religious attempt to chart the regions of the interior can be compared to Madeleine de Scudéry's highly successful "Carte de Tendre," which appeared in the first volume of *Clélie, histoire romaine* (1654). Scudéry's mapping differed from the efforts of the soul's anatomists in that the interpretive grill applied to the space of the interior was borrowed not from medical science, but from the tools of colonialism: the exterior exploration of the New World suggested a need for similar interior explorations.

36. Certeau has chronicled the succession of these terms, showing how "mystique" insinuated itself only slowly into use, as the adjective was nominalized twice, first into "la mystique" (roughly, "mysticism"), then finally into "un mystique" (a [male] mystic) (cf. *Fable mystique*, 138ff). As Jeremy Ahearne has pointed out, Certeau's subject in *La Fable mystique* is the invention and use of the word "la mystique," over a determinate time-span, to designate (or invent) a certain area of experience — and not mysticism as a transhistorical phenomenon (Jeremy Ahearne, *Michel de Certeau: Interpretation and Its Other* [Stanford, Calif.: Stanford University Press, 1995], 95–96).

37. Saint François de Sales, *Oeuvres*, ed. André Ravier, vol. 1 (Paris: Gallimard/Pléiade, 1969), 620 (my emphasis).

38. Originally, before English meaning stabilized, experiment could refer to experience, and vice versa. (The OED gives examples of the imbrication of the two terms at various historical junctures.) The matter is further complicated by the distinction, made within scientific circles, between *experimentum* and *experientia* — the latter referring to common sense or observations about nature (we all know that a dropped

feather falls to earth more slowly than an apple), the former to the way nature behaves under certain specific manipulated circumstances (what happens if the feather and the apple are dropped within a vacuum?). *Experimentum* is thus singular and local, the experiment of an observing subject; *experientia* is universal, rooted in the shared knowledge of the community. (Cf. Licoppe, *Formation de la pratique scientifique*, 21–24.) It has recently been suggested that Surin's approach to exorcism consists precisely in substituting *experimentum* for *experientia*. See Sophie Houdard, "Expérience et écriture des 'choses de la vie' chez Jean-Joseph Surin," *Littératures Classiques*, 39 (2000), 331–47.

39. "I admit nothing but on the faith of the eyes," wrote Bacon (qtd. by Martin Jay, *Downcast Eyes: The Denigration of Vision in Twentieth-Century Thought* [Berkeley: University of California Press, 1993], 64). Jay provides a excellent overview of conflicting attitudes towards the visual from the classical age to the early modern period.

40. See Licoppe, *Formation de la pratique scientifique*, 53–66. Note that in keeping with general usage in this type of autobiographical writing, "vision" and "vue" for Surin often denote an act of (sudden) understanding, rather than a truly optical event. On occasion he goes much further, though, referring to sight literally, and providing for the disbelief of his reader: "[Dieu] se déclare par des épreuves fort délicates ... en sorte que même l'oeil aperçoit—ceci paraîtra du tout incroyable, et peut-être à quelques-uns une vraie imagination—ces divines personnes" ([God] declares himself through very subtle tests ... such that—this will seem altogether incredible, and perhaps to some a mere figment of the imagination—the eye itself perceives these divine persons) (285). Nevertheless, such sight is still never exterior, in that the circuit of seer and seen takes place inside the subject.

41. Pierre Adnès, "Mystique: XVIe–XXe siècles," in *Dictionnaire d'ascétique et de mystique*, ed. Marcel Viller, vol. 10 (Paris: Beauchesne, 1937–94), col. 1921.

42. Michel Beaujour has similarly described the Middle Ages as characterized by what he calls a confessional variant, not linked to chronology (and therefore to autobiography), but to a "movement through *sites* constituted by sins and by their subdivisions .... One can therefore speak here of a *topo-logy*, or a spatial logic, in opposition to the *chronology* of texts that are largely narrative" (Michel Beaujour, *Miroirs d'encre: Rhétorique de l'autoportrait* [Paris: Seuil, 1980], 34).

43. One example among many: "Having gone through so much myself, I am sorry for those who begin with books alone. For it is strange what a difference there is between understanding a thing and subsequently knowing it by experience" (Saint Teresa of Avila, *The Life of Saint Teresa of Avila by Herself*, trans. J. M. Cohen [London: Penguin, 1957], 93).

44. Taking my cue from John Lyons, I will construe example in a general sense. (Lyons defines it as "a dependent statement qualifying a more general and independent statement by naming a member of the class established by the general statement" [John D. Lyons, *Exemplum: The Rhetoric of Example in Early Modern France and Italy* (Princeton: Princeton University Press, 1989), x].) My considerations will therefore not be limited by the literary term *exemplum*, which strictly speaking is "a short narrative used to illustrate a moral point" (9). For an analysis of the breakdown of historical exemplarity in early modern Europe, see Timothy Hampton, *Writing from His-*

tory: The Rhetoric of Exemplarity in Renaissance Literature (Ithaca: Cornell University Press, 1990).

45. On John's status as a Surinian intertext, see Michel de Certeau, "Jean-Joseph Surin, interprète de saint Jean de la Croix," *Revue d'ascétique et de mystique* 46 (1970), 45–70.

46. Lyons, *Exemplum*, 28.

47. "Whoever reads the *Exercices* sees at first glance that its material is subjected to an incessant, meticulous and obsessional process of separation; or more exactly, the *Exercices* themselves are this separation, which nothing pre-exists" (Roland Barthes, *Sade, Fourier, Loyola* [Paris: Seuil, 1971], 58).

48. Passages like these still adhere, therefore, to a medieval realist ontology — according to which "all treatment of language was in itself an experience or a manipulation of the real" (Certeau, *Fable mystique*, 170).

49. Michel de Certeau, "Folie du nom et mystique du sujet," in *Folle vérité: Vérité et vraisemblance du texte psychotique*, ed. Julia Kristeva and Jean-Michel Ribettes (Paris: Seuil, 1979), 285.

50. This passage occurs on page 209 of the published edition; I have substituted the reading of Bibliothèque nationale ms. f.f. 25253, "m'appliquer," for Cavallera's less telling "m'expliquer."

51. For general works on the crisis of authority, history, and exemplarity in the Renaissance, see, e.g., Antoine Compagnon, *La Seconde main, ou le travail de la citation* (Paris: Seuil, 1979), Thomas Greene, *The Light in Troy: Imitation and Discovery in Renaissance Poetry* (New Haven: Yale University Press, 1982), and Hampton, *Writing from History*.

52. Not coincidentally, obedience was a close cousin of exemplarity; the Jesuit Louis Lallemant, for example, one of the early seventeenth century's major spiritual figures, classed it as one of six kinds of imitation. See Edouard Cothenet, Etienne Ledor, and Pierre Adnès, "Imitation du Christ," in *Dictionnaire de spiritualité ascétique et mystique*, ed. Marcel Viller, vol. 7 (Paris: Beauchesne, 1939–94), col. 1581.

53. Jean Auvray, *L'Enfance de Jésus et sa famille, honorée en la vie de soeur Marguerite du Saint-Sacrement* (Paris: Imprimerie Royale, 1654), 363.

54. See Chapter 3.

55. The whole of Part II, after all, is entitled: "Seconde partie . . . en laquelle le Père Surin parle des maux qui lui sont arrivés" (Second part . . . in which Father Surin speaks of the evils/pains that befell him).

56. Jean de La Bruyère, *Les Caractères* (Paris: Livre de Poche, 1973), 316–17 (Des jugements, ¶10).

57. Certeau, *Fable mystique*, 263.

58. Surin is rather, though not entirely, certain that it is that of his good angel. The notion of divine breath (*pneuma* in Greek, *spiritus* in Latin, *ruah* in Hebrew) is an age-old one — in many creation myths, God's breath enters matter and gives it life; in ascetic traditions especially the idea was important, for it linked the spiritual to the physical. Analogs exist in Eastern religions as well (*prana* in Hinduism, *ch'i* in Taoism). We might note that Surin's "respir" is a much more bodily version of the "esprit" which was so popular in the seventeenth century but which had long since lost its traditional theological association with the physical.

59. The analysis of apophatic language that follows is indebted to the excellent exploration of the phenomenon given in Michael Sells, *Mystical Languages of Unsaying* (Chicago: University of Chicago Press, 1994). On seventeenth-century use of Dionysius's apophatic tradition, see more specifically Certeau, *Fable mystique*, 129.

60. Sells, *Mystical Languages of Unsaying*, 3.

61. Jacques Derrida, "Post-scriptum: Aporias, Ways, and Voices," in *Derrida and Negative Theology*, ed. Harold Coward and Tony Fosham (Albany: State University of New York Press, 1992), 284.

62. Mino Bergamo in particular has opposed texts by writers such as Bonaventura and François de Sales in order to show how the localization of the mystic experience undergoes a marked change in the seventeenth century. See Bergamo, *L'Anatomie de l'âme*, 23–136.

63. Teresa of Avila is again paradigmatic: her superiors, having doubts about the value and veracity of her experience, ordered her to compose her *Life*. In the letter to Garcia de Toledo that accompanies the *Life*, she writes: "I very much hope that Father Avila will be ordered to read this, since it was for this purpose that I began to write. Then if he thinks I am on the right road I shall be greatly comforted" (*The Life of Saint Teresa of Avila by Herself*, 315).

64. Surin's efforts to express himself as best he can lead to an exploded syntax, as many of the passages I have been citing confirm. One might note particularly the tendency of his sentences to curl, to fold in on themselves, as Surin multiplies adverbs of opposition, such as "mais" (but), and "quoique" and "combien que" (although). For a stylistic analysis of the *Science expérimentale*, so different from Surin's straightforward didactic writings, see Frank Paul Bowman, "Suffering, Madness and Literary Creation in Seventeenth-Century Spiritual Autobiography," *French Forum* 1 (1976), 44–46.

65. When systematic description fails, however, there remain the descriptive possibilities of the corporeal anecdote, a bit in the manner of Montaigne, who, in his escape from an impossible exemplarity, hits upon isolated bodily experiences—say, the fall from a horse, the loss of a tooth, or his kidney stone. (On Montaigne's post-exemplary body, see Hampton, *Writing from History*, 134–97.) Instead of a science of experience, Surin delivers a poetics of the body; see Certeau, "Voyage et prison."

66. See Michel Foucault, *Technologies of the Self*, ed. L. Martin, H. Gutman, and P. H. Hutton (Amherst: University of Massachusetts Press, 1988), as well as my discussion of Stoic "technologies of the self" in Chapter 1.

67. It should go without saying that France's canonized autobiographical "first" —Rousseau's *Confessions*—owes its originary status in part to its insistence on origins themselves: "Qui croirait," writes Rousseau, "que ce châtiment d'enfant reçu à huit ans par la main d'une fille de trente a décidé des mes goûts, de mes désirs, de mes passions, de moi pour le reste de ma vie" (Who would believe that this childhood punishment received at eight years of age from the hand of a girl of thirty determined my tastes, my desires, my passions, myself, for the rest of my life) (Jean-Jacques Rousseau, *Oeuvres complètes*, ed. Bernard Gagnebin and Marcel Raymond, vol. 1 [Paris: Gallimard, 1959], 15). Unlike Surin, Rousseau situates this origin in his childhood— childhood becomes the hidden explanation of the adult subject, an explanation uncoverable by autobiography (or eventually psychoanalysis). In a secularized world,

the child takes over the spot previously occupied by the mystic—as the person on whom non-mediated experience is most easily projected. On the importance of youth as lost origin for the modern interiorized subject, see Carolyn Steedman, *Strange Dislocations: Childhood and the Idea of Human Interiority, 1780–1930* (Cambridge, Mass.: Harvard University Press, 1995).

68. John Lyons, analyzing Lafayette's novel as a struggle between example and experience, concludes that she "creates a dynamic of the exceptional, where the energy of the narrative comes from failures of what is experienced to coincide with what is said about experience" (*Exemplum*, 223).

69. Marie-Madeleine Pioche de La Vergne, comtesse de Lafayette, *Romans et nouvelles*, ed. Alain Niderst (Paris: Garnier, 1990), 416.

70. Surin, *Correspondance*, 544.

71. Cf. Stanislas Breton, *Deux mystiques de l'excès: J.-J. Surin et Maître Eckhart* (Paris: Cerf, 1985), 70. Breton cites no source for this contention.

72. Michel de Certeau, "Les Oeuvres de Jean-Joseph Surin: Histoire des textes," *Revue d'ascétique et de mystique* 40 (1964), 446. "The disappearance of the author," continues Certeau, "intensified the dismantling of a work from which anyone could extract as he pleased materials for his devotions" (443).

73. Cited in Cavallera, "L'autobiographie du P. Surin," 146. Cavallera's classification of the mass of manuscripts is largely accurate and I will follow it here, with the exception that I refer to one manuscript apparently unknown to him (Archives du Séminaire de Saint Sulpice ms. 589) and consider another (Bibliothèque nationale f.f. 25253) as an amalgam of two distinct parts.

74. Possible dates are 1697 or 1704. See Cavallera, "L'Autobiographie du P. Surin," *Revue d'ascétique et de mystique* 6 (Oct. 1925), 405nn23 and 24.

75. Archives du Séminaire de Saint Sulpice, ms. 585, 4. The Solitaire's "Avertissement" has been reprinted, but only partially, in Cavallera, "L'Autobiographie du P. Surin," 406–8. The following citations come from the Saint Sulpice manuscript, pp. 2, 1, and 3.

76. Jean-Joseph Surin, *Histoire abrégée de la possession des Ursulines de Loudun et des peines du père Surin* (Paris: Association catholique du Sacré-Coeur, 1828).

77. Cited in Cavallera, "L'Autobiographie du P. Surin," 410.

78. Half of what was bound as BN f.f. 25253 consists of a carefully-copied rendering attentive to the meandering of Surin's sinuous prose; ms. 589 of the Archives du Séminaire de Saint Sulpice gives much the same text as the former with several particularities—the copyist puts the text uniformly in the first person, admits to some additions, suppressions, and even wholesale elimination of chapters that contain "rien d'extraordinaire" (230) or "de particulier" (257) (nothing particular or extraordinary).

79. Archives du Séminaire de Saint Sulpice, ms. 585, 11.

80. Mentioning as he does the *Science expérimentale* in a list of Surin's unpublished writings, Boudun surely knew of the text; see Henri-Marie Boudun, *La Vie du R. P. Seurin [sic] de la Compagnie de Jésus, ou l'homme de Dieu* (Chartres: Nicolas Le Clerc, 1689), 295–96.

81. Cavallera published the *Autobiographie* in the second volume of his edition of Surin's letters (Jean-Joseph Surin, *Lettres spirituelles du P. Jean-Joseph Surin*, ed. Louis

Michel and Ferdinand Cavallera, vol. 2 [Toulouse: Editions de la Revue d'acétique et de mystique, 1928]). Conscious of potential anachronism, Cavallera chose his title only as shorthand (vii).

82. Hans Robert Jauss, *Toward an Aesthetic of Reception* (Minneapolis: University of Minnesota Press, 1982), 35.

83. Michel de Certeau, *L'Ecriture de l'histoire* (Paris: Gallimard, 1975), 10.

Conclusion

Note to epigraph: Denis Diderot, *Les Bijoux indiscrets* (Paris: Garnier-Flammarion, 1968), 172. Diderot's text makes it clear that the approaching giant is male.

1. For a thorough history of the word *autobiography*, see Robert Folkenflik, "Introduction: The Institution of Autobiography," in *The Culture of Autobiography: Constructions of Self-Representation*, ed. Robert Folkenflik (Stanford, Calif.: Stanford University Press, 1993), 1–7.

2. Steven Shapin, *The Scientific Revolution* (Chicago: University of Chicago Press, 1996), 1; Bruno Latour, *We Have Never Been Modern*, trans. Catherine Porter (Cambridge, Mass.: Harvard University Press, 1993).

3. Ideological mirages, Fredric Jameson has written, end up nevertheless as a sort of objective reality: "For the lived experience of individual consciousness as a monadic and autonomous center of activity is not some mere conceptual error, which can be dispelled by the taking of thought and by scientific rectification: it has a quasi-institutional status, performs ideological functions, and is susceptible to historical causation and produced and reinforced by other objective instances, determinants, and mechanisms" (Fredric Jameson, *The Political Unconscious: Narrative as a Socially Symbolic Act* [Ithaca: Cornell University Press, 1981], 153). Jameson's then-timely warning did little to stem the tide of 1980s efforts to break the supposed spell of the Enlightenment with a wave of the wand.

4. Georges Bataille, *L'Expérience intérieure* (1943; Paris: Gallimard, 1954), 15.

5. Jean-Paul Sartre, *La Nausée* (1938; Paris: Le Livre de Poche, n.d.), 100.

6. Martin Jay, *Cultural Semantics: Keywords of Our Time* (Amherst: University of Massachusetts Press, 1998), 66–67; the Foucault passage is from a 1978 interview.

7. Bataille, *L'Expérience intérieure*, 24

8. For two pioneering collections of essays, see Domna C. Stanton and Jeanine Parisier Plottel, eds., *The Female Autograph* (New York: New York Literary Forum, 1984), and Estelle C. Jelinek, ed. *The Tradition of Women's Autobiography from Antiquity to the Present* (Boston: Twayne, 1986).

9. Roland Barthes, "Le Discours de l'histoire," *Poétique* 49 (Feb. 1982), 13–21.

10. For additional examples of the frequently large proportions of source citation in *Annales*-type scholarship, see Philippe Carrard, *Poetics of the New History: French Historical Discourse from Braudel to Chartier* (Baltimore: Johns Hopkins University Press, 1992), 152–53.

11. Cf. Jay's discussion of the way in which *Alltagsgeschichte* ("history of everyday life") has been used in Germany to suggest the noncomplicity of "average" Germans in Nazi atrocities (*Cultural Semantics*, 37–46).

12. Michel Foucault, ed., *Moi, Pierre Rivière . . . : Un Cas de parricide au dix-neuvième siècle* (Paris: Gallimard/Julliard, 1973), 12.

13. Gayatri Chakravorty Spivak, *Outside in the Teaching Machine* (New York: Routledge, 1993), 56.

14. Philippe Lejeune, *Je est un autre: L'Autobiographie de la littérature aux médias* (Paris: Seuil, 1980), 229; the wordplay of the original is untranslatable: "On leur 'donne la parole'—c'est-à-dire qu'on la leur prend, pour en faire de l'écriture." As Amelang has remarked, "[t]he fabrication of autobiographies of the oppressed by the well-intentioned" is nothing peculiar to our own time, but is, rather, a long-standing Western tradition (James S. Amelang, *The Flight of Icarus: Artisan Autobiography in Early Modern Europe* [Stanford, Calif.: Stanford University Press, 1998], 17).

15. On the ambiguities that inhere to the case of Menchú and to *testimonio* in general, see Georg M. Gugelberger, ed., *The Real Thing: Testimonial Discourse and Latin America* (Durham, N.C.: Duke University Press, 1996).

16. Michel Foucault, *Les Mots et les choses: Une Archéologie des sciences humaines* (Paris: Gallimard, 1966), 290. Of course the Dandy is other things as well, for example a consummate early consumer—consumerism being able to mesh with either the psychology of depth (shopping as sexual craving—as in Zola's *Au bonheur des dames*—or as an expression of one's true personality—as in Perec's *Les Choses*), or the anti-psychology of surface (as with the Dandy, or as in the venerable Hollywood fantasy of the "makeover").

17. See the foundational book on the subject, Stephen Greenblatt, *Renaissance Self-Fashioning: From More to Shakespeare* (Chicago: University of Chicago Press, 1980).

18. Denis Diderot, "Paradoxe sur le comédien," in *Oeuvres complètes*, ed. H. Dieckmann and J. Varloot, vol. 20 (Paris: Hermann, 1995), 104.

19. See, respectively, e.g., Jean Baudrillard, *De la séduction* (Paris: Denoël, 1979); and Judith Butler, *Gender Trouble: Feminism and the Subversion of Identity* (New York: Routledge, 1990), and Sue-Ellen Case and Janelle G. Reinelt, eds., *The Performance of Power: Theatrical Discourse and Politics* (Iowa City: University of Iowa Press, 1991).

Index

Abercrombie, Nigel, 250 nn. 87–88
Absolu, Jeanne, 206
Acarie, Barbe Avrillot. *See* Marie de l'Incarnation, soeur
Adnès, Pierre, 282 n. 41, 283 n. 52
Ahearne, Jeremy, 281 n. 36
Aignan du Sendat, Etienne d', 93
Alacoque. *See* Marguerite-Marie Alacoque, Saint
Althusser, Louis, 120, 247 n. 44
Amelang, James, 9, 279 n. 19, 287 n. 14
Amelotte, Denis, 259 n. 54
Anatomy, 37–39, 41, 47, 196–97, 240 n. 30, 247 nn. 45–47, 281 n. 35
Angélique de Saint-Jean, 121
Antoinette de Jésus, 263 n. 84, 265 nn. 124, 134
Apophasis. *See* Mysticism
Apostolate. *See* Predication
Apostolidès, Jean-Marie, 123–24, 241 n. 37
Arbouze, Marguerite d', 80
Arenal, Electa, 116, 236 n. 14, 255 n. 12, 263 n. 87
Ariès, Philippe, 122, 273 n. 57
Armstrong, Nancy, 116, 238 n. 23, 265–66 n. 135
Arnauld, Antoine, 39, 48–49, 58–59, 241 n. 36, 250 n. 86, 270 n. 37
Arnauld d'Andilly, Robert, 53–55, 58, 63, 121, 251–52 nn. 100, 103, 261 n. 68
Augustine, Saint, 6, 11, 23, 72, 137, 179, 214, 217–18, 225, 242 n. 47; interiority in the *Confessions*, 15–16, 50–53, 251–52 nn. 93–94, 98, 103; early modern translations and editions of the *Confessions*, 12, 15–16, 53–63, 73, 133–34, 156, 223, 251–52 n. 103, 253 nn. 115, 119, 254 n. 121, 281 n. 28; as model for early modern autobiographers, 46, 50, 65–69, 179, 192, 249 n. 75, 250 n. 87
Authority: institutional versus subject-centered, 17–18, 32, 180 (*see also* Author-

ship; Biography: and the disappearance of the biographer; Exemplarity; Subjectivity); oral versus written, 2, 77–78, 84–87, 99–100, 104, 125, 130–31, 174, 258 n. 42, 261 n. 69
Authorship: modern institutionalization of, 5, 24–26, 44–45, 47–48, 148–49, 167–70, 176, 187, 260 n. 56, 260–61 n. 62, 276–77 n. 98, 280 n. 20; women's access to, 16, 99–101, 110–11, 113–15, 169–70, 259 n. 44
Autobiography: as access to interior, 1, 4, 10, 12–17, 57, 63–64, 71, 78–79, 83–98, 100–113, 120, 155–61; and the bourgeoisie, 8, 27, 123, 239 n. 27; and community, 64, 150–51, 161–62, 188, 217–19; contestatory nature of, 4–5, 13–14, 120–21, 142–43, 149, 172–78, 218–19, 229–30, 233; critical approaches to, 4–10, 229–31, 239–40 n. 29; and the culture of print, 7–8, 11, 13–16, 18, 60, 69–70, 113, 228, 238 n. 22; early modern conceptual resistance to, 8–9, 15, 65–70, 135–36, 187–89, 193–95, 222–25, 280 n. 19; gendering of, 14, 16, 18, 68–71, 78–79, 99–101, 113–16, 229–30, 266 n. 6, 268 n. 22; and the imperative of self-expression, 32, 45–47, 93, 100–101, 134, 138, 187, 236 n. 10; and judicial and public scrutiny, 14, 17, 46, 48, 106–13, 119–22, 127–28, 132, 136, 143–50, 154, 156–57, 161, 167–78, 259 n. 44, 266 n. 5, 266–67 n. 7, 270 n. 39, 272–73 nn. 55–57, 59; as metonymical presence (or relic), 79, 84, 95, 101–4, 111–12, 260 n. 60; in premodern times, 6, 84, 97–98, 243 n. 5, 267 n. 7; as private text, 25–26, 63–64, 87, 105–8, 187–94, 215–19, 263 n. 99, 277 n. 99, 280 n. 19; and Protestantism, 8, 121, 125–27, 238–39 n. 24, 249 n. 75, 269–70 n. 36; and the temporal development of the individual, 21–23, 40, 127, 132–35, 139–43, 148, 216–17, 272 n. 50, 284–85 n. 67; and typographical distinctions, 8, 16, 79,

Acknowledgments

First and foremost, I would like to thank Joan DeJean and Frank Paul Bowman, who with much patience oriented this project from its inception. I could not have got it all together without their personal and professional example — nor would I even have wanted to. The Doreen B. Townsend Center for the Humanities at Berkeley both funded a teaching leave and provided a forum in which to work through many of the ideas in this book; my thanks especially to the Center fellows for many stimulating lunchtime discussions. Many friends, colleagues, and mentors at Berkeley and elsewhere have patiently read and critiqued drafts: Karl Britto, Terence Cave, Juliette Cherbuliez, Lance Donalson-Evans, Gary Ferguson, Lynn Festa, Tim Hampton, David Hult, Lynn Hunt, Priya Joshi, Tom Kavanagh, Debarati Sanyal, Derek Schilling, Mary Ann Smart. My deepest gratitude for all their efforts to make this better in spite of my stubbornness. Thanks as well to Jeff Fort for help with the translations; to the editors of *Cahiers de l'Association Internationale des Etudes Françaises* (49 [1997]) and *Romance Language Annual* (1995) for permission to revise in Chapters 2 and 4 material that first appeared in their pages; and especially to Jérôme Picon and Isabel Violante, who came through in the clinch with the perfect cover illustration. Finally, personal thanks to Henri, *ami fort intérieur*; to Marie, *ex extraordinaire*; and to my mother, for all her patience, support, and love. This book is dedicated to the memory of my father and grandfather.